HMH Florida Science

Grade 7

This Write-In Book belongs to

_____

Teacher/Room

_____

The manatee is also known as a sea cow. This plant-eating mammal can measure up to more than 4 meters in length.

Houghton Mifflin Harcourt

Consulting Authors

Michael A. DiSpezio
Global Educator
North Falmouth, Massachusetts

Marjorie Frank
*Science Writer and Content-Area Reading
   Specialist*
Brooklyn, New York

Michael R. Heithaus, Ph.D.
Dean, College of Arts, Sciences & Education
Professor, Department of Biological Sciences
Florida International University
Miami, Florida

Houghton Mifflin Harcourt.

Cover: ©Andrew Pearson/Alamy

Printed in the U.S.A.

ISBN   978-1-328-78126-0

7 8 9 10   0690   26 25 24 23 22 21 20 19
4500746681   BCDEFG

Contents in Brief

I want to know what fossils can tell me about the past.

Contents

Knowledge of dinosaurs is gained by studying fossils.

Earth's surface changes
because of Earth's layers.

A mammoth's fossils are preserved because they froze.

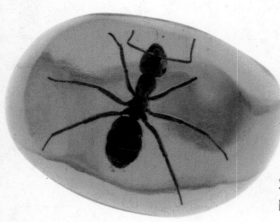

Sticky tree sap hardens and preserves insect fossils.

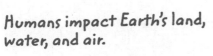
Humans impact Earth's land, water, and air.

Water waves move up and down as well as back and forth

© Houghton Mifflin Harcourt Publishing Company

©Derek Croucher/Alamy

The girls warm their cold hands by holding the warm mugs.

Thousands of years ago, the Florida landscape looked like a cool, dry, and open savannah.

This colorful ladder models DNA.

The coral reef is a diverse marine ecosystem in Florida.

REFERENCES

🧭 Available in Online Resources.

- **Reference Tables**
- **Reading and Study Skills**
- **Science Skills**
- **Math Refresher**

Nature of Science

FLORIDA BIG IDEA 1

The Practice of Science

FLORIDA BIG IDEA 2

The Characteristics of Scientific Knowledge

FLORIDA BIG IDEA 3

The Role of Theories, Laws, Hypotheses, and Models

Special power drills that can be used in low gravity environments were developed to drill for moon samples. Today, astronauts use these drills for space-station repairs.

What Do You Think?

Technology helps people perform different tasks, from the everyday to the amazing. How might technology need to be modified for use in space? As you explore this unit, gather evidence to help you state and support a claim.

Nature of Science

CITIZEN SCIENCE

Launching Humanity Into Space

The idea of exploring space was first popularized by science-fiction writers of the late 19th- and early 20th-centuries. It took until the 1940s and 1950s for advances in rocket technology to make the idea of launching humans into space even seem possible. As of today, 12 astronauts have landed on the moon and teams of astronauts have lived on space stations. What is the next step for space exploration?

1926

Robert Goddard was inspired by turn-of-the-century science fiction to develop his theories about rockets that could travel to the moon. In 1926, he launched the world's first liquid-propellant rocket—but the media thought the idea of going to the moon was just too wild.

Robert Goddard and his liquid-propellant rocket.

Sputnik 1

The space shuttle **Columbia**

Buzz Aldrin

1957

It took several decades to perfect the rocket technology that allowed the Soviet Union to launch the first man-made object into orbit. The Sputnik 1, which weighed only 84 kg, took 96 minutes to orbit Earth.

1981–2010

The new challenge for humans became getting to space as safely and as cost-efficiently as possible. *Columbia* was the first space shuttle NASA developed as a reusable vehicle that could protect astronauts from launch to re-entry.

1969

It only took another 12 years before humans were walking on the moon. Neil Armstrong and Buzz Aldrin became the first humans to set foot on the lunar surface. Back home on Earth, millions of people watched on television.

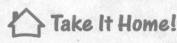 **Take It Home!**

Closer to Home

 Think About It

In 2011, the space shuttle program entered retirement. NASA has explored many different options for future launches. Are you familiar with any of the replacement programs? What are they called?

_____
_____
_____
_____

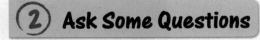 **Ask Some Questions**

Do some internet research to learn more about the plans NASA has for updating the technology we use for space travel.

- Have new, more stable materials been developed that could be used in construction?

- Have our goals for space exploration changed?

- Are there any new fuels that are more efficient for use in space travel?

- What lessons have we learned from the shuttle program about space travel?

③ Make A Plan

Identify two vehicles designed to replace the space shuttle and transport astronauts. Design a brochure that describes each option, its features, and its design history. Be sure to include the following information:

- Cost information

- Safety features

Scientific Knowledge

ESSENTIAL QUESTION

What are the types of scientific knowledge?

By the end of this lesson, you should be able to differentiate the methods that scientists use to gain empirical evidence in a variety of scientific fields and explain how this leads to scientific change.

SC.7.N.1.5 Describe the methods used in the pursuit of a scientific explanation as seen in different fields of science such as biology, geology, and physics. **SC.7.N.1.6** Explain that empirical evidence is the cumulative body of observations of a natural phenomenon on which scientific explanations are based. **SC.7.N.1.7** Explain that scientific knowledge is the result of a great deal of debate and confirmation within the science community. **SC.7.N.2.1** Identify an instance from the history of science in which scientific knowledge has changed when new evidence or new interpretations are encountered. **SC.7.N.3.1** Recognize and explain the difference between theories and laws and give several examples of scientific theories and the evidence that supports them.

Under water may seem like an odd place to conduct a science experiment. But scientists often go to faraway places to gather data.

✋ Lesson Labs

Quick Labs
• What's in the Box?
• Pluto on Trial

Exploration Lab
• Mapping the Ocean Floor

🧠 Engage Your Brain

1 Predict Check T or F to show whether you think each statement is true or false.

T   F

☐ ☐ All branches of science have scientific theories.

☐ ☐ A scientist can use only one method to investigate.

☐ ☐ Theories are scientific ideas that have not yet been tested.

☐ ☐ Scientific laws describe what happens in the world.

2 Claims • Evidence • Reasoning An aeolipile is a device powered by steam. When heated, water in the bulb produces steam. The bulb rotates as the steam escapes from the nozzles. People were making these devices as long as 2,000 years ago. How do you think they came up with the idea even though they did not have our modern understanding of science? State your claim. Provide evidence to support the claim, and explain your reasoning.

aeolipile

_____

_____

_____

_____

ACTIVE **READING**

3 Infer The word *empirical* comes from the Greek word *empeirikos*, meaning "experienced." Based on this information, infer how scientists get empirical evidence.

_____

_____

_____

_____

Vocabulary Terms

• empirical evidence
• theory
• law

4 Apply As you learn the definition of each vocabulary term in this lesson, create your own definition or sketch to help you remember the meaning of the term.

...From the Beginning

i Think Outside the Book

5 Define Before you begin reading the lesson, write down what you think science and scientific knowledge are. Reread your definition at the end of the lesson. Has your definition changed?

What is science?

Science is the study of the natural world. Scientists study everything from the deepest parts of the ocean to the objects in outer space. Some scientists study living things. Others study forces such as gravity and magnetism. Name anything you see around you. Chances are, there is a scientist who studies it.

The natural sciences are divided into three areas: biology or life science, geology or Earth science, and physics or physical science. The three areas differ in the subjects they study and the methods they use. Biology is the study of living things. Biologists study everything from the tiniest organisms to human beings. Geology is the study of Earth: what it's made of and the processes that shape it. Physical science is the study of nonliving matter and energy. Chemistry often is included under physical science. A scientist's work sometimes may overlap two or more areas. For example, a biologist often must know chemistry to understand the processes in living things.

Each of the photographs below relates to one of the areas of science in some way. From the captions, can you identify to which area each belongs?

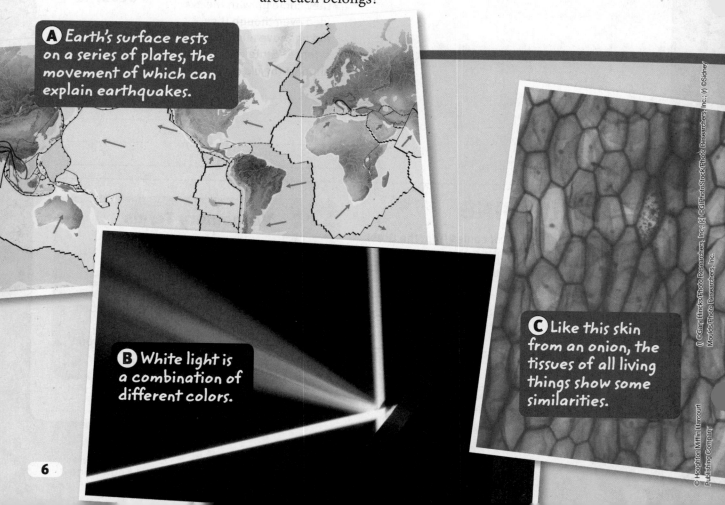

A Earth's surface rests on a series of plates, the movement of which can explain earthquakes.

B White light is a combination of different colors.

C Like this skin from an onion, the tissues of all living things show some similarities.

What does science tell us?

ACTIVE READING

6 Identify Underline what a theory is in science.

You may think that what you read in a science book is accepted by everyone and is unchanging. That is not always the case. The "facts" of science are simply the most widely accepted explanations. Scientific knowledge is and probably always will be changing.

What we learn when we study science are what most scientists agree are the best explanations about how things happen. They are *theories* scientists have about the world. Commonly, we think of a theory as a kind of guess or "hunch." In science, a theory is much more. A scientific theory is an explanation supported by a large amount of evidence. Theories are what most scientists agree to be the best explanations based upon what we now know.

The table below lists three important scientific theories. Each theory relates to one of the areas of science described before. Each also corresponds to a photograph on the previous page. Can you think of what kinds of evidence would support each theory?

👁 Visualize It!

7 Claims • Evidence • Reasoning For each of the three theories listed in the table below, write the letter of the corresponding photograph at the left. On the lines provided, summarize the evidence that supports each theory. Explain your reasoning.

Scientific Theories

	What scientists think	What is some evidence?
Biology	____Cell theory: Living things are made up of cells that perform the basic functions of life.	
Geology	____Plate tectonics: Earth's surface is made up of plates that move.	
Physics	____Wave theory of light: Each color of visible light has a wave of a specific wavelength.	

You Can't Break

How do scientific theories differ from laws?

ACTIVE READING

8 Identify As you read, underline a real-world example of Boyle's law.

To understand the nature of scientific knowledge, you must understand how scientists use certain words. Often, the meanings are very specialized. *Law* and *theory* are two familiar words that have very special scientific meanings.

○ Laws Describe Principles of Nature

A scientific **law** is a description of a specific relationship under given conditions in the natural world. In short, scientific laws describe the way the world works. They hold anywhere in the universe. You can't escape them.

Boyle's law is one scientific law. According to Boyle's law, at a constant temperature, as the pressure on a gas increases, its volume decreases. To get an appreciation of Boyle's law, think of how it would feel to squeeze a partially deflated beach ball. If you apply pressure by squeezing, the volume, or size, of the ball gets smaller.

You can feel the effects of Boyle's law. A membrane or *eardrum* separates your middle ear from outer ear. Normally, the air spaces on either side are at equal pressure. But sometimes, the pressure on the outer ear can change. For example, the scuba diver in the photo feels an increase in pressure on her eardrum as she descends in the water. By holding her nose and blowing gently, she can force more air into her middle ear. The action momentarily opens the *eustachian tube* connecting the middle ear to the throat. This allows more air from the mouth to rush into the middle ear and equalize the pressure between the two spaces.

Divers need to be aware of Boyle's law and equalize the pressure in their ears.

◉ Visualize It!

9 Label Label the middle ear, the outer ear, and eardrum in the illustration.

Air pressure is equalized in the ear by momentarily opening the eustachian tube. You may feel this as a "pop" in your ear.

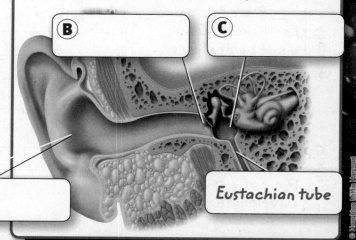

B

C

A

Eustachian tube

Theories Describe How Things Happen

While laws describe what happens, scientific theories attempt to explain how things happen. A scientific **theory** is a well-supported explanation of nature. Theories help us understand the laws we observe.

For example, the kinetic theory of gases can explain Boyle's law. The kinetic theory describes a gas as being composed of quickly-moving particles. The particles of gas constantly bounce off of the walls of the container they occupy. The pressure of the gas increases the more frequently the particles bounce off the sides of the container.

Two factors increase how frequently the particles of a gas will bounce off the walls of their container: temperature and volume. If the temperature of a gas increases, the particles move more quickly. The particles, therefore, come into contact with the container's walls more often. Decreasing volume also increases the encounters because the particles have less distance to travel before hitting the wall. The container walls can be anything: a metal cylinder, a beach ball, or your eardrum. The illustration below will give you some of idea of how this works.

👁 Visualize It!

10 Compare In the table below, circle the signs that show the relationships between the volumes, pressures, and temperatures of the gases in the two cylinders. The first is done for you.

Cylinder 1	Relationship			Cylinder 2
Volume	<	=	(>)	Volume
Pressure	<	=	>	Pressure
Temperature	<	=	>	Temperature

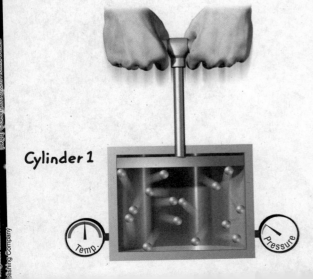

Cylinder 1

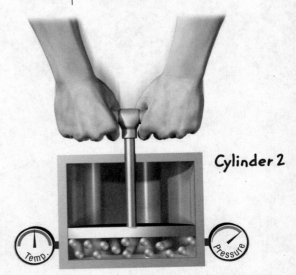

Cylinder 2

Houghton Mifflin Harcourt
Publishing Company

What's Your Evidence?

Where do scientists get their evidence?

Scientists are curious. They look at everything going on around them and ask questions. They collect any information that might help them answer these questions.

Scientific knowledge is based on *empirical evidence*. **Empirical evidence** is all the measurements and data scientists gather in support of a scientific explanation. Scientists get empirical evidence in many different places. Generally, scientific work is categorized as field or laboratory work.

ACTIVE **READING**

11 Identify Underline the definition of empirical evidence.

This scientist is a paleontologist. A paleontologist looks for fossilized bones. Here, he is carefully excavating the remains of a 10,000 year-old rhinoceros.

👁 Visualize It!

12 Gather Evidence What empirical evidence might the scientist in the photograph be trying to gather? Explain your reasoning.

_____

_____

_____

In the Field

Generally, gathering empirical evidence outdoors or where conditions cannot be controlled is known as working in the field or *fieldwork*. Fieldwork gives scientists the opportunity to collect data in an original setting. Biologists and geologists do fieldwork.

A biologist might observe how animals behave in their natural environment. They may look at how the animals gather food or interact with other animals. A geologist may be interested in the minerals in rocks found in a certain area. They may be trying to determine how the rocks formed.

In the Laboratory

In a laboratory, scientists have the opportunity to collect data in a controlled environment. Unlike in the field, the laboratory allows scientists to control conditions like temperature, lighting, and even what is in the surrounding air. A laboratory is where scientists usually do experiments. In an experiment, scientists try to see what happens under certain conditions. A chemist might be trying to see how two substances react with each other. A physicist might study the energy of a new laser. Even scientists who mainly work in the field, like paleontologists and geologists, may wish to look at a bone or rock in the laboratory.

Laboratories come in many varieties. They can be in the ocean or in the sky. Robotic laboratories even have been sent to Mars!

ACTIVE READING

13 Gather Evidence What might a scientist look for to collect evidence about the formation of a volcano? Explain your reasoning.

_____

_____

_____

_____

👁 Visualize It!

14 Claims • Evidence • Reasoning The paleontologists in the photo above have taken a specimen back to the laboratory. Make a claim about what they might be looking for. Provide evidence to support the claim, and explain your reasoning.

_____

_____

_____

The **Debate** Continues

How do scientific ideas change?

Recall that scientific knowledge is agreed-upon knowledge. It is what scientists think are the most-likely explanations for what we see. Over time, these most-likely explanations can change. Sometimes, these changes are very large. More often, they are very small. Why do scientific ideas and explanations change? It's usually because new evidence was found or someone found a better way of explaining the old evidence.

○ By New Evidence

The theory of atoms is a good example of how new evidence can modify an established theory. By the mid-1800s, most scientists agreed matter was made of atoms. However, they were not sure what atoms looked like. At first, they thought atoms probably looked like tiny, solid marbles. They assumed atoms of different substances probably differed by their masses.

Later evidence suggested that atoms most likely contained even smaller parts. Scientists observed that these smaller parts carried electric charges and that most of an atom's mass was concentrated at its center. Scientists still saw atoms as extremely small and still often treated them like they were tiny marbles. They came to realize, however, that to explain how atoms interact in the best way, they needed a more complex picture of them.

Today, scientists are still trying to refine the picture of the atom. Much of what they do involves literally smashing atoms into one another. They examine the patterns made by the crashes. It is almost like an atomic game of marbles.

ACTIVE **READING**

15 Identify Underline an example of a scientific idea that was modified after it was first introduced.

👁 Visualize It!

16 Claims • Evidence • Reasoning How does the early model of the atom differ from the current model? What is similar about the two models? State your claim. Provide evidence to support the claim, and explain your reasoning.

_____

_____

_____

_____

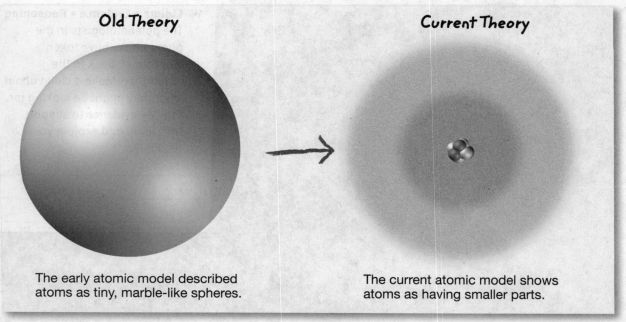

Old Theory

Current Theory

The early atomic model described atoms as tiny, marble-like spheres.

The current atomic model shows atoms as having smaller parts.

By Collaboration and Debate

Most scientists do not work in isolation. They collaborate and share ideas. In a way, all scientists are trying to solve a puzzle. Often, many brains are better than one when solving a puzzle.

Scientists regularly gather at meetings to discuss and debate ideas. This helps them to come to an agreement on their ideas. Many ideas are not accepted at first. It is the nature of science to question every idea. Many times, challenges are even welcomed. This rigorous evaluation ensures that scientific knowledge is solidly supported.

i Think Outside the Book

17 Evaluate Describe a time when you had to ask someone's help in solving a problem. Why did you ask for help?

To the left is an example of how scientists study atoms today. The "streaks" show the paths of subatomic particles after two atoms collide. The scientists below study and discuss images like these in a group in hopes to better understand atoms.

(t) ©CERN/Photo Researchers, Inc; (b) ©Fabrice Coffrini/AFP/Getty Images

Publishing Company

Visual Summary

To complete this summary, fill in the blanks with the correct word or phrase. You can use this page to review the main concepts of the lesson.

The facts we may think of as science are simply the most widely accepted explanations.

18 A scientific_____ describes what happens, but a scientific _____ describes for what reasons it happens.

Scientific Knowledge

Empirical evidence is all the measurements and data scientists gather in support of a scientific explanation.

19 Empirical evidence about rocks might be collected by a _____ doing _____

20 Empirical evidence about how substances combine might be collected by a _____ doing work in the _____

Scientific knowledge often changes with new evidence or new interpretations.

21 Scientists often_____ and _____ to help them interpret complex ideas.

22 **Claims • Evidence • Reasoning** Could a scientific theory be thought of as a scientific law that doesn't have as much evidence supporting it? State your claim, and explain your reasoning.

Lesson Review

Vocabulary

Circle the term that best completes each of the following sentences.

1 A scientific *law / theory* is an explanation for how something occurs. It is supported by a great deal of evidence.

2 Scientists look for *empirical evidence / law* either in the field or in the laboratory.

3 A basic principle that applies everywhere and in all situations is best described as a scientific *law / theory*.

Key Concepts

4 List Into what three areas are the natural sciences commonly divided?

_____

_____

5 Distinguish How is the use of the word *theory* in science different from its more common use?

_____

_____

_____

6 Differentiate How would you distinguish a scientific theory from a scientific law?

_____

_____

_____

7 Identify Name two methods scientists use to obtain empirical evidence.

_____

_____

8 Apply What is a difference between research in the field and in the laboratory?

_____

_____

_____

Critical Thinking

Use this picture to answer the following question.

9 Claims • Evidence • Reasoning As the flames heat the gases in the balloon, the volume of the gases increases. At constant pressure, the volume of all gases increases with increasing temperature. Is this statement a scientific theory or law? Provide evidence to support your claim, and explain your reasoning.

_____

_____

10 Claims • Evidence • Reasoning Someone tells you that scientific knowledge cannot be changed or modified. Is this statement true or false? State your claim. Provide evidence to support the claim, and explain your reasoning.

_____

_____

11 Claims • Evidence • Reasoning Each year, the American Chemical Society holds a national meeting and many regional meetings for chemists. Reports of these meetings are then circulated all over the world. Make a claim about why you think this has become standard practice. Provide evidence to support the claim, and explain your reasoning.

_____

_____

SC.7.N.1.5 Describe the methods used in the pursuit of a scientific explanation as seen in different fields of science such as biology, geology, and physics.

Dijanna Figueroa

MARINE BIOLOGIST

Dijanna Figueroa has wanted to be a marine biologist for as long as she can remember. Like many scientists, she now wears a lab coat and safety glasses most days. She spends up to 12 hours a day in the lab. There, she studies the metabolisms of creatures that live in extreme environments. These creatures live more than two kilometers below the ocean's surface, in a habitat that sunlight never reaches. The water pressure is so great that it would crush a human being. Creatures living in these conditions must therefore produce foods in ways that were unknown until only recently. In order to get specimens of these animals for her lab, Dr. Figueroa had to go down to where they live.

Dr. Figueroa's job has taken her onto the big screen, too. She appeared in the IMAX film *Aliens of the Deep*, with other scientists. The film shows footage of expeditions down to the deep-sea ocean vents. These vents may be one of the harshest environments on the planet. The scientists traveled in *Alvin*, a deep-sea submarine.

Dr. Figueroa works to get young people interested in real-life science through fun and exciting hands-on activities. She currently works as the science coordinator for a private school in California.

Dr. Figueroa in Alvin—2,400 m deep!

📖 Language Arts Connection

Think of a science-related job that you would like to know more about. Research the job and write a plan for a documentary film that teaches what you have learned about the job.

(bkgd) ©Science Source/Photo Researchers, Inc.; (br) Courtesy of Dijanna Figueroa
on Mifflin Harcourt

JOB BOARD

Museum Educational Interpreter

What You'll Do: Tell students and groups visiting a museum about what they are looking at. You might create educational programs, give tours, and answer questions.

Where You Might Work: Likely places are a science museum or a museum of technology.

Education: Educational interpreters usually need a bachelor's degree in science, and may need extra training in museums or in teaching.

Other Job Requirements: You need to enjoy working with people, be good at public speaking, and be able to answer questions clearly.

Pyrotechnician

What You'll Do: Work with explosives to create explosions and fireworks for special effects. Blow things up in the safest way possible, using a lot of safety measures to keep things from getting out of hand.

Where You Might Work: A company that designs special effects or that creates and performs fireworks shows is a possibility. A pyrotechnician spends time in the workshop and on-site, so you may find yourself on a film set blowing up cars, or on a hillside setting off fireworks.

Education: You need a high-school diploma with additional training in pyrotechnics and safety.

Other Job Requirements: Strong math skills, ability to concentrate, and careful attention to detail are required.

PEOPLE IN SCIENCE NEWS

Jon BOHMER

Cooking with Sunlight

Jon Bohmer isn't the first person to invent an oven that uses sunlight to heat food and water. He's one of many people to use cardboard, foil, and sunlight to build an oven. In some countries, people use firewood for most of their cooking, and must boil all of their water before they drink it. Jon's Kyoto Box oven uses two cardboard boxes painted black on the inside and coated with foil on the outside. It costs only about $5 to make, but it gets hot enough to boil water and cook food.

Scientific Investigations

ESSENTIAL **QUESTION**

How are scientific investigations conducted?

By the end of this lesson, you should be able to summarize the processes and characteristics of different kinds of scientific investigations.

SC.7.N.1.2 Differentiate replication (by others) from repetition (multiple trials). **SC.7.N.1.3** Distinguish between an experiment (which must involve the identification and control of variables) and other forms of scientific investigation and explain that not all scientific knowledge is derived from experimentation. **SC.7.N.1.4** Identify test variables (independent variables) and outcome variables (dependent variables) in an experiment. **SC.7.N.1.5** Describe the methods used in the pursuit of a scientific explanation as seen in different fields of science such as biology, geology, and physics.

Geologists are able to create artificial earthquakes on this model of a portion of Earth's crust. They can investigate the rock types through which seismic waves travel, all from a computer!

© Chris Sattlberger/Photo Researchers, Inc.

© Houghton Mifflin Harcourt

Lesson Labs

Quick Labs
• Identifying Minerals
• Soil Structure and Water Flow

Engage Your Brain

1 Predict Check T or F to show whether you think each statement is true or false.

T   F

☐   ☐   There is only one correct way to conduct a scientific investigation.

☐   ☐   A hypothesis is a conclusion you draw after you conduct a scientific experiment.

☐   ☐   In a controlled experiment, scientists try to control all but one variable.

☐   ☐   Scientists may come up with different interpretations of the same data.

2 Formulate. Observe the hills shown in the picture. Write some questions you would like to investigate about the sedimentary rock layers.

_____

_____

_____

_____

ACTIVE **READING**

3 Synthesize You can often define an unknown word if you know the meaning of its word parts. Use the word part and sentence below to make an educated guess about the meaning of the term *independent variable*.

Word part	Meaning
in-	not

Example sentence
In an experiment about how light affects plant growth, the underlined independent variable is the number of hours that a plant is exposed to light.

Independent variable:

_____

_____

Vocabulary Terms

• experiment
• hypothesis
• dependent variable
• observation
• independent variable
• data

4 Identify This list contains the vocabulary terms you'll learn in this lesson. As you read, underline the definition of each term.

Detective Story

What are some types of scientific investigations?

The two basic types of scientific investigations are *experiments* and *observations*. Most scientists use both experiments and observations. Experiments are often based on observations, and they produce additional observations while they are conducted. But observations do not always lead to experiments.

ACTIVE READING

5 Identify As you read these two pages, underline characteristics of the different types of scientific investigations discussed.

Scientific Investigations

Experiments

An **experiment** is an organized procedure to study something under controlled conditions. Scientists often conduct experiments to find out the cause of something they have observed.

In 1928, Alexander Fleming found a fungus growing on a glass plate that was coated with bacteria. He noticed that there were no bacteria around the fungus. He thought that the fungus produced something that killed the bacteria.

Fleming conducted experiments showing that the fungus produced a chemical that could kill bacteria. He named the chemical penicillin after the fungus that produced it. Based on Fleming's work, scientists produced the first antibiotic drugs.

Experiments such as Fleming's are done in a laboratory. Most variables that might affect the outcome of an experiment can be controlled in a laboratory. Experiments can also be done in the field, but fewer conditions can be controlled. However, a field experiment may be needed to show that something found in a laboratory also occurs in nature.

These scientists work in a laboratory called a clean room. A clean room must be free of all possible contaminants.

ACTIVE READING

6 Claims • Evidence • Reasoning Make a claim about why it is harder to control variables in the field than in a laboratory? Provide evidence to support the claim, and explain your reasoning.

_____

_____

Other Types of Investigations

Scientists can make discoveries without conducting experiments. **Observation** is the process of obtaining information by using the senses. The term can also refer to the information obtained by using the senses.

For example, an archaeologist observes a bone at a prehistoric site. The bone is small and does not look like other bones collected there. Based on its size and shape, the scientist wonders if it came from a small animal. She compares the bone to those from various other small animals. After making these observations, she concludes that people kept pets at the site.

Another type of investigation is the creation of models. Models are representations of an object or system. Models are useful for studying things that are very small, large, or complex. For example, computer models of Earth's atmosphere help scientists forecast the weather.

This scientist is observing flies in their natural habitat.

👁 Visualize It!

7 Assess Compare and contrast the kinds of investigations shown in each photo.

Experiment in Clean Room

Both

Observing Flies in Nature

Parts of a Whole

What are some parts of scientific investigations?

Scientists study all aspects of the natural world. The work they do varies, but their investigations have some basic elements in common.

Hypothesis

A **hypothesis** [hy•PAHTH•i•sis] is a testable idea or explanation that leads to scientific investigation. A scientist may make a hypothesis after making observations or after reading about other scientists' investigations. The hypothesis can be tested by experiment or observation.

Hypotheses must be carefully constructed so they can be tested in a practical and meaningful way. The hypothesis that birds eat plants is too broad to be meaningful. A better hypothesis would be that parrots eat foods of a particular size and shape. This hypothesis could be tested with a variety of different foods.

👁 Visualize It!

8 Develop Write a hypothesis that could be tested on the plants shown in this photo.

_____
_____
_____
_____
_____

These plants are being grown in a laboratory and tested under carefully controlled conditions. A scientist could conduct a variety of experiments with these plants.

© Houghton Mifflin Harcourt

Independent Variables

Variables are factors that can change in a scientific investigation. An **independent variable**, or test variable, is the factor that is deliberately manipulated in an investigation. The hypothesis determines what the independent variable will be. For example, consider the hypothesis that parrots eat foods of a particular size and shape. The independent variable in an investigation testing that hypothesis is the type of food.

An experiment should have one independent variable. Scientists try to keep all other variables in an experiment constant, or unchanged, so they do not affect the results. However, it may not always be possible to control all the other variables.

Dependent Variables

A **dependent variable**, or outcome variable, is the factor that changes as a result of manipulation of one or more independent variables.

In Fleming's experiments with bacteria, the independent variable was the penicillin fungus. The fungus was either present or absent. The dependent variable was survival of the bacteria. The bacteria either lived or died.

Dependent variables can be measured outside of experiments. Consider the hypothesis that crickets chirp at higher temperatures. The independent variable would be the temperature. The dependent variable would be the cricket chirps. By measuring the dependent variable, you test the hypothesis.

9 Apply Complete the missing parts of the table below, which describes three experiments.

Investigation	Independent Variable	Dependent Variable
How is plant height affected by amount of sunlight it receives?	Hours of sunlight per day	
	Altitude of water	Boiling temperature
How does a person's heart rate change as speed of movement increases?		Heart rate

Observations and Data

Data are information gathered by observation or experimentation that can be used in calculating or reasoning. Everything a scientist observes must be recorded. The setup and procedures of an experiment also need to be recorded. By carefully recording this information, scientists will not forget important information.

Scientists analyze data to determine the relationship between the independent and dependent variables in an investigation. Then they draw conclusions about whether the data supports the investigation's hypothesis.

ACTIVE READING

10 Identify As you read, underline the types of data that scientists record.

Many Methods

What are some scientific methods?

Conducting experiments and other scientific investigations is not like following a cookbook recipe. Scientists do not always use the same steps in every investigation or use steps in the same order. They may even repeat some of the steps. The following graphic shows one path a scientist might follow while conducting an experiment.

👁 Visualize It!

11 Diagram Using a different color, draw arrows showing another path a scientist might follow if the data from an experiment did not support the hypothesis.

Defining a Problem

After making observations or reading scientific reports, a scientist might be curious about some unexplained aspect of a topic. A scientific problem is a specific question that a scientist wants to answer. The problem must be well-defined, or precisely stated, so that it can be investigated.

Planning an Investigation

A scientific investigation must be carefully planned so that it tests a hypothesis in a meaningful way. Scientists need to decide whether an investigation should be done in the field or in a laboratory. They must also determine what equipment and technology are required and how materials for the investigation will be obtained.

Forming a Hypothesis and Making Predictions

When scientists form a hypothesis, they are making an educated guess about a problem. A hypothesis must be tested to see if it is true. Before testing a hypothesis, scientists usually make predictions about what will happen in an investigation.

Identifying Variables

The independent variable of an experiment is identified in the hypothesis. But scientists need to decide how the independent variable will change. They also must identify other variables that will be controlled. In addition, scientists must determine how they will measure the results of the experiment. The dependent variable often can be measured in more than one way. For example, if the dependent variable is plant growth, a scientist could measure height, weight, or even flower or fruit production.

Collecting and Organizing Data

The data collected in an investigation must be recorded and properly organized so that they can be analyzed. Data such as measurements and numbers are often organized into tables, spreadsheets, or graphs.

Interpreting Data and Analyzing Information

After they finish collecting data, scientists must analyze this information. Their analysis will help them draw conclusions about the results. Scientists may have different interpretations of the same data because they analyze it using different methods.

Drawing and Defending Conclusions

Scientists conclude whether the results of their investigation support the hypothesis. If the hypothesis is not supported, scientists may think about the problem some more and try to come up with a new hypothesis to test. Or they may repeat an experiment to see if any mistakes were made. When they publish the results of their investigation, scientists must be prepared to defend their conclusions if they are challenged by other scientists.

Make it Work

ⓘ Think Outside the Book

12 Gather Evidence Choose a plant or animal you would like to study. How would you learn about what it needs to live, grow, and reproduce? Write a paragraph describing the kinds of investigations you would conduct and the type of evidence you would collect to learn more about this organism. Explain your reasoning.

How are scientific methods used?

Scientific methods are used in physical, life, and earth science. The findings of scientific investigations support previous work and add new knowledge.

Different Situations Require Different Methods

After forming a hypothesis, scientists decide how they will test it. Some hypotheses can only be tested through observation. Others must be tested in experiments. However, observation and experiments are often used together to build scientific knowledge.

For example, a biologist wants to study the effects of air pollution on a plant species. He makes observations in the field. He gathers data on the plants and the amount of pollutants in the air. Then he conducts experiments under controlled conditions. He exposes plants to different levels of pollution to test how they are affected. He compares his laboratory data with his field data.

If an investigation does not support a hypothesis, it is still useful. The data can help scientists form a better hypothesis. Scientists often go through many cycles of testing and data analysis before they arrive at a hypothesis that is supported.

This photo shows the large jaw of SuperCroc and the smaller jaw of a modern crocodile.

Scientific Methods Are Used in Earth Science

Earth science includes the study of fossils, which are the remains of organisms that lived long ago. Scientific methods allow scientists to learn about species that died out millions of years ago.

One team of scientists found dinosaur fossils in the Sahara Desert. They found a set of jaws 1.8 meters (6 feet) long. They could tell from the shape of the jaws and teeth that it was not from a dinosaur. They also knew that rivers once flowed through this now extremely dry region. The team hypothesized that the jaws belonged to a giant crocodile that lived in rivers.

To support their hypothesis, the scientists needed more data. They later found skulls, vertebrae, and limb bones. They assembled about half of a complete crocodile skeleton. The scientists measured the fossils and compared them with the bones of modern crocodiles. Their analysis showed that the crocodile grew to a length of 12 meters (40 feet) and weighed as much as 10 tons.

The scientists concluded that the fossils supported their original hypothesis. They published their findings about the crocodile and nicknamed it "SuperCroc."

ACTIVE READING

13 Identify As you read, underline a scientific method when it is used and name the method on the lines below.

_____

_____

_____

_____

After scientists find fossils, scientific artists draw representations of the animals. This drawing shows the large size of SuperCroc.

Quality Control

What are some characteristics of good scientific investigations?

The standards for scientific investigations are rigorous. Experiments should be verified through repetition and replication. Before a report on an investigation is published in a scientific journal, it should undergo a peer review by scientists not involved in the investigation. Together, these checks help ensure that good scientific practices are followed.

Evaluating Investigations

How is repetition different from replication?

There are two ways that scientific investigations can be retested. First, the scientist who conducted the original investigation can repeat the study. Multiple repetitions of an investigation with similar results provide support for the findings. Second, other scientists can replicate the investigation. Reproduction of the findings by different scientists in different locations also provides support.

14 Classify Read each of the scenarios below. Check one of the boxes next to each statement to classify each scenario as an example of repetition, replication, or both.

Scenario 1: You go to a neighborhood park five times and take notes on the birds you see and hear. You write up your notes.

☐ Replication
☐ Repetition
☐ Both

Scenario 2: You go to the same neighborhood park with a friend. You give your friend a copy of the notes you took when you went to the park on your own. You and your friend both take notes on the birds you see and hear.

☐ Replication
☐ Repetition
☐ Both

Scenario 3: Your friend goes by himself to the same neighborhood park. Your friend takes notes on the birds he sees and hears.

☐ Replication
☐ Repetition
☐ Both

How can you evaluate the quality of scientific information?

The most reliable scientific information is published in peer-reviewed scientific journals. However, these articles are often difficult to understand for people who aren't scientists. Sometimes, reliable summaries of scientific investigations are published in newspapers or magazines or on the Internet.

Many scientists write books for the public. These books are trustworthy if the scientist is writing about his or her field of study. Reliable books and articles may also be written by people who are not scientists but who are knowledgeable about a particular field. The most reliable Internet sources are government or academic webpages. Commercial webpages are often unreliable because they are trying to sell something.

Think Outside the Book

15 Claims • Evidence • Reasoning
For one week, keep a notebook of different science articles that you find in newspapers or magazines or on the Internet. State a claim about which articles are reliable and which are not. Provide evidence to support the claim, and explain your reasoning.

Repetition occurs when an activity is repeated by the same person. When a person bakes a cake multiple times using the same recipe, it should be the same each time. When a scientist repeats her experiment, she should achieve similar results each time.

Replication occurs when an activity is repeated by a different person. When a person bakes a cake using a recipe from someone else, it should be the same as the first person's cake. When a scientist replicates another person's experiment, he should achieve the same results.

Visual Summary

To complete this summary, fill in the blanks with the correct word or phrase. You can use this page to review the main concepts of the lesson.

Scientific Investigations

Types of Scientific Investigations

Scientific investigations may involve observations, experiments, and models.

16 Scientific investigations can be conducted in a _____ or in the _____

17 The _____ of an experiment must be testable.

Scientific Methods

Scientific methods include making observations, planning experiments, collecting data, and drawing conclusions.

18 In an experiment, the variable that a scientist plans to change is the _____ variable.

19 The results of an experiment are the _____ collected.

Characteristics of Good Scientific Investigations

In addition to controlling variables, good scientific investigations should have results that can be reproduced.

20 If your classmate repeats an experiment that you have already conducted, that is an example of _____

21 One way that the quality of scientific information is evaluated is that it is reviewed by _____

22 Claims • Evidence • Reasoning Suppose that you soak ten seeds in water and ten seeds in a mixture of water and vinegar to see how acidity affects the sprouting of seeds. You observe them for two weeks. What are the independent and dependent variables of this experiment? What evidence supports your claim? Explain your reasoning.

Lesson Review

Vocabulary

Circle the term that best completes each of the following sentences.

1 A(n) *hypothesis/observation* is tested in an experiment.

2 In an experiment, the *independent/ dependent* variable is the one that scientists manipulate on purpose.

3 The *data/hypothesis* is/are the result(s) obtained from an experiment.

Key Concepts

4 **Explain Your Reasoning** What is a basic requirement that a scientific hypothesis must have?

_____

_____

5 **Claims • Evidence • Reasoning** Where are most experiments done? Make a claim about the benefits of this choice. Provide evidence to support the claim, and explain your reasoning.

_____

_____

_____

6 **Claims • Evidence • Reasoning** Make a claim about the difference between repetition and replication of an investigation? Provide evidence to support your claim, and explain your reasoning.

_____

_____

_____

7 **List** Write a list of at least five scientific methods.

_____

_____

_____

Critical Thinking

Use this photograph to answer the following questions.

8 **Compile** Record your observations about the fossil in the photograph. Be sure to include as much detail as you can observe.

_____

_____

9 **Produce** Write a hypothesis about this fossil that you could test in an investigation.

_____

_____

10 **Gather Evidence** Describe how you would test your hypothesis. You don't need to identify specific tests or instruments. Rather, describe the kinds of evidence you would want to collect. Explain your reasoning.

_____

_____

_____

Representing Data

ESSENTIAL **QUESTION**

How do scientists organize, analyze, and present data?

By the end of this lesson, you should be able to use tables, graphs, and models to display and analyze scientific data.

The letters here represent just a tiny portion of the human genome. The letters correspond to the bases that make up DNA, the carrier of genetic information. These letters are part of a genetics exhibition panel, located in the French museum City of Science and Industry.

SC.7.N.1.5 Describe the methods used in the pursuit of a scientific explanation as seen in different fields of science such as biology, geology, and physics. **SC.7.N.3.2** Identify the benefits and limitations of the use of scientific models.

✋ Lesson Labs

Quick Labs
• Heart Rate and Exercise
• Interpreting Models
Exploration Lab
• Exploring Convection

🧠 Engage Your Brain

1 Describe Fill in the blank with the word or phrase that you think correctly completes the following sentences.

Graphs are visual representations of _____.

A map of Florida is an example of a(n) _____.

_____ help show patterns, or trends, in data.

2 Claims • Evidence • Reasoning Identify two things you can understand by looking at this model of our solar system that would be difficult to see if you looked at the sky from Earth. Provide evidence to support your claim, and explain your reasoning.

_____

_____

_____

_____

_____

_____

ACTIVE **READING**

3 Apply Many words, such as *model,* have multiple meanings. Use context clues to write your own definition for each meaning of the word *model.*

Example sentence
Sports stars are role <u>models</u> for thousands of young people.
model:

_____

_____

Example sentence
They used a computer to <u>model</u> the possible effects of global warming.
model:

_____

_____

Vocabulary Term

• model

4 Apply As you learn the definition of the vocabulary term in this lesson, create your own definition or sketch to help you remember the meaning of the term.

Get Organized!

How do scientists make sense of data?

There are many different kinds of scientific investigations, all of which involve the collection of data. *Data* are the facts, figures, and other evidence scientists gather when they conduct an investigation. The more data a scientist collects, the greater is the need for the data to be organized in some way. Data tables are one easy way to organize a lot of data.

○ Scientists Organize the Data

Scientists design and build tables to hold their data in an orderly way. Typical data include quantities, times, and *frequencies,* or the number of times something happens. Scientists decide where to put each type of data and label the columns and rows accordingly. They include units of measurement, such as feet or seconds, in the column headings.

Scientists use these tables to record observations and measurements during their investigations. Later the data tables become tools of analysis.

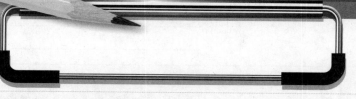

Jasmine conducted a survey to determine the types of movies students prefer. She polled 100 students in the seventh grade. Then she organized the data that she collected into the table.

Movie-Type Preferences

Type of movie	Number of students
Action	40
Comedy	30
Drama	15
Horror	5
Other	10
Total	100

👁 Visualize It!

5 Gather Evidence What other kind of evidence could you collect about student preferences?

_____

_____

_____

○ Scientists Graph and Analyze the Data

In order to analyze data for patterns and trends, it is often helpful to construct a graph. The type of graph you use depends upon the data collected and what you want to show.

A *circle graph* is an ideal way to display data that are parts of a whole. Each section of the circle represents a category of the data. The entire circle represents all of the data. For example, in the movie preference data, the types of movies are the categories.

If you think of a complete circle as 100%, you can express sections of a circle graph as percentages. The table below shows how to find the percentage of students who prefer each type of movie. As shown in the last column, divide the number of students who prefer each movie type by the total number of students. Then multiply by 100 percent to get the percentage.

ACTIVE READING

6 Claims • Evidence • Reasoning
Make a claim about the sum of the percentages in a circle graph. Provide evidence to support your claim, and explain your reasoning.

Movie-Type Preferences

Type of movie	Number of students	Percentage of students
Action	40	$\frac{40}{100} \times 100\% = 40\%$
Comedy	30	$\frac{30}{100} \times 100\% = 30\%$
Drama	15	$\frac{15}{100} \times 100\% = 15\%$
Horror	5	$\frac{5}{100} \times 100\% = 5\%$
Other	10	$\frac{10}{100} \times 100\% = 10\%$

◉ Visualize It!

Each section of the circle graph represents the percentage of students who prefer each type of movie. Compare the sizes of the sections to determine how they are related.

7 Claims • Evidence • Reasoning Would you expect the next student Jasmine polled to prefer action movies or horror movies? State your claim. Provide evidence to support the claim, and explain your reasoning.

_____

_____

_____

Movie-Type Preferences

Horror 5%
Other 10%
Action 40%
Drama 15%
Comedy 30%

Circle up!

What do graphs show?

Graphs show data in a visual way. Data displayed in a graph are often easier to understand than data displayed in a table. There are many kinds of graphs.

A *circle graph,* or pie chart, is used when showing how each group of data relates to all of the data. A *bar graph* is used to display and compare data in a number of categories. A *line graph* is most often used to show continuous change. Line graphs are useful for showing changes in variables over time.

✚➖ Do the Math
✖➗

You Try It

Cara observes the bird feeder in her yard for 3 hours at the same time each day for 3 days. She writes down the types and numbers of birds that visit the feeder. In total, she sees 60 birds. Her data are shown at the right.

Cardinal	卌 卌 卌
Finch	卌 IIII
Mockingbird	卌 卌 卌 卌 IIII
Wren	卌 卌 II

8 Calculate Use the table below to organize the data that Cara collected. In the last column, find the percentage of each bird that Cara saw by dividing the number of each type of bird by the total number of birds and multiplying by 100%.

Type of bird	Number of birds	Percentage of birds

◉ Visualize It!

The circle graph below is divided into equal sections that are 5% of the total circle. Remember that a complete circle is 100%.

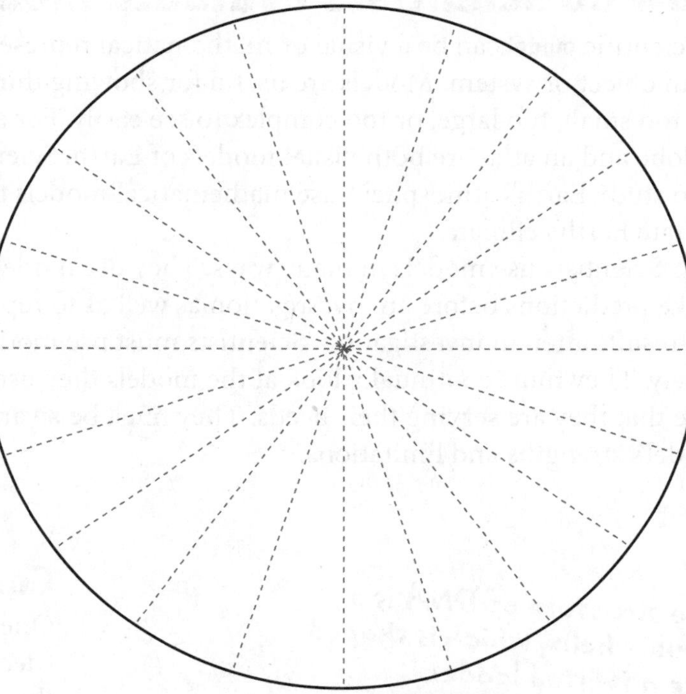

9 Graph Make a circle graph using the percentages you calculated for the bird study. Make appropriately sized pie-shaped slices of the graph for each type of bird. Label each section of the graph with the name of the bird type and the total number of birds of that type counted. Then add an appropriate title.

_____

10 Identify Describe something that is easier to see in the circle graph than it is to see in the table.

_____

_____

_____

11 Interpret How does the size of each section of your circle graph relate to the percentage that it represents?

_____

_____

_____

ⓘ Think Outside the Book

12 Hypothesize Could you have plotted the bird study results in a bar graph? If so, which variable would be shown on the horizontal axis and which would be shown on the vertical axis?

Test Drive the New Model

How do scientists evaluate models?

A scientific **model** can be a visual or mathematical representation of an object or system. Models are useful for showing things that are too small, too large, or too complex to see easily. For example, a globe and an atlas are both visual models of Earth. Scientists who study Earth's atmosphere use mathematical models to try to imitate Earth's climate.

Scientists use models in many ways. They use models to make predictions before an investigation as well as to represent the results after an investigation. Scientists must use models wisely. They must continually look at the models they use to make sure that they are serving their needs. They must be aware of the model's strengths and limitations.

ACTIVE READING

13 Apply As you read, underline examples of scientific models.

◯ By How Much They Can Explain

One famous scientific model is that of the DNA (deoxyribonucleic acid) double helix. DNA is the molecule responsible for passing genetic information from one generation to the next. Evidence and data from biology, chemistry, and physics went into developing the DNA model. The model, in a way, is a representsation of that data and evidence.

Models can be created out of a variety of materials. They can be simple or complex. For example, a DNA double helix model can be brightly colored and three-dimensional, similar to the one at the left, or it can be lines on a piece of paper. The important thing is for the model to show what it must in order to be a good representation.

14 Claims • Evidence • Reasoning Explain why it is valuable for some objects to be shown by more than one kind of model. Provide evidence to support your claim.

_____

_____

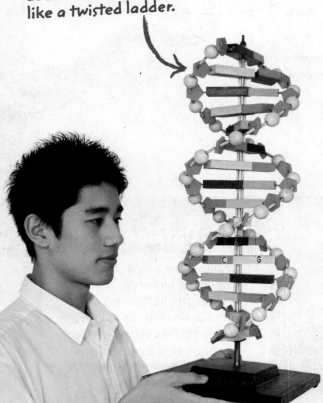

The structure of DNA is a double helix, which is shaped like a twisted ladder.

© Houghton Mifflin Harcourt

©GoGo Images Corporation/Alamy

👁 Visualize It!

15 Compare Both the photo and model below show a plant cell. Identify an advantage and a disadvantage for using the model instead of the photo to study cells.

_____

_____

_____

_____

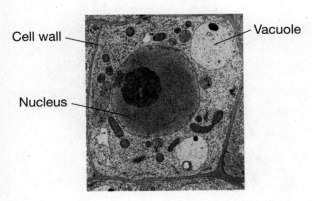

Cell wall

Vacuole

Nucleus

The details of the actual plant cell in this photograph can be fuzzy.

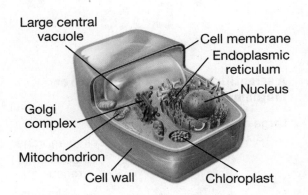

Large central vacuole

Cell membrane

Endoplasmic reticulum

Nucleus

Golgi complex

Mitochondrion

Cell wall

Chloroplast

The model of the plant cell shows distinct parts.

○ By How Well They Can Adapt

When building models, scientists often hope to discover new information. The best models may even explain something that had been puzzling to scientists.

For example, scientists already knew that DNA carries genetic information from one generation to the next. How DNA did this was not obvious. Look at the model at the left. Notice the colors of the horizontal pieces. These pieces represent the way that parts of the molecule attach to one another. The model shows that these attachments follow a certain pattern. The order and pairing of the parts gave scientists a way to speculate about how genetic information is carried.

Scientists had created the model from evidence. Then the model gave scientists more information about how DNA carries genetic information from one generation to the next.

○ By the Fewest Limitations

Scientists often choose models depending on their limitations. For example, would you want to learn about the parts of a cell using the photo at the top left? The photo is of a plant cell, and many of the cell structures are barely visible. The model of the plant cell at the top right, however, shows the plant cell more clearly. After studying the model for a while, you may even be able to pick out structures in the photo that you did not see before.

Sometimes after building a model scientists find data that do not fit the model they created. So, the model may not take certain data into account. To make sense of the information they gathered, scientists must know the ways in which a model does not act exactly as the real object or system does.

Visual Summary

To complete this summary, check the box that indicates true or false. You can use this page to review the main concepts of the lesson.

Representing Data

A scientific model can be a visual or mathematical representation.

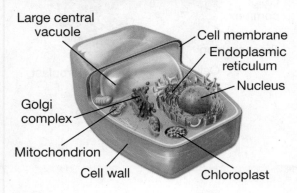

- Large central vacuole
- Cell membrane
- Endoplasmic reticulum
- Nucleus
- Golgi complex
- Mitochondrion
- Cell wall
- Chloroplast

T F

16 ☐ ☐ *Because models are simplified versions of real objects, they often have limitations.*

19 Claims • Evidence • Reasoning Sketch a simple model of your yard or a neighborhood park. Include some animals, some plants, and some environmental factors. Make a claim about the limitations of your model. Provide evidence to support the claim, and explain your reasoning.

Different types of graphs can be used to show different types of data.

Movie-Type Preferences

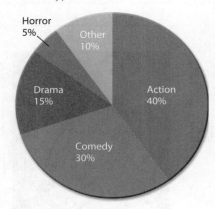

- Horror 5%
- Other 10%
- Action 40%
- Drama 15%
- Comedy 30%

T F

17 ☐ ☐ *According to this circle graph, more students preferred horror movies than comedies.*

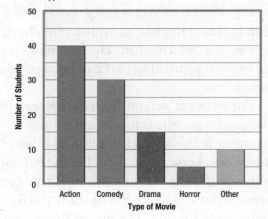

Movie-Type Preferences

Number of Students

Type of Movie: Action, Comedy, Drama, Horror, Other

T F

18 ☐ ☐ *A bar graph is used to compare data in categories.*

Lesson Review

Vocabulary

Circle the term that best completes each of the following sentences.

1 A *hypothesis/graph* can be used to represent the results of an investigation.

2 A *model/law* uses familiar things to describe unfamiliar things.

Key Concepts

3 Define What is a model?

_____

_____

_____

4 Explain Your Reasoning Explain why scientists use models.

_____

_____

_____

5 Claims • Evidence • Reasoning Why do scientists use data tables? State your claim. Provide evidence to support the claim, and explain your reasoning.

_____

_____

_____

6 Define What is a circle graph?

_____

_____

_____

7 Explain Your Reasoning Could you use a circle graph to show data about how body mass changes with height? Explain your reasoning.

_____

_____

_____

Critical Thinking

Use this photo to answer the following questions.

8 Compare How similar is this model to a real object?

_____

_____

9 Claims • Evidence • Reasoning How might this model be useful? State your claim. Provide evidence to support the claim, and explain your reasoning.

_____

_____

_____

_____

10 Hypothesize Identify a possible limitation of a model and describe why it might make a model less useful than it could be.

_____

_____

_____

The Engineering Design Process

ESSENTIAL QUESTION

What is the engineering design process?

By the end of this lesson, you should be able to explain how the engineering design process is used to develop solutions to meet people's needs.

In 2008, Olympic swimmers competed in a large pool inside the Beijing National Aquatics Center, also known as the Beijing Water Cube. It now houses water rides, a wave pool, and a spa.

SC.7.N.1.1 Define a problem from the seventh grade curriculum, use appropriate reference materials to support scientific understanding, plan and carry out scientific investigation of various types, such as systematic observations or experiments, identify variables, collect and organize data, interpret data in charts, tables, and graphics, analyze information, make predictions, and defend conclusions. **SC.7.N.1.5** Describe the methods used in the pursuit of a scientific explanation as seen in different fields of science such as biology, geology, and physics. **SC.7.N.3.2** Identify the benefits and limitations of the use of scientific models.

Lesson Labs

Quick Labs
- Technology in Science
- Evaluate a Prototype

S.T.E.M. Lab
- Earthquake Engineering Design Challenge

 Engage Your Brain

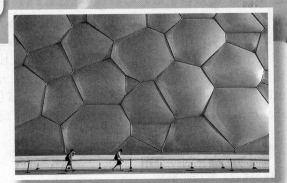

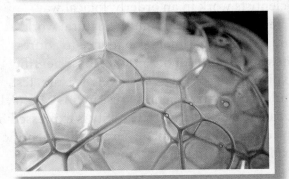

1 Predict Check T or F to show whether you think each statement is true or false.

T	F	
☐	☐	The Beijing Water Cube is an example of technology.
☐	☐	Creativity is not part of the engineering design process.
☐	☐	Nature can inspire new designs.

2 Observe Both the shape of a structure and the shapes of its individual parts affect the overall strength of a structure. Identify the repeating shapes in each image. List at least two differences between the walls of the Water Cube and the milk bubbles.

_____

_____

ACTIVE **READING**

3 Synthesize You can often define an unknown word if you know the meanings of its word parts. Use the word parts and sentence below to make an educated guess about the meaning of the word *technology*.

Word part	Meaning
techno	skill
logy	study of

Example sentence
The development of smartphones is viewed as an important advance in computer technology.

technology:

_____

_____

Vocabulary Terms

- engineering
- prototype
- technology

4 Identify This list contains the vocabulary terms you'll learn in this lesson. As you read, underline the vocabulary words whenever they appear in the text.

It's All Relative

How does the goal of science compare to the goal of engineering?

Scientists observe, collect data, and form hypotheses. **Engineering** is the use of scientific and mathematical knowledge to solve practical problems. The goal of engineering is to meet the needs of society while the goal of science is to understand the natural world. Scientists study how the parts of nature work alone and together. Engineers develop ways of improving the quality of life for human beings.

Science Strives to Explain the Natural World

Scientists work in an orderly, logical way. They ask questions about the natural world and gather experimental evidence to address those questions. In order to form a scientific explanation, scientists observe, measure, test, and record data. Scientific research is careful, but it can also be creative. Creativity is expressed in the design of experiments and in the scientific explanations of observations.

Engineering Strives to Meet the Needs of Society

Humans have always needed tools, such as knives and fire, to help them survive. Beginning in the 1700s, people have increasingly used industrial processes. There is a growing need for energy to operate machines and services to support urban populations. Engineers apply scientific discoveries to develop technologies such as electrical power, sanitation systems, and new ways of communicating.

ACTIVE READING

5 Claims • Evidence • Reasoning How do engineers contribute to the area where you live? State your claim. Provide evidence to support the claim, and explain your reasoning.

_____

👁 Visualize It!

6 Compare In what ways is the modern lamp a better design than the antique lamp? Explain your reasoning.

_____

_____

_____

_____

A wick carries oil into the globe of this lamp where it burns to produce light.

This light-emitting diode (LED) boat light stays cool. Almost 100% of its energy production is light.

What is the relationship between technology, engineering, math, and science?

Science is the study of the natural world. Engineering applies knowledge to develop technology to solve real-life problems. **Technology** includes the use of tools, materials, or processes to meet human needs. Scientists depend on technology such as digital cameras and instruments to observe and measure when they collect data. With computers, they analyze data to support scientific explanations. Engineers build advances in science into new instruments and processes. Science and engineering support one another to advance our knowledge of the natural world and create technologies to manipulate it. Engineers use science and math to develop new technologies. Scientists use technology in research, and engineers use research results to develop technology.

8 Claims • Evidence • Reasoning How could a biologist studying bird migration use global positioning satellite (GPS) technology? Provide evidence, and explain your reasoning.

_____

_____

_____

9 Support Your Claim Why does the graphic show arrows between technology and both science and engineering? Provide evidence to support your claim.

_____

_____

_____

The Right Tool For the Job

How is technology used in scientific investigations?

Scientists investigate the natural world by making observations and doing experiments. They use tools to measure, collect, and analyze data. Many investigations focus on things that are very big or very small, or located in places that are dangerous or hard to reach. Scientists and engineers design specialized technologies for these investigations. For example, biologists observe bacteria through microscopes. Huge accelerators produce high energy collisions between atoms and other particles. Astronomers probe deep into space using digital cameras with telescopes. Robots transmit data from distant planets and ocean depths. The purpose of all of these tools is to collect samples, take pictures, and acquire data.

Think Outside the Book

11 **Apply** Imagine a place or situation that would be interesting to explore but is inaccessible to humans. Design, sketch, and label your own explorer. Think about the tasks that the explorer will need to do and the environment in which it will be working.

👁 Visualize It!

10 **Identify** Label each part with one of the following tasks: generating energy, measuring properties, recording information, communicating data.

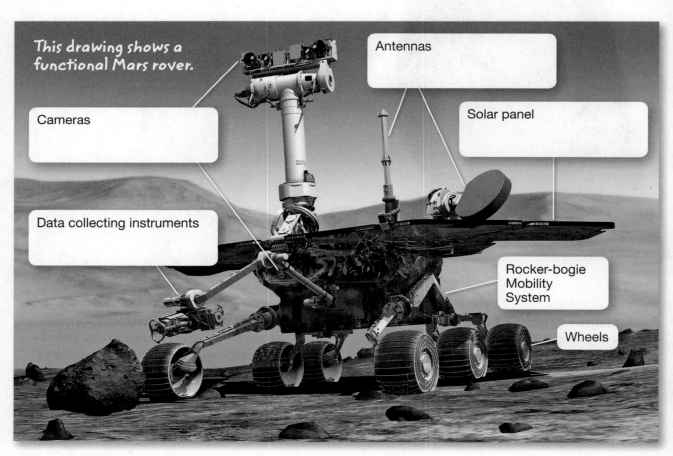

This drawing shows a functional Mars rover.

Antennas

Cameras

Solar panel

Data collecting instruments

Rocker-bogie Mobility System

Wheels

© Houghton Mifflin Harcourt

Students learning about engineering design develop such technical skills as learning to build and test a prototype.

What skills are needed for engineering design?

Look at the world around you. You see computers, cell phones, microwave ovens, and machines for washing dishes and clothes. You see motor vehicles on roads and bridges. You see a world that was designed by engineers.

The goal of engineering design is to meet people's needs. When engineers design solutions to problems, they employ a set of skills that work together.

ACTIVE READING

12 Apply Which type of skills below do you use most often? Give an example.

_____

_____

_____

Research Skills

Engineering design starts with good research skills. Engineers learn all they can about the problem they want to solve, including how similar problems were tackled in the past. Then they must determine whether previous solution attempts were successful and how to adapt them to the current problem. To build on existing approaches, engineers examine new scientific research and apply the results to their design. These adaptations often improve on or replace the previous solutions.

Technical Skills

In solving practical problems, engineers must apply their technical skills in math and science. For example, determining how much weight a bridge can bear requires knowledge of materials and structure and the ability to perform complex calculations. Modern engineering design depends on computer skills in using specialized software for computer-aided design and analysis. Engineering design also requires skill in building **prototypes**, special models built to test a product.

Thinking Skills

Methodical, orderly thinking skills are essential for engineers who must carefully go through every step in the design process. While engineers must pay close attention to every detail in building and testing a prototype, the engineering design process also calls for creativity. Engineers form teams to brainstorm ways of thinking about a problem and proposing solutions. Sometimes they turn a disadvantage into an advantage by finding creative ways to use existing knowledge to solve problems.

Step Right Up

What are the steps of the engineering design process?

When you need to solve a problem, an organized approach leads to the best solution. The steps in the engineering design process provide a logical way of developing a new product or system to solve a real-world problem. People using the process often work in teams. As you will see on the next page, once the need has been identified, the steps of the process often become a cycle.

ACTIVE READING

13 Identify What is the purpose of breaking the engineering design process into specific steps?

1. Identifying a Need

What is the problem? Who has the problem? Why must it be solved? These are the types of questions that identify a problem that needs a technical solution.

2. Conducting Research

By doing research, the design team learns as much as possible about the need that must be met or the problem that must be solved. The research frequently turns up similar problems and the different solutions that have been tried. The design team works more efficiently by learning from the past efforts of others and by identifying new resources and possibilities.

3. Brainstorming and Selecting Solutions

Team members think of possible solution ideas during a brainstorming session. The goal of brainstorming is to come up with as many engineering design solutions as possible. Any idea, even if it does not seem promising, is open for discussion. Then each idea is evaluated: Is the device or product safe? Does it address the problem? What would it cost? Would it be easy to make? The team selects the best solution based on how well it meets the requirements of the need or problem.

4. Building a Prototype

The design team builds a prototype of the device or product they selected as the best technical solution to the need or problem. The team uses the prototype as a working model to test and evaluate how well the product works under real-life conditions. A prototype usually does not work perfectly right away. The team uses the prototype to find out how the solution can be improved and for troubleshooting—finding out why parts of the product or device do not work as expected.

👁 Visualize It!

14 Design In the space provided, sketch a prototype device for rescuing the trapped cat.

5. Testing, Evaluating, and Redesigning a Prototype

The engineering design process calls for testing and changing the prototype until a solution is reached. The team tests the prototype and records the results. After discussing the results, changes are made to improve the prototype design. Testing and redesigning the prototype continues until the prototype addresses the need.

6. Communicating Results

The final step in the engineering design process is communicating the results. It is very important to take good notes and communicate all details about the product or solution. Such details enable others to duplicate the results. Student teams can communicate the results to others in a final report or by posting their results on a display board. Professional engineers often communicate their results through reports in engineering journals.

15 List You want to tell others how you rescued the cat. How will you communicate the results? List two possible ways below.

_____

_____

How does the engineering design process work?

The steps of the engineering design process call for engineers to use both technical skills and creativity. From identifying a need to finding a good solution, engineers are always asking questions. Instead of simply moving from one step to the next, the process goes back and forth between the steps. In the chart below, the rectangles contain steps, and the diamonds contain questions or decision points. Try answering the questions in different ways and see how the path that you follow through the design process depends on the answers to the questions. Keep in mind that the goal is to design a solution to a problem, whether it is rescuing a cat or focusing a beam of charged particles on a tiny target.

Start

Identify a Need The first step in the engineering design process is to select a need to address.

Conduct Research To find an engineering design solution, you need to find out as much about the need as you can.

Do you have enough information?

NO

YES

Does the prototype work well? — YES

NO

Redesign to Improve Make design changes to improve your model so that it better solves your problem.

YES

Brainstorm Solutions Cooperate with others to come up with as many possible solutions as you can. These are not final solutions. They are ideas to try.

Do you have an idea worth trying? — YES

NO

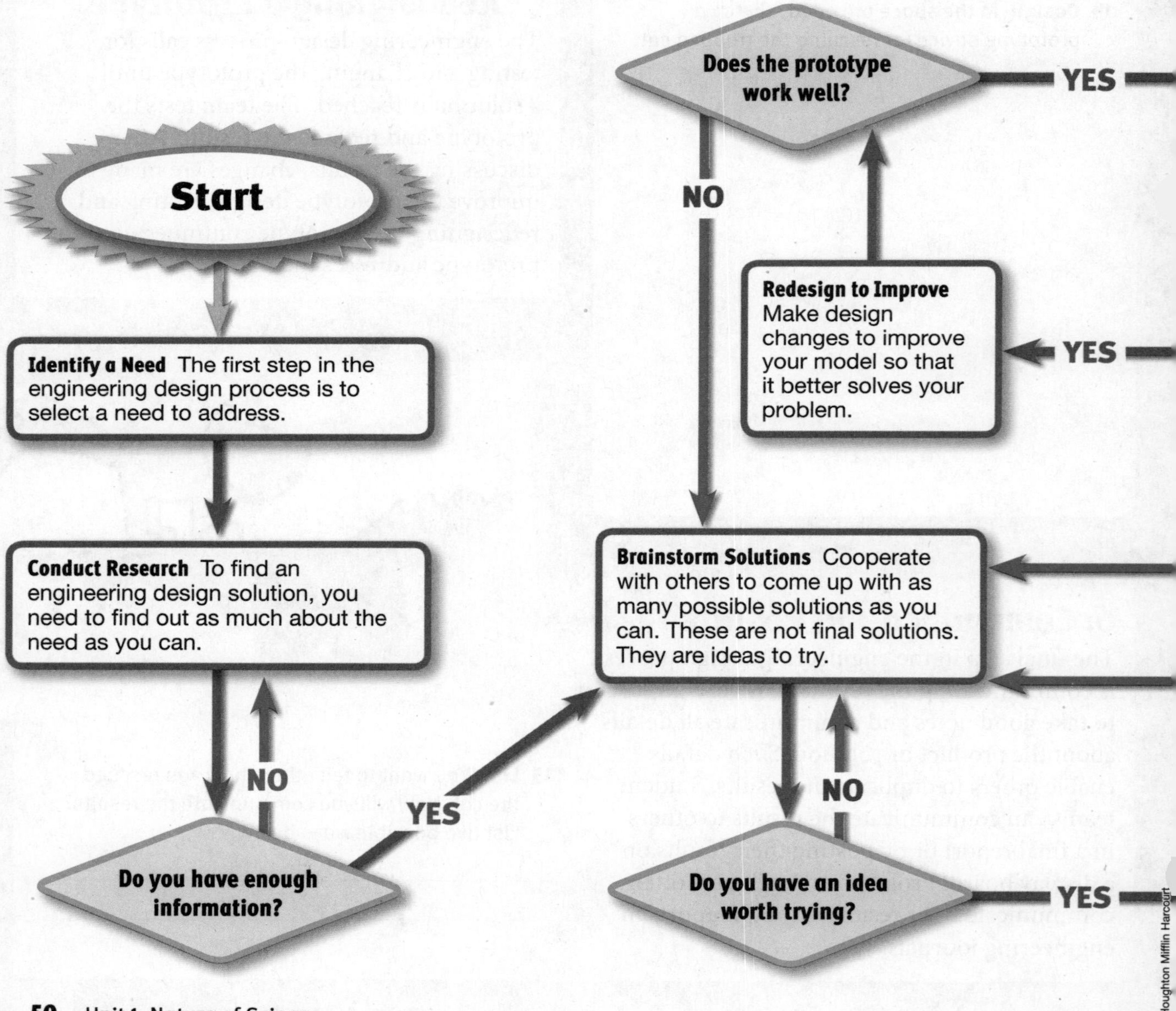

© Houghton Mifflin Harcourt

This superconducting magnet assembly is one of many magnets designed to focus a beam of charged particles on a target the size of an atom in the Large Hadron Collider. Engineers followed the engineering design process to develop every component of the magnet.

Communicate Your Results When your prototype is finished, you have designed a solution to your problem. Tell others how you did it!

→ **End!**

Test and Evaluate Your prototype probably won't be perfect the first time you try it, but it should be on the right track.

Does the prototype show promise?

NO

Build a Prototype Your prototype should be a working model of your solution to the problem.

YES

Can you make a prototype?

NO

Select a Solution Which of your ideas do you want to try? Pick one, and plan how you want to try it.

👁 Visualize It!

17 Apply Oh, no! The test results of your most recent prototype indicate that it doesn't meet the need for which it was designed. List the next four steps in the engineering design process that you might follow.

_____

_____

_____

_____

Visual Summary

To complete this summary, fill in each blank with the correct word or phrase. You can use this page to review the main concepts of this lesson.

The goal of science is to understand the natural world. The goal of engineering is to meet the needs of society.

18 Engineering applies _____ and math to develop technology.

The Engineering Design Process

The first steps in the process are identifying and doing research about a need.
The next steps involve brainstorming and selecting a solution.

20 Before selecting the final design, engineers built and tested a _____

Engineering design starts with good research skills. Engineering design requires a variety of technical skills.

19 Engineering design calls for both logical and creative _____ skills.

21 **Claims • Evidence • Reasoning** As part of an engineering team, you are designing a tool for tracking packages being shipped. Provide some suggestions to be discussed as part of the brainstorming process. Make a claim about your suggested solutions, and support your claim with evidence. Explain your reasoning.

Lesson Review

Vocabulary

Fill in the blank with the term that best completes the following sentences.

1 Engineers solve real-life problems by developing new _____.

2 Developing new products and systems that meet human needs is the goal of _____.

3 A working model that engineers use to test a design is called a _____.

Key Concepts

4 Relate How are scientific discoveries used in engineering design?

_____

_____

5 Summarize List the basic steps in the engineering design process.

_____

_____

6 Claims • Evidence • Reasoning Make a claim about why engineering design calls for good research skills. Provide evidence to support the claim, and explain your reasoning.

_____

_____

7 Claims • Evidence • Reasoning Make a claim about why the engineering design process does not move smoothly from step to step but instead goes back and forth between the steps. Provide evidence to support the claim, and explain your reasoning.

_____

_____

Critical Thinking

8 Infer After an engineering design team communicates its results, how could those results be used?

_____

_____

_____

Use this diagram to answer the following questions.

9 Claims • Evidence • Reasoning Make a claim about the qualities that engineers could test using the prototype of this bicycle. Provide evidence to support your claim, and explain your reasoning.

_____

_____

10 Claims • Evidence • Reasoning Make a claim about one or more changes that could be made to this prototype to reduce wind resistance and increase speed. Provide evidence to support your claim, and explain your reasoning.

_____

_____

Methods of Analysis

ESSENTIAL QUESTION

How can we evaluate technology?

By the end of this lesson you should be able to explain how scientists and engineers determine the costs, benefits, and risks of a new technology.

X-rays expose the body to harmful radiation, but they allow doctors to see inside the body without surgery. Do the benefits outweigh the risks?

SC.7.N.1.1 Define a problem from the seventh grade curriculum, use appropriate reference materials to support scientific understanding, plan and carry out scientific investigation of various types, such as systematic observations or experiments, identify variables, collect and organize data, interpret data in charts, tables, and graphics, analyze information, make predictions, and defend conclusions. **SC.7.N.1.5** Describe the methods used in the pursuit of a scientific explanation as seen in different fields of science such as biology, geology, and physics **SC.7.N.2.1** Identify an instance from the history of science in which scientific knowledge has changed when new evidence or new interpretations are encountered. **SC.7.N.3.2** Identify the benefits and limitations of the use of scientific models.

 ## Engage Your Brain

1 Predict Check T or F to show whether you think each statement is true or false.

T	F	
☐	☐	Sometimes people accept certain risks in exchange for other benefits.
☐	☐	Technology never causes problems.
☐	☐	When comparing technology, you need to examine each feature.
☐	☐	A product only affects the environment when it is thrown away.

2 Identify List advantages and disadvantages of each of the writing utensils shown here.

Advantages	Disadvantages
A	
B	

ACTIVE **READING**

3 Infer The term *life cycle* often describes the stages an organism goes through from birth to death. What do you think *life cycle* means when it is used to talk about a product?

_____

_____

_____

_____

Vocabulary Terms

• trade-off
• risk-benefit analysis
• life cycle analysis
• Pugh chart

4 Apply As you learn the definition of each vocabulary term in this lesson, create your own definition or sketch to help you remember the meaning of the term.

Better or Worse

How can the effects of technology be described?

Technology is the application of science for practical purposes and can include products, processes, and systems. New technology may affect society, the environment, or the economy in several ways. The effects of a new technology can be classified in four ways:

- expected and favorable
- expected and unfavorable
- unexpected and favorable
- unexpected and unfavorable

◯ Expected Effects

When people develop technology, they try to predict the effects that it may have. The goal for any new technology is to keep the expected favorable effects greater than any expected unfavorable effects. People make trade-offs when they adopt new technology. A **trade-off** means accepting risks in exchange for benefits or giving up one benefit to gain another. The control of fire is one of the earliest human technologies. Fire improves food and increases the odds of surviving winter. But fire can also destroy homes, crops, and habitats. For thousands of years, people have accepted the risk of fire because the expected benefits outweigh the risk.

Control of fire is one of the earliest technologies to be developed by humans.

◯ Unexpected Effects

People cannot always predict the effects of new technology. For example, scientists developed instruments to study how atoms interact with one another. An unexpected favorable result was magnetic resonance imaging (MRI). MRI is a medical technique that looks inside the body without using harmful radiation.

In the mid-twentieth century, nontoxic chemicals made it possible to make better refrigerators for homes. An unexpected unfavorable effect was that these chemicals began destroying the protective ozone layer in the upper atmosphere.

ACTIVE READING

5 Claims • Evidence • Reasoning What is the difference between expected effects and unexpected effects of technology? Provide evidence to support your claim, and explain your reasoning.

Think Outside the Book

6 Claims • Evidence • Reasoning Use the Internet to find out how infectious diseases can spread rapidly from one continent to another. How would you classify the spread of disease as an effect of air travel? State your claim. Provide evidence to support the claim, and explain your reasoning.

Before the invention of freezer technology, many vegetables and fruits could only be eaten during a few months of the year.

	Expected	Unexpected
Favorable	When frozen foods were developed, it was expected that frozen food would last longer than food that was not frozen. As a result, people save money because frozen vegetables do not spoil. Also, people can eat healthy foods even when they are not in season.	Surprisingly, frozen fruits and vegetables turned out to be more nutritious than fresh produce. Produce begins to lose nutrients as soon as it is picked. Food processors usually freeze fruits and vegetables soon after picking so nutrients remain in the product.
Unfavorable	An expected unfavorable effect of selling frozen foods is that local farmers and markets that provide fresh fruits and vegetables lose customers. In addition, frozen foods need more packaging than fresh foods. This adds to the cost of the food and the environmental costs of supplying it. People are willing to make these trade-offs in order to have frozen food.	When frozen foods were first developed, no one could have predicted the variety of frozen foods that would become available. Many frozen foods today contain more fat, sugar, and salt than fresh foods do. Eating too much of these substances can have unfavorable health effects.

7 Analyze Use the comparison table below to analyze the expected and unexpected effects of the development of the World Wide Web.

	Expected	Unexpected
Favorable		
Unfavorable		

Risky Business

How is technology analyzed?

There are many ways to analyze new technology. Three methods that people use are *risk-benefit analysis, life cycle analysis,* and *Pugh charts.*

◯ Risk-Benefit Analysis

A **risk-benefit analysis** compares the risks, or unfavorable effects, to the benefits, or favorable effects, of a decision or technology. For example, x-rays are a way for doctors to look inside the body to evaluate broken bones and diagnose disease. However, as x-rays pass through the body, they can damage living cells. Medical x-rays expose patients to very small doses of radiation, so the benefits are considered greater than the risks. At one time, some shoe stores used x-rays to match shoes to customers' feet. This is no longer done because the benefit was very small compared to the risk.

Risks and Benefits of X-rays	
Risks	**Benefits**
damage to cells	quick
increased risk of cancer	painless
	saves lives

Skate parks are popular attractions. But there are definite risks involved for the skaters and the owners of the park.

8 Analyze Fill in the chart below with the risks and benefits of building a new skate park in your community.

Risks and Benefits of a New Skate Park	

Life Cycle Analysis

When analyzing technology, it is important to consider the real cost. This is done using a life cycle analysis. A **life cycle analysis** is an evaluation of the materials and energy used for the manufacture, transportation, sale, use, and disposal of a product. This analysis includes everything that the product affects, from obtaining raw materials through disposal. The costs of all of these steps are added together to find the real cost of the product. For example, a life cycle analysis of a glass bottle examines the cost of repairing environmental damage from the mining of raw materials, the cost of fuels consumed to transport materials and finished bottles, and the cost of disposal. A major reason for doing a life cycle analysis is to include environmental effects in the cost. Life cycle analyses are important to manufacturers because the analyses help engineers compare the real costs of different products and find ways to improve production.

Life Cycle of a Television

Resources
A life cycle analysis includes the cost to mine materials for television parts, for manufacturing packaging, and for repairing environmental damage.

Production
The cost of manufacturing is just one part of the overall economic effect of a television.

Consumer Use
Another part of the life cycle analysis is the cost in money and energy when people buy and use the product.

👁 Visualize It!

9 Infer Write a title and a description for the final step in the life cycle of a television.

_____

_____

_____

_____

_____

Pugh Chart

A **Pugh chart** is a table used to compare the features of multiple items. Each row of the table shows a different product or solution. Each column of the chart lists one feature. In some Pugh charts, various options are marked as being either present or missing. Other Pugh charts rank each product as being better or worse than a standard for each feature. Another type ranks each product by feature using a numerical scale.

By looking at the table, a person can analyze and compare items. For example, a Pugh chart comparing cell phones would list different phones in the first column on the left. Then each column would be titled based on a characteristic that is important to consumers. These characteristics could include battery life, sound quality, and messaging systems. A quick look at the Pugh chart would tell you which cell phone was the best based on the qualities that you were looking for.

10 Analyze Evaluate the features of different types of containers. Place an X in each box where the quality applies to the container. Then use the chart to answer the following questions.

	Lightweight	Waterproof	Durable	Inexpensive	Transparent	Reusable
Glass jar						
Plastic bag	X					
Cardboard box	X					
Metal box						

11 Infer Suppose that you have a collection of interesting seashells. Use the chart to help you decide which container you would use to display the collection on shelves in your room. Explain your reasoning.

_____

_____

_____

_____

_____

12 Claims • Evidence • Reasoning Why do manufacturers choose cardboard containers for products such as breakfast cereal? State your claim. Provide evidence to support the claim, and explain your reasoning.

_____

_____

_____

_____

_____

Building Coral Reefs

Recycling large vehicles—ships, jetliners, or railroad cars—is expensive and difficult. Scuba divers exploring wrecked ships found an unexpected solution. Aquatic organisms had moved into the sunken ships and built new coral reefs.

Potential Hazards?
Before sinking, a risk-benefit analysis is done to look for any unfavorable effects such as pollution by leftover fuel.

New Shelters
To the coral organisms, the airplane walls are like an underwater cave. As the new reef grows, many different organisms find their perfect habitat.

This airplane does not look much like a coral reef yet.

Extend

13 Identify How can an artificial reef be considered an unexpected favorable effect of building a plane?

14 Research Use the Internet to investigate other positive or negative effects of sinking ships or planes to build artificial reefs. What did you find?

15 Claims • Evidence • Reasoning Some people feel that sinking ships and planes on purpose is like dumping our trash in the ocean. In your opinion, do the possible negative effects outweigh the benefits? Provide evidence to support the claim, and explain your reasoning.

Visual Summary

To complete this summary, fill in the blanks with the correct word or phrase. You can use this page to review the main concepts of the lesson.

The effects of technology can be expected favorable, expected unfavorable, unexpected favorable, and unexpected unfavorable.

16 When an effect is predicted and desired, it is an

_____ effect.

Methods of Analysis

Three methods for analyzing technology are risk-benefit analysis, life-cycle analysis, and Pugh charts.

17 A _____
examines every aspect of a product from obtaining raw materials through disposal or recycling.

18 A _____
uses a table to compare features of similar products.

19 An analysis that compares the favorable and unfavorable effects of a decision or technology is a

_____

20 Claims • Evidence • Reasoning Why do scientists use analysis methods when developing new technology? Provide evidence to support your claim, and explain your reasoning.

Lesson Review

Vocabulary

Fill in the blank with the term that best completes the following sentences.

1 A _____ happens when some benefits are lost to gain other benefits.

2 The evaluation of the materials and energy used for making, selling, using, and disposing of a product is called a _____

_____

3 A _____ is the comparison of the favorable and unfavorable effects of a technology.

Key Concepts

4 Identify What are the four types of effects that can result from technology?

_____

_____

5 Claims • Evidence • Reasoning Which type of analysis would be most useful to someone buying a product at a store? State your claim. Provide evidence to support the claim, and explain your reasoning.

_____

_____

6 Claims • Evidence • Reasoning How is a life cycle analysis used to make decisions about technology? Provide evidence to support your claim, and explain your reasoning.

_____

_____

_____

7 Describe When do the results of a risk-benefit analysis indicate that a technology should be used?

_____

_____

_____

Critical Thinking

Use the Pugh chart below to answer the following questions about digital cameras.

+ = excellent; 0 = good; − = poor

	Zoom	Picture quality	Ease of use	Price
Camera A	−	−	+	0
Camera B	+	−	+	−
Camera C	+	0	0	+

8 Analyze Which camera received the highest overall ratings? Explain your reasoning.

_____

_____

9 Infer If someone chose Camera A based on the ratings in the Pugh chart, which feature was most important to that user?

_____

_____

10 Predict Imagine that a new surgical procedure has been developed to treat spinal cord injury. What are some possible risks and benefits of receiving this procedure?

_____

_____

_____

_____

11 Claims • Evidence • Reasoning How has the development of social networking on the Internet had favorable and unfavorable effects? State your claim. Provide evidence to support the claim, and explain your reasoning.

SC.7.N.1.1 Define a problem from the seventh grade curriculum, use appropriate reference materials to support scientific understanding, plan and carry out scientific investigation of various types, such as systematic observations or experiments, identify variables, collect and organize data, interpret data in charts, tables, and graphics, analyze information, make predictions, and defend conclusions. SC.7.N.3.2 Identify the benefits and limitations of the use of scientific models.

S.T.E.M. ENGINEERING & TECHNOLOGY

Analyzing Technology

Skills
✔ Identify benefits and risks
✔ Evaluate cost of technology
✔ Evaluate environmental impact
Propose improvements
Propose risk reduction
Compare technology
✔ Communicate results

Objectives
Identify the benefits of a specific technology.
Identify the risks of a specific technology.
Conduct a risk-benefit analysis of a specific technology.

Risks and Benefits of Electric Transportation

The growing population in many areas has led to significant transportation problems. People need to move around to get to work, school, or shopping areas. However, without other options, they often end up driving around in cars all by themselves. This contributes to traffic problems, wear and tear on the roads, pollution, and wasted fuel.

Many traffic problems are caused by too many cars on the roads.

(c) ©Thinkstock Images/Comstock Images/Getty Images

1 Observe From a safe place, observe the number of cars driving by your school or driving on a main street in your neighborhood. Record how many cars drive by in a certain amount of time and also how many of those cars contain only the driver.

Cars	Only driver

2 Claims • Evidence • Reasoning What are some of the benefits of people driving around in cars, even though they may often be by themselves? State your claim. Provide evidence to support the claim, and explain your reasoning.

_____

_____

_____

Electric Scooters

Electric scooters are small, open vehicles that use a battery-operated electric motor to propel the rider. Some people say electric scooters are the solution to modern transportation problems. A benefit is something that provides an advantage. Some benefits are that electric scooters take up less space on the road and in parking lots. Electric scooters also do not emit exhaust and can be cheaper to own and operate than cars. A risk is the chance of a dangerous or undesirable outcome.

3 Claims • Evidence • Reasoning Make a claim about some of the problems or risks that could result from the widespread use of electric scooters. Provide evidence to support the claim, and explain your reasoning.

_____

_____

_____

Risk
Even though electric vehicles don't emit exhaust, the power plants that deliver their electricity do have negative environmental effects.

Benefit
Electric scooters take up less room on the road than cars.

✋ You Try It!

Now it's your turn to evaluate the risks and benefits of students using electric scooters to travel to and from your school.

You Try It!

Now it's your turn to evaluate the risks and benefits of students using electric scooters to travel to and from your school.

1 Identify Risks and Benefits

Suppose all of the students at your school used electric scooters to ride from home to school and back. Think of all the positive and negative aspects of all students riding electric scooters. In the table below, list all of these risks and benefits. List any negative aspects under the "Risks" heading and list any positive aspects under the "Benefits" heading. You may need to add to the table as you complete the rest of this activity.

Risks	Benefits

2 Evaluate Cost of Technology

A Imagine that every student in your school rides the school bus. Research the cost per student per year of your school's bus system. To do this, estimate how many miles the students have to ride to and from school and how much gas is needed to travel that distance.

_____

_____

_____

B Research the cost of electric scooters that students might be able to use to get to and from your school. How much would it cost each student to buy a scooter? What other costs do you need to consider?

_____

_____

S.T.E.M. ENGINEERING & TECHNOLOGY

③ Evaluate Environmental Impact

In what specific ways would the environment be affected by all students riding electric scooters to and from your school? Be sure to think about both positive and negative effects on the environment.

_____
_____
_____
_____
_____
_____

④ Communicate Results

A Based on all the risks and benefits you listed, what conclusion would you make about whether all students should drive electric scooters to and from your school? Explain your reasoning.

_____
_____
_____
_____
_____
_____
_____

B Write a persuasive letter to your local school board attempting to convince members to adopt your conclusion about the use of electric scooters at your school. Be sure to support your argument with evidence from your risk-benefit analysis.

_____
_____
_____
_____
_____
_____
_____
_____
_____

Engineering and Our World

ESSENTIAL QUESTION

How are engineering and society related?

By the end of this lesson, you should be able to explain how engineering, technology, and society affect each other.

Washing machines, dryers, and other appliances are engineered to make our lives easier.

SC.7.N.2.1 Identify an instance from the history of science in which scientific knowledge has changed when new evidence or new interpretations are encountered. **SC.7.N.3.2** Identify the benefits and limitations of the use of scientific models.

© Houghton Mifflin Harcourt

Lesson Labs

Quick Labs
- Inventor Trading Cards
- Investigate Energy Efficiency

 Engage Your Brain

1 Describe Write a caption explaining what is going on in this photo.

_____

_____

_____

2 Infer Every kind of technology has advantages and disadvantages. Think of some disadvantages to washing clothes by hand. Think of some advantages. Write your answers below.

_____

_____

_____

_____

_____

ACTIVE **READING**

3 Apply Use context clues to write your own definition for the words *technology* and *design*.

Example sentence
The tools of modern farming <u>technology</u> include chemical fertilizers, diesel-powered tractors, and automatic irrigation systems.

technology:

_____

_____

Example sentence
Landscape engineers <u>design</u> parks so that people have room to relax and play.

design:

_____

_____

Vocabulary

4 Identify As you read, place a question mark next to any words that you don't understand. When you finish reading the lesson, go back and review the text that you marked. If the information is still confusing, consult a classmate or teacher.

Got Tech?

What makes up the designed world?

Your environment is made of a designed world within a natural world. The natural world includes all the parts of the environment that were not made by people. The designed world includes all the parts of the environment that were made by people.

◯ Big Structures and Large Machines

Look around you. What do you see? You might see houses, apartments, your school, and roads and bridges and the vehicles on them. These structures are all parts of the designed world. The designed world includes skyscrapers, cars, trains, planes, and other complex technology that require careful engineering. The highways, railroad tracks, and airports needed for transportation have also been engineered.

Other parts of the designed world are not as obvious. For example, within a city park, trees and other plants are used with engineered lights, paths, and bridges. Landscape designers use these natural and human-made things to create natural-looking spaces within cities.

ACTIVE READING

5 Identify What is the designed world?

_____

_____

👁 Visualize It!

6 Identify List all of the engineered objects that you can see in the photo.

_____

_____

_____

A city is a designed environment within the natural world. Architects and engineers design the buildings, roads, and parks that people use and enjoy.

Products You Use Every Day

The designed world also includes all the products you use every day. Soap, clocks, chairs, and lamps are all engineered to help you live well at home. Books, eyeglasses, and lab equipment are engineered to help you learn at school. Helmets, in-line skates, tennis rackets, and other pieces of sports equipment are designed to help you have fun safely.

Some designed products, such as hand-held games, cell phones, and computers, are complex. Other designed products, such as dinner plates and towels, are fairly simple technology. Some products are a combination of simple and complex. Shoes and waterproof clothing may be made from natural cotton cloth and materials designed by chemical engineers. All of the products you wear and use are part of a designed world.

Personal music players are engineered to store digital music and replay it through earbuds.

Books are a form of technology that people have used for centuries.

Clothing is engineered to be durable, comfortable, and attractive.

Skateboards are engineered to be durable, easy to steer, and fast.

i Think Outside the Book

7 Apply Write a script for a podcast ad for a spoon. Imagine that your audience has never seen a spoon before, so describe the spoon's design carefully!

Why is technology developed?

The designed world depends on technology. Technology includes all the inventions, processes, and tools that have been developed to meet our needs and wants.

○ To Meet People's Needs

Basic needs include food, water, clothing, shelter, protection, transportation, and communication. Some simple technology has been meeting people's needs for a long time. For example, people learned how to cook food over fire, use ditches to water crops, weave cloth, and use animals for work and transportation thousands of years ago.

Technology used today still meets these same needs. Modern stoves use electricity or gas to cook food. Modern farms use mechanical irrigation to water crops more efficiently and tractors to pull farm equipment. Clothes are woven using both traditional and new materials. Protective gear is made of modern plastics. Engines power cars, buses, and trains. Modern medical technology helps keep you healthy.

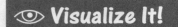 **Visualize It!**

Needs

8 Classify Identify the need that each of the items in the photos addresses.

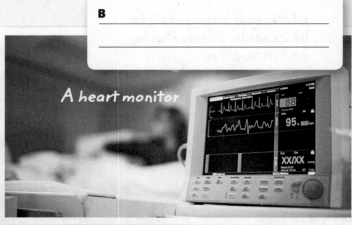

B
_____
_____

A heart monitor

An irrigation system

A
_____
_____

C
_____
_____
_____

A bicycle helmet

© Houghton Mifflin Harcourt

(bl) ©Lisa Kyle Young/Photodisc/Getty Images; (tr) ©Helen Ashford/Workbook Stock/Getty

Wants

A _____

Beads

Electronic keyboard

Video game

B _____

C _____

👁 Visualize It!

9 Classify Identify the want that each of the items in the photos addresses.

To Meet People's Wants

ACTIVE **READING**

10 Identify As you read, underline two factors that shape people's wants.

Wants are things that people do not require to survive, but desire anyway. Wants include the desire to be more comfortable, to play, to have beautiful things, or to make music.

Inventors and engineers use technology to develop devices that meet people's wants, such as air conditioners, radios, and telephones. Plastics and other materials are used to meet the desire for play or decoration. The desire for realistic computer games has advanced the field of computer graphics.

People's technological wants often depend on their values and culture. Some cultures embrace all modern technology. Others accept only some technology. For example, some farmers choose to farm using horses instead of tractors. Additionally, wants vary from one culture to another. The definition of beautiful music, art, and fashion differs depending on whom you ask.

> **ⓘ 11 Claims • Evidence • Reasoning** Would you classify a cellular phone as a want or a need? State your claim. Provide evidence to support the claim, and explain your reasoning.
>
> _____
> _____
> _____
> _____
> _____

Growing and Changing

Why is technology revised?

Technology is revised as society's needs and wants change. New technology often leads to new needs and wants. These new needs and wants then fuel the development of even newer technology.

Needs and Wants Change

Needs and wants change when society changes. For example, years ago, most people in the United States lived on farms. When new technology made farming more efficient, fewer farmers were needed to grow food. Many people left farms and moved to cities.

The people in cities had new needs. For example, now that they were not growing food, they needed to buy and store food. Refrigerators were developed to keep food fresh. People also had more free time, and new wants. New forms of entertainment, such as movies and recorded music, were developed. All of these wants and needs drove the development of new technology and products.

12 Claims • Evidence • Reasoning
Before you read, make a claim about why you think technology is revised. Provide evidence to support your claim, and explain your reasoning.

_____

_____

_____

_____

👁 Visualize It!

Computer technology was developed as society's needs changed. Computers have gotten smaller and more reliable over time. They process data faster and can share data more easily.

In the 1960s and 1970s, computers were large and processed data stored on reels of magnetic tape. Data were shared by moving the reels to another computer.

In the 1980s, engineers worked on making computers smaller. Improved hardware led to the development of personal computers.

Personal computers stored and shared information on floppy disks.

(tr) ©Bettmann/Corbis; (bl) ©SuperStock/Getty Images; (br) ©Andrzei Tokarski/Alamy

© Houghton Mifflin Harcourt

New Technology Generates New Needs

ACTIVE **READING**

13 Identify As you read, underline two examples of new technology creating new needs.

When people begin using new technology, they often develop new needs. For example, when people in cities began driving cars, they needed a way of coordinating traffic. So traffic lights were invented. One technology led to another.

Likewise, computers were developed in the 1950s to meet the need to process data. Early computers were very big machines that stored data on giant spools of magnetic tape. Even though they could process large amounts of data, they could not share that data easily. Computer scientists needed a better way to share information. As a result, engineers developed disk storage technology. As computers became smaller and more affordable, more people began using them and more information needed to be shared. Disks improved, and now one DVD can hold more data than an early computer could. Today, computers can transfer data electronically over the Internet. The Internet connects computers directly to each other and makes sharing data and images easy.

Now, computers all over the world can share data quickly over the Internet. Although the Internet was developed for scientists, people now use it for everyday activities, such as talking to friends.

14 Illustrate How do you think data storage and computer communication will change next? Draw and describe your answer.

Publishing Company

How are society and technology related?

Society and technology affect each other. For example, when people choose to buy a technology, manufacturers continue to make and improve it. When people stop buying a technology, manufacturers no longer make it.

Society's technology choices can change in unpredictable ways. For example, in the 1940s, American society had hopes that nuclear technology could supply limitless, clean, and cheap energy. So, in the mid-1950s, engineers planned the first nuclear power plants. However, people discovered that nuclear technology has its disadvantages, too. For example, the plants are costly to build. They need expensive controls to operate safely, and they make dangerous radioactive waste. Accidents at nuclear plants in the 1980s reminded people of the risks of nuclear energy. Companies stopped building nuclear plants and built more plants that burned fossil fuels.

But fossil fuels are limited and becoming more scarce. And a new disadvantage of that technology emerged. Power plants that burn fossil fuels add greenhouse gases to the atmosphere. So the advantages of using nuclear power are being discussed again. The debate is still going on. Modern society needs energy. The values and priorities of society help us select which technology we use.

ACTIVE READING

15 Identify As you read, underline the ways society affects which technology is developed.

16 Identify List some advantages and disadvantages of nuclear energy in the table below.

Advantages	Disadvantages

Society will choose whether nuclear power plants meet our energy needs in the future.

Going Up?

Which technology allows people to climb tall buildings with the push of a button? Elevators! The addition of elevators changed the height of buildings, the skyline of cities, and people's ability to reach the sky.

Need for Skyscrapers

In the middle 1800s, more people started moving to cities. More space was needed for homes and offices. But land in cities was limited and expensive. Building upward was less expensive than spreading out. So architects began designing taller buildings, which meant climbing more stairs to reach the upper floors.

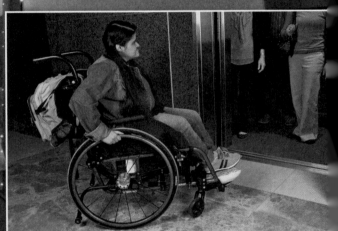

Need for Elevators

Putting elevators in buildings eliminated the need to climb stairs. Elevators make it possible for people who cannot climb stairs to move around easily in any building that has more than one floor.

ℹ Extend

17 Gather Evidence Why might someone put an elevator in a single-family home? Provide evidence to support your claim.

18 Explain Your Reasoning What might be one disadvantage of elevator technology? Explain your reasoning.

19 Compare Investigate and describe three types of elevator designs: hydraulic, pneumatic, and roped. Describe the advantages and drawbacks of each of the three elevator designs.

Visual Summary

To complete this summary, fill in the blanks with the correct word or phrase. You can use this page to review the main concepts of the lesson.

Engineering and Our World

The designed world includes large structures and machines and small products. Every product we use is part of the designed world.

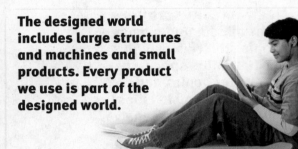

20 Large structures in the designed world include _____

As needs and wants change, technologies are revised, too.

22 The need to process, store, and share growing amounts of information led to improved _____

Technologies are developed to meet needs and wants.

21 Clothing, shelter, food, communication, transportation are considered

_____

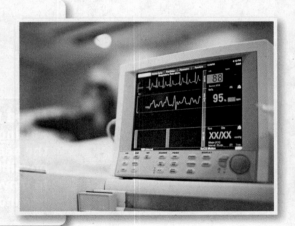

23 Claims • Evidence • Reasoning Make a claim about how society's need to replace coal, oil, and other fossil fuels as energy sources could lead to new technology for automobiles and other motor vehicles. Provide evidence to support the claim, and explain your reasoning.

Lesson Review

Vocabulary

In your own words define the following term.

1 designed world

_____

_____

Key Concepts

2 Identify What makes up the designed world?

_____

_____

3 Apply What drives companies to make batteries that cost less and last longer?

_____

_____

_____

_____

4 Claims • Evidence • Reasoning Why does the designed world change? State your claim. Provide evidence to support the claim, and explain your reasoning.

_____

_____

_____

_____

5 Claims • Evidence • Reasoning Why did computer floppy disks develop? State your claim. Provide evidence to support the claim, and explain your reasoning.

_____

_____

_____

6 Distinguish What is the difference between the designed world and the natural world?

_____

_____

_____

Critical Thinking

Use this table to answer the following question.

Solar Energy	
Advantages	**Disadvantages**
Solar cells use free solar energy.	Solar cells are expensive to make.
Solar cells reduce the need for fossil fuels.	Solar energy cannot supply all of our energy needs right now.
Solar cells do not make pollution.	Solar cells cannot generate electricity at night.

7 Claims • Evidence • Reasoning How would switching to solar power affect a city environmentally and financially? State your claim. Provide evidence to support the claim, and explain your reasoning.

_____

_____

_____

_____

_____

8 Analyze What parts of the designed world were developed to make air travel practical?

_____

_____

_____

9 Claims • Evidence • Reasoning Some farmers in the United States still use horse-drawn equipment. Make a claim about why they might choose to use older technology. Provide evidence to support the claim, and explain your reasoning.

_____

_____

_____

_____

Publishing Company

PEOPLE IN SCIENCE

SC.7.N.1.5 Describe the methods used in the pursuit of a scientific explanation as seen in different fields of science such as biology, geology, and physics.

Mitchell W. Pryor
ROBOTICS ENGINEER

Do you think of robots as mostly science fiction? Can you imagine going to college to learn how to build robots? One place where you can do just that is the University of Texas at Austin (UT). Dr. Mitchell Pryor and his colleagues conduct robot research on a regular basis. Dr. Pryor's research group develops and tests new ways to use robots. They are on the cutting edge of robotics.

The group works on robots that operate both with and without human assistance. Today's robots do not look like typical robots from science fiction movies, but they do complete a wide range of tasks. In industrial settings, for example, robots are used to weld, paint, and move and assemble parts. Unlike people, the robots can perform their tasks exactly the same way every time. They also work quickly, do not get injured, can generally work for long periods of time without breaks, and do not require daily pay (although they are not cheap to make or purchase!).

Dr. Pryor, who received his Ph.D. from UT, also teaches graduate and undergraduate courses in mechanical engineering at the university. His ongoing research group gives students an opportunity for some hands-on learning, a dream for many science fiction fans!

This robot cleans areas too hazardous for humans. The robot is controlled by an operator watching a video feed.

📖 Language Arts Connection

Robot speech must be clear, concise, and grammatically correct. Work in a group to generate acceptable robot speech for the information below. Assume that your robot is limited to eight-word statements.

- The lid on the container must be tightened before you can move the container.
- The yellow paint is finished. Red paint will be added next, after drying for 20 minutes.

JOB BOARD

Computer Scientist

What You'll Do: Computer scientists work in a wide range of jobs including Software or Website development, Systems Analyst, Systems Administrator, and Information Technology Specialist.

Where You Might Work: At a computer company, government agency, manufacturing company, software company, large office, or academic institution.

Education: At a minimum a bachelor's degree, but often an advanced degree is needed.

Other Job Requirements: You need research, critical thinking, and problem-solving skills along with knowledge of computer security management and the latest technology.

Materials Scientist

What You'll Do: Study the composition and structure of matter to build new and better products such as shoes, computer chips, vehicles, blue jeans, and baking pans.

Where You Might Work: At a manufacturing plant, environmental consulting firm, or computer company.

Education: A minimum of a bachelor's degree, but typically a master's degree or doctorate in physics or chemistry.

Other Job Requirements: Research skills, verbal and written communication skills, and the ability to solve problems.

PEOPLE IN SCIENCE NEWS

Agnes Riley

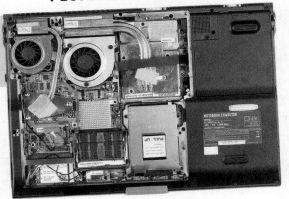

A Job for a Problem Solver

A computer is a great time-saving machine—right up until it doesn't work. If your computer isn't working right, you should try some simple steps, such as restarting it. If you are unable to solve the problem yourself, you might need to call an expert. Agnes Riley from Budapest, Hungary, is one such expert. Give her a computer that isn't working correctly, and she will take it apart, find the problem, and fix it.

Agnes learned how to fix computers by trial and error. She worked for a company in Hungary that had old computers, which needed constant repair. By experimenting, she learned to fix them.

In 1999, Agnes moved to New York City and took the exam to become a licensed computer technician. She enjoys the challenge of solving computer problems for people. If you enjoy solving problems, you might want to become a computer technician too!

Nature of Science

involves

Scientific Investigations

lead to constantly changing

display data for

Tables and Graphs

Scientific Knowledge

1 Interpret According to the Graphic Organizer, there is a relationship between scientific investigations and scientific knowledge. Explain this relationship.

_____

_____

_____

_____

2 Claims • Evidence • Reasoning Why are tables and graphs useful for organizing scientific data? State your claim. Provide evidence to support the claim and explain your reasoning.

_____

_____

_____

_____

_____

3 Claims • Evidence • Reasoning Why is science important for our understanding of the natural world? State your claim. Provide evidence to support the claim and explain your reasoning.

_____

_____

_____

_____

_____

_____

_____

_____

_____

_____

_____

Vocabulary

Name _____

Fill in each blank with the term that best completes the following sentences.

1 Applying science and mathematics to solve real-world problems is called _____.

2 Testing and evaluating a(n) _____ is an important step in the design process.

3 Engineers perform a(n) _____ to compare the possible negative effects of making a decision involving technology with the possible positive effects.

4 To determine how a technology might affect the environment from the time it is made, sold, and used to the time it must be disposed of, engineers make a(n)_____.

5 A(n) _____ must be supported by empirical evidence.

Key Concepts

Identify the choice that best completes the statement or answers the question.

6 Raoul is studying areas of the United States to find the best location for high-rise senior citizen housing.

Major Earthquakes in Northern California						
Year	1906	1911	1979	1980	1984	1989
Magnitude	7.8	6.5	5.7	5.8	6.2	6.9

To help with his decision on the best location, how could Raoul use this table listing the major earthquakes that have occurred in northern California?

A to develop a list of building materials

B to perform a life cycle analysis

C to create a model

D to perform a risk-benefit analysis

7 Jason wants to know how far a shot-putter from the track team can throw a shot. During the experiment, Jason measures test and outcome variables. The drawings below show three trials from the experiment.

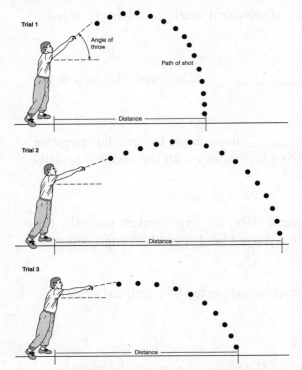

Assuming the shot-putter hurls the shot with the same force each time, what is the test variable?

F force exerted on the shot

G distance traveled by the shot

H angle at which the shot is thrown

I time it takes the shot to hit the ground

8 Which of the following is not a tool used in engineering and technology?

A computer design program

B electron microscope

C suspension bridge

D power drill

9 In the early 1900s, geologist Alfred Wegener described a process he called *continental drift.* He proposed that Earth's continents had once been a single landmass that had broken up and the continents had then moved apart. At first, scientists were skeptical, but they accepted Wegener's idea when new discoveries supported it. Which term describes continental drift?

F hypothesis   **H** law

G theory   **I** empirical evidence

10 Bryan recorded the mass of a kitten in the table below. What would be the best scale to use for the *mass* variable when making a line graph of the data shown?

Growth of a Kitten

Age (weeks)	Mass (g)
6	2,560
7	2,790
8	2,850
9	2,920
10	3,120

A 0 to 3,500 in units of 10

B 0 to 3,500 in units of 500

C 2,500 to 3,500 in units of 50

D 2,000 to 3,500 in units of 100

11 Which statement best describes technology?

F the tools, machines, materials, and processes that are used for practical purposes

G the application of science and mathematics to solve problems, meeting the needs of society and improving the quality of life

H the study of the natural world

I the exploration of the nature of science

Critical Thinking

Answer the following question in the space provided.

12 Technology used in developing automobiles had some favorable and unfavorable effects.

What is a favorable and unfavorable effect of the automobile shown in the illustration? Use reasoning to explain your answer.

_____

_____

_____

13 The development of refrigeration and frozen-food technology has benefited society in different ways. Identify two ways in which refrigeration has helped people. Support your claims with evidence by identifying two products that developed because of frozen-food technology.

_____

_____

_____

Earth's Structures

FLORIDA **BIG IDEA** 6

Earth Structures

This delta may look different
than it did 10 years ago.

What Do You Think?

Earth is continuously changing. How did the rock cycle change the
delta over time? As you explore this unit, gather evidence to help you
state and support a claim.

Earth's Structures

CITIZEN SCIENCE

Stable Structures

The building on the right, located in San Francisco, was engineered to protect it from earthquakes.

1 Think About It

People in different parts of the United States—and all over the world—need to make buildings earthquake-proof. Where would it be of most importance to have earthquake-proof buildings?

_____
_____

The taller the building, the more difficult it is to make it safe during an earthquake. Why do you think this is?

_____
_____
_____

Some materials survive the shaking from an earthquake, while others crumble or crack. What materials might withstand an earthquake? Why?

_____
_____
_____
_____
_____
_____

Image Credits: ©Dennis Hallinan/Alamy

©Houghton Mifflin Harcourt

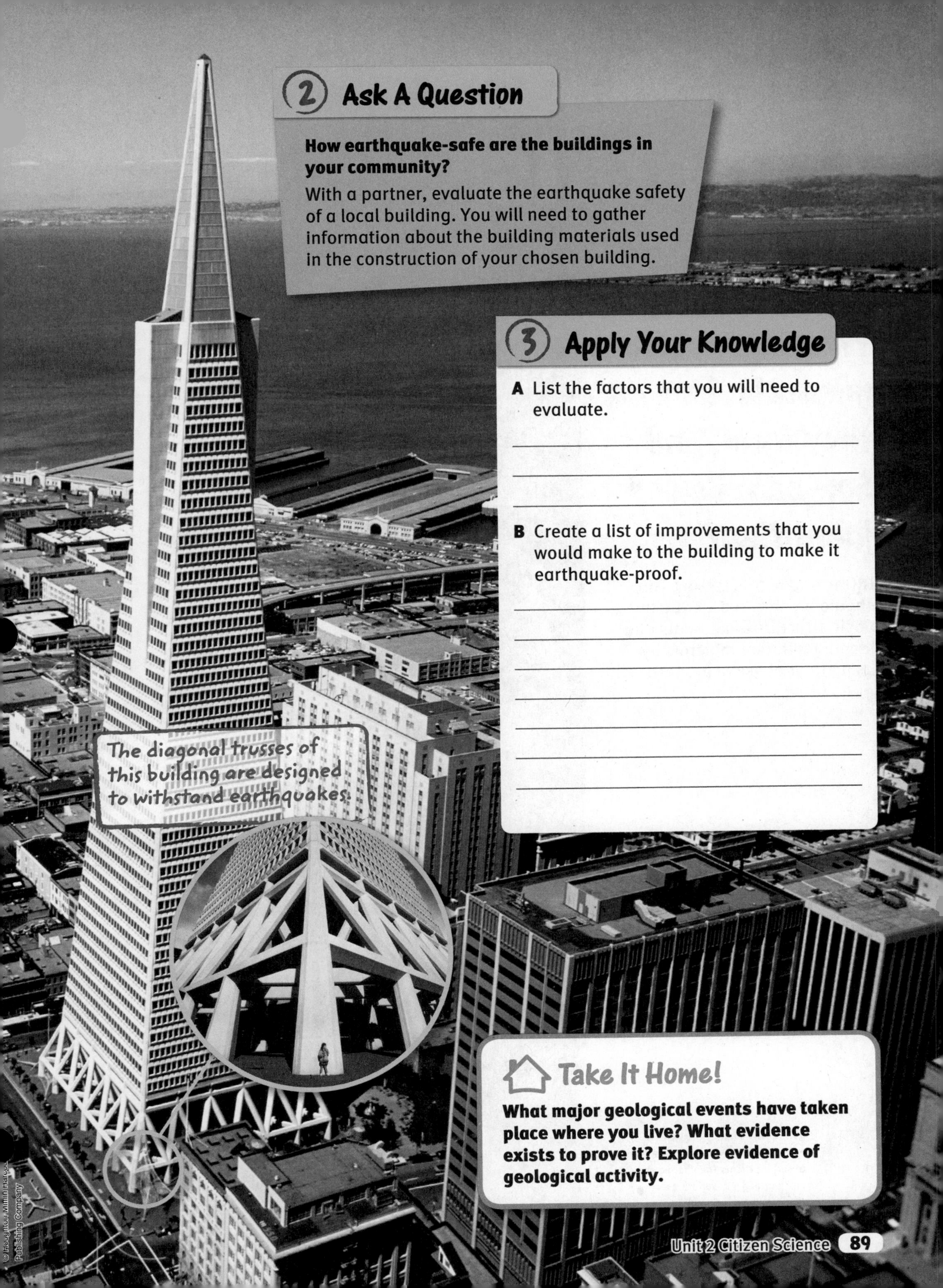

② Ask A Question

How earthquake-safe are the buildings in your community?

With a partner, evaluate the earthquake safety of a local building. You will need to gather information about the building materials used in the construction of your chosen building.

③ Apply Your Knowledge

A List the factors that you will need to evaluate.

_____

_____

_____

B Create a list of improvements that you would make to the building to make it earthquake-proof.

_____

_____

_____

_____

_____

_____

_____

The diagonal trusses of this building are designed to withstand earthquakes.

🏠 Take It Home!

What major geological events have taken place where you live? What evidence exists to prove it? Explore evidence of geological activity.

Minerals

ESSENTIAL QUESTION

What are minerals, how do they form, and how can they be identified?

By the end of this lesson, you should be able to describe the basic structure of minerals and identify different minerals by using their physical properties.

This cave was once full of water. Over millions of years, dissolved minerals in the water slowly formed these gypsum crystals, which are now considered to be the largest mineral crystals in the world!

SC.7.E.6.2 Identify the patterns within the rock cycle and relate them to surface events (weathering and erosion) and sub-surface events (plate tectonics and mountain building).

Lesson Labs

Quick Labs
• Evaporation Rates
• Cooling Rate and Crystal Size
• Scratch Test

Exploration Lab
• Intrinsic Identification of Minerals

Engage Your Brain

1 Identify Which of the materials listed below is a mineral?

Yes	No	
☐	☐	ice
☐	☐	gold
☐	☐	wood
☐	☐	diamond
☐	☐	table salt

2 Explain Describe how you think the minerals in the picture below may have formed.

_____

_____

_____

_____

ACTIVE **READING**

3 Synthesize Many of this lesson's vocabulary terms are related to each other. Locate the terms in the Glossary and see if you can find connections between them. When you find two terms that are related to each other, write a sentence using both terms in a way that shows the relationship. An example is done for you.

Example Sentence
Each element is made of only one kind of atom.

_____

_____

_____

_____

Vocabulary Terms

• mineral
• element
• atom
• compound
• matter
• crystal
• streak
• luster
• cleavage

4 Apply As you learn the definition of each vocabulary term in this lesson, create your own definition or sketch to help you remember the meaning of the term.

What do minerals have in common?

When you hear the word *mineral,* you may think of sparkling gems. But, in fact, most minerals are found in groups that make up rocks. So what is a mineral? A **mineral** is a naturally occurring, usually inorganic solid that has a definite crystalline structure and chemical composition.

○ Definite Chemical Composition

To understand what a definite chemical composition is, you need to know a little about elements. **Elements** are pure substances that cannot be broken down into simpler substances by ordinary chemical means. Each element is made of only one kind of atom. All substances are made up of atoms, so **atoms** can be thought of as the building blocks of matter. Stable particles that are made up of strongly bonded atoms are called *molecules.* And, if a substance is made up of molecules of two or more elements, the substance is called a **compound.**

The chemical composition of a mineral is determined by the element or compound that makes up the mineral. For example, minerals such as gold and silver are composed of only one element. Such a mineral is called a *native element.* The mineral quartz is a compound in which silicon atoms can each bond with up to four oxygen atoms in a repeating pattern.

> **5 Claim • Evidence • Reasoning** Make a claim about the relationship between elements, atoms, and compounds. Summarize evidence to support the claim and explain your reasoning.

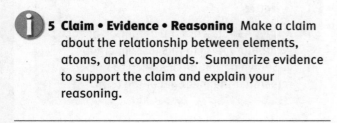

○ Solid

Matter is anything that has volume and mass. *Volume* refers to the amount of space an object takes up. For example, a golf ball has a smaller volume than a baseball does. Matter is generally found in one of three states: solid, liquid, or gas. A mineral is a solid—that is, it has a definite volume and shape. A substance that is a liquid or a gas is not a mineral. However, in some cases its solid form is a mineral. For instance, liquid water is not a mineral, but ice is because it is solid and has all of the other mineral characteristics also.

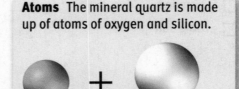

Atoms The mineral quartz is made up of atoms of oxygen and silicon.

Oxygen (O)   Silicon (Si)

Compound An atom of silicon can typically bond with up to four oxygen atoms to form a molecule. One or more of these molecules form a compound.

or Mineral?

Usually Inorganic

Most substances made by living things are categorized as organic substances, such as kidney stones and wood. However, a few substances made by animals, such as clam shells, are categorized as inorganic. An inorganic substance is usually one that is not made up of living things or the remains of living things. And, although a few organic substances such as kidney stones are categorized as minerals, most minerals are inorganic. And, unlike clam shells, most of the processes that form minerals usually take place in the non-living environment.

Crystalline Structure

Minerals have a crystalline structure because they are composed of crystals. A **crystal** is a solid, geometric form that results from a repeating pattern of atoms or molecules. A crystal's shape is produced by the arrangement of the atoms or molecules within the crystal. This arrangement is determined by the kinds of atoms or molecules that make up the mineral and the conditions under which it forms. All minerals can be placed into crystal classes according to their specific crystal shape. This diagram shows how silica compounds can be arranged in quartz crystals.

Crystal Structure In crystals, molecules are arranged in a regular pattern.

Naturally Occurring

Minerals are formed by many different natural processes that occur on Earth and throughout the universe. On Earth, the mineral halite, which is used for table salt, forms as water evaporates and leaves behind the salt it contained. Some minerals form as molten rock cools. Talc, a mineral that can be used to make baby powder, forms deep in Earth as high temperature and pressure change the rock. Some of the other ways in which minerals form are on the next page.

6 Classify Circle *Y* for "yes" or *N* for "no" to determine whether the two materials below are minerals.

	Cardboard	Topaz
Definite chemical composition?	Y (N)	(Y) N
Solid?	Y N	(Y) N
Inorganic?	Y N	Y N
Naturally occurring?	Y N	Y N
Crystalline structure?	Y (N)	Y N
Mineral?	Y N	Y N

Mineral Crystal Billions of molecules arranged in a crystalline structure form these quartz crystals.

(t) ©Bryan Ladswell/Alamy; (c) ©Joel Arem/Photo Researchers, Inc; (br) ©GC Minerals/Alamy

Publishing Company

Crystal Clear!

How are minerals formed?

Minerals form within Earth or on Earth's surface by natural processes. Recall that each type of mineral has its own chemical makeup. Therefore, which types of minerals form in an area depends in part on which elements are present there. Temperature and pressure also affect which minerals form.

As Magma and Lava Cool

Many minerals grow from magma. Magma—molten rock inside Earth—contains most of the types of atoms that are found in minerals. As magma cools, the atoms join together to form different minerals. Minerals also form as lava cools. Lava is molten rock that has reached Earth's surface. Quartz is one of the many minerals that crystallize from magma and lava.

By Metamorphism

Temperature and pressure within Earth cause new minerals to form as bonds between atoms break and reform with different atoms. The mineral garnet can form and replace the minerals chlorite and quartz in this way. At high temperatures and pressures, the element carbon in rocks forms the mineral diamond or the mineral graphite, which is used in pencils.

👁 Visualize It!

7 Claims • Evidence • Reasoning Make a claim about the ways in which pluton and pegmatite form in a similar fashion. Summarize evidence to support the claim and explain your reasoning.

_____

_____

Cooling Magma Forms Plutons
As magma rises, it can stop moving and cool slowly. This forms rocks like this granite, which contains minerals like quartz, mica, and feldspar.

Cooling Magma Forms Pegmatites
Magma that cools very slowly can form pegmatites. Some crystals in pegmatites, such as this topaz, can grow quite large.

Metamorphism Minerals like these garnets form when temperature and pressure causes the chemical and crystalline makeup of minerals to change.

◯ From Solutions

Water usually has many substances dissolved in it. As water evaporates, these substances form into solids and come out of solution, or *precipitate*. For example, the mineral gypsum often forms as water evaporates. Minerals can also form from hot water solutions. Hot water can dissolve more materials than cold water. As a body of hot water cools, dissolved substances can form into minerals such as dolomite, as they precipitate out of solution.

8 Summarize Describe three ways minerals form.

A _____

_____

B _____

_____

C _____

_____

Precipitating from an Evaporating Solution When a body of salt water evaporates, minerals such as this halite precipitate and are left behind on the shoreline.

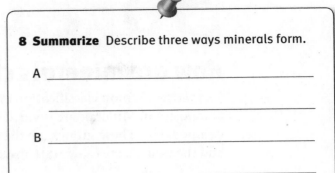

Precipitating from a Cooling Solution on Earth's Surface Dissolved materials can come out of a solution and accumulate. Dolomite, can form this way.

Precipitating from a Cooling Solution Beneath Earth's Surface Water works its way downward and is heated by magma. It then reacts with minerals to form a solution. Dissolved elements, such as gold, precipitate once the fluid cools to form new mineral deposits.

Think Outside the Book

9 Apply Find out what your state mineral is and how it forms.

Sort It Out

How are minerals classified?

The most common classification of minerals is based on chemical composition. Minerals are divided into two groups based on their composition. These groups are the silicate (SIL'ih•kayt) minerals and the nonsilicate (nawn•SIL'ih•kayt) minerals.

Silicate Minerals

Silicon and oxygen are the two most common elements in Earth's crust. Minerals that contain a combination of these two elements are called *silicate minerals*. Silicate minerals make up most of Earth's crust. The most common silicate minerals in Earth's crust are feldspar and quartz. Most silicate minerals are formed from basic building blocks called *silicate tetrahedrons*. Silicate tetrahedrons are made of one silicon atom bonded to four oxygen atoms. Most silicate minerals, including mica and olivine, are composed of silicate tetrahedrons combined with other elements, such as aluminum or iron.

ACTIVE READING

10 Claims • Evidence • Reasoning Make a claim about why Earth's crust is made up mostly of silicate materials. Summarize evidence to support the claim and explain your reasoning.

_____

_____

The mineral zircon is a silicate mineral. It is composed of the element zirconium and silicate tetrahedrons.

Nonsilicate Minerals

Minerals that do not contain the silicate tetrahedron building block form a group called the *nonsilicate minerals.* Some of these minerals are made up of elements such as carbon, oxygen, fluorine, iron, and sulfur. The table on the next page shows the most important classes of nonsilicate minerals. A nonsilicate mineral's chemical composition determines its class.

➕➖ Do the Math
✖️➗

You Try It

11 Calculate Calculate the percent of non-silicates in Earth's crust to complete the graph's key.

Minerals in Earth's Crust

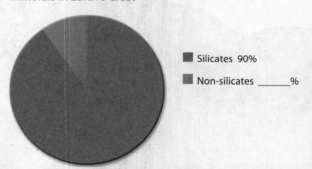

■ Silicates 90%

■ Non-silicates _____%

Classes of Nonsilicate Minerals

Native elements are minerals that are composed of only one element. Copper (Cu) and silver (Ag) are two examples. Native elements are often used to make electronics.

Silver, Ag

Carbonates are minerals that contain carbon (C) and oxygen (O) in the form of the carbonate ion CO_3^{2-}. We use carbonate minerals in cement, building stones, and fireworks.

Calcite, $CaCO_3$

Halides are compounds that form when elements such as fluorine (F) and chlorine (Cl), combine with elements such as calcium (Ca). Halides are used in the chemical industry and in detergents.

Fluorite, CaF_2

Oxides are compounds that form when an element, such as aluminum (Al) or iron (Fe), combines with oxygen. Oxide minerals are used to make abrasives, aircraft parts, and paint.

Corundum, Al_2O_3

Sulfates are minerals that contain sulfur (S) and oxygen (O) in the form of the sulfate ion SO_4^{2-}. Sulfates are used in cosmetics, toothpaste, cement, and paint.

Barite, $BaSO_4$

Sulfides are minerals that contain one or more elements, such as lead (Pb), or iron (Fe), combined with sulfur (S). Sulfide minerals are used to make batteries and medicines.

Pyrite, FeS_2

Visualize It!

12 Classify Examine the chemical formulas for the two minerals on the right. Classify each mineral as a silicate or a nonsilicate. If it is a nonsilicate, also write its class.

Gypsum, $CaSO_4 \cdot 2H_2O$

Kyanite, Al_2SiO_5

_____   _____

_____   _____

Name That Mineral!

What properties can be used to identify minerals?

If you closed your eyes and tasted different foods, you could probably determine what the foods are by noting properties such as saltiness or sweetness. You can also determine the identity of a mineral by noting different properties. In this section, you will learn about the properties that will help you identify minerals.

○ Color

The same mineral can come in different colors. For example, pure quartz is colorless. However, impurities can make quartz pink, orange, or many other colors. Other factors can also change a mineral's color. Pyrite is normally golden, but turns black or brown if exposed to air and water. The same mineral can be different colors, and different minerals can be the same color. So, color is helpful but usually not the best way to identify a mineral.

○ Streak

The color of the powdered form of a mineral is its **streak**. A mineral's streak is found by rubbing the mineral against a white tile called a *streak plate*. The mark left is the streak. A mineral's streak is not always the same as the color of the mineral, but all samples of the same mineral have the same streak color. Unlike the surface of a mineral, the streak is not affected by air or water. For this reason, streak is more reliable than color in identifying a mineral.

ACTIVE READING

13 Identify Underline the name of the property on this page that is most reliable for identifying a mineral.

👁 Visualize It!

14 Claims • Evidence • Reasoning Look at these two mineral samples. Make a claim about which property indicates that the two minerals might be the same mineral. Summarize evidence to support the claim and explain your reasoning.

_____

_____

_____

© Houghton Mifflin Harcourt

Mineral Lusters

Metallic **Silky** **Vitreous** **Waxy**

Submetallic **Pearly** **Resinous** **Earthy**

○ Luster

The way a surface reflects light is called **luster**. When you say an object is shiny or dull, you are describing its luster. The two major types of luster are metallic and nonmetallic. Pyrite has a metallic luster. It looks as if it is made of metal. A mineral with a nonmetallic luster can be shiny, but it does not appear to be made of metal. Different types of lusters are shown above.

○ Cleavage and Fracture

The tendency of a mineral to split along specific planes of weakness to form smooth, flat surfaces is called **cleavage**. When a mineral has cleavage, it breaks along flat surfaces that generally run parallel to planes of weakness in the crystal structure. For example, mica tends to split into parallel sheets. Many minerals, however, do not break along cleavage planes. Instead, they fracture, or break unevenly, into pieces that have curved or irregular surfaces. Scientists describe a fracture according to the appearance of the broken surface. For example, a rough surface has an irregular fracture, and a curved surface has a conchoidal (kahn•KOY•duhl) fracture.

◉ Visualize It!

15 Identify Write the correct description, either *cleavage* or *fracture,* under the two broken mineral crystals shown here.

_____

_____

Mohs Scale

1 Talc

2 Gypsum

Your fingernail has a hardness of about 2.5, so it can scratch talc and gypsum.

3 Calcite

4 Fluorite

5 Apatite

6 Feldspar

A steel file has a hardness of about 6.5. You can scratch feldspar with it.

7 Quartz

8 Topaz

9 Corundum

10 Diamond

Diamond is the hardest mineral. Only a diamond can scratch another diamond.

👁 Visualize It!

16 Determine A mineral can be scratched by calcite but not by a fingernail. What is its approximate hardness?

_____

_____

○ Density

If you pick up a golf ball and a table-tennis ball, which will feel heavier? Although the balls are of similar size, the golf ball will feel heavier because it is denser. *Density* is the measure of how much matter is in a given amount of space. Density is usually measured in grams per cubic centimeter. Gold has a density of 19 g/cm^3. The mineral pyrite looks very similar to gold, but its density is only 5 g/cm^3. Because of this, density can be used to tell gold from pyrite. Density can also be used to tell many other similar-looking minerals apart.

○ Hardness

A mineral's resistance to being scratched is called its *hardness*. To determine the hardness of minerals, scientists use the Mohs hardness scale, shown at left. Notice that talc has a rating of 1 and diamond has a rating of 10. The greater a mineral's resistance to being scratched, the higher its hardness rating. To identify a mineral by using the Mohs scale, try to scratch the surface of a mineral with the edge of one of the 10 reference minerals. If the reference mineral scratches your mineral, the reference mineral is as hard as or harder than your mineral.

○ Special Properties

All minerals exhibit the properties that were described earlier in this section. However, a few minerals have some additional, special properties that can help identify those minerals. For example, the mineral magnetite is a natural magnet. The mineral calcite is usually white in ordinary light, but in ultraviolet light, it often appears red. Another special property of calcite is shown below.

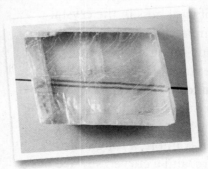

A clear piece of calcite placed over an image will cause a double image.

Made from Minerals

Many minerals contain useful substances. Rutile and several other minerals contain the metal titanium. Titanium can resist corrosion and is about as strong as steel, but it is 47% lighter than steel. These properties make titanium very valuable.

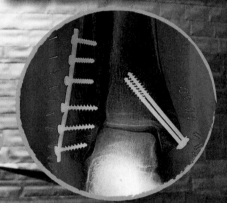

Devices for Doctors

Surgical procedures like joint replacements require metal implantations. Titanium is used because it can resist body fluid corrosion and its low density and elasticity are similar to human bone.

Marvels for Mechanics

Motorcycle exhaust pipes are often made out of titanium, which dissipates heat better than stainless steel.

An Aid to Architects

Titanium doesn't just serve practical purposes. Architect Frank Gehry used titanium panels to cover the outside of the Guggenheim Museum in Bilbao, Spain. He chose titanium because of its luster.

ℹ Extend

17 Claims • Evidence • Reasoning Make a claim about how the density of titanium-containing minerals would compare to the density of minerals used to make steel. Use evidence to support the claim and explain your reasoning.

18 List Research some other products made from minerals. Make a list summarizing your research.

19 Determine Choose one of the products you researched. How do the properties of the minerals used to make the product contribute to the product's characteristics or usefulness?

Visual Summary

To complete this summary, fill in the blanks with the correct words or phrase. You can use this page to review the main concepts of the lesson.

Minerals make up Earth's crust.

20 A mineral:

- has a definite chemical composition
- is a solid
- is usually inorganic
- is formed in nature
- _____

Minerals are classified by composition.

21 Minerals are classified in two groups as:

Quartz, SiO_2 Calcite, $CaCO_3$

_____   _____

Minerals

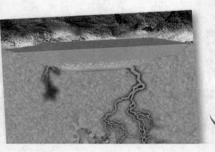

Minerals form by natural processes.

22 Minerals form by:

- metamorphism
- the cooling of magma and lava
- _____

Minerals are identified by their properties.

23 Properties used to identify minerals include:

- color and luster
- _____
- cleavage or fracture
- density and hardness
- special properties

24 Claims • Evidence • Reasoning Make a claim as to whether ice (H_2O) is a silicate or nonsilicate. Summarize evidence to support the claim and explain your reasoning.

Lesson Review

Vocabulary

Fill in the blank with the term that best completes the following sentence.

1 The way light bounces off a mineral's surface is described by the mineral's _____

2 The color of a mineral in powdered form is the mineral's _____

3 Each element is made up of only one kind of _____

Key Concepts

4 Explain How could you determine whether an unknown substance is a mineral?

_____

_____

_____

_____

5 Determine If a substance is a mineral, how could you identify what type of mineral it is?

_____

_____

_____

6 Organize In the space below, draw a graphic organizer showing how minerals can be classified. Be sure to include the six main classes of nonsilicate minerals.

Critical Thinking

Use the diagram below to answer question 7.

Carbon Bonds in Graphite

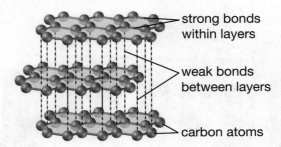

strong bonds within layers

weak bonds between layers

carbon atoms

7 Claims • Evidence • Reasoning The diagram above shows the crystal structure of graphite, a mineral made up of carbon atoms that are bonded together in a regular pattern. Make a claim about whether graphite would more likely display cleavage or fracture. Summarize evidence to support the claim and explain your reasoning.

_____

_____

_____

_____

8 Infer How do you think the hardness and density of a mineral that formed through metamorphism would compare to a mineral that formed through evaporation? Explain your reasoning.

_____

_____

_____

_____

_____

_____

_____

_____

Publishing Company

FOCUS ON **FLORIDA**

SC.7.E.6.2 Identify the patterns within the rock cycle and relate them to surface events (weathering and erosion) and sub-surface events (plate tectonics and mountain building).

Florida Minerals

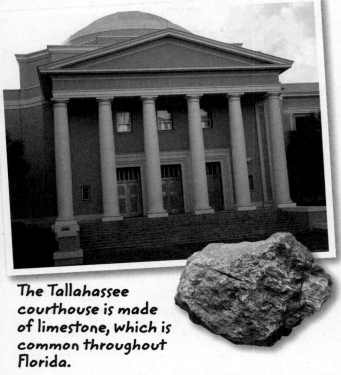

The Tallahassee courthouse is made of limestone, which is common throughout Florida.

Calcite in Limestone

Calcite is the primary mineral in limestone. Florida is the second largest producer of limestone in the United States. Most of the limestone mined in Florida is used for road construction. Limestone can also be used to produce cement, glass, and ceramics. Florida's limestone formed over millions of years. Sediment made up of the hard body parts of marine organisms was deposited in thick layers. These layers were later compressed to form limestone.

A key part of the mining process for limestone is following standards to help protect natural resources. The standards include using minimum amounts of water, replanting trees, and making sure an area is not overmined.

Mining

Sandstone, calcite, gypsum, and kaolin are some of the common minerals found in Florida. Kaolin is a clay that is used to make paper, rubber, and china. It is mined mostly in east-central Florida. Kaolin miners drill holes and take samples to locate kaolin deposits. If a deposit is large enough and is of good quality, mining can start. First, the layers of earth above the kaolin are removed—as deep as 30 m. The crude kaolin material is sent to a processing plant where it is dried and separated from other materials. Afterward, the dried kaolin is sent to roller mills, where it is ground into a fine powder. It is then packaged and sent off to manufacturers to make a variety of products. Kaolin can be hazardous. Studies have found that long-term exposure to kaolin may cause miners to develop a respiratory disease called *kaolinosis*.

🌐 Social Studies Connection

Use your school library or the Internet to learn about the state stone of Florida and the minerals it contains. Mark the locations where it can be found on the map shown.

Phosphate Minerals

Florida's phosphate industry supplies one-fourth of the world's phosphate needs. Mining for phosphate rock, which is rich in phosphate minerals, began in 1883 in Florida. Phosphate is mainly used to make fertilizer, but it is also used in other things, such as vitamins, soft drinks, and even toothpaste!

Like limestone, phosphate rock is formed from sediments of marine organisms deposited on the ocean floor. It is found in a layer of sediment located about 5–15 m below Earth's surface. To get to this layer, miners use a dragline to remove the soil above the layer. The layer is transported to a pit, where it is processed. The phosphate is separated from sediments like sand and clay.

Phosphate mining primarily uses fluoride, radon gas, and sulfur dioxide for processing. These chemicals can be dangerous to the environment and humans. Recent regulations have been put in place to control and reduce the harmful effects of phosphate mining.

This dragline is being used to mine phosphate in Florida.

The Rock Cycle

ESSENTIAL QUESTION

What is the rock cycle?

By the end of this lesson, you should be able to describe the series of processes and classes of rocks that make up the rock cycle.

It may be hard to believe, but these mountains actually move. Wyoming's Teton Mountains rise by millimeters each year. An active fault is uplifting the mountains. In this lesson, you will learn about uplift and other processes that change rock.

SC.7.E.6.2 Identify the patterns within the rock cycle and relate them to surface events (weathering and erosion) and sub-surface events (plate tectonics and mountain building).

✋ Lesson Labs

Quick Lab
• Crayon Rock Cycle
• Compression

S.T.E.M. Lab
• Modeling Rock Formation

⚙️ Engage Your Brain

1 Describe Fill in the blank with the word or phrase that you think correctly completes the following sentences.

Most of Earth is made of _____

Rock is _____ changing.

The three main classes of rock are igneous, metamorphic, and _____

2 Describe Write your own caption for this photo.

_____

_____

_____

_____

ACTIVE **READING**

3 Synthesize Many English words have their roots in other languages. Use the Latin words below to make an educated guess about the meaning of the words *erosion* and *deposition*.

Latin Word	Meaning
erosus	eaten away
depositus	laid down

Erosion:

_____

_____

Deposition:

_____

_____

Vocabulary Terms

• weathering
• erosion
• deposition
• igneous rock
• sedimentary rock

• metamorphic rock
• rock cycle
• uplift
• subsidence
• rift zone

4 Apply As you learn the definition of each vocabulary term in this lesson, create your own definition or sketch to help you remember the meaning of the term.

Let's Rock!

What is rock?

The solid parts of Earth are made almost entirely of rock. Scientists define rock as a naturally occurring solid mixture of one or more minerals that may also include organic matter. Most rock is made of minerals, but some rock is made of nonmineral material that is not organic, such as glass. Rock has been an important natural resource as long as humans have existed. Early humans used rocks as hammers to make other tools. For centuries, people have used different types of rock, including granite, marble, sandstone, and slate, to make buildings, such as the pyramids shown below.

It may be hard to believe, but rocks are always changing. People study rocks to learn how areas have changed through time.

5 List How is rock used today?

_____

_____

_____

_____

The ancient Egyptians used a rock called limestone to construct the Great Sphinx and the pyramids at Giza.

These rock formations in Goreme, Turkey, are known as fairy chimneys. They were shaped by erosion.

Think Outside the Book

6 Design Create a travel brochure for Goreme, Turkey.

What processes change rock?

Natural processes make and destroy rock. They change each type of rock into other types of rock and shape the features of our planet. These processes also influence the type of rock that is found in each area of Earth's surface.

ACTIVE **READING**

7 Identify As you read, underline the processes and factors that can change rock.

◯ Weathering, Erosion, and Deposition

The process by which water, wind, ice, and changes in temperature break down rock is called **weathering**. Weathering breaks down rock into fragments called *sediment*. The process by which sediment is moved from one place to another is called **erosion.** Water, wind, ice, and gravity can erode sediments. These sediments are eventually deposited, or laid down, in bodies of water and other low-lying areas. The process by which sediment comes to rest is called **deposition.**

◯ Temperature and Pressure

Rock that is buried can be squeezed by the weight of the rock or the layers of sediment on top of it. As pressure increases with depth beneath Earth's surface, so does temperature. If the temperature and pressure are high enough, the buried rock can change into metamorphic rock. In some cases, the rock gets hot enough to melt and forms *magma*, or molten rock. If magma reaches Earth's surface, it is called *lava*. The magma or lava eventually cool and solidify to form new rock.

Classified Information!

What are the classes of rocks?

Rocks fall into three major classes based on how they form. **Igneous rock** forms when magma or lava cools and hardens to become solid. It forms beneath or on Earth's surface. **Sedimentary rock** forms when minerals that form from solutions or sediment from older rocks get pressed and cemented together. **Metamorphic rock** forms when pressure, temperature, or chemical processes change existing rock. Each class can be divided further, based on differences in the way rocks form. For example, some igneous rocks form when lava cools on Earth's surface, and others form when magma cools deep beneath the surface. Therefore, igneous rock can be classified based on how and where it forms.

ACTIVE READING

8 Identify As you read the paragraph, underline the three main classes of rocks.

i Think Outside the Book

9 Claims • Evidence • Reasoning Make a claim about the processes that might have shaped the rock formations in the Valley of Fire State Park. Summarize evidence to support the claim and explain your reasoning.

These formations in Valley of Fire State Park in Nevada are made of sandstone, a sedimentary rock.

sandstone

○ Sedimentary Rock

Sedimentary rock is composed of minerals formed from solutions or sediments from older rock. Sedimentary rock forms when the weight from above presses down on the layers of minerals or sediment, or when minerals dissolved in water solidify between sediment pieces and cement them together.

Sedimentary rocks are named according to the size and type of the fragments they contain. For example, the rock shown here is made of sand and is called sandstone. Rock made primarily of the mineral calcite (calcium carbonate) is called limestone.

Enchanted Rock in Texas is a large dome made of granite, an intrusive igneous rock.

○ Igneous Rock

Igneous rock forms from cooling lava and magma. As molten rock cools and becomes solid, the minerals crystallize and grow. The longer the cooling takes, the more time the crystals have to grow. The granite shown here cooled slowly and is made of large crystals. Rock that forms when magma cools beneath Earth's surface is called intrusive igneous rock. Rock that forms when lava cools on Earth's surface is called extrusive igneous rock.

granite

○ Metamorphic Rock

Metamorphic rock forms when high temperature and pressure change the texture and mineral content of rock. For example, a rock can be buried in Earth's crust, where the temperature and pressure are high. Over millions of years, the solid rock changes, and new crystals are formed. Metamorphic rocks may be changed in four ways: by temperature, by pressure, by temperature and pressure combined, or by fluids or other chemicals. Gneiss, shown here, is a metamorphic rock. It forms at high temperatures deep within Earth's crust.

gneiss

Gneiss is a metamorphic rock that is made up of bands of light and dark minerals.

10 Compare Fill in the chart to compare and contrast sedimentary, igneous, and metamorphic rock.

Classes of Rocks

Sedimentary rock	Igneous rock	Metamorphic rock

Publishing Company

What is the rock cycle?

ACTIVE READING

11 Apply As you read, underline the rock types that metamorphic rock can change into.

Rocks may seem very permanent, solid, and unchanging. But over millions of years, any of the three rock types can be changed into another of the three types. For example, igneous rock can change into sedimentary or metamorphic rock, or back into another kind of igneous rock. This series of processes in which rock changes from one type to another is called the **rock cycle**. Rocks may follow different pathways in the cycle. Examples of these pathways are shown here. Factors, including temperature, pressure, weathering, and erosion, may change a rock's identity. Where rock is located on a tectonic plate and whether the rock is at Earth's surface also influence how it forms and changes.

When igneous rock is exposed at Earth's surface, it may break down into sediment. Igneous rock may also change directly into metamorphic rock while still beneath Earth's surface. It may also melt to form magma that becomes another type of igneous rock.

When sediment is pressed together and cemented, the sediment becomes sedimentary rock. With temperature and pressure changes, sedimentary rocks may become metamorphic rocks, or they may melt and become igneous rock. Sedimentary rock may also be broken down at Earth's surface and become sediment that forms another sedimentary rock.

Under certain temperature and pressure conditions, metamorphic rock will melt and form magma. Metamorphic rock can also be altered by heat and pressure to form a different type of metamorphic rock. Metamorphic rock can also be broken down by weathering and erosion to form sediment that forms sedimentary rock.

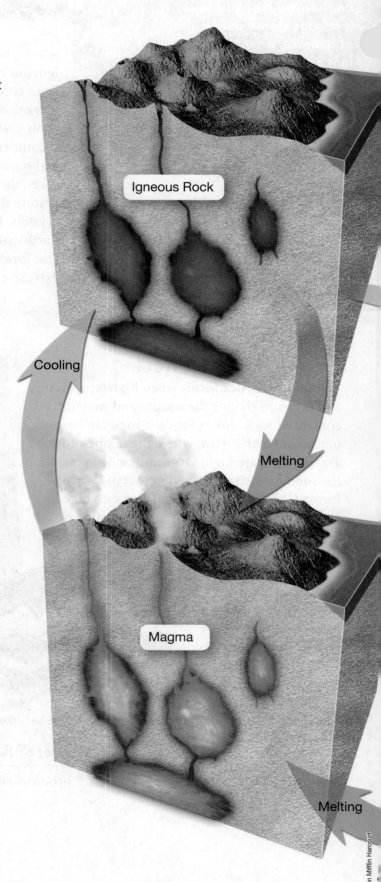

Igneous Rock

Cooling

Melting

Magma

Melting

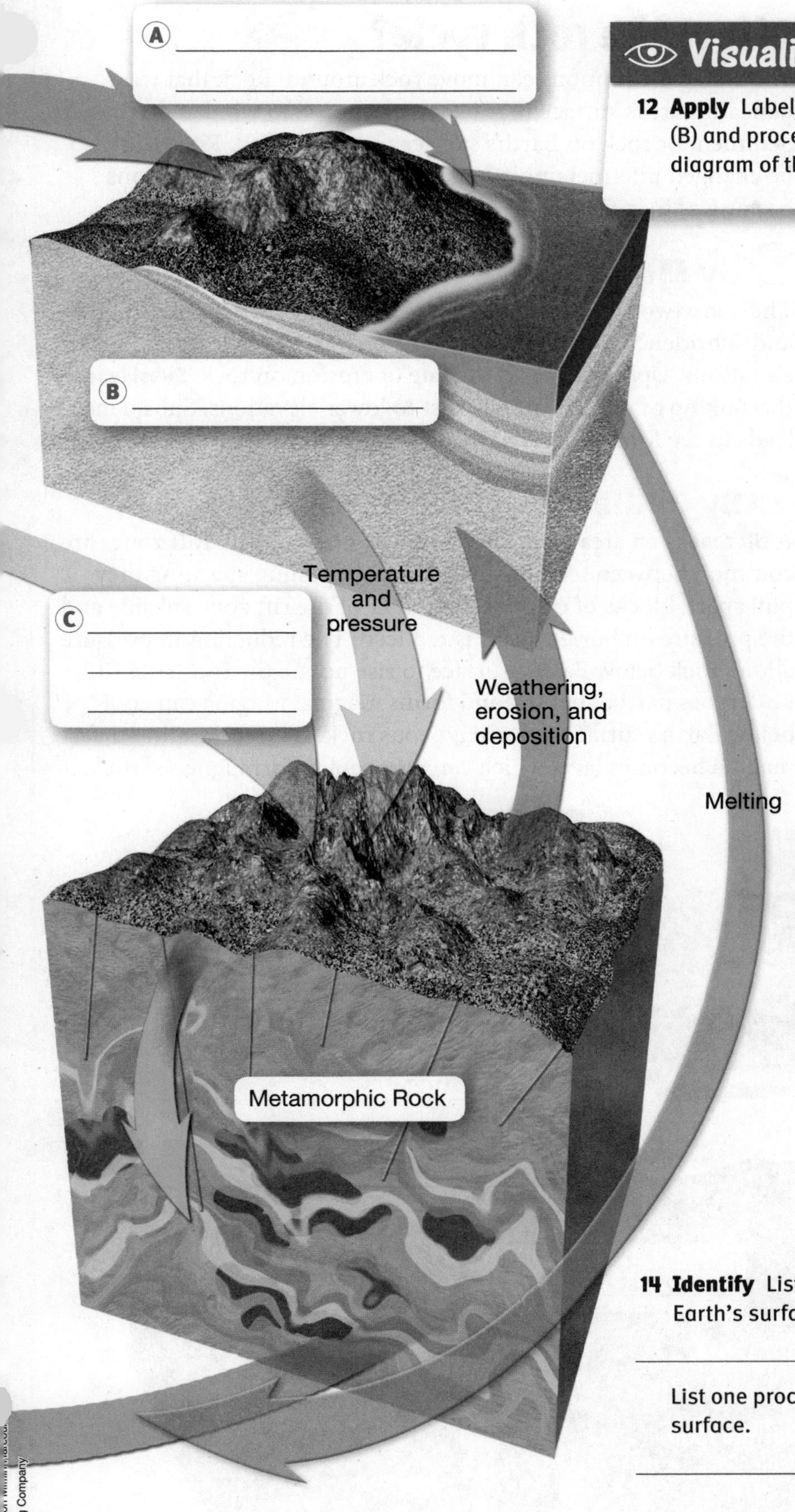

(A) _____
_____

👁 **Visualize It!**

12 Apply Label the missing rock type (B) and processes (A and C) on the diagram of the rock cycle.

(B) _____

Temperature
and
pressure

(C) _____
_____
_____

Weathering,
erosion, and
deposition

Melting

Think Outside the Book

13 Apply Write a series of blog entries from the viewpoint of igneous rock that is changing into sedimentary rock.

Metamorphic Rock

14 Identify List one process that happens above Earth's surface.

_____

List one process that happens below Earth's surface.

_____

How do tectonic plate motions affect the rock cycle?

Tectonic plate motions can move rock around. Rock that was beneath Earth's surface may become exposed to wind and rain. Sediment or rock on Earth's surface may be buried. Rock can also be changed into metamorphic rock by tectonic plate collisions because of increased temperature and pressure.

◯ By Moving Rock Up or Down

There are two types of vertical movements in Earth's crust: uplift and subsidence. **Uplift** is the rising of regions of the crust to higher elevations. Uplift increases the rate of erosion on rock. **Subsidence** is the sinking of regions of the crust to lower elevations. Subsidence leads to the formation of basins where sediment can be deposited.

◯ By Pulling Apart Earth's Surface

A **rift zone** is an area where a set of deep cracks form. Rift zones are common between tectonic plates that are pulling apart. As they pull apart, blocks of crust in the center of the rift zone subside and the pressure on buried rocks is reduced. The reduction in pressure allows rock below Earth's surface to rise up. As the rock rises, it undergoes partial melting and forms magma. Magma can cool below Earth's surface to form igneous rock. If it reaches the surface, magma becomes lava, which can also cool to form igneous rock.

15 Claims • Evidence • Reasoning
Make a claim about how uplift differs from subsidence. Summarize evidence to support the claim and explain your reasoning.

_____

_____

_____

_____

👁 Visualize It!

16 Claims • Evidence • Reasoning Label uplift and subsidence on this diagram. Make a claim about what pathway in the rock cycle might take next if it is subject to uplift. Use evidence to support the claim and explain your reasoning.

_____

_____

_____

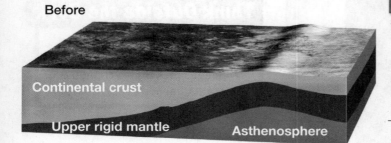

Before

Continental crust

Upper rigid mantle

Asthenosphere

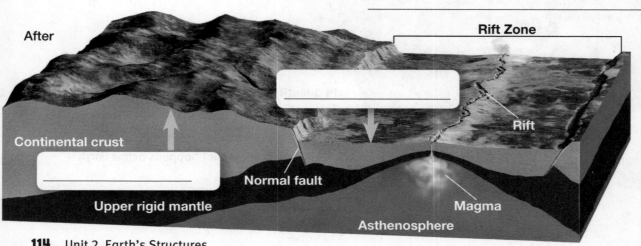

After

Rift Zone

Continental crust

Normal fault

Rift

Upper rigid mantle

Magma

Asthenosphere

WHY IT MATTERS

Cliff Dwellings

Can you imagine living on the side of a cliff? Some ancient peoples could! They created dwellings from cliff rock. They also decorated rock with art, as you can see in the pictographs shown below.

Cliff Palace
This dwelling in Colorado is called the Cliff Palace. It was home to the Ancient Puebloans from about 550 to 1300 CE.

Cliff Art
These pictographs are located at the Gila Cliff Dwellings in New Mexico.

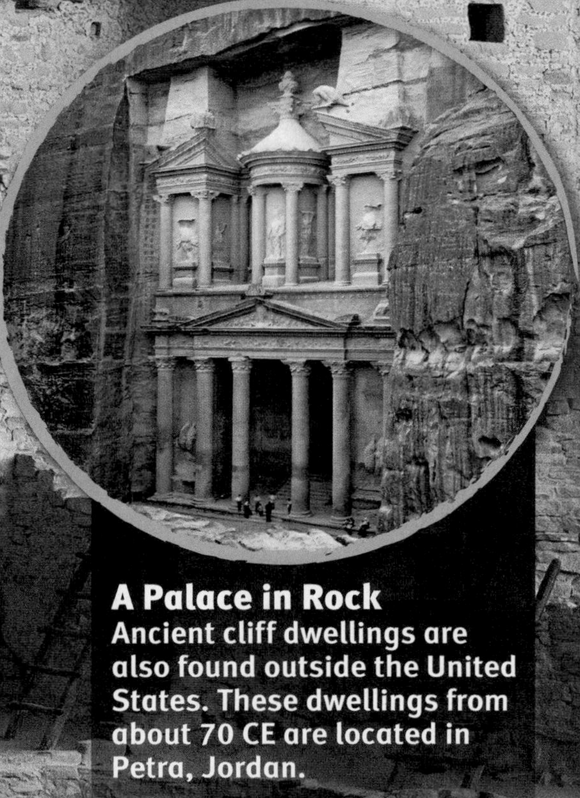

A Palace in Rock
Ancient cliff dwellings are also found outside the United States. These dwellings from about 70 CE are located in Petra, Jordan.

ⓘ Extend

17 Claims • Evidence • Reasoning Make a claim about how ancient people used rock to create shelter. Summarize evidence to support the claim and explain your reasoning.

18 Research Find out how people lived in one of the cliff dwelling locations. How did living in a rock environment affect their daily lives?

19 Produce Illustrate how the people lived by doing one of the following: write a play, write a song, or create a graphic novel.

Visual Summary

To complete this summary, use what you know about the rock cycle to fill in the blanks below. You can use this page to review the main concepts of the lesson.

Each rock type can change into another of the three types.

20 When sediment is pressed together and cemented, the sediment becomes

_____

21 When lava cools and solidifies,

_____

forms.

22 Metamorphic rock can be altered by temperature and pressure to form a different type of

_____

Rock Cycle

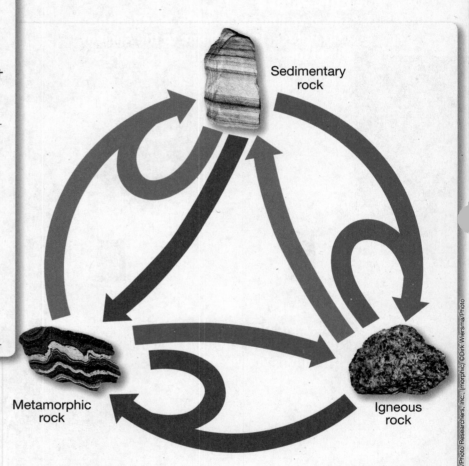

Sedimentary rock

Metamorphic rock

Igneous rock

23 **Claims • Evidence • Reasoning** Make a claim about what factors and processes can affect the pathway that igneous rock takes in the rock cycle. Summarize evidence to support the claim and explain your reasoning.

Lesson Review

Vocabulary

In your own words, define the following terms.

1 Rock cycle

_____

_____

2 Weathering

_____

_____

3 Rift zone

_____

_____

Key Concepts

Use these photos to classify the rock as sedimentary, igneous, or metamorphic.

Example	Type of rock
4 Classify This rock is made up of the mineral calcite, and it formed from the remains of organisms that lived in water.	 _____
5 Classify Through high temperature and pressure, this rock formed from a sedimentary rock.	 _____
6 Classify This rock is made of tiny crystals that formed quickly when molten rock cooled at Earth's surface.	_____

7 Describe How can sedimentary rock become metamorphic rock?

_____

_____

8 Explain How can subsidence lead to the formation of sedimentary rock?

_____

_____

_____

9 Explain Why are rift zones common places for igneous rock to form?

_____

_____

_____

Critical Thinking

10 Claims • Evidence • Reasoning Make a claim about what would happen to the rock cycle if erosion did not occur. Summarize evidence to support the claim and explain your reasoning.

_____

_____

11 Criticize A classmate states that igneous rock must always become sedimentary rock next, according to the rock cycle. Explain why this statement is not correct.

_____

_____

12 Claims • Evidence • Reasoning Granite is an igneous rock that forms from magma cooled below Earth's surface. Make a claim about why granite would have larger crystals than igneous rocks formed from lava cooled above Earth's surface. Support your claim with evidence and explain your reasoning.

SC.7.N.1.1 Define a problem from the seventh grade curriculum, use appropriate reference materials to support scientific understanding, plan and carry out scientific investigation of various types, such as systematic observations or experiments, identify variables, collect and organize data, interpret data in charts, tables, and graphics, analyze information, make predictions, and defend conclusions.

S.T.E.M. ENGINEERING & TECHNOLOGY

Analyzing Technology

Skills
Identify risks
Identify benefits
✔ Evaluate cost of technology
✔ Evaluate environmental impact
✔ Propose improvements
Propose risk reduction
✔ Compare technology
✔ Communicate results

Objectives
Analyze the life cycle of an aluminum can.
Analyze the life cycle of a glass bottle.
Evaluate the cost of recycling versus disposal of technology.
Analyze the environmental impact of technology.

Analyzing the Life Cycles of Aluminum and Glass

A life cycle analysis is a way to evaluate the real cost of a product. The analysis considers how much money an item costs to make. It also examines how making the product affects the economy and the environment through the life of the product. Engineers, scientists, and technologists use this information to improve processes and to compare products.

Costs of Production

Have you ever wondered where an aluminum soda can comes from? Have you wondered where the can goes when you are done with it? If so, you have started a life cycle analysis by asking the right questions. Aluminum is a metal found in a type of rock called *bauxite.* To get aluminum, first bauxite must be mined. The mined ore is then shipped to a processing plant. There, the bauxite is melted to get aluminum in a process called *smelting.* After smelting, the aluminum is processed. It may be shaped into bicycle parts or rolled into sheets to make cans. Every step in the production involves both financial costs and environmental costs that must be considered in a life cycle analysis.

Many bicycles are made of aluminum because it is lightweight and strong.

Costs of Disposal

After an aluminum can is used it can travel either to a landfill or to a recycling plant. The process of recycling an aluminum can does require the use of some energy. However, the financial and environmental costs of disposing of a can and mining ore are much greater than the cost of recycling a can. Additionally, smelting bauxite produces harmful wastes. A life cycle analysis of an aluminum can must include the cost and environmental effects of mining, smelting, and disposing of the aluminum can.

1 Claims • Evidence • Reasoning Make a claim about which steps are no longer part of a can's life cycle after the can is recycled. Summarize evidence to support the claim and explain your reasoning.

_____

_____

_____

Bauxite mining

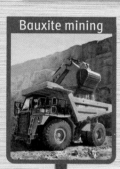

Most bauxite mining occurs far away from where aluminum is used. Large ships or trains transport the ore before it is made into aluminum products.

Smelting

Aluminum is one of the easiest materials to recycle. Producing a ton of aluminum by shredding and remelting uses about 5% of the energy needed to process enough bauxite to make a ton of aluminum.

Remelting **Shredding** **Recycling** **Fabrication** **Manufacturing** **Consumer use**

Life Cycle of an Aluminum Can

2 Evaluate In the life cycle shown here, which two steps could include an arrow to indicate disposal?

_____

_____

 **You Try It!**

Now it's your turn to analyze the life cycle of a product.

 **You Try It!**

Now, apply what you have learned about the life cycle of aluminum to analyze the life cycle of a glass bottle. Glass is made by melting silica from sand or from mineral deposits mined from the Earth. A kiln heats the silica until it melts to form a red-hot gob. Then, the glass is shaped and cooled to form useful items.

1 Evaluate Cost of Technology

As a group, discuss the steps that would be involved in making a glass bottle. List the steps in the space below. Start with mining and end at a landfill. Include as many steps in the process as you can think of. Beside each step, tell whether there would be financial costs, environmental costs, or both.

Life Cycle of a Glass Bottle

2 Evaluate Environmental Impact

Use the table below to indicate which of the steps listed above would have environmental costs, and what type of cost would be involved. A step can appear in more than one column.

Cause pollution	Consume energy	Damage habitat

(3) Propose Improvements

In your group, discuss how you might improve the life cycle of a glass bottle and reduce the impact on the environment. Draw a life cycle that includes your suggestions for improvement.

(4) Compare Technology

Claims • Evidence • Reasoning How does your improved process decrease the environmental effects of making and using glass bottles? Provide evidence to support your claim and explain your reasoning.

_____
_____
_____
_____

(5) Communicate Results

Imagine that you are an accountant for a company that produces glass bottles. In the space below, write an argument for using recycled glass that is based on financial savings for your company.

_____
_____
_____
_____

Earth's Layers

ESSENTIAL QUESTION

What are Earth's layers?

By the end of this lesson, you should be able to identify Earth's compositional and physical layers and describe their properties.

If you could dig below this canyon, you would discover that Earth is made up of different layers below its surface.

SC.7.E.6.1 Describe the layers of the solid Earth, including the lithosphere, the hot convecting mantle, and the dense metallic liquid and solid cores.
SC.7.E.6.7 Recognize that heat flow and movement of material within Earth causes earthquakes and volcanic eruptions, and creates mountains and ocean basins.

Lesson Labs

Quick Labs
- Tectonic Ice Cubes
- Layers of Earth

S.T.E.M. Lab
- Models of Earth

 ## Engage Your Brain

1 Predict Check T or F to show whether you think each statement is true or false.

T   F

☐   ☐   The outermost layer of solid Earth is sometimes called the crust.

☐   ☐   The crust is the densest layer.

☐   ☐   The mantle is the layer between the crust and the core.

☐   ☐   Earth's core is divided into five parts.

2 Describe If you were asked to describe this apple, how many layers would you say it has? How would you describe the layers?

_____

_____

_____

_____

_____

ACTIVE **READING**

3 Synthesize You can often define an unknown word if you know the meaning of its word parts. Use the word parts and sentence below to make an educated guess about the meaning of the word *mesosphere*.

Word part	Meaning
meso-	middle
-sphere	ball

Example sentence
The <u>mesosphere</u> is more than 2,000 km thick.

Mesosphere:

_____

_____

Vocabulary Terms

- crust
- mantle
- convection
- core
- lithosphere
- asthenosphere
- mesosphere

4 Apply As you learn the definition of each vocabulary term in this lesson, create your own definition or sketch to help you remember the meaning of the term.

Peeling the Layers

What is inside Earth?

If you tried to dig to the center of Earth, what do you think you would find? Would Earth be solid or hollow? Would it be made of the same material throughout? Actually, Earth is made of several layers. The materials that make up each layer have characteristic properties that vary from layer to layer. Scientists think about Earth's layers in two ways—in terms of their chemical composition and in terms of their physical properties.

i Think Outside the Book

5 Claims • Evidence • Reasoning
Make a claim about why scientists might have two ways for thinking about Earth's layers. Summarize evidence to support the claim and explain your reasoning.

What are Earth's compositional layers?

Earth can be divided into three layers based on chemical composition. These layers are called the *crust*, the *mantle*, and the *core*. Each compositional layer is made up of a different mixture of chemicals.

Earth is divided into three layers based on the chemical composition of each layer.

crust

mantle

core

continental crust

oceanic crust

mantle

Continental crust is thicker than oceanic crust.

Crust

The outermost solid layer of Earth is the **crust.** There are two types of crust—continental and oceanic. Both types are made mainly of the elements oxygen, silicon, and aluminum. However, the denser oceanic crust has almost twice as much iron, calcium, and magnesium. These elements form minerals that are denser than those in the continental crust.

ACTIVE **READING**

6 Identify List the compositional layers in order of most dense to least dense.

_____

_____

Mantle

The **mantle** is located between the core and the crust. It is a region of hot, slow-flowing, solid rock. When convection takes place in the mantle, cooler rock sinks and warmer rock rises. **Convection** is the movement of matter that results from differences in density caused by variations in temperature. Scientists can learn about the mantle by observing mantle rock that has risen to Earth's surface. The mantle is denser than the crust. It contains more magnesium and less aluminum and silicon than the crust does.

Core

The **core** extends from below the mantle to the center of Earth. Scientists think that the core is made mostly of iron and some nickel. Scientists also think that it contains much less oxygen, silicon, aluminum, and magnesium than the mantle does. The core is the densest layer. It makes up about one-third of Earth's mass.

ACTIVE **READING**

7 Identify What element makes up most of Earth's core?

_____

What are Earth's physical layers?

Earth can also be divided into layers based on physical properties. The properties considered include whether the layer is solid or liquid, and how the layer moves or transmits waves. The five physical layers are the *lithosphere*, *asthenosphere*, *mesosphere*, *outer core*, and *inner core*.

ACTIVE READING

8 Label Write the names of the compositional layers shown below in the spaces provided.

Lithosphere

The outermost, rigid layer of Earth is the **lithosphere.** The lithosphere is made of two parts—the crust and the rigid, upper part of the mantle. The lithosphere is divided into pieces called *tectonic plates*.

Asthenosphere

The **asthenosphere** is a layer of weak or soft mantle that is made of rock that flows slowly. Tectonic plates move on top of this layer.

Mesosphere

The strong, lower part of the mantle is called the **mesosphere.** Rock in the mesosphere flows more slowly than rock in the asthenosphere does.

Outer Core

The outer core is the liquid layer of Earth's core. It lies beneath the mantle and surrounds the inner core.

Inner Core

The inner core is the solid, dense center of our planet that extends from the bottom of the outer core to the center of Earth, which is about 6,380 km beneath the surface.

9 Claims • Evidence • Reasoning Make a claim about which of Earth's compositional layers make up the lithosphere. Summarize evidence to support the claim and explain your reasoning.

_____

A

B

C

Sample Problem

Here's an example of how to find the percentage thickness of the core that is the outer core.

Physical	Compositional
Continental lithosphere (150 km)	Continental crust (50 km)
Asthenosphere (250 km)	Mantle (2,900 km)
Mesosphere (2,550 km)	
Outer core (2,200 km)	Core (3,430 km)
Inner core (1,230 km)	

Identify

A. What do you know?

core = 3,430 km   outer core = 2,200 km

B. What do you want to find out?

Percentage of core that is outer core

Plan

C. Write the formula:

Percentage (%) of core that is outer core =

$$\left(\frac{\text{thickness of outer core}}{\text{thickness of core}} \right) \times 100\%$$

D. Substitute into the formula:

$$\% = \frac{(2,200)}{(3,430)} \times 100\%$$

Solve

E. Calculate and simplify:

$$\% = 0.6414 \times 100\% = 64.14\%$$

Answer: 64.14%

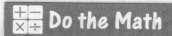

You Try It

10 Calculate What percentage thickness of the continental lithosphere is continental crust?

Identify

A. What do you know?

B. What do you want to find out?

Plan

C. Write the formula:

D. Substitute into the formula:

Solve

E. Calculate and simplify:

Answer:

Visual Summary

To complete this summary, fill in the blanks with the correct word or phrase. You can use this page to review the main concepts of the lesson.

Earth is divided into three compositional layers.

11 The outermost compositional layer of the Earth is the _____ .

12 The _____ is denser than the crust and contains more magnesium.

Earth is divided into five physical layers.

13 The _____ is divided into pieces called tectonic plates.

14 The _____ core is the liquid layer of Earth's core.

Earth's Layers

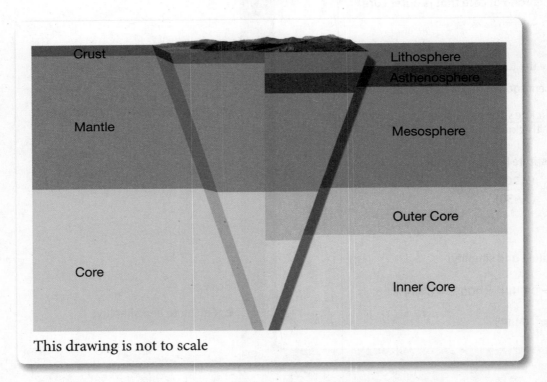

Crust

Mantle

Core

Lithosphere
Asthenosphere
Mesosphere
Outer Core
Inner Core

This drawing is not to scale

15 **Claims • Evidence • Reasoning** Make a claim about which physical layers correspond to which compositional layers. Give evidence to support the claim and explain your reasoning.

Lesson Review

Vocabulary

Fill in the blank with the term that best completes the following sentence.

1 The _____ is a region of hot, slow-flowing, solid rock between the core and the crust.

2 The _____ is the densest compositional layer and makes up one-third of Earth's mass.

3 The _____ is the outermost, rigid physical layer of Earth.

Key Concepts

Use this diagram to answer the following questions.

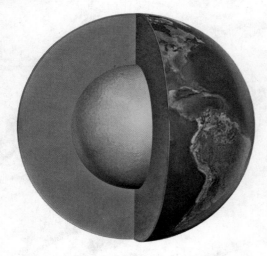

4 Identify Which model of Earth's interior does this image show?

_____

5 Identify Which of these layers is made mostly of iron and nickel?

_____

6 Compare Explain the differences between the inner core and the outer core.

_____

Critical Thinking

7 Compare Explain the difference between the lithosphere and the crust.

_____

_____

_____

8 Claims • Evidence • Reasoning Scientists find dense rock on Earth's surface that is made of magnesium and smaller amounts of aluminum and silicon. Make a claim about which layer of Earth this rock might help scientists study. Summarize evidence to support the claim and explain your reasoning.

_____

_____

_____

_____

_____

_____

9 Apply In a model of Earth's layers that is determined by physical properties, how might the atmosphere be classified? Would it be part of the lithosphere, or a separate layer? Explain your answer.

_____

_____

_____

_____

_____

_____

_____

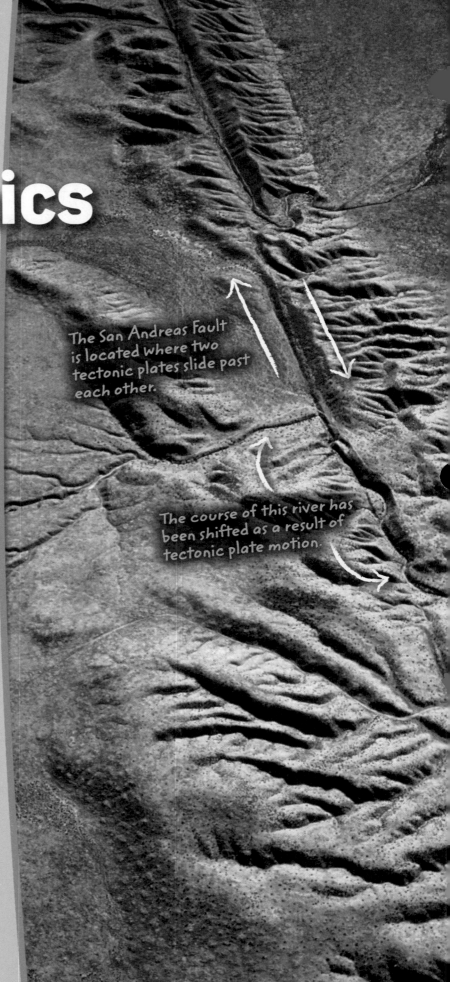

The San Andreas Fault is located where two tectonic plates slide past each other.

The course of this river has been shifted as a result of tectonic plate motion.

Plate Tectonics

ESSENTIAL QUESTION

What is plate tectonics?

By the end of this lesson, you should be able to explain the theory of plate tectonics, to describe how tectonic plates move, and to identify geologic events that occur because of tectonic plate movement.

SC.7.E.6.1 Describe the layers of the solid Earth, including the lithosphere, the hot convecting mantle, and the dense metallic liquid and solid cores. **SC.7.E.6.2** Identify the patterns within the rock cycle and relate them to surface events (weathering and erosion) and sub-surface events (plate tectonics and mountain building). **SC.7.E.6.5** Explore the scientific theory of plate tectonics by describing how the movement of Earth's crustal plates causes both slow and rapid changes in Earth's surface, including volcanic eruptions, earthquakes, and mountain building. **SC.7.E.6.7** Recognize that heat flow and movement of material within Earth causes earthquakes and volcanic eruptions, and creates mountains and ocean basins.

 **Lesson Labs**

Quick Labs
- Reconstructing Land Masses
- What Happens When Objects Collide?
- Mantle Convection

Exploration Lab
- Seafloor Spreading

 Engage Your Brain

1 Identify Check T or F to show whether you think each statement is true or false.

T   F

☐ ☐ Earth's surface is all one piece.

☐ ☐ Scientists think the continents once formed a single landmass.

☐ ☐ The sea floor is smooth and level.

☐ ☐ All tectonic plates are the same.

2 Predict Imagine that ice cubes are floating in a large bowl of punch. If there are enough cubes, they will cover the surface of the punch and bump into one another. Parts of the cubes will be below the surface of the punch and will displace the punch. Will some cubes displace more punch than others? Explain your answer.

_____

_____

_____

_____

_____

_____

ACTIVE **READING**

3 Apply Many scientific words, such as *divergent* and *convergent,* also have everyday meanings or are related to words with everyday meanings. Use context clues to write your own definition for each underlined word.

Example sentence
They argued about the issue because their opinions about it were <u>divergent</u>.

divergent:

_____

_____

Example sentence
The two rivers <u>converged</u> near the town.

convergent:

_____

_____

Vocabulary Terms
- Pangaea
- sea-floor spreading
- plate tectonics
- tectonic plates
- convergent boundary
- divergent boundary
- transform boundary
- convection

4 Identify This list contains key terms you'll learn in this lesson. As you read, underline the definition of each term.

Puzzling Evidence

What evidence suggests that continents move?

Have you ever looked at a map and noticed that the continents look like they could fit together like puzzle pieces? In the late 1800s, Alfred Wegener proposed his hypothesis of continental drift. He proposed that the continents once formed a single landmass, broke up, and drifted. This idea is supported by several lines of evidence. For example, fossils of the same species are found on continents on different sides of the Atlantic Ocean. These species could not have crossed the ocean. The hypothesis is also supported by the locations of mountain ranges and rock formations and by evidence of the same ancient climatic conditions on several continents.

Geologic evidence supports the hypothesis of continental drift.

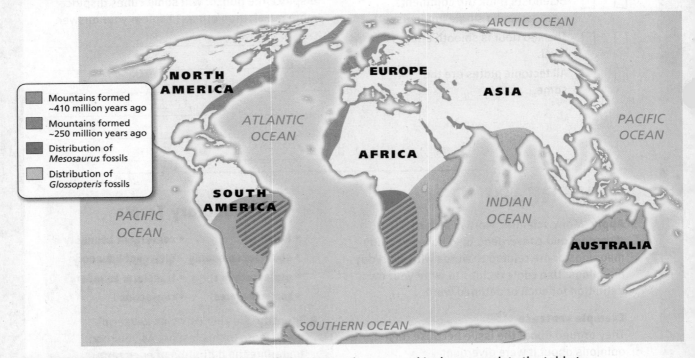

Key:
- Mountains formed ~410 million years ago
- Mountains formed ~250 million years ago
- Distribution of *Mesosaurus* fossils
- Distribution of *Glossopteris* fossils

5 Summarize Using the map and its key, complete the table to describe evidence that indicates each continent pair was once joined.

👁 Visualize It!

	Fossil evidence	Mountain evidence
South America and Africa		
North America and Europe		

What is Pangaea?

ACTIVE READING

6 Identify As you read, underline the description of how North America formed from Pangaea.

Using evidence from many scientific fields, scientists can construct a picture of continental change throughout time. Scientists think that about 245 million years ago, the continents were joined in a single large landmass they call **Pangaea** (pan•JEE•uh). As the continents collided to form Pangaea, mountains formed. A single, large ocean called Panthalassa surrounded Pangaea.

About 200 million years ago, a large rift formed and Pangaea began to break into two continents—*Laurasia* and *Gondwana*. Then, Laurasia began to drift northward and rotate slowly, and a new rift formed. This rift separated Laurasia into the continents of North America and Eurasia. The rift eventually formed the North Atlantic Ocean. At the same time, Gondwana also broke into two continents. One continent contained land that is now the continents of South America and Africa. The other continent contained land that is now Antarctica, Australia, and India.

About 150 million years ago, a rift between Africa and South America opened to form the South Atlantic Ocean. India, Australia, and Antarctica also began to separate from each other. As India broke away from Australia and Antarctica, it started moving northward, toward Eurasia.

As India and the continents moved into their present positions, new oceans formed while others disappeared. In some cases, continents collided with other continents. About 50 million years ago, India collided with Eurasia, and the Himalaya Mountains began to form. Mountain ranges form as a result of these collisions, because a collision welds new crust onto the continents and uplifts some of the land.

The Breakup of Pangaea

245 million years ago

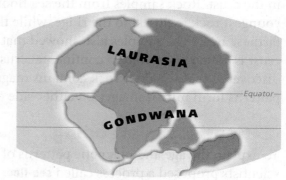

200 million years ago

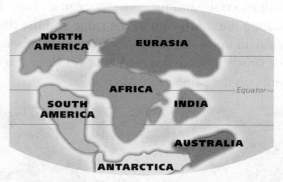

65 million years ago

3 million years ago

What discoveries support the idea of continental drift?

Wegener's ideas of continental drift were pushed aside for many years because scientists could not determine how continents moved. Then, in the mid-1900s, scientists began mapping the sea floor. They expected the floor to be smooth and level. Instead, they found huge under-water mountain ranges called *mid-ocean ridges*. The discovery of mid-ocean ridges eventually led to the theory of plate tectonics, which built on some of Wegener's ideas.

○ Age and Magnetic Properties of the Sea Floor

Scientists learned that the mid-ocean ridges form along cracks in the crust. Rock samples from the sea floor revealed that the youngest rock is closest to the ridge, while the oldest rock is farthest away. The samples also showed that even the oldest ocean crust is young compared to continental crust. Scientists also discovered that sea-floor rock contains magnetic patterns. These patterns form mirror images on either side of a mid-ocean ridge.

○ Sea-Floor Spreading

To explain the age and magnetic patterns of sea-floor rocks, scientists proposed a process called **sea-floor spreading**. In this process, molten rock from inside Earth rises through the cracks in the ridges, cools, and forms new oceanic crust. The old crust breaks along the mid-point of the ridge and the two pieces of crust move away in opposite directions from each other. In this way, the sea floor slowly spreads apart. As the sea floor moves, so do the continents on the same piece of crust.

7 Claims • Evidence • Reasoning
Make a claim about why many scientists would not accept the hypothesis of continental drift. Give evidence to support the claim and explain your reasoning.

_____

_____

_____

This map shows where mid-ocean ridges are located.

Ocean Trenches

If the sea floor has been spreading for millions of years, why is Earth not getting larger? Scientists discovered the answer when they found huge trenches, like deep canyons, in the sea floor. At these sites, dense oceanic crust is sinking into the asthenosphere as shown in the diagram below. Older crust is being destroyed at the same rate new crust is forming. Thus, Earth remains the same size.

With this new information about the sea floor, sea-floor spreading, and ocean trenches, scientists could begin to understand how continents were able to move.

Publishing Company

ACTIVE READING

8 Claims • Evidence • Reasoning
Make a claim about why Earth isn't getting larger if the sea floor is spreading. Summarize evidence to support the claim and explain your reasoning.

_____

_____

_____

👁 Visualize It!

9 Provide Label the youngest rock and the oldest rock on this diagram of sea-floor spreading.

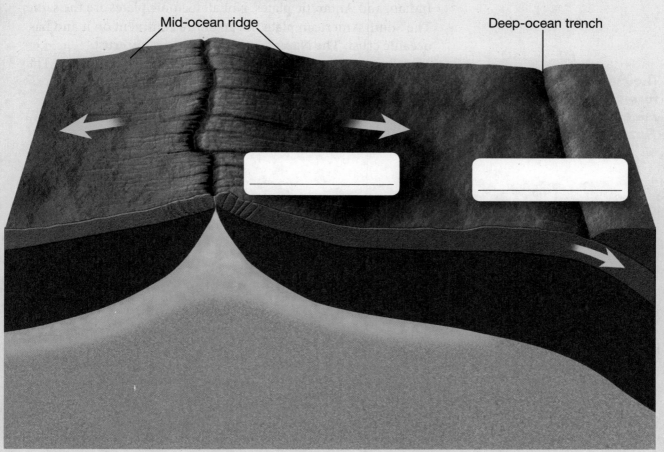

Sea-floor spreading takes place at mid-ocean ridges.

Mid-ocean ridge

Deep-ocean trench

A Giant Jigsaw

What is the theory of plate tectonics?

As scientists' understanding of continental drift, mid-ocean ridges, and sea-floor spreading grew, scientists formed a theory to explain these processes and features. **Plate tectonics** describes large-scale movements of Earth's lithosphere, which is made up of the crust and the rigid, upper part of the mantle. Plate tectonics explains how and why features in Earth's crust form and continents move.

What is a tectonic plate?

The lithosphere is divided into pieces called **tectonic plates.** These plates move around on top of the asthenosphere. The plates are moving in different directions and at different speeds. Each tectonic plate fits together with the plates that surround it. The continents are located on tectonic plates and move around with them. The major tectonic plates include the Pacific, North American, Nazca, South American, African, Australian, Eurasian, Indian, and Antarctic plates. Not all tectonic plates are the same. The South American plate has an entire continent on it and has oceanic crust. The Nazca plate has only oceanic crust.

Tectonic plates cover the surface of the asthenosphere. They vary in size, shape, and thickness. Thick tectonic plates, such as those with continents, displace more asthenosphere than thin oceanic plates do. But, oceanic plates are much more dense than continental plates are.

ACTIVE READING

11 Identify As you read, underline the definition of *tectonic plates*.

The Andes Mountains formed where the South American plate and Nazca plate meet.

12 Locate Which letter marks where the Andes Mountains are located on the map of tectonic plates, A, B, or C? _____

The tectonic plates fit together like the pieces of a jigsaw puzzle.

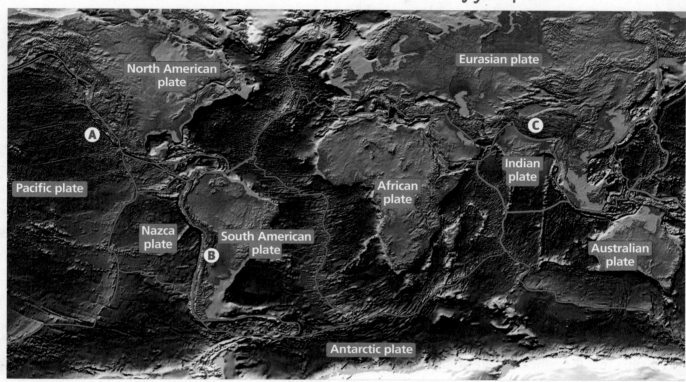

North American plate

Eurasian plate

A

Pacific plate

African plate

C

Indian plate

Nazca plate

South American plate

B

Australian plate

Antarctic plate

The thickest part of the South American plate is the continental crust. The thinnest part of this plate is in the Atlantic Ocean.

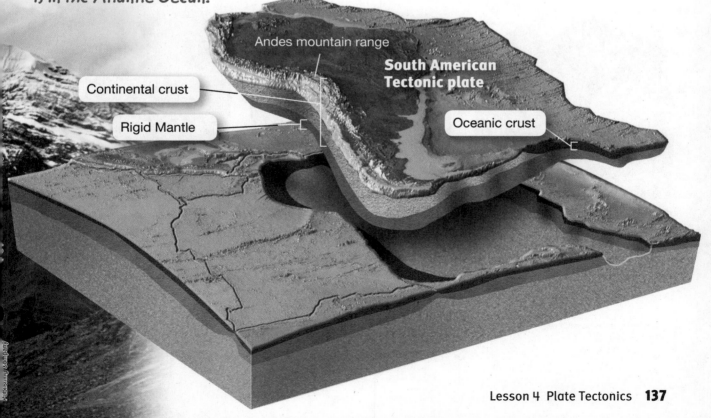

Andes mountain range

South American Tectonic plate

Continental crust

Rigid Mantle

Oceanic crust

Boundaries

What are the three types of plate boundaries?

The most dramatic changes in Earth's crust occur along plate boundaries. Plate boundaries may be on the ocean floor, around the edges of continents, or even within continents. There are three types of plate boundaries: divergent boundaries, convergent boundaries, and transform boundaries. Each type of plate boundary is associated with characteristic landforms.

ACTIVE READING

13 Identify As you read, underline the locations where plate boundaries may be found.

Convergent Boundaries

Convergent boundaries form where two plates collide. Three types of collisions can happen at convergent boundaries. When two tectonic plates of continental lithosphere collide, they buckle and thicken, which pushes some of the continental crust upward. When a plate of oceanic lithosphere collides with a plate of continental lithosphere, the denser oceanic lithosphere sinks into the asthenosphere. Boundaries where one plate sinks beneath another plate are called subduction zones. When two tectonic plates of oceanic lithosphere collide, one of the plates subducts, or sinks, under the other plate.

 14 Claims • Evidence • Reasoning Make a claim about why the denser plate subducts in a collision. Support the claim with evidence and explain your reasoning.

_____

_____

_____

Continent-Continent Collisions
When two plates of continental lithosphere collide, they buckle and thicken. This causes mountains to form.

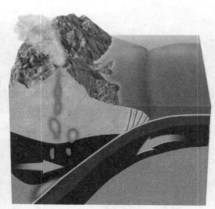

Continent-Ocean Collisions
When a plate of oceanic lithosphere collides with a plate of continental lithosphere, the oceanic lithosphere subducts because it is denser.

Ocean-Ocean Collisions
When two plates of oceanic lithosphere collide, the older, denser plate subducts under the other plate.

Divergent Boundaries

At a **divergent boundary**, two plates move away from each other. This separation allows the asthenosphere to rise toward the surface and partially melt. This melting creates magma, which erupts as lava. The lava cools and hardens to form new rock on the ocean floor.

As the crust and the upper part of the asthenosphere cool and become rigid, they form new lithosphere. This lithosphere is thin, warm, and light. This warm, light rock sits higher than the surrounding sea floor because it is less dense. It forms mid-ocean ridges. Most divergent boundaries are located on the ocean floor. However, rift valleys may also form where continents are separated by plate movement.

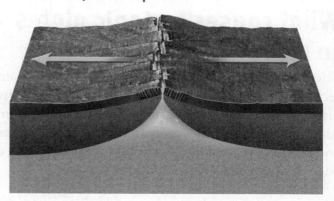

At divergent boundaries, plates separate.

Transform Boundaries

A boundary at which two plates move past each other horizontally is called a **transform boundary**. However, the plate edges do not slide along smoothly. Instead, they scrape against each other in a series of sudden slippages of crustal rock that are felt as earthquakes. Unlike other types of boundaries, transform boundaries generally do not produce magma. The San Andreas Fault in California is a major transform boundary between the North American plate and the Pacific plate. Transform motion also occurs at divergent boundaries. Short segments of mid-ocean ridges are connected by transform faults called fracture zones.

At transform boundaries, plates slide past each other horizontally.

ACTIVE **READING**

15 Claims • Evidence • Reasoning How are transform boundaries different from convergent and divergent boundaries? Provide evidence to support the claim and explain your reasoning.

_____

_____

_____

Hot Plates

What causes tectonic plates to move?

Scientists have proposed three mechanisms to explain how tectonic plates move over Earth's surface. Mantle convection drags plates along as mantle material moves beneath tectonic plates. Ridge push moves plates away from mid-ocean ridges as rock cools and becomes more dense. Slab pull tugs plates along as the dense edge of a plate sinks beneath Earth's surface.

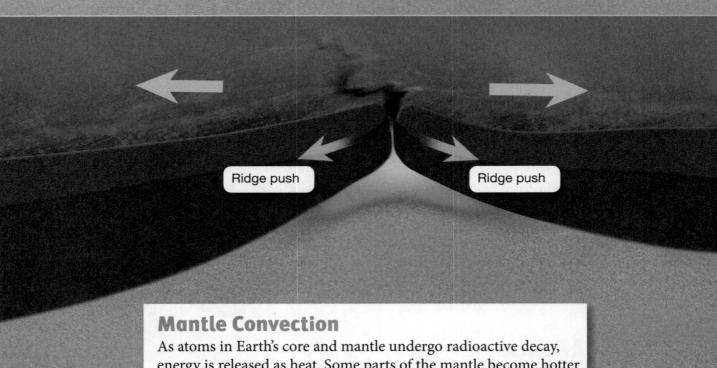

Ridge push   Ridge push

Mantle Convection

As atoms in Earth's core and mantle undergo radioactive decay, energy is released as heat. Some parts of the mantle become hotter than others parts. The hot parts rise as the sinking of cooler, denser material pushes the heated material up. This kind of movement of material due to differences in density is called **convection**. It was thought that as the mantle convects, or moves, it would drag the overlying tectonic plates along with it. However, this hypothesis has been criticized by many scientists because it does not explain the huge amount of force that would be needed to move plates.

Ridge Push

Newly formed rock at a mid-ocean ridge is warm and less dense than older, adjacent rock. Because of its lower density, the new rock rests at a higher elevation than the older rock. The older rock slopes downward away from the ridge. As the newer, warmer rock cools, it also becomes more dense. These cooling and increasingly dense rocks respond to gravity by moving down the slope of the asthenosphere, away from the ridge. This force, called ridge push, pushes the rest of the plate away from the mid-ocean ridge.

Slab Pull

At subduction zones, a denser tectonic plate sinks, or subducts, beneath another, less dense plate. The leading edge of the subducting plate is colder and denser than the mantle. As it sinks, the leading edge of the plate pulls the rest of the plate with it. This process is called slab pull. In general, subducting plates move faster than other plates do. This evidence leads many scientists to think that slab pull may be the most important mechanism driving tectonic plate motion.

Slab pull

17 Compare Complete the chart with brief descriptions to compare and contrast mantle convection, ridge push, and slab pull.

Mechanisms

Mantle convection	Ridge push	Slab pull

Visual Summary

To complete this summary, fill in the blanks to complete the label or caption. You can use this page to review the main concepts of the lesson.

The continents were joined in a single landmass.

18 Scientists call the landmass _____

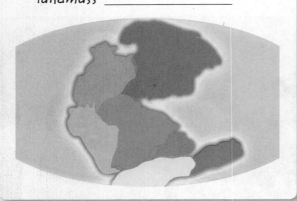

Tectonic plates differ in size and composition.

19 The United States lies on the _____ plate.

There are three types of plate boundaries: convergent, divergent, and transform.

20 This image shows a _____ boundary.

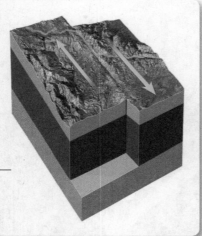

Three mechanisms may drive plate motion. These are mantle convection, slab pull, and ridge push.

21 The mechanism that scientists think is most important is _____

22 **Synthesize** How does the flow of energy as heat in Earth's interior contribute to the movement of tectonic plates? Make a claim about what would happen if Earth were not a convecting system. Use evidence to support your claim, and explain your reasoning.

Lesson Review

Vocabulary

Fill in the blanks with the term that best completes the following sentences.

1 The lithosphere is divided into pieces called

_____

2 The theory that describes large-scale movements of Earth's lithosphere is called

_____

3 The movement of material due to differences in density that are caused by differences in temperature is called _____

_____

Key Concepts

Use this diagram to answer the following questions.

4 Identify What type of plate boundary is shown?

_____

5 Identify Which types of lithosphere are colliding at this boundary?

_____

_____

6 Identify What landforms are likely to form at this boundary?

_____

_____

7 Describe How is continental lithosphere different from oceanic lithosphere?

_____

_____

_____

8 Compare How are convergent boundaries different from divergent boundaries?

_____

_____

_____

Critical Thinking

9 Claims • Evidence • Reasoning Make a claim about why cool rock material sinks when convection takes place in the mantle. Summarize evidence to support the claim and explain your reasoning.

_____

_____

_____

_____

_____

_____

10 Defend A friend says that Earth's continents are too large and massive to move. Explain to your friend why continents move. Defend your claim with evidence.

_____

_____

_____

_____

_____

_____

PEOPLE IN SCIENCE

SC.7.N.1.5 Describe the methods used in the pursuit of a scientific explanation as seen in different fields of science such as biology, geology, and physics.

Estella Atekwana

GEOPHYSICIST

Dr. Estella Atekwana studies changes on Earth's surface. Some of the changes may tell us how life on Earth developed. Others may help us to detect whether life exists somewhere else in the universe.

Some of Dr. Atekwana's work takes her to Botswana and Zambia in Africa. There she is studying the formation of a new rift valley. Rift valleys are places where continents break apart. (For example, long ago a rift valley formed, and Africa broke apart from South America.) Studying this rift valley, Dr. Atekwana hopes to learn more about how new landmasses form. Further, the ground reveals the remains of plants and animals that once lived there. These remains can tell us more about the climate that existed there millions of years ago.

Currently, Dr. Atekwana is doing brand new research in a new field of geology known as biogeophysics. She is looking at the effects that microorganisms have on rocks. She is using new technologies to study how rock changes after microorganisms have mixed with it. This research may one day help scientists detect evidence of life on other planets. Looking for the same geophysical changes in the rocks on Mars might be a way of detecting whether life ever existed on that planet. If the rocks show the same changes as the rocks on Earth, it could be because microorganisms once lived in them.

Dr. Atekwana's research included this visit to Victoria Falls on the Zambezi River in Africa.

🌐 Social Studies Connection

Dr. Atekwana studies rift valleys—areas where the tectonic plates are pulling apart. Research to find out where else in the world scientists have located rift valleys.

JOB BOARD

Surveying and Mapping Technicians

What You'll Do: Help surveyors take measurements of outdoor areas. Technicians hold measuring tapes and adjust instruments, take notes, and make sketches.

Where You Might Work: Outdoors and indoors entering measurements into a computer.

Education: Some post-secondary education to obtain a license.

Other Job Requirements: Technicians must be able to visualize objects, distances, sizes, and shapes. They must be able to work with great care, precision, and accuracy because mistakes can be expensive. They must also be in good physical condition.

Petroleum Technician

What You'll Do: Measure and record the conditions in oil or gas wells to find out whether samples contain oil and other minerals.

Where You Might Work: Outdoors, sometimes in remote locations and sometimes in your own town or city.

Education: An associate's degree or a certificate in applied science or science-related technology.

Other Job Requirements: You need to be able to take accurate measurements and keep track of many details.

Geologist

What You'll Do: Study the history of Earth's crust. Geologists work in many different businesses. You may explore for minerals, oil, or gas. You may find and test ground water supplies. You may work with engineers to make sure ground is safe to build on.

Where You Might Work: In the field, where you collect samples, and in the office, where you analyze them. Geologists work in mines, on oil rigs, on the slopes of volcanoes, in quarries, and in paleontological digs.

Education: A four-year bachelor's degree in science.

Other Job Requirements: Geologists who work in the field must be in good physical condition. Most geologists do field training. Geologists need strong math skills, analytical skills, and computer skills. They also need to be able to work well with other members of a team.

Publishing Company

Mountain Building

The highest peak in the Alps mountain range is Mont Blanc at just over 4,800 m tall.

ESSENTIAL QUESTION

How do mountains form?

By the end of this lesson, you should be able to describe how the movement of Earth's tectonic plates causes mountain building.

SC.7.N.1.1 Define a problem from the seventh grade curriculum, use appropriate reference materials to support scientific understanding, plan and carry out scientific investigation of various types, such as systematic observations or experiments, identify variables, collect and organize data, interpret data in charts, tables, and graphics, analyze information, make predictions, and defend conclusions. **SC.7.E.6.5** Explore the scientific theory of plate tectonics by describing how the movement of Earth's crustal plates causes both slow and rapid changes in Earth's surface, including volcanic eruptions, earthquakes, and mountain building. **SC.7.E.6.7** Recognize that heat flow and movement of material within Earth causes earthquakes and volcanic eruptions, and creates mountains and ocean basins.

© Houghton Mifflin Harcourt

Lesson Labs

Quick Labs
- Modeling Geologic Processes
- Modeling Strike-Slip Faults

 Engage Your Brain

1 Predict Check T or F to show whether you think each statement is true or false.

T   F

☐ ☐ Mountains can originate from a level surface that is folded upward.

☐ ☐ Rocks can be pulled apart by the movement of tectonic plates.

☐ ☐ All mountains are created by volcanoes.

☐ ☐ A mountain range can form only at the edge of a tectonic plate.

Rocky Mountains

Appalachian Mountains

2 Hypothesize The Appalachian Mountains were once taller than the Rocky Mountains. What do you think happened to the mountains? Explain your reasoning.

_____

_____

_____

ACTIVE READING

3 Compare The terms *compression* and *tension* have opposite meanings. Compare the two sentences below, then write your own definition for *compression* and *tension*.

Vocabulary	Sentence
compression	The stack of books on Jon's desk caused the bottom book to be flattened by <u>compression</u>.
tension	Keisha pulled the piece of string so hard, the <u>tension</u> caused the string to break.

compression:

_____

_____

tension:

_____

_____

Vocabulary Terms

- **deformation**
- **folding**
- **fault**
- **shear stress**
- **tension**
- **compression**

4 Apply As you learn the definition of each vocabulary term in this lesson, create your own definition or sketch to help you remember the meaning of the term.

Stressed Out

How can tectonic plate motion cause deformation?

The movement of tectonic plates places stress on rocks. A tectonic plate is a block of lithosphere that consists of crust and the rigid outermost part of the mantle. *Stress* is the amount of force per unit area that is placed on an object. Rocks can bend or break under stress. In addition, low temperatures make materials more brittle, or easily broken. High temperatures can allow rock to bend.

When a rock is placed under stress, it deforms, or changes shape. **Deformation** (dee•fohr•MAY•shuhn) is the process by which rocks change shape when under stress. Rock can bend if it is placed under high temperature and pressure for long periods of time. If the stress becomes too great, or is applied quickly, rock can break. When rocks bend, folds form. When rocks break, faults form.

ACTIVE READING

5 Identify As you read, list some objects near you that can bend or break from deformation.

_____

_____

_____

_____

_____

By applying stress, the boy is causing the spaghetti to deform. Similarly, stress over a long period of time can cause rock to bend.

Like the spaghetti, stress over a short period of time or great amounts of stress can cause rock to break.

👁 Visualize It!

6 Claims • Evidence • Reasoning Make a claim about how the same material might bend in one situation but break in another. Provide evidence to support the claim and explain your reasoning.

_____

_____

_____

_____

What are two kinds of folds?

Folded rock layers appear bent or buckled. **Folding** occurs when rock layers bend under stress. The bends are called *folds*. Scientists assume that all rock layers start out as horizontal layers deposited on top of each other over time. Sometimes, different layers of rocks can still be seen even after the rocks have been folded. When scientists see a fold, they know that deformation has happened. Two common types of folds are synclines and anticlines.

○ Synclines and Anticlines

Folds are classified based on the age of the rock layers. In a *syncline* (SIN•klyn), the youngest layers of rock are found at the core of a fold. The oldest layers are found on the outside of the fold. Synclines usually look like rock layers that are arched upward, like a bowl. In an *anticline* (AN•tih•klyn), the oldest layers of rock are found at the core of the fold. The youngest layers are found on the outside of the fold. Anticlines often look like rock layers that are arched downwards and high in the middle. Often, both types of folds will be visible in the same rock layers, as shown below.

👁 Visualize It!

8 Claims • Evidence • Reasoning Make a claim about which rock layers are youngest and oldest. Summarize evidence to support the claim and explain your reasoning.

_____

_____

_____

_____

The hinge is the middle point of the bend in a syncline or anticline.

Faulted

What are the three kinds of faults?

Rock can be under so much stress that it cannot bend and may break. The crack that forms when large blocks of rock break and move past each other is called a **fault**. The blocks of rock on either side of the fault are called *fault blocks*. The sudden movement of fault blocks can cause earthquakes.

Any time there is a fault in Earth's crust, rocks tend to move in predictable ways. Earth has three main kinds of faults: strike-slip faults, normal faults, and reverse faults. Scientists classify faults based on the way fault blocks move relative to each other. The location where two fault blocks meet is called the *fault plane*. A fault plane can be oriented horizontally, vertically, or at any angle in between. For any fault except a perfectly vertical fault, the block above the fault plane is called the *hanging wall*. The block below the fault plane is the *footwall*.

The movement of faults can create mountains and other types of landforms. At any tectonic plate boundary, the amount of stress on rock is complex. Therefore, any of the three types of faults can occur at almost all plate boundaries.

ACTIVE READING

9 Identify As you read, underline the direction of movement of the fault blocks in each type of fault.

Strike-Slip Faults

In a strike-slip fault, the fault blocks move past each other horizontally. Strike-slip faults form when rock is under shear stress. **Shear stress** is stress that pushes rocks in parallel but opposite directions as seen in the image. As rocks are deformed deep in Earth's crust, energy builds. The release of this energy can cause earthquakes as the rocks slide past each other. Strike-slip faults are common along transform boundaries, where tectonic plates move past each other. The San Andreas fault system in California is an example of a strike-slip fault.

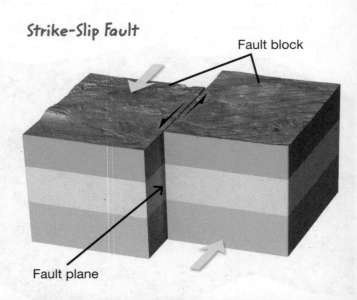

Strike-Slip Fault

Fault block

Fault plane

© Houghton Mifflin Harcourt

Normal Faults

In the normal fault shown on the right, the hanging wall moves down relative to the footwall. The faults are called normal because the blocks move in a way that you would *normally* expect as a result of gravity. Normal faults form when the rock is under tension. **Tension** (TEN•shun) is stress that stretches or pulls rock apart. Therefore, normal faults are common along divergent boundaries. Earth's crust can also stretch in the middle of a tectonic plate. The Basin and Range area of the southwestern United States is an example of a location with many normal fault structures.

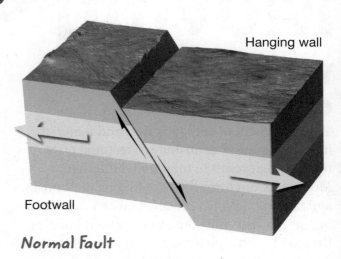

Hanging wall

Footwall

Normal Fault

Reverse Faults

In the reverse fault shown on the right, the hanging wall moves up relative to the footwall. The faults are called reverse because the hanging blocks move up, which is the reverse of what you would expect as a result of gravity. Reverse faults form when rocks undergo compression. **Compression** (kuhm•PRESH•uhn) is stress that squeezes or pushes rock together. Reverse faults are common along convergent boundaries, where two plates collide. The San Gabriel Mountains in the United States are caused by reverse faults.

Reverse Fault

👁 Visualize It!

10 Identify Label the fault plane, hanging wall, and footwall on the reverse fault to the right.

🛈 Think Outside the Book

11 Compile Create a memory matching game of the types of faults. Create as many cards as you can with different photos, drawings, or written details about the types of faults. Use the cards to quiz yourself and your classmates.

Moving On Up

What are the three kinds of mountains?

The movement of energy as heat and material in Earth's interior contribute to tectonic plate motions that result in mountain building. Mountains can form through folding, volcanism, and faulting. *Uplift,* a process that can cause land to rise can also contribute to mountain building. Because tectonic plates are always in motion, some mountains are constantly being uplifted.

ACTIVE READING

12 Identify As you read, underline examples of folded, volcanic, and fault-block mountains.

Folded Mountains

Folded mountains form when rock layers are squeezed together and pushed upward. They usually form at convergent boundaries, where plates collide. For example, the Appalachian Mountains (ap•uh•LAY•chun) formed from folding and faulting when the North American plate collided with the Eurasian and African plates millions of years ago.

In Europe, the Pyrenees (PIR•uh•neez) are another range of folded mountains, as shown below. They are folded over an older, pre-existing mountain range. Today, the highest peaks are over 3,000 m tall.

The Pyrenees Mountains are folded mountains that separate France from Spain.

👁 Visualize It!

13 Claims • Evidence • Reasoning What evidence do you see that the Pyrenees Mountains are folded mountains? Summarize evidence to support the claim and explain your reasoning.

_____

_____

_____

Volcanic Mountains

Volcanic mountains form when melted rock erupts onto Earth's surface. Many major volcanic mountains are located at convergent boundaries. Volcanic mountains can form on land or on the ocean floor. Volcanoes on the ocean floor can grow so tall that they rise above the surface of the ocean, forming islands. Most of Earth's active volcanoes are concentrated around the edge of the Pacific Ocean. This area is known as the Ring of Fire. Many volcanoes, including Mt. Griggs in the image to the right, are located on the Northern rim of the Pacific plate in Alaska.

Mt. Griggs volcano on the Alaskan Peninsula is 2,317 m high.

The Teton Mountains in Wyoming are fault-block mountains.

Fault-Block Mountains

Fault-block mountains form when tension makes the lithosphere break into many normal faults. Along the faults, pieces of the lithosphere drop down compared with other pieces. The pieces left standing form fault-block mountains. The Teton Mountains (TEE•tuhn) and the Sierra Nevadas are fault-block mountains.

14 Identify Draw a simple version of each type of mountain below.

Folded	Volcanic	Faulted

Visual Summary

To complete this summary, fill in the blanks with the correct word or phrase. You can use this page to review the main concepts of the lesson.

Mountain Building

Rocks can bend or break under stress.

15 The process by which rocks change shape under stress is called _____

Folds occur when rock layers bend.

16 A rock structure with the oldest rocks at the core of the fold is called a/an _____

Faults occur when rock layers break.

Footwall

Hanging wall

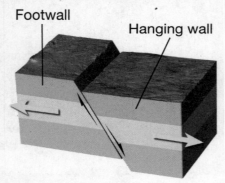

17 The type of fault pictured is a _____ fault.

Mountains form through folding, volcanism, and faulting.

18 The type of mountains pictured are _____ mountains.

19 Claims • Evidence • Reasoning The middle of tectonic plates tend to have fewer mountains than locations near tectonic plate boundaries. Make a claim about what might be one possible explanation for this. Summarize evidence to support the claim and explain your reasoning.

Lesson Review

Vocabulary

Fill in the blank with the term that best completes the following sentences.

1 A normal fault is a result of a type of stress known as _____

2 A strike-slip fault is a result of _____ stress.

3 A reverse fault is caused by a type of stress known as _____

Key Concepts

Fill in the table below by identifying the type of mountain described in the example question.

Example	Type of Mountain
4 Identify The Basin and Range province is characterized by many normal faults.	
5 Identify The Cascade Range in the United States has many eruptive mountains.	
6 Identify The Pyrenees Mountains have many syncline and anticline structures.	

7 Describe How does the movement of tectonic plates cause deformation in rock?

_____

_____

8 Compare How do folded, volcanic, and fault-block mountains differ?

_____

_____

_____

Critical Thinking

Use the diagram below to answer the following questions.

9 Correlate What type of stress caused the fault shown in the image?

_____

10 Claims • Evidence • Reasoning Make a claim about along which type of tectonic plate boundary this fault would be common. Provide evidence to support the claim and explain your reasoning.

_____

_____

11 Claims • Evidence • Reasoning Make a claim about whether a rock can undergo compression, tension, and shear stress all at once. Summarize evidence to support the claim and explain your reasoning.

_____

_____

_____

12 Conclude Imagine you are walking along a roadway and see a syncline. What can you conclude about the formation of that fold?

_____

_____

_____

_____

Earthquakes

ESSENTIAL QUESTION

Why do earthquakes happen?

By the end of this lesson, you should be able to describe the causes of earthquakes and to identify where earthquakes happen.

SC.7.N.1.1 Define a problem from the seventh grade curriculum, use appropriate reference materials to support scientific understanding, plan and carry out scientific investigation of various types, such as systematic observations or experiments, identify variables, collect and organize data, interpret data in charts, tables, and graphics, analyze information, make predictions, and defend conclusions. **SC.7.E.6.5** Explore the scientific theory of plate tectonics by describing how the movement of Earth's crustal plates causes both slow and rapid changes in Earth's surface, including volcanic eruptions, earthquakes, and mountain building. **SC.7.E.6.7** Recognize that heat flow and movement of material within Earth causes earthquakes and volcanic eruptions, and creates mountains and ocean basins.

The 1995 Kobe earthquake in Japan destroyed more than 200,000 buildings and structures including this railroad track.

© Pacific Press Service/Alamy

© Houghton Mifflin Harcourt

Lesson Labs

Quick Labs
- Elastic Rebound
- Earthquake Vibrations
- Earthquakes and Buildings

S.T.E.M. Lab
- Use a Seismograph to Determine the Amount of Energy in an Earthquake

 ## Engage Your Brain

1 Predict Fill in any words or numbers that you think best complete each of the statements below.

Each year there are approximately _____ earthquakes detected around the world.

In the United States, the state with the most earthquakes on average is _____

Every year, earthquakes cause _____ of dollars in damages in the United States.

Most earthquakes only last for several _____ of time.

2 Analyze Using the image, list in column 1 some of the hazards that can occur after an earthquake. In column 2, explain why you think these items or situations would be hazardous.

_____

_____

Hazards	Why?

ACTIVE **READING**

3 Synthesize You can often define an unknown word if you know the meaning of its word parts. Use the word parts and sentence below to make an educated guess about the meaning of the word *epicenter*.

Word part	Meaning
epi-	on, upon, or over
-center	the middle

Example sentence
The <u>epicenter</u> of the earthquake was only 3 km from our school.

epicenter:

_____

_____

Vocabulary Terms
- earthquake
- focus
- epicenter
- tectonic plate boundary
- fault
- deformation
- elastic rebound

4 Apply As you learn the definition of each vocabulary term in this lesson, create your own definition or sketch to help you remember the meaning of the term.

Let's Focus

ACTIVE READING

5 Identify As you read, underline the definitions of *focus* and *epicenter*.

What is an earthquake?

Earthquakes can cause extreme damage and loss of life. **Earthquakes** are ground movements that occur when blocks of rock in Earth move suddenly and release energy. The energy is released as seismic waves which cause the ground to shake and tremble.

Earthquake waves can be tracked to a point below Earth's surface known as the focus. The **focus** is a place within Earth along a fault at which the first motion of an earthquake occurs. Motion along a fault causes stress. When the stress on the rock is too great, the rock will rupture and cause an earthquake. The earthquake releases the stress. Directly above the focus on Earth's surface is the **epicenter** (EP•i•sen•ter). Seismic waves flow outward from the focus in all directions.

👁 Visualize It!

6 Identify Label the epicenter, focus, and fault on the diagram.

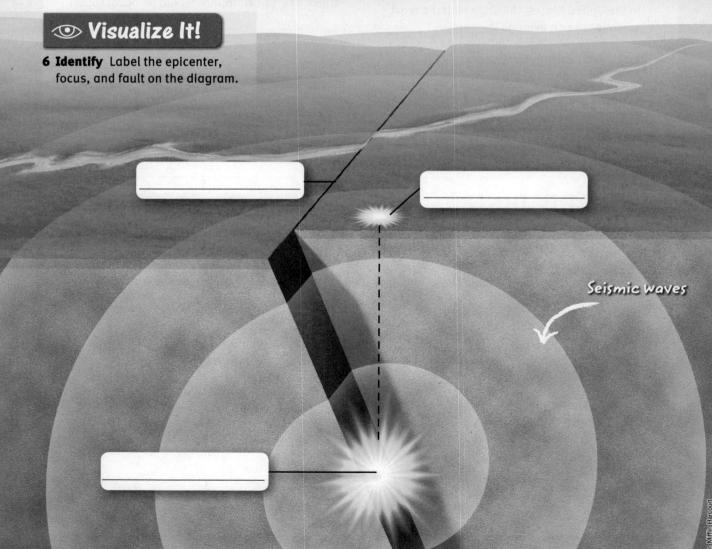

Seismic waves

What causes earthquakes?

Most earthquakes occur near the boundaries of tectonic plates. A **tectonic plate boundary** is where two or more tectonic plates meet. As tectonic plates move, pressure builds up near the edges of the plates. These movements break Earth's crust into a series of faults. A **fault** is a break in Earth's crust along which blocks of rock move. The release of energy that accompanies the movement of the rock along a fault causes an earthquake.

◯ Elastic Rebound

When rock is put under tremendous pressure, stress may deform, or change the shape of, the rock. **Deformation** (dee•for•MAY•shun) is the process by which rock becomes deformed and changes shape due to stress. As stress increases, the amount of energy that is stored in the rock increases, as seen in image B to the right.

Stress can change the shape of rock along a fault. Once the stress is released, rock may return to its original shape. When rock returns to nearly the same shape after the stress is removed, the process is known as *elastic deformation*. Imagine an elastic band that is pulled tight under stress. Once stress on the elastic band is removed, there is a *snap!* The elastic band returns to its original shape. A similar process occurs during earthquakes.

Similar to an elastic band, rock along tectonic plate boundaries can suddenly return to nearly its original shape when the stress is removed. The sudden *snap* is an earthquake. The return of rock to its original shape after elastic deformation is called **elastic rebound**. Earthquakes accompany the release of energy during elastic rebound. When the rock breaks and rebounds, it releases energy as seismic waves. The seismic wave energy radiates from the focus of the earthquake in all directions. This energy causes the ground to shake for a short time. Most earthquakes last for just a few seconds.

⊙ Visualize It!

7 Claims • Evidence • Reasoning Make a claim about whether an earthquake occurred between images A and B or between images B and C. Summarize evidence to support the claim and explain your reasoning.

_____

_____

A

Along a fault, rocks are pushed or pulled in different directions and at different speeds.

B

As stress increases and energy builds within the rock, the rock deforms but remains locked in place.

C

Too much stress causes the rock to break and rebound to its original shape, releasing energy.

© Houghton Mifflin Harcourt Publishing Company

Unstable Ground

Where do earthquakes happen?

ACTIVE READING

8 Identify As you read, underline the locations where earthquakes occur.

Each year, approximately 500,000 earthquakes are detected worldwide. The map below shows some of these earthquakes. Movement of material and energy in the form of heat in Earth's interior contribute to plate motions that result in earthquakes.

Most earthquakes happen at or near tectonic plate boundaries. Tectonic plate boundaries are areas where Earth's crust experiences a lot of stress. This stress occurs because the tectonic plates are colliding, separating, or grinding past each other horizontally. There are three main types of tectonic plate boundaries: divergent, convergent, and transform. The movement and interactions of the plates causes the crust to break into different types of faults. Earthquakes happen along these faults.

Plate Tectonic Boundaries and Earthquake Locations Worldwide

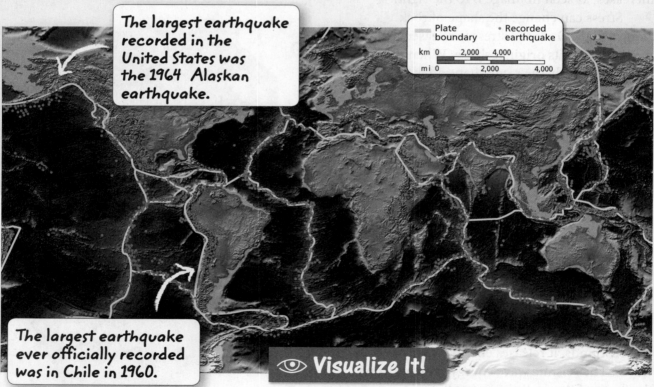

The largest earthquake recorded in the United States was the 1964 Alaskan earthquake.

The largest earthquake ever officially recorded was in Chile in 1960.

Plate boundary • Recorded earthquake

km 0   2,000   4,000
mi 0   2,000   4,000

👁 Visualize It!

9 Claims • Evidence • Reasoning Make a claim about where most of Earth's earthquakes are located. Summarize evidence to support the claim and explain your reasoning.

_____

_____

At Divergent Boundaries

At a divergent boundary, plates pull apart, causing the crust to stretch. Stress that stretches rock and makes rock thinner is called *tension*. Normal faults commonly result when tension pulls rock apart.

Most of the crust at divergent boundaries is thin, so the earthquakes tend to be shallow. Most earthquakes at divergent boundaries are no more than 20 km deep. A mid-ocean ridge is an example of a divergent boundary where earthquakes occur.

At divergent boundaries, earthquakes are common along _____ faults.

At Convergent Boundaries

Convergent plate boundaries occur when plates collide, causing rock to be squeezed. Stress that shortens or squeezes an object is known as *compression*. Compression causes the formation of reverse faults. Rocks are thrust over one another at reverse faults.

When two plates come together, both plates may crumple up to form mountains. Or one plate can subduct, or sink, underneath the other plate and into the mantle. The earthquakes that happen at convergent boundaries can be very strong. Subduction zone earthquakes occur at depths of up to 700 km.

At convergent boundaries, earthquakes are common along _____ faults.

At Transform Boundaries

A transform boundary is a place where two tectonic plates slide past each other horizontally. Stress that distorts a body by pushing different parts of the body in opposite directions is called *shear stress*. As the plates move, rocks on both sides of the fault are sheared, or broken, as they grind past one another in opposite directions.

Strike–slip faults are common at transform boundaries. Most earthquakes along the faults at transform boundaries are relatively shallow. The earthquakes are generally within the upper 50 km of the crust.

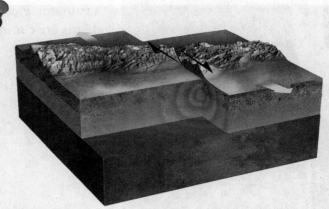

At transform boundaries, earthquakes are common along _____ faults.

11 Design You are an emergency management professional. You have been assigned to create an earthquake safety brochure for your town. Create a brochure that demonstrates ways people can protect themselves during an earthquake.

Although most of this building is left standing, the entire area is a hazard to citizens in the town.

What are some effects of earthquakes?

Many earthquakes do not cause major damage. However, some strong earthquakes can cause billions of dollars in property damage. Earthquakes may even cause human injuries and loss of life. In general, areas closest to the epicenter of an earthquake experience the greatest damage.

Danger to People and Structures

The shaking of an earthquake can cause structures to move vertically and horizontally. When structures cannot withstand the shaking, major destruction can occur. Following the release of seismic waves, buildings can shake so violently that a total or partial collapse can happen, as shown below.

Much of the injury and loss of life that happen during and after earthquakes is caused by structures that collapse. In addition, fires, gas leaks, floods, and polluted water supplies can cause secondary damages following an earthquake. The debris left after an earthquake can take weeks or months to clean up. Bridges, roadways, homes, and entire cities can become disaster zones.

Tsunamis

An earthquake under the ocean can cause a vertical movement of the sea floor that displaces an enormous amount of water. This displacement may cause a tsunami to form. A *tsunami* (sue•NAH•mee) is a series of extremely long waves that can travel across the ocean at speeds of up to 800 km/h. Tsunami waves travel outward in all directions from the point where the earthquake occurred. As the waves approach a shoreline, the size of the waves increases. The waves can be taller than 30 m. Tsunami waves can cause major destruction and take many lives as they smash and wash away anything in their path. Many people may drown during a tsunami. Floods, polluted water supplies, and large amount of debris are common in the aftermath.

12 Identify List some of the hazards associated with earthquakes on land and underwater.

On Land	Underwater

Killer Quake

Imagine losing half the people in your city. On December 26, 2004, a massive tsunami destroyed approximately one-third of the buildings in Banda Aceh, Indonesia, and wiped out half the population.

A CHANGING WORLD

Epicenter
Affected coastal areas

INDIA
BANGLADESH
MYANMAR
THAILAND
Andaman Is.
SRI LANKA
Nicobar Is.
MALDIVES
Banda Aceh
MALAYSIA
INDONESIA
INDIAN OCEAN

Before

How Tsunamis Form
In the ocean, tsunami waves are fast but not very tall. As the waves approach a coast, they slow down and get much taller.

Before the Earthquake
The Banda Aceh tsunami resulted from a very strong earthquake in the ocean. Banda Aceh was very close to the epicenter.

Major Damages
The destruction to parts of Asia were so massive that geographers had to redraw the maps of some of the countries.

After

(i) Extend

13 Identify In what ocean did the earthquake occur?

14 Research Investigate one other destructive tsunami and find out where the earthquake that caused it originated.

15 Claims • Evidence • Reasoning Many of the people affected by the tsunami were poor. Make a claim about why earthquakes might be more damaging in poor areas of the world. Support the claim with evidence, and explain your reasoning.

Visual Summary

To complete this summary, fill in the correct word. You can use this page to review the main concepts of the lesson.

Earthquakes

Earthquakes occur along faults.

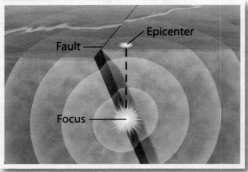

16 The epicenter of an earthquake is directly above the _____

Rocks break and snap back to their original shape in an earthquake.

17 Earthquakes happen when rocks bend and snap back in a process called _____

Earthquakes usually happen along plate boundaries.

18 The three types of plate boundaries are

_____

_____

_____

Earthquakes can cause a lot of damage.

19 An example of the dangers of earthquakes is _____

20 **Claims • Evidence • Reasoning** Make a claim about whether or not earthquakes can be prevented. Summarize evidence to support the claim and explain your reasoning.

Lesson Review

Vocabulary

In your own words, define the following terms.

1 Elastic rebound

_____

_____

_____

2 Focus

_____

_____

_____

3 Fault

_____

_____

_____

Key Concepts

Example	Type of Boundary
4 Identify Most of the earthquakes in Japan are a result of one plate sinking under another.	
5 Identify The African Rift Valley is a location where plates are moving apart.	
6 Identify The San Andreas fault is a location where tectonic plates move horizontally past each other.	

7 Explain What causes an earthquake?

_____

_____

_____

Critical Thinking

Use the image to answer the following questions.

8 Claims • Evidence • Reasoning Make a claim about how the image above demonstrates that a deformation has taken place. Summarize evidence to support the claim and explain your reasoning.

_____

_____

_____

_____

9 Apply How do Earth's surface and the structures on the surface change as a result of an earthquake?

_____

_____

_____

_____

10 Claims • Evidence • Reasoning Make a claim about why there is often only a short amount of time to evacuate an area before an earthquake. Use evidence to support the claim and explain your reasoning.

_____

_____

_____

SC.7.N.1.3 Distinguish between an experiment (which must involve the identification and control of variables) and other forms of scientific investigation and explain that not all scientific knowledge is derived from experimentation.

S.T.E.M. ENGINEERING & TECHNOLOGY

Engineering Design Process

Skills
Identify a need
Conduct research
✓ Brainstorm solutions
✓ Select a solution
Design a prototype
✓ Build a prototype
✓ Test and evaluate
✓ Redesign to improve
✓ Communicate results

Objectives
Explain how scientists measure the energy of earthquakes.
Design a model seismometer to measure motion.
Test and modify a prototype to achieve a desired result.

Building a Seismometer

An earthquake occurs when rocks beneath the ground move suddenly. The energy of this movement travels through Earth in waves. Sometimes the shaking is detected hundreds or thousands of miles away from the origin of the earthquake. Scientists can learn about earthquakes by measuring the earthquake waves.

Measuring Motion

A seismometer is a device for measuring the motion of the ground beneath it. To develop seismometers, scientists had to solve a problem: How do you keep one part of the device from moving when the ground moves? The solution can be seen in the design shown here. A spring separates a heavy weight from the frame of the seismometer. Attached to the weight is a pen. The tip of the pen touches the surface of a circular drum that is covered in paper and slowly turning. When the ground moves, the frame and the rotating drum move along with it. The spring absorbs the ground's movement, so the weight and pen do not move. The pen is always touching the paper on the rotating drum. When the ground is not moving, the pen draws a straight line. When the ground moves, the pen draws this movement.

Waves move the instrument, but the spring and weight keep the pen still.

1 Claims • Evidence • Reasoning This instrument measures the up-and-down motion of earthquake waves. Make a claim about how to change the instrument to measure the side-to-side motion of an earthquake. Support the claim with evidence and explain your reasoning.

_____

_____

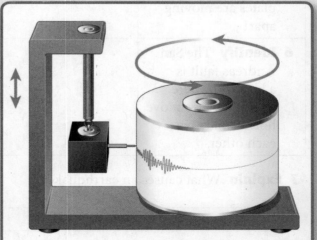

2 Infer In the oval below, write *moves* or *still* to indicate whether the labeled part moves during an earthquake or remains still.

The spring in this older type of seismometer absorbs energy. Modern seismometers use electronic components instead of giant springs.

Drawing the Waves

The drawing produced by a seismometer is called a *seismogram*. A seismogram shows two kinds of earthquake waves: P waves and S waves. P waves move though Earth's crust faster than S waves do. Seismologists measure the time between the arrival of P waves and the arrival of S waves to calculate how far away the earthquake occurred.

Seismogram

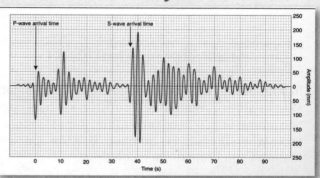

3 Claims • Evidence • Reasoning Make a claim about how geologists might use seismograms to find the exact location of an earthquake. Support the claim with evidence, and explain your reasoning.

_____

_____

_____

_____

_____

🖐 You Try It!

Now it's your turn to design and build a seismometer.

You Try It!

Now you will build a seismometer that can detect motion. You will use your seismometer to record the motion of a table. To do this, you will need to determine which parts of your seismometer will move and which parts will remain still. After you design and build the prototype, slowly shake the table back and forth. You may need to redesign and try again.

You Will Need

- ✓ large square wooden frame
- ✓ metal weights
- ✓ string
- ✓ fine point felt tip pen
- ✓ long strips or roll of paper
- ✓ tape
- ✓ various hooks and hardware

① Brainstorm Solutions

In your group, brainstorm ideas for a seismometer that will measure side-to-side movement of a surface, such as a table. When the seismometer is placed on a table, it must record the motion of the table when the table is bumped. Use the space below to record ideas as you brainstorm a solution.

_____

_____

_____

_____

② Select a Solution

Draw a prototype of your group's seismometer idea in the space below. Be sure to include all the parts you will need and show how they will be connected.

(3) Build a Prototype

In your group, build the seismometer. As the group builds it, are there some aspects of the design that cannot be assembled as predicted? What did the group have to revise in the prototype?

_____
_____
_____
_____

(4) Test and Evaluate

Bump or shake the table under the seismometer. Did the prototype record any motion on the paper strip? If not, what can you revise?

_____
_____
_____
_____

(5) Redesign to Improve

Choose one aspect to revise, and then test again. Keep making revisions, one at a time, until your seismometer records the motion of the table. How many revisions did the group make?

_____
_____

(6) Communicate Results

Claims • Evidence • Reasoning Report your observations about the prototype seismometer. Include changes that improved its performance or decreased its performance. Make a claim about ways you could have built a more accurate seismometer, including what additional materials you would need and what they would be used for. Provide evidence to support the claim and explain your reasoning.

_____
_____
_____

Volcanoes

ESSENTIAL QUESTION

How do volcanoes change Earth's surface?

By the end of this lesson, you should be able to describe what the various kinds of volcanoes and eruptions are, where they occur, how they form, and how they change Earth's surface.

SC.7.E.6.5 Explore the scientific theory of plate tectonics by describing how the movement of Earth's crustal plates causes both slow and rapid changes in Earth's surface, including volcanic eruptions, earthquakes, and mountain building.
SC.7.E.6.7 Recognize that heat flow and movement of material within Earth causes earthquakes and volcanic eruptions, and creates mountains and ocean basins.

The Arenal volcano in Costa Rica has been active since 1968. The volcano has erupted on and off for over 7,000 years.

Lesson Labs

Quick Lab
• Modeling an Explosive Eruption
• Volcano Mapping

Engage Your Brain

1 Predict Check T or F to show whether you think each statement is true or false.

T	F	
☐	☐	Volcanoes create new landforms such as mountains.
☐	☐	Tectonic plate boundaries are the only locations where volcanoes form.
☐	☐	Volcanic eruptions are often accompanied by earthquakes.
☐	☐	Volcanoes form new rocks and minerals.

2 Hypothesize You are a news reporter assigned to cover a story about the roadway in the image below. Describe what you think happened in this photo.

_____

_____

_____

ACTIVE READING

3 Synthesize You can often define an unknown word if you know the meaning of its word parts. Use the word parts and sentence below to make an educated guess about the meaning of the word *pyroclastic*.

Word part	Meaning
pyro-	heat or fire
-clastic	pieces

Example sentence
<u>Pyroclastic</u> material was ejected into the atmosphere with explosive force during the eruption of the volcano.

pyroclastic: _____

_____

Vocabulary Terms

- volcano
- magma
- lava
- vent
- tectonic plate
- hot spot

4 Apply As you learn the definition of each vocabulary term in this lesson, create your own definition or sketch to help you remember the meaning of the term.

Magma MAGIC

What is a volcano?

What do volcanoes look like? Most people think of a steep mountain with smoke coming out of the top. In fact, a **volcano** is any place where gas, ash, or melted rock come out of the ground. A volcano can be a tall mountain, as shown below, or a small crack in the ground. Volcanoes occur on land and underwater. There are even volcanoes on other planets. Not all volcanoes actively erupt. Many are *dormant*, meaning an eruption has not occurred in a long period of time.

Volcanoes form as rock below the surface of Earth melts. The melted rock, or **magma**, is less dense than solid rock, so it rises toward the surface. **Lava** is magma that has reached Earth's surface. Lava and clouds of ash can erupt from a **vent**, or opening of a volcano.

👁 Visualize It!

5 Identify Label the parts of the volcano. Include the following terms: *magma, lava, vent, ash cloud*.

Lava can reach temperatures of more than 1,200 °C.

What are the kinds of volcanic landforms?

The location of a volcano and the composition of magma determine the type of volcanic landforms created. Shield volcanoes, cinder cones, composite volcanoes, lava plateaus, craters, and calderas are all types of volcanic landforms.

◯ Volcanic Mountains

Materials ejected from a volcano may build up around a vent to create volcanic mountains. *Viscosity* (vyz•SKAHZ•ih•tee) is the resistance of a liquid material, such as lava, to flow. The viscosity of lava determines the explosiveness of an eruption and the shape of the resulting volcanic mountain. Low-viscosity lava flows easily, forms low slopes, and erupts without large explosions. High-viscosity lava does not flow easily, forms steep slopes, and can erupt explosively. *Pyroclastic materials* (py•roh•KLAHZ•tyk), or hot ash and bits of rock, may also be ejected into the atmosphere.

ACTIVE READING

7 Identify As you read, underline the main features of each type of volcanic mountain.

ⓘ Think Outside the Book

6 Apply Small fragments of rock material that are ejected from a volcano are known as *volcanic ash*. Volcanic ash is a form of pyroclastic material. The material does not dissolve in water and is very abrasive, meaning it can scratch surfaces. Ash can build up to great depths in locations around a volcano. Write a cleanup plan for a town that explains how you might safely remove and dispose of volcanic ash.

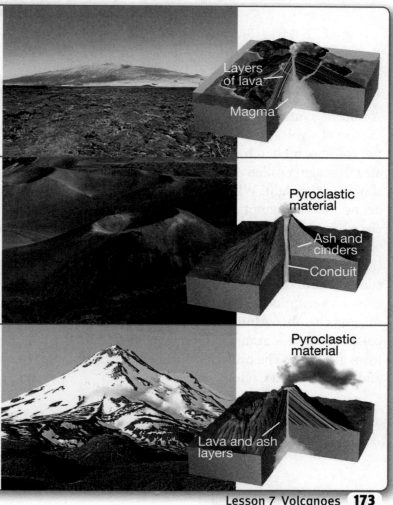

- **Shield Volcanoes** Volcanoes with a broad base and gently sloping sides are *shield volcanoes*. Shield volcanoes cover a wide area and generally form from mild eruptions. Layers of lava flow out from the vent, harden, and slowly build up to form the cone. The Hawaiian Islands are shield volcanoes.

  Layers of lava
  Magma

- **Cinder Cones** Sometimes, ash and pieces of lava harden in the air and can fall to the ground around a small vent. The hardened pieces of lava are called cinders. The cinders and ash build up around the vent and form a steep volcano called a *cinder cone*. A cinder cone can also form at a side vent on other volcanic mountains, such as on shield or composite volcanoes.

  Pyroclastic material
  Ash and cinders
  Conduit

- **Composite Volcanoes** Alternating layers of hardened lava flows and pyroclastic material create *composite volcanoes* (kuhm•PAHZ•iht). During a mild eruption, lava flows cover the sides of the cone. During an explosive eruption, pyroclastic material is deposited around the vent. Composite volcanoes commonly develop into large and steep volcanic mountains.

  Pyroclastic material
  Lava and ash layers

Fissures and Lava Plateaus

Fissure eruptions (FIH•shohr ee•RUHP•shuhnz) happen when lava flows from giant cracks, or *fissures*, in Earth's surface. The fissures are found on land and on the ocean floor. A fissure eruption has no central opening. Lava flows out of the entire length of the fissure, which can be many kilometers long. As a result, a thick and mostly flattened layer of cooled lava, called a *lava plateau* (plah•TOH), can form. One example of a lava plateau is the Columbia Plateau Province in Washington, Oregon, and Idaho, as shown to the right.

The Palouse Falls in Washington plunge deep into exposed layers of the Columbia lava plateau.

Craters and Calderas

A *volcanic crater* is an opening or depression at the top of a volcano caused by eruptions. Inside the volcano, molten rock can form an expanded area of magma called a *magma chamber*, as shown to the right. When the magma chamber below a volcano empties, the roof of the magma chamber may collapse and leave an even larger, basin-shaped depression called a *caldera* (kahl•DAHR•uh). Calderas can form from the sudden drain of a magma chamber during an explosive eruption or from a slowly emptied magma chamber. More than 7,000 years ago, the cone of Mount Mazama in Oregon collapsed to form a caldera. The caldera later filled with water and is now called Crater Lake.

A caldera can be more than 100 km in diameter.

Visualize It!

8 Claims • Evidence • Reasoning Make a claim about how the appearance of land surfaces change before and after a caldera forms. Summarize evidence to support the claim and explain your reasoning.

Before

Expanded magma chamber

After

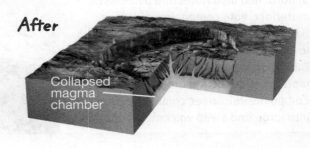

Collapsed magma chamber

ERUPTION!

Where do volcanoes form?

Volcanoes can form at plate boundaries or within the middle of a plate. Recall that **tectonic plates** are giant sections of lithosphere on Earth's surface. Volcanoes can form at *divergent plate boundaries* where two plates are moving away from each other. Most fissure eruptions occur at divergent boundaries. Shield volcanoes, fissure eruptions, and cinder cones can also occur away from plate boundaries within a plate at *hot spots*. The type of lava normally associated with these volcanoes has a relatively low viscosity, few trapped gases, and is usually not explosive.

Composite volcanoes are most common along *convergent plate boundaries* where oceanic plates subduct. In order for the rock to melt, it must be hot and the pressure on it must drop, or water and other fluids must be added to it. Extra fluids from ocean water form magma of higher viscosity with more trapped gases. Thus, composite volcanoes produce the most violent eruptions. The *Ring of Fire* is a name used to describe the numerous explosive volcanoes that form on convergent plate boundaries surrounding the Pacific Ocean.

ACTIVE READING

9 Identify As you read, underline three locations where volcanoes can form.

Plate Tectonic Boundaries and Volcano Locations Worldwide

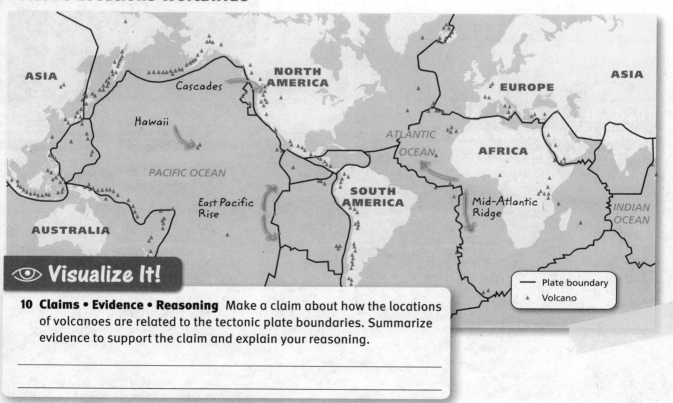

Visualize It!

10 Claims • Evidence • Reasoning Make a claim about how the locations of volcanoes are related to the tectonic plate boundaries. Summarize evidence to support the claim and explain your reasoning.

_____

_____

At Divergent Boundaries

At divergent boundaries, plates move away from each other. The lithosphere stretches and gets thinner, so the pressure on the mantle rock below decreases. As a result, the asthenosphere bulges upward and magma forms. This magma rises through fissures in the lithosphere, out onto the land or the ocean floor.

Most divergent boundaries are on the ocean floor. When eruptions occur in these areas, undersea volcanoes develop. These volcanoes and other processes lead to the formation of a long, underwater mountain range known as a *mid-ocean ridge*. Two examples of mid-ocean ridges are the East Pacific Rise in the Pacific Ocean and the Mid-Atlantic Ridge in the Atlantic Ocean. The youngest rocks in the ocean are located at mid-ocean ridges.

Shield volcanoes and cinder cones are common in Iceland, where the Mid-Atlantic Ridge runs through the country. As the plates move away from each other, new crust forms. When a divergent boundary is located in the middle of a continent, the crust stretches until a rift valley is formed, as shown below.

ACTIVE READING

11 Claims • Evidence • Reasoning Make a claim about what types of volcanic landforms occur at divergent plate boundaries. Support your claim with evidence. Explain your reasoning.

_____

_____

_____

Divergent plate boundaries create fissure eruptions and shield volcanoes.

Fissure

The Great Rift Valley in Africa is a location where the crust is stretching and separating.

Tectonic plates move away from each other at divergent boundaries.

⭕ At Convergent Boundaries

At convergent boundaries, two plates move toward each other. In most cases, one plate sinks beneath the other plate. As the sinking plate dives into the mantle, fluids in the sinking plate become super heated and escape. These escaping fluids cause the rock above the sinking plate to melt and form magma. This magma rises to the surface and erupts to form volcanoes.

The magma that forms at convergent boundaries has a high concentration of fluids. As the magma rises, decreasing pressure causes the fluid trapped in the magma to form gas bubbles. But, because the magma has a high viscosity, these bubbles cannot escape easily. As the bubbles expand, the magma rises faster. Eventually, the magma can erupt explosively, forming calderas or composite volcanoes. Gas, ash, and large chunks of rock can be blown out of the volcanoes. The Cascade Range is a chain of active composite volcanoes in the northwestern United States, as shown to the right. In 1980, Mt. St. Helens erupted so violently that the entire top of the mountain was blown away.

Tectonic plates move toward each other at convergent boundaries.

Oceanic crust

Continental crust

👁️ Visualize It!

12 Identify Draw two arrows in the white boxes to indicate the direction of motion of the plates that formed the Cascade volcanoes.

Mt. Rainier ●
Mt. St Helens ●

Crater Lake ●

Mt. Shasta ●

The Cascade Range of volcanic mountains

13 Summarize List the characteristics of divergent-boundary volcanoes and convergent-boundary volcanoes below.

Volcanoes at divergent boundaries	Volcanoes at convergent boundaries

At Hot Spots

Volcanoes can form within a plate, away from the plate boundaries. A **hot spot** is a location where a column of extremely hot mantle rock, called a *mantle plume*, rises through the asthenosphere. As the hot rock reaches the base of the lithosphere, it melts partially to form magma that can rise to the surface and form a volcano. Eruptions at a hot spot commonly form shield volcanoes. As tectonic plates move over a mantle plume, chains of volcanic mountains can form, as shown below.

The youngest Hawaiian island, the Big Island, is home to Kilauea (kih•loh•AY•uh). The Kilauea volcano is an active shield volcano located over a mantle plume. To the north and west of Kilauea is a chain of progressively-older shield volcanoes. These volcanoes were once located over the same mantle plume. Hot spots can also occur on land. Yellowstone National Park, for example, contains a huge volcanic caldera that was formed by the same mantle plume that created the Columbia Plateau.

👁 Visualize It!

14 Claims • Evidence • Reasoning Make a claim about which location, A, B, or C, is the oldest volcano. Give evidence to support the claim and explain your reasoning.

_____

_____

_____

Hot spots form over mantle plumes within a tectonic plate.

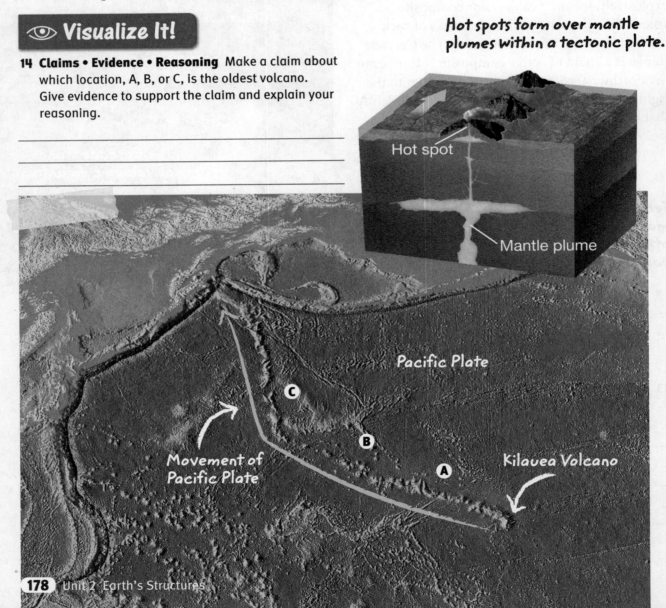

Hot spot

Mantle plume

Pacific Plate

C

B

A

Movement of Pacific Plate

Kilauea Volcano

Living Near a
Volcano

Volcanoes occur around the world. Many people live near volcanoes because the soils around a volcano can be very rich with essential minerals. These minerals make the soils fertile for growing a variety of crops. Living near a volcano also has its hazards. Sudden and unexpected eruptions can cause people to lose their homes and their lives.

Not All Bad
Volcanic rocks are used in jewelry, in making concrete, and in water filtration systems. Even cat litter and facial scrubs can contain volcanic rock.

Destruction
Earthquakes, fires, ash, and lava flows during an eruption can destroy entire cities.

Ash in the Air
Volcanic ash can cause breathing problems, bury crops, and damage engines. The weight of falling ash can cause buildings to collapse.

ⓘ Extend

15 **Claims • Evidence • Reasoning** Make a claim about whether all characteristics of volcanoes are dangerous. Summarize evidence to support the claim and explain your reasoning.

16 **Apply** Research the eruption of a specific volcano of your choice. Describe how the volcano affected the environment and the people near the volcano.

17 **Design** Create a poster that outlines a school safety plan for events that can occur before, during, and after a volcanic eruption.

Visual Summary

To complete this summary, check the box that indicates true or false. You can use this page to review the main concepts of the lesson.

Lava and magma are different.

T F
18 ☐ ☐ Lava is inside Earth's crust and may contain trapped gases.

The three types of volcanic mountains are shield volcanoes, cinder cones, and composite volcanoes.

T F
19 ☐ ☐ The type of volcano shown is a shield volcano.

Volcanoes

Volcanoes can form at tectonic plate boundaries.

T F
20 ☐ ☐ At divergent plate boundaries, plates move toward each other.

Volcanoes can form at hot spots.

T F
21 ☐ ☐ Hot spots are restricted to tectonic plate boundaries.

22 **Claims • Evidence • Reasoning** Make a claim about how volcanoes contribute to the formation of new landforms. Summarize evidence to support the claim and explain your reasoning.

Lesson Review

Vocabulary

Write 1 or 2 sentences that describe the differences between the two terms.

1 magma   lava

_____

_____

2 volcano   vent

_____

_____

_____

3 tectonic plate   hot spot

_____

_____

Key Concepts

Use the image to answer the following question.

4 Identify How did the composite volcano in the image get its layered interior?

_____

_____

5 Analyze Is pyroclastic material likely to form from low-viscosity lava or high-viscosity lava? Explain your answer.

_____

_____

_____

Describe the location and characteristics of the types of volcanic landforms in the table below.

Volcanic landform	Description
6 Hot-spot volcanoes	
7 Cinder cones	
8 Calderas	

Critical Thinking

9 Claims • Evidence • Reasoning In Iceland, the Mid-Atlantic Ridge runs through the center of the country. Make a claim about the appearance of Iceland many thousands of years from now. Summarize evidence to support the claim and explain your reasoning.

_____

_____

10 Analyze Why do you think the location surrounding the Pacific Ocean is known as the Ring of Fire?

_____

_____

_____

UNIT 2
Summary

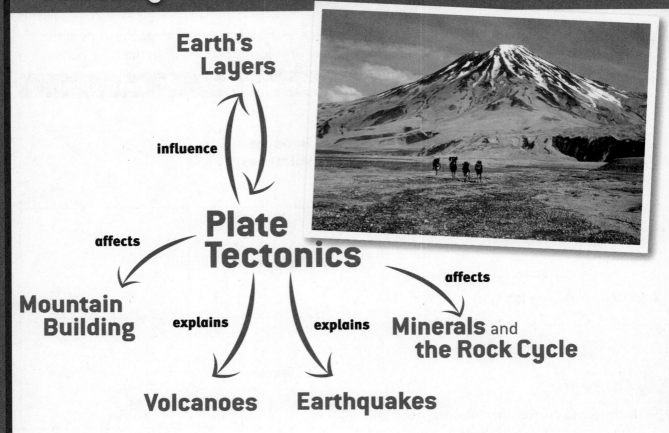

Earth's Layers

influence

Plate Tectonics

affects → **Mountain Building**

explains → **Volcanoes**

explains → **Earthquakes**

affects → **Minerals and the Rock Cycle**

1 Claims • Evidence • Reasoning The Graphic Organizer above shows how Earth's surface changes because of Earth's layers. Make a claim about changes on a planet that has the same composition from core to surface. Use evidence to support the claim and explain your reasoning.

_____

_____

_____

_____

_____

_____

_____

_____

_____

2 Relate How are Earth's crust and mantle involved in the formation of new rock?

_____

_____

_____

_____

3 Apply Explain how a volcanologist can piece together the history of a volcano by studying the rock that makes up the volcano.

_____

_____

_____

_____

_____

_____

Vocabulary

Fill in each blank with the term that best completes the following sentences.

1 The hot, convecting _____ is the layer of rock between the Earth's crust and core.

2 _____ is the theory that explains how large pieces of Earth's outermost layer move and change shape.

3 _____ is the bending of rock layers due to stress.

4 A(n) _____ is a vent or fissure in the Earth's surface through which magma and gases are expelled.

5 A(n) _____ is a movement or trembling of the ground that is caused by a sudden release of energy when rocks move along a fault.

Key Concepts

Identify the choice that best completes the statement or answers the question.

6 One way of measuring the amount of energy released by an earthquake is the Richter scale. Each increase of one unit on the Richter scale shows a 10-fold increase in the strength of the earthquake. What determines how strong an earthquake will be?

A distance from the epicenter of the earthquake

B amount of stress released by the elastic rebound of rock

C the temperature of the rock just before the earthquake begins

D the density of population and buildings near the epicenter of the earthquake

7 Earth's core is composed of two separate layers: the inner core and the outer core. What is one difference between these two layers?

F One is iron, and one is zinc.

G One is liquid, and one is gas.

H One is solid, and one is liquid.

I One is iron, and one is nickel.

8 Scientists study different parts of earthquakes and how they are related. This illustration shows a cross section of the lithosphere when an earthquake is taking place.

Cross Section of Lithosphere during an Earthquake

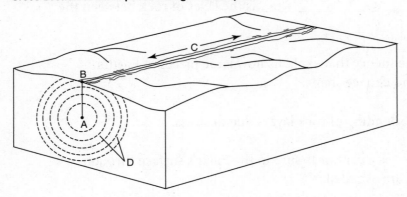

Where is the epicenter of this earthquake located?

A point A

B point B

C along the line labeled C

D along the line between points A and B

9 Convection currents in the mantle contribute to tectonic plate movement. What is a convection current?

F the transfer of energy through materials in direct contact

G the transfer of energy due to the movement of matter

H the transfer of energy as electromagnetic waves

I the transfer of energy from a region of lower temperature to a region of higher temperature

10 Granite forms when liquid magma slowly cools within Earth's crust. If the granite is exposed to intense heat and pressure, it can change to gneiss. Which type of change takes place when granite turns into gneiss?

A Sedimentary rock changes into igneous rock.

B Igneous rock changes into metamorphic rock.

C Metamorphic rock changes into igneous rock.

D Sedimentary rock changes into metamorphic rock.

Name _____

11   Imagine you could travel in a straight line through Earth from a point on one side and come out on the other side. What compositional layer would you travel through in the exact center of Earth?

F core

G crust

H lithosphere

I mesosphere

12   Earth can be divided into three layers: the core, the mantle, and the crust. How are these three layers identified?

A by their plate tectonics

B by their structural features

C by their physical properties

D by their chemical composition

13   The forces of volcanic eruptions vary. Some eruptions explode violently, and others are slow and quiet. Which type of eruption is happening when pyroclastic materials are released?

F a quiet eruption

G a violent eruption

H a moderate eruption

I quiet eruptions alternating with moderate eruptions

14   Unlike Florida, a transform boundary passes through California. What happens at a transform boundary that can cause an earthquake?

A Two plates collide.

B Two plates move in the same direction.

C Two plates move away from each other.

D Two plates slide or glide past each other.

15   Sometimes tectonic plates move toward each other and squeeze large blocks of rocks together, creating folded mountains. Which of the following terms describes a kind of fold in which the youngest rock layers are in the center of the fold?

F syncline

G anticline

H symmetrical fold

I asymmetrical fold

16 Quartz, feldspar, and mica are silicate minerals. Silicate minerals contain atoms of silicon and oxygen and often other elements bonded together. What must be **true** of silicate minerals?

A They are pure elements.

B They are made up of compounds.

C They melt at very low temperatures.

D They are made up of only one kind of atom.

17 The following steps are part of a laboratory exercise that Florida sixth-grade students are doing in their science class.

Step	Procedure
1	Get an ice cube that has been darkly colored with food coloring.
2	Use tongs to place the ice cube in a beaker containing warm water. Be sure to lower the ice cube slowly to keep the water as still as possible.
3	Observe the ice cube and water mixture for at least 5 min.

What are these students modeling?

F plate boundary

G continental drift

H movement of tectonic plates

I convection currents in the mantle

18 Mr. Garcia told his seventh-grade class that as a tectonic plate moves farther from a mid-ocean ridge, it cools and becomes denser. This can cause the plate to sink below another, less dense tectonic plate. The weight of the sinking plate then drags the rest of the plate downward. What is Mr. Garcia describing?

A slab pull

B ridge push

C continental drift

D convection current

Name _____

19 The figure below shows mountains that were formed when large blocks of rock were squeezed together as two tectonic plates collided.

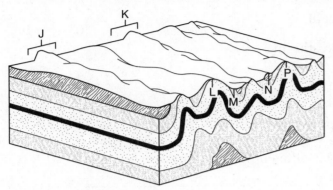

What does the letter K represent?

F syncline

G anticline

H reverse fault

I normal fault

20 Ruben made the chart below to describe the classes of nonsilicate minerals.

Class	Description	Example
Carbonates	contain carbon and oxygen compounds	calcite
Halides	contain ions of chlorine, fluorine, iodine, and bromine	halite
Native elements	contain only one type of atom	gold
Oxides	contain oxygen compounds	hematite
Sulfides	contain sulfur compounds	pyrite

There are actually six classes of nonsilicate minerals. Which class is missing from Ruben's chart?

A feldspars

B micas

C silicates

D sulfates

21 Declan observed a rock that he found at the beach. The rock felt hard, it was yellow, and it appeared to be made of layers. Declan concluded that the rock was sedimentary. Which observation **best** supports this conclusion?

F the yellow color

G the layers within the rock

H the hardness of the rock

I the location where the rock was found

22 Mount Everest formed when two tectonic plates collided. Which process then took place to create Mount Everest?

A erosion

C uplift

B subsidence

D weathering

Critical Thinking

Answer the following questions in the space provided.

23 Explain how a convergent boundary is different from a transform boundary.

_____

_____

Then name one thing that commonly occurs along both convergent boundaries and transform boundaries.

_____

_____

24 The diagram below shows the five physical layers of Earth.

Identify the physical layers A, B, and C. Is the relationship between these layers important to understanding plate tectonics? Use evidence to support your claim and explain your reasoning.

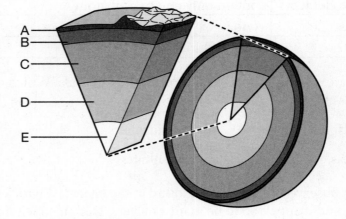

_____

_____

_____

_____

_____

FLORIDA **BIG IDEA 6**

Earth Structures

Florida's unique topog
answers questions abo
Florida's past.

What Do You Think?

Earth's landscape is constantly changing. But Earth's history has not been erased. Look closely at the prominent features of this saber-toothed cat skull. What might the environment have been like when this animal was alive? As you explore this unit, gather evidence to state and support your claim.

Earth's History

Preserving the Past

Fossils are found throughout Florida. These fossils contain information about the organisms that lived both on land and in the ocean. How would you research Florida's fossil history?

1 Think About It

Where can people find fossils?

_____

_____

What are the most common types of fossils found in Florida?

_____

_____

Many important fossil discoveries have been made in Florida. Use the internet to research a fossil discovery site in Florida. Take notes on your findings on a separate sheet of paper.

Scientists use grids to record where things are found.

Ammonite fossils in limestone

② Ask A Question

Is your area home to fossils?

As a class, evaluate the area in which you live and determine the likelihood of fossils being present. Consider natural changes like weather or earthquakes that might ruin fossil sites, as well as human factors like construction.

What to consider

☐ What kind of rock is common in your area?

☐ Are there any undeveloped areas that will have undisturbed rock?

③ Apply Your Knowledge

A List the kinds of rock in which fossils are found in Florida.

_____
_____
_____
_____
_____
_____

B Use a geologic map to determine where rock that contains fossils can be found close to where you live. Determine how long it will take to travel to one of these sites.

C If you can, plan a trip to a site where you can find fossils. Describe how you will search for fossils.

_____
_____
_____
_____
_____
_____

🏠 Take It Home!

What was your local community like long ago? Research to find out what the most common fossils from your area are. How were the fossils formed?

Geologic Change over Time

ESSENTIAL **QUESTION**

How do we learn about Earth's history?

By the end of this lesson, you should be able to explain how Earth materials, such as rock, fossils, and ice, show that Earth has changed over time.

Scientists learn about Earth's history by studying materials such as these rhinoceros fossils in Nebraska.

SC.7.N.1.1 Define a problem from the seventh grade curriculum, use appropriate reference materials to support scientific understanding, plan and carry out scientific investigation of various types, such as systematic observations or experiments, identify variables, collect and organize data, interpret data in charts, tables, and graphics, analyze information, make predictions, and defend conclusions. **SC.7.N.1.5** Describe the methods used in the pursuit of a scientific explanation as seen in different fields of science such as biology, geology, and physics. **SC.7.E.6.4** Explain and give examples of how physical evidence supports scientific theories that Earth has evolved over geologic time due to natural processes.

Lesson Labs

Quick Labs
- Fossil Flipbook
- Connecting Fossils to Climates
- Timeline of Earth's History

S.T.E.M. Lab
- Exploring Landforms

Engage Your Brain

1 Predict Check T or F to show whether you think each statement is true or false.

T	F	
☐	☐	Once rock forms, it never changes.
☐	☐	Fossils can tell us which animals lived at a certain time.
☐	☐	The climate is exactly the same all over the world.
☐	☐	A volcano erupting is an example of a geologic process.

2 Explain What can you infer about the environment in which this fossil probably formed?

_____

_____

_____

ACTIVE READING

3 Synthesize You can often define an unknown word if you know the meaning of its word parts. Use the word parts and sentence below to make an educated guess about the meaning of the word *uniformitarianism*.

Word part	Meaning
uniform-	the same in all cases and at all times
-ism	a system of beliefs or actions

Example sentence
The idea that erosion has occurred the same way throughout Earth's history is an example of <u>uniformitarianism</u>.

uniformitarianism:

_____

_____

Vocabulary Terms

- uniformitarianism
- fossil
- trace fossil
- climate
- ice core

4 Identify This list contains vocabulary terms you'll learn in this lesson. As you read, circle the definition of each term.

Been There,

This inactive volcano last erupted over 4,000 years ago.

What is the principle of uniformitarianism?

The principle of **uniformitarianism** (yoo•nu h•fohr•mi•TAIR•ee•uh•niz•uhm) states that geologic processes that happened in the past can be explained by current geologic processes. Processes such as volcanism and erosion that go on today happened in a similar way in the past. Because geologic processes tend to happen at a slow rate, this means that Earth must be very old. In fact, scientists have shown that Earth is about 4.6 billion years old.

Most geologic change is slow and gradual, but sudden changes have also affected Earth's history. An asteroid hitting Earth may have led to the extinction of the dinosaurs. However, scientists see these as a normal part of geologic change.

ACTIVE READING

5 Describe In your own words, describe the principle of uniformitarianism.

_____

_____

_____

_____

👁 Visualize It!

6 Identify How do these photos show the principle of uniformitarianism?

_____

_____

_____

This is an active volcano.

Done That

How do organisms become preserved as fossils?

Fossils are the trace or remains of an organism that lived long ago, most commonly preserved in sedimentary rock. Fossils may be skeletons or body parts, shells, burrows, or ancient coral reefs. Fossils form in many different ways.

👁 Visualize It!

Trapped in Amber

Imagine that an insect is caught in soft, sticky tree sap. Suppose that the insect is covered by more sap, which hardens with the body of the insect inside. Amber is formed when hardened tree sap is buried and preserved in sediment. Some of the best insect fossils, such as the one shown below, are found in amber. Fossil spiders, frogs, and lizards have also been found in amber.

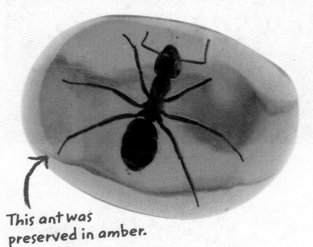

This ant was preserved in amber.

7 Analyze What features of the ant can you still see in this fossil?

_____

_____

_____

Trapped in Asphalt

There are places where asphalt wells up at Earth's surface in thick, sticky pools. One such place is La Brea Tar Pits in California. These asphalt pools have trapped and preserved many fossils over the past 40,000 years, such as the one shown below. Fossils such as these show a lot about what life was like in Southern California in the past.

This water beetle was preserved in asphalt.

8 Claims • Evidence • Reasoning Make a claim about how this organism became a fossil. Support your claim with evidence, and explain your reasoning.

_____

_____

_____

Buried in Rock

When an organism dies, it often starts to decay or is eaten by other organisms. Sometimes, however, organisms are quickly buried by sediment when they die. The sediment slows down decay and can protect parts of the body from damage. Hard parts of organisms, such as shells and bones, do not break down as easily as soft parts do. So, when sediments become rock, the hard parts of animals are preserved and become part of the rock as the sediments harden.

👁 Visualize It!

9 Gather Evidence What part of the organism was preserved as a fossil in this rock? Support your claim with evidence.

_____

_____

Ammonites once lived in shells in ancient seas.

Become Frozen

In very cold places on Earth, the soil can be frozen all the time. An animal that dies there may also be frozen. It is frozen with skin and flesh, as well as bones. Because cold temperatures slow down decay, many types of frozen fossils are preserved from the last ice age.

👁 Visualize It!

10 Compare What information can this fossil give that fossils preserved in rock cannot?

_____

_____

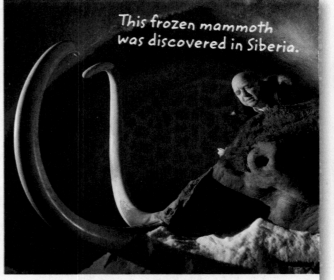

This frozen mammoth was discovered in Siberia.

Become Petrified

Petrification (pet•ruh•fi•KAY•shuhn) happens when an organism's tissues are replaced by minerals. In some petrified wood, minerals have replaced all of the wood. A sample of petrified wood is shown at the right. This wood is in the Petrified Forest National Park in Arizona.

A similar thing happens when the pore space in an organism's hard tissue, such as bone, is filled up with minerals.

This petrified wood is in Arizona.

What are trace fossils?

ACTIVE READING

11 Identify As you read, underline examples of trace fossils.

Fossils of organisms can tell us a lot about the bodies of life forms. Another type of fossil may also give evidence about how some animals behaved. A **trace fossil** is a fossilized structure that formed in sedimentary rock by animal activity on or in soft sediment.

Tracks, like the ones across this page, are one type of trace fossil. They are footprints made by animals in soft sediment that later became hard rock. Tracks show a lot about the animal that made them, such as how it lived, how big it was, and how fast it moved. For example, scientists have found paths of tracks showing that a group of dinosaurs moved in the same direction. This has led scientists to hypothesize that some dinosaurs moved in herds.

Burrows are another kind of trace fossil. Burrows are pathways or shelters made by animals, such as clams on the sea floor or rodents on land, that dig in sediment. Some scientists also classify animal dung, called coprolite (KAHP•ruh•lyt), as a trace fossil. Some coprolites are shown at the right.

---

i ◉ Visualize It!

12 Illustrate Draw two sets of tracks that represent what you might leave for future scientists to study. Draw one set of you walking and another set of you running.

Walking

_____

Running

These tracks were made by dinosaurs that once lived in Utah.

Time Is on Our Side

13 Claims • Evidence • Reasoning
Based on these fossils of tropical plants from Antarctica, make a claim about what the climate was once like. Support your claim with evidence, and explain your reasoning.

_____

_____

_____

A piece of Antarctica's past

Antarctica today

ACTIVE READING

14 Identify As you read, underline two types of changes on Earth that fossils can give information about.

What can fossils tell us?

All of the fossils that have been discovered on Earth are called the _fossil record_. The fossil record shows part of the history of life on Earth. It is only part of the history because some things are still unknown. Not all the organisms that ever lived have left behind fossils. Also, there are many fossils that have not been discovered yet. Even so, fossils that are available do provide important information about Earth's history.

Fossils can tell scientists about environmental changes over time. The types of fossils preserved in sedimentary rock show what the environment was like when the organisms were alive. For example, fish fossils indicate that an aquatic environment was present. Palm fronds mean a tropical environment was present. Scientists have found fossils of trees and dinosaurs in Antarctica, so the climate there must have been warm in the past.

Fossils can also tell scientists how life forms have changed over time. Major changes in Earth's environmental conditions and surface can influence an organism's survival and the types of adaptations that a species must have to survive. To learn about how life on Earth has changed, scientists study relationships between different fossils and between fossils and living organisms.

How does sedimentary rock show Earth's history?

Rock and mineral fragments move from one place to another during erosion. Eventually, this sediment is deposited in layers. As new layers of sediment are deposited, they cover older layers. Older layers become compacted. Dissolved minerals, such as calcite and quartz, separate from water that passes through the sediment. This forms a natural cement that holds the rock and mineral fragments together in sedimentary rock.

Scientists use different characteristics to classify sedimentary rock. These provide evidence of the environment that the sedimentary rock formed in.

Composition

The composition of sedimentary rock shows the source of the sediment that makes up the rock. Some sedimentary rock forms when rock or mineral fragments are cemented together. Sandstone, shown below, forms when sand grains are deposited and buried, then cemented together. Other sedimentary rock forms from the remains of once-living plants and animals. Most limestone forms from the remains of animals that lived in the ocean. Another sedimentary rock, called coal, forms underground from partially decomposed plant material that is buried beneath sediment.

ACTIVE READING

15 Describe What processes can cause rock to break apart into sediment?

_____

_____

_____

Texture and Features

The texture of sedimentary rock shows the environment in which the sediment was carried and deposited. Sedimentary rock is arranged in layers. Layers can differ from one another, depending on the kind, size, and color of their sediment. Features on sedimentary rock called *ripple marks* record the motion of wind or water waves over sediment. An example of sedimentary rock with ripple marks is shown below. Other features, called *mud cracks,* form when fine-grained sediments at the bottom of a shallow body of water are exposed to the air and dry out. Mud cracks show that an ancient lake, stream, or ocean shoreline was once a part of an area.

👁 Visualize It!

16 Identify Which arrow shows the direction that water was moving to make these ripple marks?

_____

Sandstone

These are ripple marks in sandstone.

What do Earth's surface features tell us?

Earth's surface is always changing. Continents change position continuously as tectonic plates move across Earth's surface.

○ Continents Move

The continents have been moving throughout Earth's history. For example, at one time the continents formed a single landmass called *Pangaea* (pan•JEE•uh). Pangaea broke apart about 200 million years ago. Since then, the continents have been slowly moving to their present locations, and continue to move today.

Evidence of Pangaea can be seen by the way rock types, mountains, and fossils are now distributed on Earth's surface. For example, mountain-building events from tectonic plate movements produced different mountain belts on Earth. As the map below shows, rock from one of these mountain belts is now on opposite sides of the Atlantic Ocean. Scientists think this mountain belt separated as continents have moved to their current locations.

Today's continents were once part of a landmass called Pangaea.

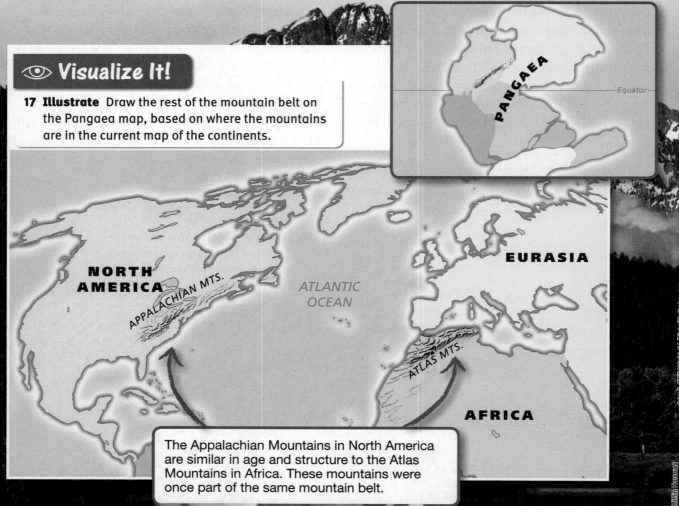

◉ Visualize It!

17 Illustrate Draw the rest of the mountain belt on the Pangaea map, based on where the mountains are in the current map of the continents.

The Appalachian Mountains in North America are similar in age and structure to the Atlas Mountains in Africa. These mountains were once part of the same mountain belt.

Mifflin Harcourt

Landforms Change over Time

The movement of tectonic plates across Earth has resulted in extraordinary events. When continental plates collide, mountain ranges such as the ones shown below can form. As they pull apart, magma can be released in volcanic eruptions. When they grind past one another, breaks in Earth's surface form, where earthquakes can occur. Collisions between oceanic and continental plates can also cause volcanoes and the formation of mountains.

In addition to forces that build up Earth's surface features, there are forces that break them down as well. Weathering and erosion always act on Earth's surface, changing it with time. For example, high, jagged mountains can become lower and more rounded over time. So, the height and shape of mountains can tell scientists about the geologic history of mountains.

Think Outside the Book

19 Support Find out about how the continents continue to move today. Draw a map that shows the relative motion along some of the tectonic plate boundaries.

Visualize It!

18 Analyze Label the older and younger mountains below. Explain your reasoning about how you decided which was older and which was younger.

____

____

____

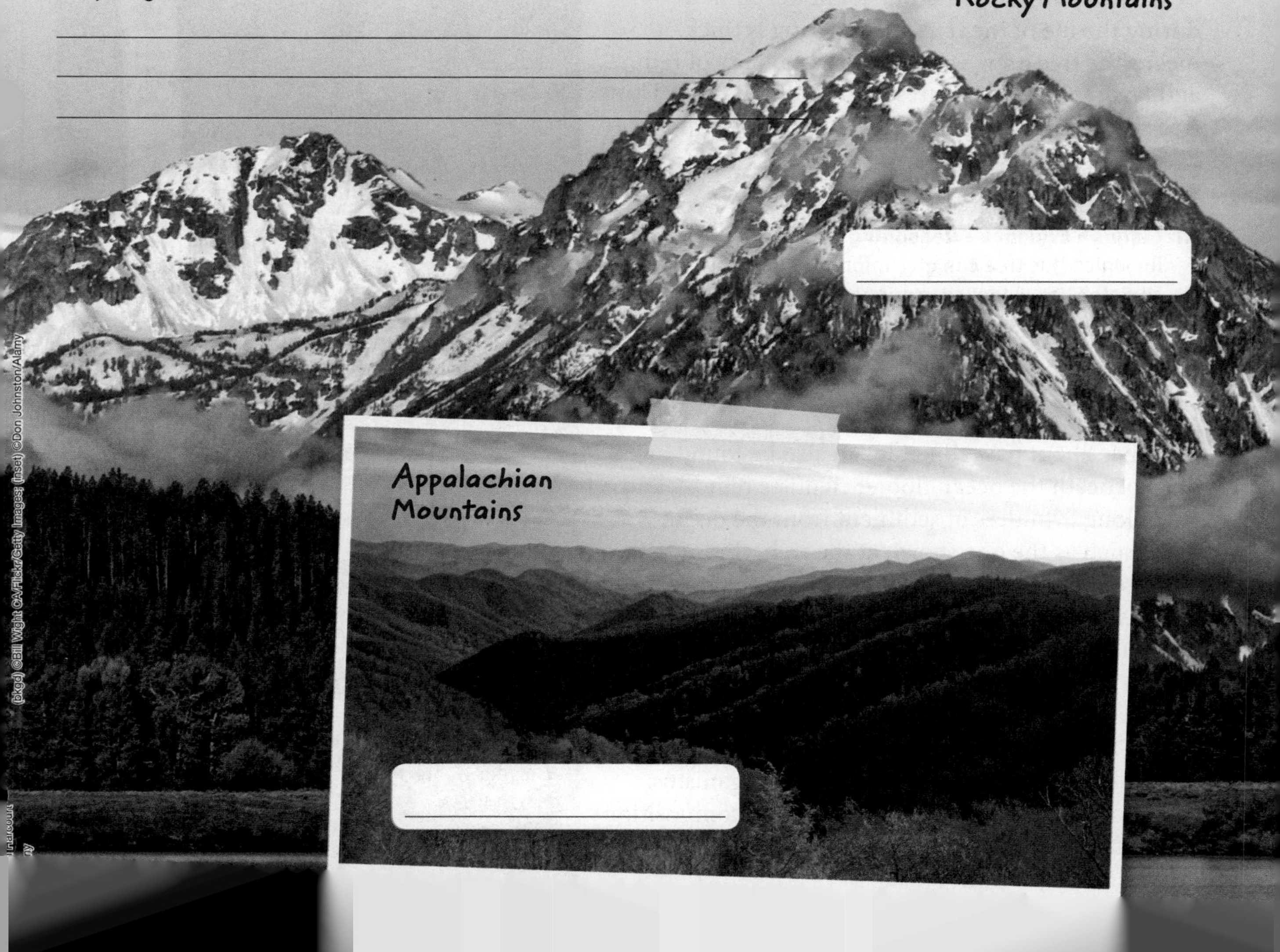

Rocky Mountains
Appalachian Mountains

(bkgd) ©Bill Wight CA/Flickr/Getty Images; (inset) ©Don Johnston/Alamy

Back to the Future

What other materials tell us about Earth's climate history?

The **climate** of an area describes the weather conditions in the area over a long period of time. Climate is mostly determined by temperature and precipitation. In addition to using fossils, scientists also analyze other materials to study how Earth's climate and environmental conditions have changed over time.

ACTIVE READING

20 **Identify** As you read the next two pages, underline the evidence that scientists use to learn about Earth's climate history.

Trees

When most trees grow, a new layer of wood is added to the trunk every year. This forms rings around the circumference (suhr•KUHM•fuhr•uhns) of the tree, as shown at the right. These rings tell the age of the tree. Some trees are over 2,000 years old. Scientists can use tree rings to find out about the climate during the life of the tree. If a tree ring is thick, it means the tree grew well—there was plenty of rain and favorable temperatures existed at that time. Thin tree rings mean the growing conditions were poor.

👁 Visualize It!

21 **Claims • Evidence • Reasoning** What is the time frame for which this tree can give information about Earth's climate? Use evidence to support your claim, and explain your reasoning.

Tree rings tell the age of a tree and what the climate was like.

Sea-Floor Sediments

Evidence about past climates can also be found deep beneath the ocean floor. Scientists remove and study long cylinders of sediment from the ocean floor, such as the one shown at the right. Preserved in these sediments are fossil remains of microscopic organisms that have died and settled on the ocean floor. These remains build up in layers, over time. If certain organisms are present, it can mean that the climate was particularly cold or warm at a certain time. The chemical composition of sediments, especially of the shells of certain microorganisms, can also be important. It shows what the composition was of the ocean water and atmosphere when the organisms were alive.

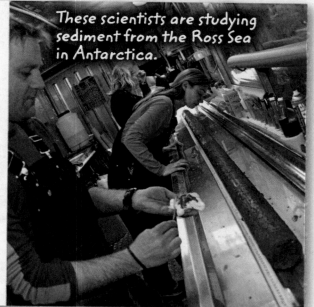

These scientists are studying sediment from the Ross Sea in Antarctica.

Ice

Icecaps are found in places such as Iceland and islands in the Arctic. The icecaps formed as older snow was squeezed into ice by new snow falling on top of it. Scientists can drill down into icecaps to collect a long cylinder of ice, called an **ice core**.

Ice cores, such as the ones shown in these photographs, give a history of Earth's climate over time. Some ice cores have regular layers, called bands, which form each year. Band size shows how much precipitation fell during a given time. The composition of water and concentration of gases in the ice core show the conditions of the atmosphere at the time that the ice formed.

Scientists study ice cores to find out about amounts of precipitation in the past.

22 State Your Claim Fill in the table by reading the evidence and making a claim about what it could mean.

Evidence	What it could mean
A. A scientist finds a fossil of a shark tooth in a layer of rock that is high in the mountains.	
B. Rocks from mountains on two different continents were found to have formed at the same time and to have the same composition.	
C. Upon studying an ice core, scientists find that a particular band is very wide.	

Visual Summary

To complete this summary, check the box that indicates true or false. You can use this page to review the main concepts of the lesson.

Fossils give information about changes in Earth's environments and life forms.

23 Trace fossils give information about animal activity and movement.

☐ True
☐ False

Sedimentary rocks provide information about Earth's geologic history.

24 These are ripple marks in sedimentary rock.

☐ True
☐ False

Studying Earth's History

Earth's surface features reflect its geologic history.

25 Tall, jagged mountains are older than rounded, smaller mountains.

☐ True
☐ False

Besides fossils, other materials give information about Earth's climate history.

26 Scientists study the width of tree rings to learn about past climate conditions.

☐ True
☐ False

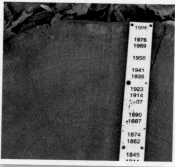

27 **Claims • Evidence • Reasoning** At one point in history, Florida was completely submerged in water. Use evidence to support a claim about which material (wood, sea-floor sediments, ice) would be the most useful in studying Florida's fossil record. Explain your reasoning.

Lesson Review

Vocabulary

In your own words, define the following terms.

1 uniformitarianism _____

_____

_____

2 trace fossil _____

_____

_____

Key Concepts

3 Identify How old is Earth?

_____

4 Explain How can sedimentary rock show Earth's history?

_____

_____

_____

_____

5 List Name three examples of trace fossils.

_____

_____

6 Explain Name five ways that organisms can be preserved as fossils, and explain what fossils can show about Earth's history.

_____

_____

_____

_____

7 Describe How do Earth's surface features indicate changes over time?

_____

_____

_____

8 Describe What are two ways that scientists can study Earth's climate history?

_____

_____

_____

_____

Critical Thinking

9 Claims • Evidence • Reasoning Make a claim about whether or not a piece of pottery is an example of a fossil? Summarize evidence to support your claim and explain your reasoning.

_____

_____

_____

Use this photo to answer the following questions.

10 Synthesize How does the erosion of these mountains support the principle of uniformitarianism? Explain your reasoning.

_____

_____

_____

11 Infer The type and age of rocks found in this mountain range are also found on another continent. What might this mean?

_____

_____

_____

_____

Publishing Company

Relative Dating

ESSENTIAL QUESTION

How are the relative ages of rock measured?

By the end of this lesson, you should be able to summarize how scientists measure the relative ages of rock layers and identify gaps in the rock record.

Studying these rock layers can tell scientists a great deal about the order in which the different layers formed.

SC.7.N.1.5 Describe the methods used in the pursuit of a scientific explanation as seen in different fields of science such as biology, geology, and physics. **SC.7.E.6.3** Identify current methods for measuring the age of Earth and its parts, including the law of superposition and radioactive dating.

Lesson Labs

Quick Labs
• Layers of Sedimentary Rock
• Ordering Rock Layers

Exploration Lab
• Earth's History

 Engage Your Brain

1 Describe Fill in each blank with the word or phrase that you think completes the following sentences.

An example of something young is

_____

An example of something old is

_____

An example of something that is horizontal is

_____

An example of something older than you is

_____

The Liberty Bell

2 Explain Which came first, the bell or the crack in the bell? Explain your reasoning.

_____

_____

_____

_____

ACTIVE **READING**

3 Synthesize You can often define an unknown word if you know the meaning of its word parts. Use the word parts below to make an educated guess about the meaning of the word *superposition*, when used to describe layers of rock.

Word part	Meaning
super-	above
-position	specific place

superposition:

_____

_____

Vocabulary Terms

• relative dating
• superposition
• unconformity
• fossil
• geologic column

4 Apply As you learn the definition of each vocabulary term in this lesson, make your own definition or sketch to help you remember the meaning of the term.

Who's First?

What is relative dating?

Imagine that you are a detective at a crime scene. You must figure out the order of events that took place before you arrived. Scientists have the same goal when studying Earth. They try to find out the order in which events happened during Earth's history. Instead of using fingerprints and witnesses, scientists use rocks and fossils. Determining whether an object or event is older or younger than other objects or events is called **relative dating**.

The telephones shown below show how technologies have changed over time. Layers of rock also show how certain things took place in the past. Using different pieces of information, scientists can find the order in which rock layers formed. Once they know the order, a relative age can be determined for each rock layer. Keep in mind, however, that this does not give scientists a rock's age in years. It only allows scientists to find out what rock layer is older or younger than another rock layer.

ⓘ Think Outside the Book

5 Model In groups of 6–10 people, form a line. Place the oldest person in the front of the line and the youngest person at the end of the line. What is your relative age compared to the person in front of you? Compared to the person behind you?

👁 Visualize It!

6 Explain Use the numbers 1, 2, and 3 to rate these telephones from oldest (1) to youngest (3). Explain your reasoning. Does this tell you the years that the telephones were made?

_____

_____

_____

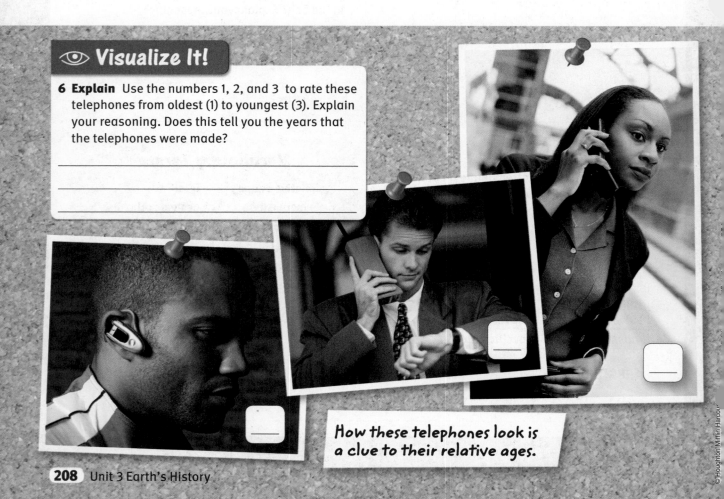

How these telephones look is a clue to their relative ages.

© Houghton Mifflin Harcourt

How are undisturbed rock layers dated?

To find the relative ages of rocks, scientists study the layers in sedimentary rocks. Sedimentary rocks form when new sediments are deposited on top of older rock. As more sediment is added, it is compressed and hardens into rock layers.

Scientists know that gravity causes sediment to be deposited in layers that are horizontal (hohr•ih•ZAHN•tuhl). Over time, different layers of sediment pile up on Earth's surface. Younger layers pile on top of older ones. If left undisturbed, the sediment will remain in horizontal layers. Scientists use the order of these layers to date the rock of each layer.

ACTIVE **READING**

7 Explain Why does gravity cause layers of sediment to be horizontal? Explain your reasoning.

_____

_____

_____

Using Superposition

Suppose that you have a brother who takes pictures of your family and piles them in a box. Over time, he adds new pictures to the top of the pile. Where are the oldest pictures—the ones taken when you were a baby? Where are the most recent pictures—the ones taken last week? The oldest pictures will be at the bottom of the pile. The youngest pictures will be at the top of the pile. Layers of rock are like the photographs shown below. As you go from top to bottom, the layers get older.

This approach is used to determine the relative age of sedimentary rock layers. The law of **superposition** (soo•per•puh•ZISH•uhn) is the principle that states that younger rocks lie above older rocks if the layers have not been disturbed.

Rock layers are like photographs that have been put in a pile over time.

👁 Visualize It!

8 Claims • Evidence • Reasoning Make a claim about the relative ages of these rock layers. Support your claim with evidence. Explain your reasoning.

_____

_____

How Disturbing!

How are sedimentary rock layers disturbed?

If rock layers are not horizontal, then something disturbed them after they formed. Forces in Earth can disturb rock layers so much that older layers end up on top of younger layers. Some of the ways that rock layers can be disturbed are shown below and on the next page.

By Tilting and Folding

Tilting happens when Earth's forces move rock layers up or down unevenly. The layers become slanted. *Folding* is the bending of rocks that can happen when rock layers are squeezed together. The bending is from stress on the rock. Folding can cause rock layers to be turned over by so much that older layers end up on top of younger layers.

By Faults and Intrusions

Scientists often find features that cut across existing layers of rock. A *fault* is a break or crack in Earth's crust where rocks can move. An *intrusion* (in•TROO•zhuhn) is igneous rock that forms when magma is injected into rock and then cools and becomes hard.

Folding, tilting, faults, and intrusions can make finding out the relative ages of rock layers difficult. This can be even more complicated when a layer of rock is missing. Scientists call this missing layer of rock an *unconformity*.

👁 Visualize It!

9 Describe Write a caption for this group of images.

_____

_____

Tilting

Faults

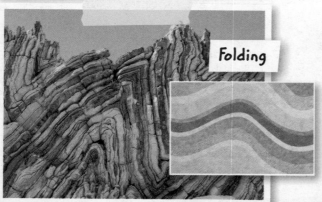

Folding

Intrusions

By Unconformities

A missing layer of rock forms a gap in Earth's geologic history, also called the geologic record. An **unconformity** (uhn•kuhn•FAWR•mih•tee) is a break in the geologic record that is made when rock layers are eroded or when sediment is not deposited for a long period of time. When scientists find an unconformity, they must question if the "missing layer" was simply never present or if it was removed. Two examples of unconformities are shown below.

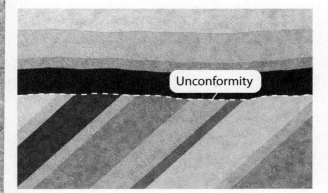

An unconformity can happen between horizontal layers and layers that are tilted or folded. The older layers were tilted or folded and then eroded before horizontal layers formed above them.

ACTIVE READING

10 Claims • Evidence • Reasoning Make a claim about two ways that a rock layer can cause a gap in the geologic record. Support your claim with evidence, and explain your reasoning.

_____

_____

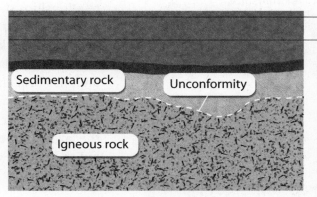

Sedimentary rock

Unconformity

Igneous rock

An unconformity can also happen when igneous or metamorphic rocks are exposed at Earth's surface and become eroded. Later, deposited sediment causes the eroded surface to become buried under sedimentary rock.

11 Illustrate Choose two of the following: tilting, folding, fault, intrusion, and an unconformity. Draw and label each one.

I'm Cutting In!

How are rock layers ordered?

Often, the order of rock layers is affected by more than one thing. Finding out what happened to form a group of rock layers is like piecing together a jigsaw puzzle. The law of superposition helps scientists to do this.

The idea that layers of rock have to be in place before anything can disturb them is also used. The law of crosscutting relationships states that a fault or a body of rock, such as an intrusion, must be younger than any feature or layer of rock that the fault or rock body cuts through. For example, if a fault has broken a rock layer, the fault is younger than the rock layer. If a fault has broken through igneous rock, the igneous rock must have been in place, and cool, before it could have been broken. The same is true for an unconformity. Look at the image below and use the laws of superposition and crosscutting relationships to figure out the relative ages of the rock layers and features.

ACTIVE **READING**

12 **Identify** As you read, underline the law of crosscutting relationships.

◉ Visualize It!

13 **Claims • Evidence • Reasoning** Make a claim about the order in which features A through J formed. Support your claim with evidence from the illustration. Fill in the lines according to the relative ages of the layers or features. Explain your reasoning.

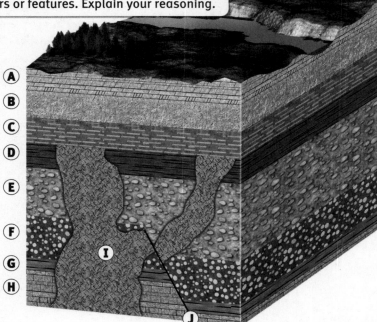

Youngest

_____
_____
_____
_____
_____
_____
_____
_____
_____

Oldest

© Houghton Mifflin Harcourt

Dating Mars

NASA's Mars Odyssey orbiter and the Hubble Space Telescope have produced a large collection of images of the surface of Mars. These are studied to find the relative ages of features on Mars, using the laws of superposition and crosscutting relationships. Here are two examples of crosscutting relationships.

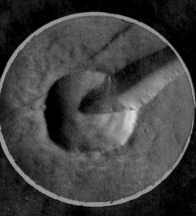

The Crater Came First

A crater can be cut by another feature, such as a fracture.

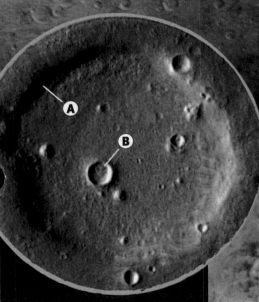

Crater in a Crater

A crater (A) can be cut by another crater (B) that formed from a later impact.

Hellas Crater

The many craters on Mars are studied to determine relative ages of features. This is Hellas Impact Basin, which is almost 2100 km wide.

Extend

14 **Claims • Evidence • Reasoning** Make a claim about the relative ages of crater A and crater B. Provide evidence to support your claim, and explain your reasoning.

15 **Apply** How can scientists use erosion as a way to determine the relative ages of craters on Mars? Describe how erosion could change the appearance of a crater over time.

16 **Research** Find out how scientists have used relative dating to study the geologic history of other planets, such as Venus. Present what you found out by drawing a graphic novel or making a poster.

How are fossils used to determine relative ages of rocks?

Fossils are the traces or remains of an organism that lived long ago, most commonly preserved in sedimentary rock. Fossil forms of plants and animals show change over time, as they evolve. Scientists can classify fossilized (FAHS•uh•lyzd) organisms based on these changes. Then they can use that classification of fossils to find the relative ages of the rocks in which the fossils are found. Rock that contains fossils of organisms similar to those that live today is most likely younger than rock that contains fossils of ancient organisms. For example, fossilized remains of a 47 million-year-old primate are shown below. Rock that contains these fossils is younger than rock that contains the fossils of a dinosaur that lived over 200 million years ago.

17 Claims • Evidence • Reasoning Make a claim about whether fossils of species that did not change noticeably over time would be useful in determining the relative ages of rocks. Summarize your evidence to support your claim, and explain your reasoning.

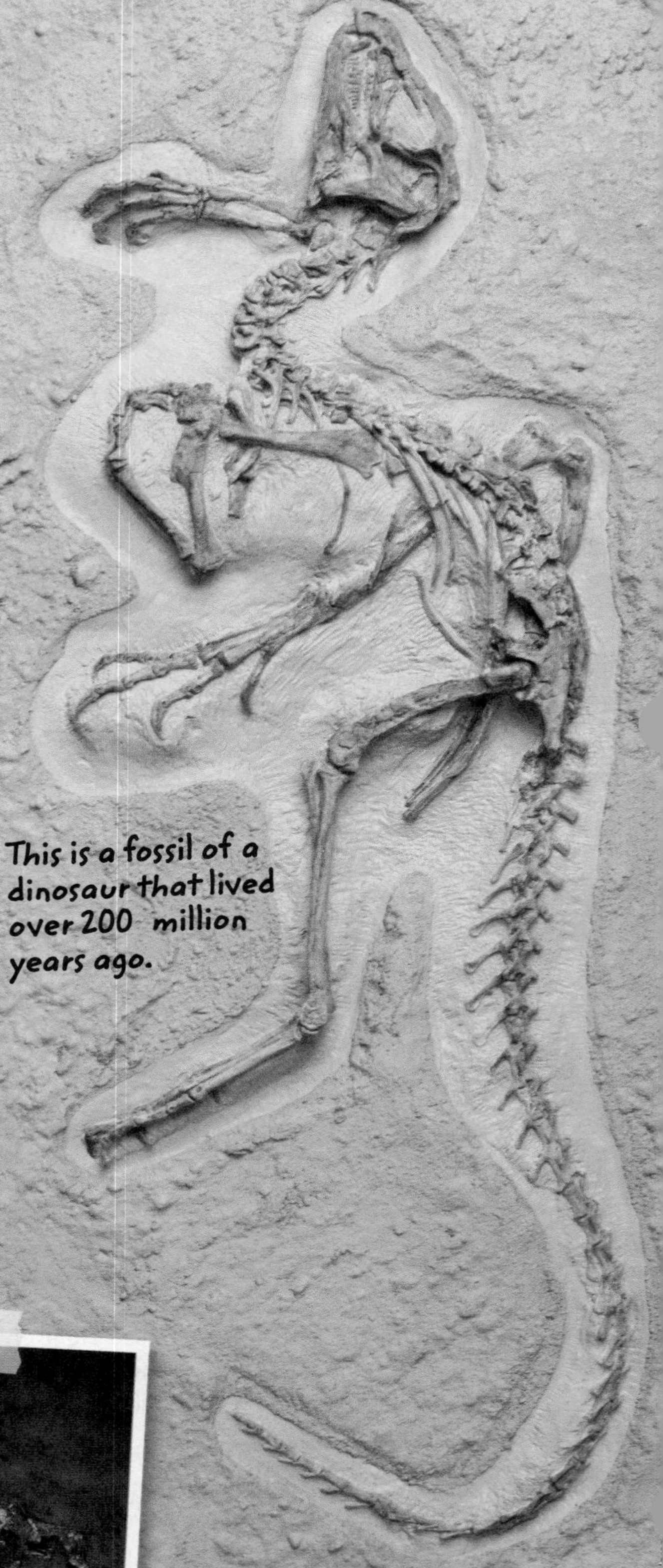

_____

_____

_____

This is a fossil of a dinosaur that lived over 200 million years ago.

This is a fossil of a primate that lived about 47 million years ago.

How are geologic columns used to compare relative ages of rocks?

Relative dating can also be done by comparing the relative ages of rock layers in different areas. The comparison is done using a geologic column. A **geologic column** is an ordered arrangement of rock layers that is based on the relative ages of the rocks, with the oldest rocks at the bottom of the column. It is made by piecing together different rock sequences from different areas. A geologic column represents an ideal image of a rock layer sequence that doesn't actually exist in any one place on Earth.

The rock sequences shown below represent rock layers from different outcrops at different locations. Each has certain rock layers that are common to layers in the geologic column, shown in the middle. Scientists can compare a rock layer with a similar layer in a geologic column that has the same fossils or that has the same relative position. If the two layers match, then they probably formed around the same time.

ACTIVE **READING**

18 Identify As you read, underline the description of how rock layers are ordered in a geologic column.

👁 Visualize It!

19 Identify Draw lines from the top and bottom of each outcrop to their matching positions in the geologic column.

Outcrop 1

Geologic Column

Outcrop 2

Rock layers from different outcrops can be compared to a geologic column.

Visual Summary

To complete this summary, circle the correct words. You can use this page to review the main concepts of the lesson.

If undisturbed, sedimentary rock exists as horizontal layers.

20 For undisturbed rock layers, younger rocks are above/below older rocks.

Forces in Earth can cause horizontal layers of rock to be disturbed.

21 This photo shows folding/tilting.

Relative Dating

Fossils can be used to determine the relative ages of rock layers.

22 In undisturbed rock layers, fossils of a more recent organism will be in rock that is above/below rock containing fossils of older organisms.

Rock layers from different areas can be compared to a geologic column.

23 In geologic columns, the oldest rock layers are at the bottom/top.

24 Claims • Evidence • Reasoning Make a claim as to how the law of superposition relates to a stack of magazines that you have been saving over the past few years. Use evidence to support your claim and explain your reasoning.

Lesson Review

Vocabulary

In your own words, define the following terms.

1 relative dating

_____

_____

2 unconformity

_____

_____

Key Concepts

3 Describe How are sedimentary rock layers deposited?

_____

4 List Name five ways that the order of rock layers can be disturbed.

_____

_____

_____

5 Explain How are the laws of superposition and crosscutting relationships used to determine the relative ages of rocks?

_____

_____

_____

_____

_____

6 Explain How can fossils be used to determine the relative ages of rock layers?

_____

_____

_____

_____

7 Describe How is the geologic column used in relative dating?

_____

_____

_____

Critical Thinking

8 Claims • Evidence • Reasoning Make a claim about which types of rocks the law of crosscutting relationships involves. Summarize evidence to support your claim and explain your reasoning.

_____

_____

_____

Use this image to answer the following questions.

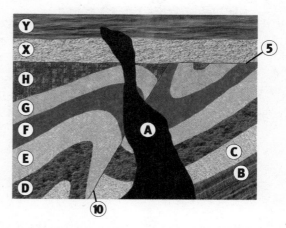

9 Analyze Is intrusion A younger or older than layer X? Explain your reasoning.

_____

_____

10 Analyze What feature is marked by 5?

_____

11 Analyze Other than intrusion and faulting, what happened in layers B, C, D, E, F, G, and H? Support your claim with evidence.

_____

SC.7.N.1.1 Define a problem from the seventh grade curriculum, use appropriate reference materials to support scientific understanding, plan and carry out scientific investigation of various types, such as systematic observations or experiments, identify variables, collect and organize data, interpret data in charts, tables, and graphics, analyze information, make predictions, and defend conclusions.

Forming a Hypothesis

When conducting an investigation to test a hypothesis, a scientist must not let personal bias affect the results of the investigation. A scientist must be open to the fact that the results of an investigation may not completely support the hypothesis. They may even contradict it! Revising or forming a new hypothesis may lead a scientist to make a breakthrough that could be the basis of a new discovery.

Tutorial

The following procedure explains the steps that you will use to develop and evaluate a hypothesis.

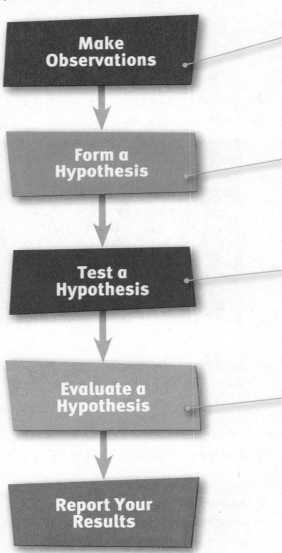

Make Observations

1 Making Observations Scientific investigations commonly begin with observations. Your observations may lead to a question. For example, you may wonder how, why, or when something happens.

Form a Hypothesis

2 Forming a Hypothesis To answer your question, you can start by forming a hypothesis. A hypothesis is a clear statement of what you expect will be the answer to your question. Start to form a hypothesis by stating the probable answer to your question based on your observations.

Test a Hypothesis

3 Testing a Hypothesis A useful hypothesis must be testable. To determine whether your hypothesis is testable, identify experiments that you can perform or observations that you can make to find out whether the hypothesis is supported or not.

Evaluate a Hypothesis

4 Evaluating a Hypothesis After analyzing your data, you can determine if your results support your hypothesis. If your data support your hypothesis, you may want to repeat your observations or experiments to verify your results. If your data do not support your hypothesis, you may have to check your procedure for errors. You may even have to reject your hypothesis and form a new one.

Report Your Results

You Try It!

The table provides observations about the latest eruptions of several volcanoes in Hawai'i.

Latest Eruption of Volcanoes in Hawai'i	
Volcano	**Year**
East Maui (Haleakala)	1460
Hualalai	1801
Mauna Loa	1984
Kilauea	still active

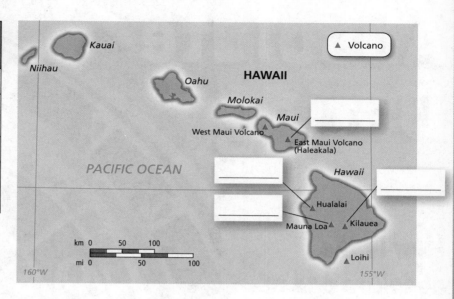

1 Making Observations On the map, label the volcanoes with the years shown. What do you observe about the dates and the locations of the volcanoes?

_____
_____
_____
_____
_____
_____
_____

2 Forming a Hypothesis Use the observations above to form a hypothesis about the history of the area. Focus on the relationship between the activity of the volcanoes and the location of the volcanoes. Your hypothesis should be supported by all of your data. Summarize your completed hypothesis in a single paragraph.

_____
_____
_____
_____
_____

3 Claims • Evidence • Reasoning Loihi is currently active, but West Maui has not erupted in recent history. Make a claim about whether these new observations support your hypothesis or disprove it. Support your claim with evidence, and explain your reasoning.

_____
_____
_____

4 Revising a Hypothesis Share your hypothesis with your classmates. Rewrite your hypothesis so that it includes the changes suggested by your classmates.

_____
_____
_____

 Take It Home!

While you already know the word *hypothesis*, you might not know the word *hypothetical*. Use the dictionary to look up the meaning of the suffix *-ical*. Combine the meanings of these two word parts, and write an original definition of *hypothetical* in your notebook.

Absolute Dating

ESSENTIAL QUESTION

How is the absolute age of rock measured?

By the end of this lesson, you should be able to summarize how scientists measure the absolute age of rock layers, including by radiometric dating.

SC.7.N.1.5 Describe the methods used in the pursuit of a scientific explanation as seen in different fields of science such as biology, geology, and physics. **SC.7.E.6.3** Identify current methods for measuring the age of Earth and its parts, including the law of superposition and radioactive dating.

A clock is one way of measuring absolute time.

Lesson Labs

Quick Labs
- Radioactive Decay
- Index Fossils

Engage Your Brain

1 Predict Check T or F to show whether you think each statement is true or false.

T	F	
☐	☐	All rocks are made of matter and all matter is made of atoms.
☐	☐	We use calendars to measure the absolute age of people.
☐	☐	Someone tells you that he is older than you are. This tells you his absolute age.
☐	☐	If you cut a clay ball in two and then cut one of the halves in two, you will end up with four pieces of clay.

2 Explain What is the age of this person? Explain your reasoning.

_____
_____
_____
_____
_____
_____

ACTIVE **READING**

3 Synthesize You can often define an unknown word if you know the meaning of its word parts. Use the word parts and sentence below to make an educated guess about the meaning of the phrase *radiometric dating*.

Word part	Meaning
radio-	relating to radiation
-metric	relating to measurement

Example sentence
By using radiometric dating, the scientist found that the rock was 25 million years old.

radiometric dating:

_____
_____

Vocabulary Terms

- absolute dating
- radioactive decay
- half-life
- radiometric dating

4 Apply As you learn the definition of each vocabulary term in this lesson, create your own definition or sketch to help you remember the meaning of the term.

It's About

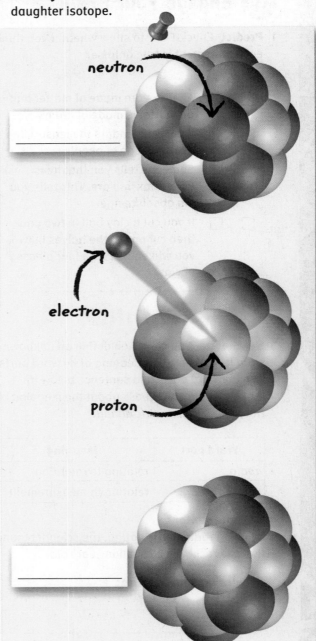

How can the absolute age of rock be determined?

Determining the actual age of an event or object in years is called **absolute dating**. Scientists use many different ways to find the absolute age of rock and other materials. One way is by using radioactive isotopes (ray•dee•oh•AK•tiv EYE•suh•tohpz).

Using Radioactive Isotopes

Atoms of the same element that have a different number of neutrons are called isotopes. Many isotopes are stable, meaning that they stay in their original form. But some isotopes are unstable, and break down to form different isotopes. The unstable isotopes are called *radioactive*. The breakdown of a radioactive isotope into a stable isotope of the same element or of another element is called **radioactive decay**. As shown on the right, radioactive decay for many isotopes happens when a neutron is converted to a proton, with the release of an electron. A radioactive isotope is called a *parent isotope*. The stable isotope formed by its breakdown is called the *daughter isotope*.

Each radioactive isotope decays at a specific, constant rate. **Half-life** is the time needed for half of a sample of a radioactive substance to undergo radioactive decay to form daughter isotopes. Half-life is always given in units of time.

ACTIVE **READING**

5 Claims • Evidence • Reasoning Make a claim about how much of a radioactive parent isotope remains after one half-life has passed? Use evidence to support your claim, and explain your reasoning.

_____

_____

6 Identify Label the parent isotope and the daughter isotope.

neutron

_____

electron

proton

_____

Time!

By Radiometric Dating

Some radioactive isotopes in mineral crystals can act as clocks. These mineral crystals record the ages of the rocks in which the minerals formed. Scientists study the amounts of parent and daughter isotopes to date samples. If you know how fast a radioactive isotope decays, you can figure out the sample's absolute age. Finding the absolute age of a sample by determining the relative percentages of a radioactive parent isotope and a stable daughter isotope is called **radiometric dating** (ray•dee•oh•MET•rik DAYT•ing). The figure on the right shows how the relative percentages of a parent isotope and a daughter isotope change with the passing of each half-life. The following is an example of how radiometric dating can be used:

- You want to determine the age of a sample that contains a radioactive isotope that has a half-life of 10 million years.
- You analyze the sample and find equal amounts of parent and daughter isotopes.
- Because 50%, or ½, of the parent isotope has decayed, you know that 1 half-life has passed.
- So, the sample is 10 million years old.

What is the best rock for radiometric dating?

Igneous rock is often the best type of rock sample to use for radiometric dating. When igneous rock forms, elements are separated into different minerals in the rock. When they form, minerals in igneous rocks often contain only a parent isotope and none of the daughter isotope. This makes the isotope percentages easier to interpret and helps dating to be more accurate.

7 Calculate Fill in the number of parent isotopes and daughter isotopes in the spaces beside the images below.

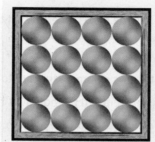

0 years
Parent isotope = 16
Daughter isotope = 0
100% of the sample is parent isotope.

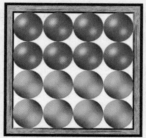

After 1 half-life
Parent isotope = 8
Daughter isotope = 8
50%, or $\frac{1}{2}$, of the sample is parent isotope.

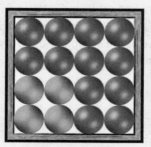

After 2 half-lives
Parent isotope = 4
Daughter isotope = ____
25%, or $\frac{1}{4}$, of the sample is parent isotope.

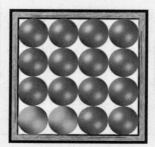

After 3 half-lives
Parent isotope = ____
Daughter isotope = ____
12.5%, or $\frac{1}{8}$, of the sample is parent isotope.

Do the Math

Sample Problem

A crystal contains a radioactive isotope that has a half-life of 10,000 years. One-fourth (25%) of the parent isotope remains in a sample. How old is the sample?

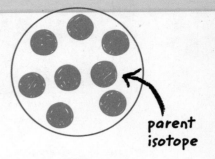

parent isotope

Identify

A. What do you know? Half-life = 10,000 years, parent isotope = 25%

B. What do you want to find out? How old the sample is. So, you need to know how many half-lives have gone by since the crystal formed.

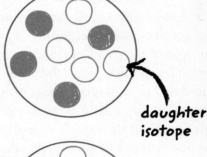

daughter isotope

Plan

C. Draw the parent-to-daughter isotope ratios for each half-life.

Solve

D. The third drawing on the right shows a sample that contains 25% parent isotope. This amount is present after 2 half-lives have passed.

E. Find the age of the sample. Because the half-life of the radioactive isotope is 10,000 years and 2 half-lives have passed, the age of the sample is: $2 \times 10,000 \ years = 20,000 \ years$

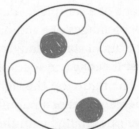

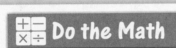 Do the Math

You Try It

8 Claims • Evidence • Reasoning A crystal contains a radioactive isotope that has a half-life of 20,000 years. You analyze a sample and find that one-eighth (12.5%) of the parent isotope remains. Make a claim about the age of the sample. Support your claim with mathematical evidence, and explain your reasoning.

Identify

A. What do you know? _____

B. What do you want to find out? _____

Plan

C. Draw the parent-to-daughter isotope ratios on the right.

Solve

D. Figure out how many half-lives have passed: _____

E. Find the age of the sample: _____

Answer: _____

Time for a Change

What are some radiometric dating methods?

Scientists use many different isotopes for radiometric dating. The half-life of an isotope is very important in determining the time range that it is useful for dating. If the half-life is too short compared with the age of the sample, there will be too little parent isotope left to measure. If the half-life is too long, there will not be enough daughter isotope to measure. Also, different methods may only be useful for certain types of materials.

ACTIVE **READING**

9 Identify As you read, underline the time frame for which radiocarbon dating is useful.

Radiocarbon Dating

The ages of wood, bones, shells, and other organic remains can be found by radiocarbon dating. The radioactive isotope carbon-14 combines with oxygen to form radioactive carbon dioxide, CO_2. Most CO_2 in the atmosphere contains nonradioactive carbon-12, but radioactive carbon-14 is also present.

Plants absorb CO_2 from the atmosphere, which they use to build their bodies through photosynthesis. As long as a plant is alive, the plant takes in carbon dioxide with the same carbon-14 to carbon-12 ratio. Similarly, animals convert the carbon from the food they eat into bone and other tissues. So, animals inherit the carbon isotope ratio of their food sources.

Once a plant or animal dies, carbon is no longer taken in. The ratio of carbon-14 to carbon-12 decreases in the dead organism because carbon-14 undergoes radioactive decay to nitrogen-14. The half-life of carbon-14 is only 5,730 years. Also, radiocarbon dating can only be used to date organic matter. So this method is used to date things that lived in the last 45,000 years.

Materials such as these woolly mammoth teeth can be radiocarbon dated.

ACTIVE **READING**

10 Claims • Evidence • Reasoning You have found a bone in a layer of rock that you think is about 500,000 years old. Make a claim about whether you would use radiocarbon dating to find the age of this bone. Use evidence to explain your reasoning. Why or why not? _____

Radiometric dating has been done on Mammoth Mountain's volcanic rock.

ACTIVE READING

11 Identify As you read this page, underline the time frame for which each method is most useful.

Potassium-Argon Dating

The element potassium (puh•TAS•ee•uhm) occurs in two stable isotopes, potassium-41 and potassium-39, and one radioactive isotope that occurs naturally, potassium-40. Potassium-40 decays to argon and calcium. It has a half-life of 1.25 billion years. Scientists measure argon as the daughter isotope. Potassium-argon dating is often used to date igneous volcanic rocks. This method is used to date rocks that are between about 100,000 years and a few billion years old.

Scientist and astronaut Harrison Schmitt collected samples of rock on the moon during the Apollo 17 mission in 1972.

Uranium-Lead Dating

An isotope of uranium (yoo•RAY•nee•uhm), called uranium-238, is a radioactive isotope that decays to lead-206. Uranium-lead dating is based on measuring the amount of the lead-206 daughter isotope in a sample. Uranium-238 has a half-life of 4.5 billion years.

Uranium-lead dating can be used to determine the age of igneous rocks that are between 100 million years and billions of years old. Younger rocks do not have enough daughter isotope to be accurately measured by this method. Uranium-lead dating was used to find the earliest accurate age of Earth.

Time Will Tell

How is radiometric dating used to determine the age of Earth?

Radiometric dating can be used to find the age of Earth, though not by dating Earth rocks. The first rocks that formed on Earth have long ago been eroded or melted, or buried under younger rocks. So, there are no Earth rocks which can be directly studied that are as old as our planet. But other bodies in space do have rock that is as old as our solar system.

Meteorites (MEE•tee•uh•rytz) are small, rocky bodies that have traveled through space and fallen to Earth's surface. Scientists have found meteorites on Earth, such as the one shown below. Rocks from the moon have also been collected. Radiometric dating has been done on these rocks from other parts of our solar system. The absolute ages of these samples show that our solar system, including Earth, is about 4.6 billion years old.

ACTIVE READING

12 Identify As you read, underline the reason why scientists cannot use rocks from Earth to measure the age of Earth.

> ## Think Outside the Book
>
> **13 Model** Develop a way to help people understand how large the number 4.6 billion is.

This 4.5 billion-year-old rock is part of a meteorite that landed in Antarctica. It is thought to be from Mars.

Showing Your Age

How can fossils help to determine the age of sedimentary rock?

Sedimentary rock layers and the fossils within these layers cannot be dated directly. But igneous rock layers on either side of a fossil layer can be dated radiometrically. Once the older and younger rock layers are dated, scientists can assign an absolute age range to the sedimentary rock layer that the fossils are found in.

Using Index Fossils

Scientists have found that particular types of fossils appear only in certain layers of rock. By dating igneous rock layers above and below these fossil layers, scientists can determine the time span in which the organisms lived. *Index fossils,* such as the ones shown below, are fossils that are used to estimate the absolute age of the rock layers in which they are found. Once the absolute age of an index fossil is known, it can be used to determine the age of rock layers that contain the same index fossil anywhere on Earth.

To be an index fossil, the organism from which the fossil formed must have lived during a relatively short geologic time span. The fossils of the organism must be relatively common and must be found over a large area. Index fossils must also have features that make them different from other fossils.

ACTIVE READING

14 Identify As you read, underline the requirements for a fossil to be an index fossil.

Phacops rana fossils are used as index fossils. This trilobite lived between 405 million and 360 million years ago.

How are index fossils used?

Index fossils act as markers for the time that the organisms lived on Earth. Organisms that formed index fossils lived during short periods of geologic time. So, the rock layer that an index fossil is found in can be dated accurately. For example, ammonites were marine mollusks, similar to a modern squid. They lived in coiled shells in ancient seas. The ammonite *Tropites* (troh•PY•teez) lived between 230 million and 208 million years ago. So, whenever scientists find a fossil of *Tropites*, they know that the rock layer the fossil was found in formed between 230 million and 208 million years ago. As shown below, this can also tell scientists something about the ages of surrounding rock layers.

Trilobite (TRY•luh•byt) fossils are another example of a good index fossil. The closest living relatives of trilobites are the horseshoe crab, spiders, and scorpions. *Phacops rana* is a trilobite that lived between 405 million and 360 million years ago. The *Phacops rana* fossil, shown on the previous page, is the state fossil of Pennsylvania.

Index fossils can also be used to date rock layers in separate areas. The appearance of the same index fossil in rock of different areas shows that the rock layers formed at about the same time.

ACTIVE READING

15 **Identify** As you read, underline examples of organisms whose fossils are index fossils. Include the time frame for which they are used to date rock.

👁 Visualize It!

16 **Explain Your Reasoning** *Tropites* fossils are found in the middle rock layer shown below. Place each of the following ages beside the correct rock layer: 215 million/500 million/100 million. Explain your reasoning.

Fossils of a genus of ammonites called Tropites are good index fossils.

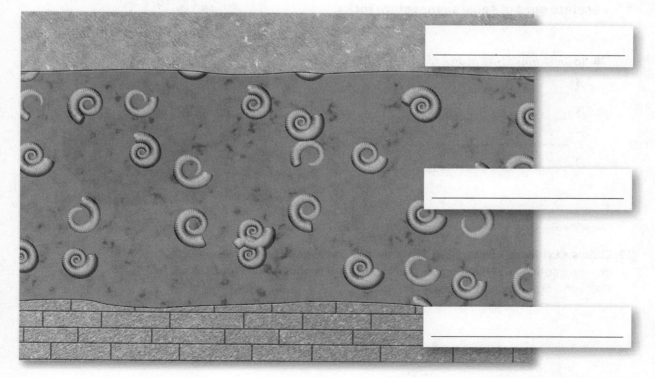

Visual Summary

To complete this summary, fill in the blanks with the correct word or phrase. You can use this page to review the main concepts of the lesson.

Radiometric dating can be used to find the absolute ages of materials such as igneous rocks. This method uses the radioactive decay of an isotope.

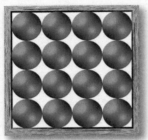 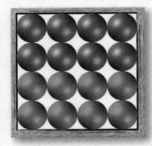 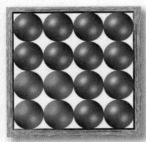

17 During radioactive decay, the amount of _____ isotope

decreases by one-half after every _____

Absolute Dating

Index fossils can be used to estimate the absolute ages of some sedimentary rocks.

18 Four things that index fossils should be:

A _____

B _____

C _____

D _____

19 **Claims • Evidence • Reasoning** Make a claim about how the use of radioactive decay in absolute dating is similar to how you use a clock. Summarize evidence to support your claim and explain your reasoning.

Lesson Review

Vocabulary

Fill in each blank with the term that best completes the following sentences.

1 The breakdown of a radioactive isotope into a stable isotope is called _____

_____

2 The _____ is the time needed for half of a sample of a radioactive isotope to break down to form daughter isotopes.

3 _____ is a method used to determine the absolute age of a sample by measuring the relative amounts of parent isotope and daughter isotope.

Key Concepts

4 Summarize How are radioactive isotopes used to determine the absolute age of igneous rock? Name two radiometric methods that are used.

_____

_____

5 Describe What happens to an isotope during radioactive decay?

_____

_____

6 Claims • Evidence • Reasoning Make a claim about why igneous rocks are the best type of rock sample for radiometric dating. Support you claim with evidence, and explain your reasoning.

_____

_____

7 Describe How old is Earth and how did scientists find this out?

_____

_____

8 Explain What are index fossils and how are they used to determine the absolute age of sedimentary rock?

_____

_____

Critical Thinking

9 Claims • Evidence • Reasoning An igneous rock sample is about 250,000 years old. Make a claim about whether you would use uranium-lead radiometric dating to find its age. Summarize evidence to support your claim and explain your reasoning.

_____

_____

10 Calculate A sample of wood contains 12.5% of its original carbon-14. What is the estimated age of this sample? Show your work.

_____

_____

Use this graph to answer the following questions.

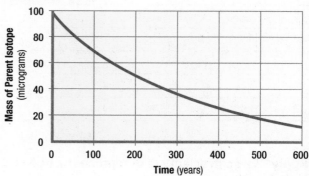

Radioactive Decay

11 Analyze What is the half-life of the radioactive isotope? Explain your reasoning.

_____

12 Analyze What mass of radioactive isotope will be left after three half-lives? Explain your reasoning.

_____

Earth's History

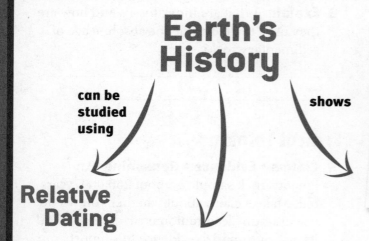

can be studied using → **Relative Dating**

→ **Absolute Dating**

shows →

Geologic Change over Time

1 Claims • Evidence • Reasoning As shown in the Graphic Organizer above, both relative and absolute dating are used to study Earth's history. Make a claim about how both techniques could be used together to date igneous and sedimentary rock that are found together. Summarize your evidence to support your claim and explain your reasoning.

_____

_____

_____

_____

_____

_____

2 Apply How can scientists determine the age of Earth?

_____

_____

_____

_____

_____

_____

3 Relate What does sedimentary rock tell us about past environments on Earth?

_____

_____

_____

_____

_____

_____

_____

_____

_____

Vocabulary

Fill in each blank with the term that best completes the following sentences.

1 A _____ is the remains of a once-living organism found in layers of rock, ice, or amber.

2 The time required for half the quantity of a radioactive material to decay is its _____.

3 _____ is the theory stating that Earth's lithosphere is made up of large plates that are in constant motion.

4 _____ is the process in which a radioactive isotope tends to break down into a stable isotope.

5 _____ is the scientific study of the origin, physical history, and structure of Earth and the processes that shape it.

Key Concepts

Identify the choice that best completes the statement or answers the question.

6 A trace fossil includes no physical remains of the organism's body but only a mark or structure that the organism left behind. Which of these choices is not an example of a trace fossil?

  A footprint in sediment   **C** burrow in the sea floor

  B coprolite in sediment   **D** insect in amber

7 Weather is not the same as climate. What is the main difference between these two concepts?

  F The main difference is how both are measured.

  G Only weather includes information about the temperature.

  H Only climate includes information about the precipitation.

  I The main difference is the length of time over which both are measured.

8 Ava visited the Grand Canyon. She was very impressed by the rock formations and decided to sketch them. This figure shows what she drew.

What type of rock did Ava see?

A fossilized

C metamorphic

B igneous

D sedimentary

9 A team of scientists is searching for specimens to understand how Earth's climate has changed in the past. The black boxes in the figure below show where this team has drilled to obtain such specimens.

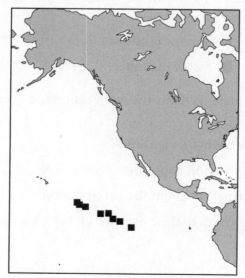

What were these scientists drilling for?

F ice cores

H sea-floor sediments

G surface landforms

I fossils preserved in amber

10 Tiny fossils provide evidence that life on Earth began at least 3.5 billion years ago. According to this fossil evidence, about how old was Earth when life first appeared on the planet?

A 4.6 billion years

B 3.5 billion years

C 2.3 billion years

D 1.1 billion years

11 A team of geologists compared the rock layers found in Florida to those found in northwest Africa. They placed all of the rock layers from the two regions in order from youngest to oldest. What did the team make?

F a geologic record

G a fossil reference

H a geologic column

I a topographic map

12 Jacob has one older brother and one younger sister. He wants to explain relative dating to them using their ages as an example. Which of these statements describes their ages using relative dating?

A Their ages are 14, 12, and 9.

B They are all about the same age.

C The boys have different ages than the girl.

D Jacob is younger than his brother but older than his sister.

13 Basalt is a gray or black igneous rock. Pilar uses an absolute dating method to study a sample of basalt. What will the method help her learn about the basalt sample?

F the age of the sample

G the composition of the sample

H the physical structure of the sample

I the geographic distribution of the sample

14 Scientists have determined an approximate age for Earth. To do this, they tested samples of meteorites, rocks from the moon, and rocks from other parts of the solar system. Which method could be used to determine the age of these samples?

A radiocarbon dating

B index fossil dating

C sedimentary rock dating

D uranium-lead dating

15 Which type of evidence acts as a record of changes in species over time and indicates major changes in Earth's surface and climate?

   F fossil record

   G movement of continents

   H ripple marks and mud cracks

   I composition of ice core samples

Critical Thinking

Answer the following questions in the space provided.

16 Scientists study how radioactive isotopes in rocks, such as carbon-14, decay to tell the age of the rock.

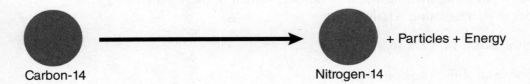

Carbon-14   Nitrogen-14   + Particles + Energy

Does knowing the half-life of Carbon 14 help scientists determine the absolute or relative age of a rock? State your claim. Use evidence to support your claim and explain your reasoning.

_____

_____

_____

_____

_____

17 Explain how fossils and other materials can tell us about the conditions of an area at the times it existed. Then explain how you could find the ages of these fossils and other materials.

_____

_____

_____

_____

_____

Human Impact on Earth

FLORIDA BIG IDEA 6

Earth Structures

The Cape Sable dam cuts through Cape Sable in Everglades National Park.

What Do You Think?

The construction of buildings, roads, parking lots, and other structures like dams and bridges can affect our water resources in a variety of ways. In what ways does human activity affect the environment? As you explore this unit, gather evidence to help you state and support a claim.

Human Impact on Earth

Investigating Water Resources

All of the water that we use comes from natural resources. Most of the water that is used in Florida is freshwater that comes from underground aquifers.

1 Think About It

What makes fresh surface water and groundwater such valuable resources?

_____

_____

How does human activity affect the availability of fresh water?

_____

_____

_____

Rain barrels collect rainwater for use at home.

② Ask A Question

Where does your water come from?

With a partner, research the source of the water used by your community. Consider contacting your local utility company as a source of information.

Things to Consider

☐ How do our water supplies get replenished?

☐ What are the most common uses for water?

③ Make A Plan

A Describe the environment that surrounds your local water source.

_____

_____

B Describe threats to your local water supply and how your water supply can be protected.

Threats	Ways to Protect Water Supply

C Determine what happens to wastewater and how it cycles through your environment.

_____

_____

_____

_____

 Take It Home!

Trace the water used in your home to its source. Use a map to determine the route by which the water you use must be transported from its source.

Natural Resources

ESSENTIAL QUESTION

What are Earth's natural resources?

By the end of this lesson, you should be able to understand the types and uses of Earth's natural resources.

Light produced from electrical energy helps people see at night. Some regions of Earth are still mostly dark once the sun sets. The people living in some of these regions rely more on sunlight.

©World Perspectives/Photographer's Choice/Getty Images

SC.7.E.6.6 Identify the impact that humans have had on Earth, such as deforestation, urbanization, desertification, erosion, air and water quality, changing the flow of water.

© Houghton Mifflin Harcourt Publishing Company

✋ Lesson Labs

Quick Labs
- How Is That Made?
- Renewable or Not?
- Production Impacts

Exploration Lab
- Natural Resources Used at Lunch

Engage Your Brain

1 Predict Check T or F to show whether you think each statement is true or false.

T   F

☐   ☐   Energy from the sun can be used to make electricity.

☐   ☐   All of Earth's resources will last forever.

☐   ☐   Food, cloth, rope, lumber, paper, and rubber come from plants.

☐   ☐   Human activity can negatively affect Earth's resources.

2 Describe Name one item that you use everyday. Describe how you think that item is made.

_____

_____

_____

_____

_____

_____

_____

ACTIVE **READING**

3 Apply Many scientific words, such as *natural* and *resource*, also have everyday meanings. Use context clues to write your own definition for each underlined word.

Oranges are a <u>natural</u> source of vitamin C.

natural:

_____

_____

His curly hair is <u>natural</u>.

natural:

_____

_____

A dictionary is a useful <u>resource</u> for learning words.

resource:

_____

_____

In the desert, water is a limited <u>resource</u>.

resource:

_____

_____

Vocabulary Terms

- **natural resource**
- **renewable resource**
- **nonrenewable resource**
- **fossil fuel**
- **material resource**
- **energy resource**

4 Identify This list contains the key terms you'll learn in this lesson. As you read, circle the definition of each term.

It's Only Natural

What are natural resources?

What do the water you drink, the paper you write on, the gasoline used in cars, and the air you breathe have in common? All of these come from Earth's natural resources. A **natural resource** is any natural material that is used by humans, such as air, soil, minerals, water, petroleum, plants, and animals.

The Earth's natural resources provide everything needed for life. The energy we get from many of these resources, such as petroleum and wind, originally comes from the sun's energy. The atmosphere contains the air we breathe, controls air temperatures, and produces rain. Rainfall from the atmosphere renews the water in oceans, rivers, lakes, and streams in the water cycle. In turn, these water sources provide food and water for drinking, cleaning, and other uses. The Earth's soil provides nutrients and a place for plants to grow. Plants provide food for some animals and humans. Petroleum is used to make fuels for cars and other machines, and also to make plastics. All of these natural resources are used to make products that make people's lives more convenient.

ACTIVE READING

5 Identify As you read, underline examples of natural resources.

👁 Visualize It!

6 Illustrate Draw or label the missing natural resources.

A

Bauxite is a rock that is used to make aluminum.

How can we categorize natural resources?

There are many different types of natural resources. Some can be replaced more quickly than others. Thus, a natural resource may be categorized as a renewable resource or a nonrenewable resource.

◯ Renewable

Some natural resources can be replaced in a relatively short time. A **renewable resource** is a natural resource that can be replaced at the same rate at which the resource is consumed. Solar energy, water, and air are considered renewable resources. However, renewable resources can be used up too quickly. For example, trees are renewable. But some forests are being cut down faster than new forests can grow to replace them. Some renewable resources are considered to be *inexhaustible resources* (in'•ig•ZAW•stuh•buhl REE•sawrs•iz) because the resources can never be used up. Solar energy and wind energy from the sun are examples of these resources.

◯ Nonrenewable

A **nonrenewable resource** is a resource that forms at a rate that is much slower than the rate at which it is consumed. Some natural resources, like minerals, form very slowly. Iron ore, aluminum, and copper are important minerals. A **fossil fuel** is a nonrenewable resource formed from buried remains of plants and animals that lived long ago. For example, coal is a fossil fuel that takes millions of years to form. Oil and natural gas are other types of fossil fuels. Once these resources are used up, humans will have to find other resources to use instead. Some renewable resources, such as water, may also be considered nonrenewable if they are not used wisely.

> **i Think Outside the Book**
>
> **7 Claims • Evidence • Reasoning**
> Make a claim about why water can be a renewable or nonrenewable resource. Summarize evidence to support each claim and explain your reasoning to a classmate.

8 Compare List some examples of renewable and nonrenewable resources.

Renewable Resources	Nonrenewable Resources

Natural fibers from cotton plants are processed to make fabric.

B

Material World

How do we use natural resources?

When you turn on a computer, take a shower, or eat food, you are using natural resources. A variety of natural resources are used to make common objects. The energy required for many of the activities that we do also comes from natural resources. Earth's natural resources can be divided into material resources and energy resources depending on how the resource is used.

ACTIVE **READING**

9 Identify As you read, underline examples of material resources and energy resources.

○ As Material Resources

A **material resource** is a natural resource that humans use to make objects or to consume as food or drink. These resources can come from Earth's atmosphere, crust, fresh waters and oceans, and from organisms, such as plants and animals.

Earth's atmosphere provides the oxygen needed by plants and animals, including humans. Minerals and rock in Earth's crust are used for construction and other industries. Salt, a mineral, comes from ocean water. Fresh water sources and the oceans provide drinking water and food. Some plants, such as cotton, produce fibers that are woven into cloth or braided into ropes. Trees supply fruit crops, lumber, and paper. The sap of some trees is used to make rubber and maple syrup. Animals provide meat, leather, and dairy and egg products.

10 State Your Claim Make a claim about what other items you can think of are made of wood.

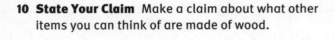

Trees are a material resource when they are used to make products, such as this guitar.

As Energy Resources

Energy resources drive the world. An **energy resource** is a natural resource that humans use to generate energy. Most of the energy used by humans comes from fossil fuels. When fossil fuels are burned, they release energy, usually in the form of heat. Power plants and machines use that heat to produce mechanical and electrical energy. In turn, electrical energy is used to power lights and most of the appliances we use every day.

Other energy resources include moving water, solar power, and wind power. Trees supply fuel in the form of heat. Horses, camels, and other animals are used as transportation in some places. All of these resources are renewable energy resources.

Trees are energy resources when they are burned in a campfire.

👁 Visualize It!

11 Claims • Evidence • Reasoning
Make a claim about what two types of energy are generated from fire. Summarize evidence to support each claim and explain your reasoning to a classmate.

_____

_____

12 List Think about all the products you use every day. Fill in the chart with three of these products and the resources needed to make them or use them.

Product	Material and Energy Resources Needed
computer	plastic, metal, glass, electricity

Visual Summary

To complete this summary, circle the correct word. You can use this page to review the main concepts of the lesson.

Natural resources can be categorized as nonrenewable resources or renewable resources depending on how quickly they can be replaced.

13 Bauxite is a nonrenewable / renewable resource.

14 Cotton plants are a nonrenewable / renewable resource.

Natural Resources

A material resource can be used to make objects or to consume as food or drink. An energy resource is used to generate energy.

15 Trees that are used to make paper products are material resources / energy resources.

16 **Claims • Evidence • Reasoning** Make a claim about how a natural resource could be used as both a material resource and an energy resource. Summarize evidence to support your claim providing examples of each. Explain your reasoning.

Lesson Review

Vocabulary

Fill in the blank with the term that best completes the following sentences.

1 Nonrenewable and renewable are the two categories of _____.

2 A(n) _____ can be used to make objects.

Key Concepts

3 Evaluate Why are natural resources important to humans? Explain your reasoning.

_____

_____

_____

_____

4 Identify Give one example of a material resource and one example of an energy resource.

_____

_____

_____

5 Claims • Evidence • Reasoning Make a claim about how nonrenewable resources and renewable resources differ. Provide evidence to support your claim and explain your reasoning.

_____

_____

_____

_____

_____

6 List Name two material resources, one renewable and one nonrenewable. Explain your answer.

_____

_____

_____

Critical Thinking

Use the graph to answer the following three questions.

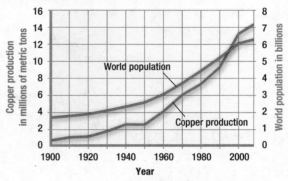

World Copper Production, 1900–2004

Sources: U.S. Bureau of Mines, U.S. Geological Survey, and U.S. Census Bureau

7 Interpret In what year was the most copper produced?

_____

8 Claims • Evidence • Reasoning Make a claim about the trend in copper production over the past 100 years. Use evidence to support your claim and explain your reasoning.

_____

_____

_____

9 State Your Claim Copper is used in making electronic devices. Make a claim about how the use of copper might change as copper becomes more scarce.

_____

_____

_____

10 Claims • Evidence • Reasoning Make a claim about how human activity affects Earth's natural resources. Provide evidence to support your claim.

_____

_____

_____

Lesson 1 Natural Resources **247**

Human Impact on Land

ESSENTIAL QUESTION

What impact can human activities have on land resources?

By the end of this lesson, you should be able to identify the impact that human activity has on Earth's land.

Human activities can carve up land features. A tunnel was cut into this mountain in Zion National Park, Utah, so that people may move around easily.

SC.7.E.6.6 Identify the impact that humans have had on Earth, such as deforestation, urbanization, desertification, erosion, air and water quality, changing the flow of water.

Lesson Labs

Quick Labs
• Debating Human Impact
• Roots and Erosion

Engage Your Brain

1 Predict Check T or F to show whether you think each statement is true or false.

T	F	
☐	☐	Urban areas have more open land than rural areas do.
☐	☐	Many building materials are made from land resources.
☐	☐	Soil provides habitat for plants but not animals.
☐	☐	Soil can erode when trees are removed from an area.

2 Illustrate Draw a picture of an object or material that is taken from the land and that is commercially important.

ACTIVE READING

3 Synthesize You can often define an unknown word if you know the meaning of its word parts. Use the word parts to make an educated guess about the meaning of the words *land degradation* and *deforestation*.

Word part	Meaning
degrade	to damage something
deforest	to remove trees from an area
-ation	action or process

Vocabulary Terms
• urbanization
• land degradation
• desertification
• deforestation

4 Apply As you learn the definition of each vocabulary term in this lesson, create your own definition or sketch to help you remember the meaning of the term.

land degradation:

_____

_____

deforestation:

_____

_____

Land of Plenty

Why is land important?

It is hard to imagine human life without land. Land supplies a solid surface for buildings and roads. The soil in land provides nutrients for plants and hiding places for animals. Minerals below the land's surface can be used for construction materials. Fossil fuels underground can be burned to provide energy. Land and its resources affect every aspect of human life.

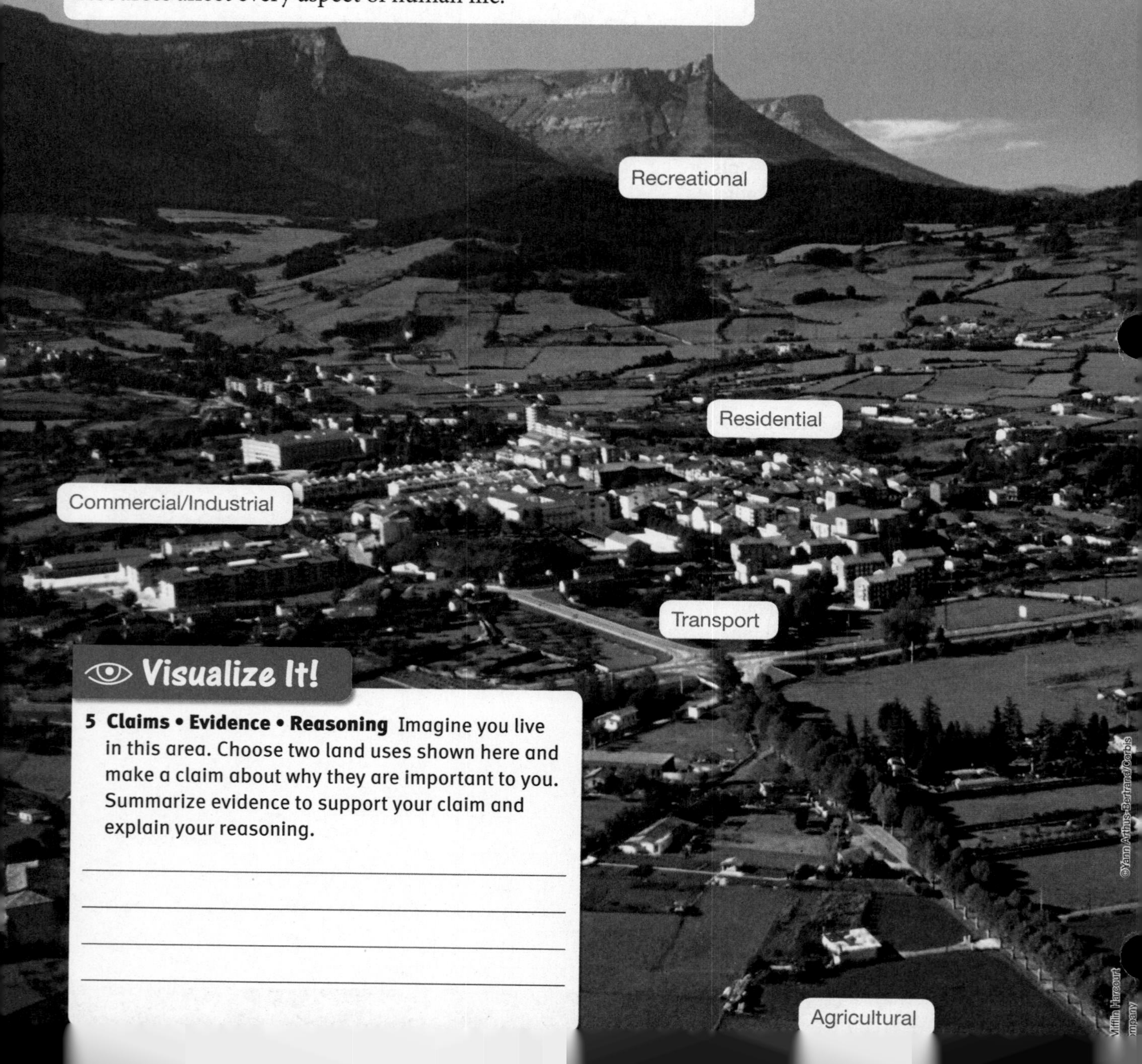

Recreational

Residential

Commercial/Industrial

Transport

Agricultural

👁 Visualize It!

5 Claims • Evidence • Reasoning Imagine you live in this area. Choose two land uses shown here and make a claim about why they are important to you. Summarize evidence to support your claim and explain your reasoning.

_____

_____

_____

_____

Mifflin Harcourt Company

What are the different types of land use?

We live on land in urban or rural areas. Cities and towns are urban areas. Rural areas are open lands that may be used for farming. Humans use land in many ways. We use natural areas for *recreation*. We use roads that are built on land for *transport*. We grow crops and raise livestock on *agricultural* land. We live in *residential* areas. We build *commercial* businesses on land and extract resources such as metals and water from the land.

Recreational

Natural areas are places that humans have left alone or restored to a natural state. These wild places include forests, grasslands, and desert areas. People use natural areas for hiking, bird-watching, mountain-biking, hunting, and other fun or recreational activities.

Transport

A large network of roads and train tracks connect urban and rural areas all across the country. Roads in the U.S. highway system cover 4 million miles of land. Trucks carry goods on these highways and smaller vehicles carry passengers. Railroads carrying freight or passengers use over 120,000 miles of land for tracks. Roads and train tracks are often highly concentrated in urban areas.

Agricultural

Much of the open land in rural areas is used for agriculture. Crops such as corn, soybeans, and wheat are grown on large, open areas of land. Land is also needed to raise and feed cattle and other livestock. Agricultural land is open, but very different from the natural areas that it has replaced. Farmland generally contains only one or two types of plants, such as corn or cotton. Natural grasslands, forests, and other natural areas contain many species of plants and animals.

ACTIVE READING

6 Identify As you read, underline the ways rural areas differ from urban areas.

Residential

Where do you call home? People live in both rural and urban areas. Rural areas have large areas of open land and low densities of people. Urban areas have dense human populations and small areas of open land. This means that more people live in a square km of an urban area than live in a square km of a rural area. **Urbanization** is the growth of urban areas caused by people moving into cities. When cities increase in size, the population of rural areas near the city may decrease. When an area becomes urbanized, its natural land surface is replaced by buildings, parking lots, and roads. City parks, which contain natural surfaces, may also be built in urban areas.

Commercial and Industrial

As cities or towns expand, commercial businesses are built too, and replace rural or natural areas. Industrial businesses also use land resources. For example, paper companies and furniture manufacturers use wood from trees harvested on forest land. Cement companies, fertilizer manufacturers, and steel manufacturers use minerals that are mined from below the land's surface. Commercial and industrial development usually includes development of roads or railways. Transporting goods to market forms the basis of commerce.

ACTIVE READING

7 Identify What effects does urbanization have on land?

_____

_____

_____

_____

_____

_____

_____

Why is soil important?

Soil is a mixture of mineral fragments, organic material, water, and air. Soil forms when rocks break down and dead organisms decay. There are many reasons why soil is important. Soil provides habitat for organisms such as plants, earthworms, fungi, and bacteria. Many plants get the water and nutrients they need from the soil. Because plants form the base of food webs, healthy soil is important for most land ecosystems. Healthy soil is also important for agricultural land, which supplies humans with food.

ACTIVE READING

8 Identify As you read, underline the ways that soil is important to plants.

It Is a Habitat for Organisms

Earthworms, moles, badgers, and other burrowing animals live in soil. These animals also find food underground. *Decomposers* are organisms that break down dead animal and plant material, releasing the nutrients into the soil. Decomposers such as fungi and bacteria live in soil. Soil holds plant roots in place, providing support for the plant. In turn, plants are food for herbivores and are habitats for organisms such as birds and insects. Many animals on Earth depend on soil for shelter or food.

It Stores Water and Nutrients

Falling rain soaks into soil and is stored between soil particles. Different types of soil can store different amounts of water. Wetland soils, for example, store large amounts of water and reduce flooding. Soils are also part of the nutrient cycle. Plants take up nutrients and water stored in soil. Plants and animals that eat them die and are broken down by decomposers such as bacteria and earthworms. Nutrients are released back into the soil and the cycle starts again.

👁 Visualize It!

Nutrients Cycle between Soil and Organisms

Earthworm

Decomposers such as earthworms break down dead organisms, releasing nutrients into the soil.

Plant roots take up nutrients, which they need to live and grow.

9 Relate A chemical spill kills many of the decomposers in the soil. How might it affect nutrient cycles in the soil?

_____

_____

Dust Bowl

In the 1930s, huge clouds of dusty soil rolled across the southern Great Plains of the United States. Areas that were once farmlands and homesteads were wiped out. What caused the soil to blow away?

Drought and Overuse

Farmers who settled in the southern Great Plains overplowed and overgrazed their land. When severe drought hit in 1931, topsoil dried out. Winds lifted the soil and carried it across the plains in huge storms that farmers called "black blizzards." The drought and dust storms continued for years.

Modern Day Dust Bowl

Today in northwest China another dust bowl is forming. Large areas of farmland were made there by clearing the natural vegetation and plowing the soil. Herds of sheep and cattle are overgrazing the land, and large dust storms are common.

Extend

10 Identify What type of land use by people contributed to the Dust Bowl? Does it remain a common use of land today?

11 Claims • Evidence • Reasoning Research another area under threat from overuse. Make a claim about what is causing the problem. Summarize evidence to explain your reasoning.

12 Illustrate Do one of the following to show how the Dust Bowl or the area you researched affected society: make a poster, write a play, write a song, or draw a cartoon strip. Present your findings to the class.

Footprints

How can human activities affect land and soil?

Human activities can have positive and negative effects on land and soil. Some activities restore land to its natural state, or increase the amount of fertile soil on land. Other activities can degrade land. **Land degradation** is the process by which human activity and natural processes damage land to the point that it can no longer support the local ecosystem. Urbanization, deforestation, and poor farming practices can all lead to land degradation.

ⓘ Think Outside the Book

13 Claims • Evidence • Reasoning
Make a claim about how you could help lessen the impact of urbanization on the land in the area where you live. Summarize evidence to support the claim and explain your reasoning.

ACTIVE READING

14 Identify As you read, underline the effects that urbanization can have on land.

◯ Urban Sprawl

When urbanization occurs at the edge of a city or town, it is called *urban sprawl*. Urban sprawl replaces forests, fields, and grasslands with houses, roads, schools, and shopping areas. Urban sprawl decreases the amount of farmland that is available for growing crops. It decreases the amount of natural areas that surround cities. It increases the amount of asphalt and concrete that covers the land. Rainwater runs off hard surfaces and into storm drains instead of soaking into the ground and filling aquifers. Rainwater runoff from urban areas can increase the erosion of nearby soils.

◯ Erosion

Erosion (ih•ROH•zhuhn) is the process by which wind, water, or gravity transports soil and sediment from one place to another. Some type of erosion occurs on most land. However, erosion can speed up when land is degraded. Roots of trees and plants act as anchors to the soil. When land is cleared for farming, the trees and plants are removed and the soil is no longer protected. This exposes soil to blowing wind and running water that can wash away the soil, as shown in this photo.

(btg) ©Skip ODonnell/iStockPhoto/Getty Images Plus/Getty Images; (r) ©John Humble/Photographer's Choice/Getty Images

© Houghton Mifflin Harcourt Publishing Company

Nutrient Depletion and Land Pollution

Crops use soil nutrients to grow. If the same crops are planted year after year, the same soil nutrients get used up. Plants need the right balance of nutrients to grow. Farmers can plant a different crop each year to reduce nutrient loss. Pollution from industrial activities can damage land. Mining wastes, gas and petroleum leaks, and chemical wastes can kill organisms in the soil. U.S. government programs such as Superfund help to clean up polluted land.

Desertification

When too many livestock are kept in one area, they can overgraze the area. Overgrazing removes the plants and roots that hold topsoil together. Overgrazing and other poor farming methods can cause desertification. **Desertification** (dih•zer•tuh•fih•KAY•shuhn) is the process by which land becomes more desertlike and unable to support life. Without plants, soil becomes dusty and prone to wind erosion. Deforestation and urbanization can also lead to desertification.

Deforestation

The removal of trees and other vegetation from an area is called **deforestation**. Logging for wood can cause deforestation. Surface mining causes deforestation by removing vegetation and soil to get to the minerals below. Deforestation also occurs in rain forests, as shown in the photo, when farmers cut or burn down trees so they can grow crops. Urbanization can cause deforestation when forests are replaced with buildings. Deforestation leads to increased soil erosion.

👁 Visualize It!

15 Claims • Evidence • Reasoning Make a claim about how human activity affected the forest in this photo. Use evidence to support your claim and explain your reasoning.

_____
_____
_____
_____
_____

Visual Summary

To complete this summary, circle the correct word or phrase.
You can use this page to review the main concepts of the lesson.

Humans use land in different ways.

16 Crops are grown on recreational/agricultural land.

Human Impact on Land

Soil is important to all organisms, including humans.

17 Decomposers/Plants that live in soil break down dead matter in the soil.

Human activities can affect land and soil

18 Poor farming practices and drought can lead to desertification/urbanization.

19 Claims • Evidence • Reasoning Make a claim about how concentrating human populations in cities help to conserve agricultural and recreational land. Summarize evidence to support your claim and explain your reasoning.

Lesson Review

Vocabulary

Draw a line to connect the following terms to their definitions.

1 urbanization

2 deforestation

3 land degradation

4 desertification

A the removal of trees and other vegetation from an area

B the process by which land becomes more desertlike

C the process by which human activity can damage land

D the formation and growth of cities

Key Concepts

5 Contrast How are natural areas different from rural areas?

_____

_____

_____

_____

6 Relate How might deforestation lead to desertification?

_____

_____

_____

_____

7 Claims • Evidence • Reasoning Think of an animal that eats other animals. Make a claim about why soil would be important to this animal. Provide evidence to support your claim and explain your reasoning.

_____

_____

_____

_____

Critical Thinking

Use this photo to answer the following questions.

8 Analyze What type of land degradation is occurring in this photo?

_____

_____

9 Claims • Evidence • Reasoning The type of soil damage shown in the photo can also occur in urban areas. Make a claim about how urbanization could lead to this type of degradation. Summarize evidence to support your claim and explain your reasoning.

_____

_____

_____

_____

_____

_____

10 Apply What kinds of land uses are around your school? Write down each type of land use. Then describe how one of these land uses might affect natural systems.

_____

_____

_____

_____

_____

SC.7.E.6.6 Identify the impact that humans have had on Earth, such as deforestation, urbanization, desertification, erosion, air and water quality, changing the flow of water.

Angel Montoya

CONSERVATION BIOLOGIST

In 1990, Angel Montoya was a student intern working at Laguna Atascosa National Wildlife Refuge in Texas. He became interested in the Aplomado falcon, a bird of prey that disappeared from the southwestern United States during the first half of the 20th century. Montoya decided to go looking for the raptors. He found a previously unknown population of Aplomados in Chihuahua, Mexico. His work helped to make it possible for the falcons to be reintroduced to an area near El Paso, Texas.

Restoration of the Aplomado falcon became Angel's lifework. He has monitored and researched the falcon since 1992. He helps release falcons that have been raised in captivity back into the wild and monitors falcons that have already been released. It isn't easy to keep tabs on a falcon, however. "Their first year they are pretty vulnerable, because they haven't had parents," Montoya says. "Just like juveniles, they're always getting into trouble. But I think they will do just fine."

Angel Montoya releases an Aplomado falcon back into the wild.

JOB BOARD

Environmental Engineering Technician

What You'll Do: Work closely with environmental engineers and scientists to prevent or fix environmental damage. Take care of water and wastewater treatment systems, as well as equipment used for recycling. Test water and air quality and keep good records.

Where You Might Work: In a water treatment facility, or an environmental laboratory.

Education: an associate's degree in engineering technology.

Other Job Requirements: Good communication skills and the ability to work well with others.

Agronomist

What You'll Do: Study the best ways to grow crops and work with farmers to help them use their land better, and get better yields. Agronomists are scientists who study crops and soil.

Where You Might Work: On a farm, in an agricultural business, for the U.S. Department of Agriculture or state or local government agencies, or for seed companies. Agronomists may work both in fields and in laboratories.

Education: a four-year college degree in agronomy, agriculture, or soil conservation.

YUMI Someya

Fueling the Family Business

Yumi Someya's family had worked in recycling for three generations, cleaning and recycling used cooking oil. In Japan, many people enjoy fried foods. They often throw out the used cooking oil. Yumi's family business collected used oil, cleaned it, and sold it for reuse.

When Yumi traveled to Nepal, she was caught in a landslide. She learned that deforestation was one cause of the landslide and began to think about environmental issues. When she returned home, she worked with her father to find new uses for the used cooking oil. They experimented with fertilizer and soap. Then, in 1992, they learned about biodiesel—fuel made from recycled soybean oil. They thought that used cooking oil might work to fuel cars, too. With a team of researchers, they created Vegetable Diesel Fuel (VDF).

Now, VDF fuels the company's oil-collecting trucks and some Tokyo buses. Yumi hopes to eventually recycle all of the cooking oil used in Japan.

Publishing Company

Human Impact on Water

ESSENTIAL QUESTION

What impact can human activities have on water resources?

By the end of this lesson, you should be able to explain the impacts that humans can have on the quality and supply of fresh water.

Humans and other organisms depend on clean water to survive. More than half of the material inside humans is water.

SC.7.E.6.6 Identify the impact that humans have had on Earth, such as deforestation, urbanization, desertification, erosion, air and water quality, changing the flow of water.

Lesson Labs

Quick Labs
- Ocean Pollution from Land
- Turbidity and Water Temperature
- Modeling Groundwater

Exploration Lab
- Filtering Water

Engage Your Brain

1 Analyze Write a list of the reasons humans need water. Next to this list, write a list of reasons fish need water. Are there similarities between your two lists?

2 Identify Circle the word that correctly completes the following sentences. The man in this photo is testing *water/air* quality. The flowing body of water next to the man is a *river/lake*.

ACTIVE READING

3 Synthesize You can often define an unknown word if you know the meaning of its word parts. Use the word parts and the sentence below to make an educated guess about the meaning of the word *nonrenewable*.

Word part	Meaning
renew	restore, make like new
-able	able to be
non-	not

Example sentence
Some of Earth's <u>nonrenewable</u> resources include coal and oil.

nonrenewable:

_____

_____

_____

_____

_____

Vocabulary Terms

- **water pollution**
- **point-source pollution**
- **nonpoint-source pollution**
- **thermal pollution**
- **eutrophication**
- **potable**
- **reservoir**

4 Identify This list contains the key terms you'll learn in this lesson. As you read, circle the definition of each term.

Close up of a
mayfly larva

Water, Water

Organisms need clean water for life
and good health. For example, young
mayflies live in water, humans drink
water, and brown pelicans eat fish
they catch in water.

Why is water important?

Earth is the only planet with large amounts of water. Water
shapes Earth's surface and affects Earth's weather and climates.
Most importantly, water is vital for life. Every living thing is
made mostly of water. Most life processes use water. Water is an
important natural resource. For humans and other organisms,
access to clean water is important for good health.

There is lots of water, so what's the problem?

About 97% of Earth's water is salty, which leaves only 3% as fresh
water. However, as you can see from the graph, over two-thirds of
Earth's fresh water is frozen as ice and snow. But a lot of the liquid
water seeps into the ground as groundwater. That leaves much
less than 1% of Earth's fresh liquid water on the surface. Water is
vital for people, so this small volume of fresh surface water and
groundwater is a limited resource.

Areas with high densities of people, such as cities, need lots
of fresh water. Cities are getting bigger, and so the need for fresh
water is increasing. *Urbanization* (ER•buh•ny•zhay•shuhn) is
the growth of towns and cities that results from the movement of
people from rural areas into the urban areas. The greater demand
for fresh water in cities is threatening the availability of water for
many people. Fresh water is becoming a natural resource that
cannot be replaced at the same rate at which it is used.

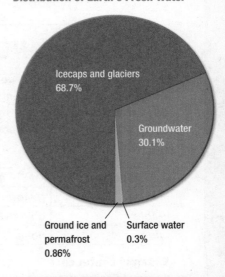

Distribution of Earth's Fresh Water

- Icecaps and glaciers 68.7%
- Groundwater 30.1%
- Ground ice and permafrost 0.86%
- Surface water 0.3%

👁 Visualize It!

5 Gather Evidence What
percentage of fresh water on
Earth is frozen? What percentage
of fresh water is liquid?

_____

_____

(bkgd) ©Luigi Masella/Flickr/Getty Images; (l) ©blickwinkel/Alamy; (c) ©Biggie Productions/Taxi/ © Houghton Mifflin Harcourt

Everywhere...

Where do we get fresh water?

Fresh water may fall directly as precipitation, or may melt from ice and snow. Earth's fresh liquid water is found as surface water and groundwater. *Surface water* is any body of water above the ground. It includes liquid salt or fresh water, or solid water, like snow and ice. Water may seep below the surface to become *groundwater*. Groundwater is found under Earth's surface, in spaces in rocks or in soil, where it can be liquid or frozen.

Aquifers and Groundwater

Aquifers and ground ice are forms of groundwater. An *aquifer* is a body of rock or sediment that can store a lot of water, and that allows water to flow easily through it. Aquifers store water in spaces, called *pores,* between particles of rock or sediment. Wells are dug into aquifers to reach the water. In polar regions, water is often frozen in a layer of soil called *permafrost.*

Rivers, Streams, and Lakes

Rivers, streams, and most lakes are fresh surface waters. A stream or river may flow into a bowl-shaped area, which may fill up to form a lake. Many millions of people around the world depend on fresh water that is taken from rivers and fresh water lakes.

What are water quality and supply?

Water quality is a measure of how clean or polluted water is. Water quality is important because humans and other organisms depend on clean water to survive. It is vital for living things to not only have water, but also to have clean water. Dirty, contaminated water can make us sick or even kill us.

   Water supply is the availability of water. Water supply influences where and when farmers grow crops, and where people can build cities. *Water supply systems* carry water from groundwater or surface waters so people can use the water. The systems can be a network of underground pipes, or a bucket for scooping water from a well. A shortage of clean, fresh water reduces quality of life for people. Many people in developing countries do not have access to clean, fresh water.

ACTIVE READING

6 List What are the different sources of fresh water?

_____

_____

ⓘ Think Outside the Book

7 Claims • Evidence • Reasoning
Keep a water diary for a day. Record every time you use water. At the end of the day, make a claim about how you could reduce your water usage. Summarize evidence to support the claim and explain your reasoning.

Many people do not have a water supply to their homes. Instead, they have to go to a local stream, well, or pump to gather water for cooking, cleaning, and drinking.

Under Threat

What threatens fresh water quality?

When waste or other material is added to water so that it is harmful to organisms that use it or live in it, **water pollution** (WAW•ter puh•LOO•shuhn) occurs. It is useful to divide pollution sources into two types. **Point-source pollution** comes from one specific site. For example, a major chemical spill is point-source pollution. Usually this type of pollution can be controlled once its source is found. **Nonpoint-source pollution** comes from many small sources and is more difficult to control. Most nonpoint-source pollution reaches water supplies by runoff or by seeping into groundwater. The main sources of nonpoint-source pollution are city streets, roads and drains, farms, and mines.

ACTIVE **READING**

8 Identify As you read, underline the sources of water pollution.

Thermal Pollution

Any heating of natural water that results from human activity is called **thermal pollution**. For example, water that is used for cooling some power plants gets warmed up. When that water is returned to the river or lake it is at a higher temperature than the lake or river water. The warm water has less oxygen available for organisms that live in the water.

Chemical Pollution

Chemical pollution occurs when harmful chemicals are added to water supplies. Two major sources of chemical pollution are industry and agriculture. For example, refineries that process oil or metals and factories that make metal or plastic products or electronic items all produce toxic chemical waste. Chemicals used in agriculture include pesticides, herbicides, and fertilizers. These pollutants can reach water supplies by seeping into groundwater. Once in groundwater, the pollution can enter the water cycle and can be carried far from the pollution source. *Acid rain* is another form of chemical pollution. It forms when gases formed by burning fossil fuels mix with water in the air. Acid rain can harm both plants and animals. It can lower the pH of soil and water, and make them too acidic for life.

Biological Pollution

Many organisms naturally live in and around water, but they are not normally polluters. *Biological pollution* occurs when live or dead organisms are added to water supplies. Wastewater may contain disease-causing microbes from human or animal wastes. *Wastewater* is any water that has been used by people for such things as flushing toilets, showering, or washing dishes. Wastewater from feed lots and farms may also contain harmful microbes. These microbes can cause diseases such as dysentery, typhoid, or cholera.

Eutrophication

Fresh water often contains nutrients from decomposing organisms. An increase in the amount of nutrients in water is called **eutrophication** (yoo•TRAWF•ih•kay•shuhn). Eutrophication occurs naturally in water. However, *artificial eutrophication* occurs when human activity increases nutrient levels in water. Wastewater and fertilizer runoff that get into waterways can add extra nutrients that upset the natural biology of the water. These extra nutrients cause the fast growth of algae over the water surface. An overgrowth of algae and aquatic plants can reduce oxygen levels and kill fish and other organisms in the water.

Water can become polluted by human activities in many different ways.

Chemical Pollution
Sulfur in smoke and vehicle exhausts contributes to the acidification of rain, leading to acid rain. Acid rain can affect areas far from the point of pollution.

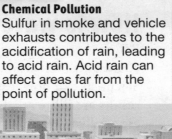

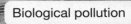

Biological pollution

Biological Pollution
Animal and human wastes can get washed into a water supply in runoff, or through leaking pipes.

Thermal pollution

Eutrophication

Chemical pollution

9 Claims • Evidence • Reasoning Make a claim about how human activity is impacting water quality in this image. Summarize evidence to support the claim and explain your reasoning.

_____

_____

_____

10 Apply Identify one point source and one nonpoint source of pollution in this image.

_____

_____

_____

_____

How is water quality measured?

Before there were scientific methods of testing water, people could only look at water, taste it, and smell it to check its quality. Scientists can now test water with modern equipment, so the results are more reliable. Modern ways of testing water are especially important for finding small quantities of toxic chemicals or harmful organisms in water.

Water is a good solvent. So, water in nature usually contains dissolved solids, such as salt and other substances. Because most dissolved solids cannot be seen, it is important to measure them. Measurements of water quality include testing the levels of dissolved oxygen, pH, temperature, dissolved solids, and the number and types of microbes in the water. Quality standards depend on the intended use for the water. For example, drinking water needs to meet much stricter quality standards than environmental waters such as river or lake waters do.

Water Quality Measurement

Quality measurement	What is it?	How it relates to water quality
Dissolved solids	a measure of the amount of ions or microscopic suspended solids in water	Some dissolved solids could be harmful chemicals. Others such as calcium could cause scaling or build-up in water pipes.
pH	a measure of how acidic or alkaline water is	Aquatic organisms need a near neutral pH (approx. pH 7). Acid rain can drop the pH too low (acidic) for aquatic life to live.
Dissolved oxygen (DO)	the amount of oxygen gas that is dissolved in water	Aquatic organisms need oxygen. Animal waste and thermal pollution can decrease the amount of oxygen dissolved in water.
Turbidity	a measure of the cloudiness of water that is caused by suspended solids	High turbidity increases the chance that harmful microbes or chemicals are in the water.
Microbial load	the identification of harmful bacteria, viruses or protists in water	Microbes such as bacteria, viruses, and protists from human and animal wastes can cause diseases.

11 State Your Claim Make a claim about the relationship between increased turbidity and the likelihood of something harmful being in the water.

_____

How is water treated for human use?

ACTIVE READING

12 Identify As you read, number the basic steps in the water treatment process.

Natural water may be unsafe for humans to drink. So, water that is to be used as drinking water is treated to remove harmful chemicals and organisms. Screens take out large debris. Then chemicals are added that make suspended particles stick together. These particles drop out of the water in a process called *flocculation*. Flocculation also removes harmful bacteria and other microbes. Chlorine is often added to kill microbes left in the water. In some cities, fluoride is added to water supplies to help prevent tooth decay. Finally, air is bubbled through the water. Water that is suitable to drink is called **potable** water. Once water is used, it becomes wastewater. It enters the sewage system where pipes carry it to a wastewater treatment plant. There the wastewater is cleaned and filtered before being released back into the environment.

Drinking water is often mixed in large basins to help remove chemicals and harmful organisms. Paddles stir the water in the basins.

Who monitors and protects our water quality?

ACTIVE READING

13 Identify As you read, underline the government agency that is responsible for enforcing water quality rules.

If a public water supply became contaminated, many people could get very sick. As a result, public water supplies are closely monitored so that any problems can be fixed quickly. The Safe Drinking Water Act is the main federal law that ensures safe drinking water for people in the United States. The act sets strict limits on the amount of heavy metals or certain types of bacteria that can be in drinking water, among other things. The Environmental Protection Agency (EPA) has the job of enforcing this law. It is responsible for setting the standards drinking water must meet before the water can be pumped into public water systems. Water quality tests can be done by trained workers or trained volunteers.

Samples of water are routinely taken to make sure the water quality meets the standards required by law.

© Houghton Mifflin Harcourt Publishing Company

(t) ©Lawrence Migdale/Photo Researchers, Inc.; (b) ©Will & Deni McIntyre/Photo Researchers, Inc.

Supply and Demand

How does water get to the faucet?

In earlier times, humans had to live near natural sources of fresh water. Over time, engineers developed ways to transport and store large amounts of water. So, humans can now live in places where fresh water is supplied by water pipes and other infrastructure. The ability to bring fresh water safely from its source to a large population has led to the urbanization of cities.

○ Creating Water Supply Systems

Freshwater supply is often limited, so we have found ways to store and transport water far from its source to where it is used. Surface water is collected and pumped to places where people need it. Groundwater can be found by digging wells into aquifers. Water can be lifted from a well by hand in buckets. It can be pumped into pipes that supply homes, farms, factories and cities. Piped water supply systems can deliver water over great distances to where humans need it. Water supply and storage systems are expensive to build and maintain.

👁 Visualize It!

A public water supply includes the water source, the treatment facilities, and the pipes and pumps that send it to homes, industries, businesses, and public facilities.

Water treatment and distribution

A Water can be moved far away from its source by pumping it through pipes to large urban areas.

Intake

Chemicals added

Lake

Tunnels

Mixing basins

Settling basins

Water treatment plant

B Water is treated to make it potable.

◯ Changing the Flow of Water

Pumping and collecting groundwater and surface waters changes how water flows in natural systems. For example, a **reservoir** (REZ•uhr•vwohr) is a body of water that usually forms behind a dam. Dams stop river waters from flowing along their natural course. The water in a reservoir would naturally have flowed to the sea. Instead, the water can be diverted into a pipeline or into artificial channels called *canals* or *aqueducts*.

What threatens our water supply?

ACTIVE READING

14 Identify As you read, underline the things that are a threat to water supply.

As the human use of water has increased, the demand for fresh water has also increased. Demand is greater than supply in many areas of the world, including parts of the United States. The larger a population or a city gets, the greater the demand for fresh water. Increased demand for and use of water can cause water shortages. Droughts or leaking water pipes can also cause water shortages. Water is used to keep our bodies clean and healthy. It is also used to grow crops for food. Water shortages threaten these benefits.

15 Infer Why would a larger city have a larger demand for water? Explain your reasoning.

_____
_____
_____
_____
_____
_____

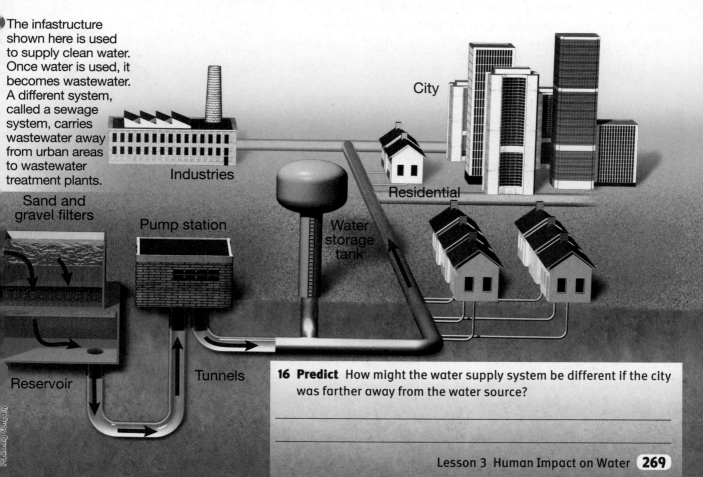

The infastructure shown here is used to supply clean water. Once water is used, it becomes wastewater. A different system, called a sewage system, carries wastewater away from urban areas to wastewater treatment plants.

Industries

City

Residential

Sand and gravel filters

Pump station

Water storage tank

Reservoir

Tunnels

16 Predict How might the water supply system be different if the city was farther away from the water source?

_____
_____

How do efforts to supply water to humans affect the environment?

Growing urban populations place a greater demand on water supplies. Efforts to increase water supply can affect the environment. For example, building dams and irrigation canals changes the natural flow of water. The environment is physically changed by construction work. The local ecology changes too. Organisms that live in or depend on the water may lose their habitat and move away or die.

Aquifers are often used as freshwater sources for urban areas. When more water is taken from an aquifer than can be replaced by rain or snow, the water table can drop below the reach of existing wells. Rivers and streams may dry up, and the soil that once held aquifer waters may collapse, or *subside*. In coastal areas, the overuse of groundwater can cause seawater to seep into the aquifer in a process called *saltwater intrusion*. In this way, water supplies can become contaminated with salt water.

Increasing population in an area can also affect water quality. The more people who use a water supply in one area, the greater the volume of wastewater that is produced in that area. Pollutants such as oil, pesticides, fertilizers, and heavy metals from city runoff, from industry, and from agriculture may seep into surface waters and groundwater. In this way, pollution could enter the water supply. This pollution could also enter the water cycle and be carried far from the initial source of the pollution.

ACTIVE READING

17 Claims • Evidence • Reasoning Make a claim about how an increased demand on water can affect the water quality. Provide evidence to support your claim and explain your reasoning.

_____

_____

_____

_____

_____

_____

Digging irrigation canals changes the flow of rivers.

Building dams disrupts water flow and affects the ecology of the land and water.

Irrigating arid areas changes the ecology of those areas.

Death of a Sea

The Aral Sea in Central Asia was once the world's fourth-largest inland salty lake. But it has been shrinking since the 1960s. In the 1940s, the courses of the rivers that fed the lake were changed to irrigate the desert, so that crops such as cotton and rice could be grown. By 1997, the lake was down to 20% of its original volume, and down to 10% by 2017. The freshwater flow into the lake was reduced and evaporation caused the lake to become so salty that most of the plants and animals in it died or left the lake.

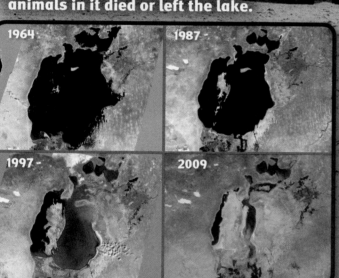

1964 1987 1997 2009

By 2017, only about 10% of the water originally in the Aral Sea remained and had split into several smaller lakes.

Polluted Land

The Aral Sea is also heavily polluted by industrial wastes, pesticides, and fertilizer runoff. Salty dust that is blown from the dried seabed damages crops and pollutes drinking water. The salt- and dust-laden air cause serious public health problems in the Aral Sea region. One of the more bizarre reminders of how large the lake once was are the boats that lie abandoned on the exposed sea floor.

ⓘ Extend

18 Identify What human activity has created the situation in the Aral Sea?

19 Apply Research the impact that of one of these two large water projects has had on people and on the environment: The Three Gorges Dam or the Columbia Basin Project.

20 Claims • Evidence • Reasoning Research a current or past water project in the area where you live. Make a claim about the benefits of the project for people in the area. Make another claim about what risks there might be to the environment. Summarize evidence to support the claim and explain your reasoning.

Visual Summary

To complete this summary, fill in the blanks with the correct word or phrase. You can use this page to review the main concepts of the lesson.

Human Impact on Water

Organisms need clean water for life and good health.

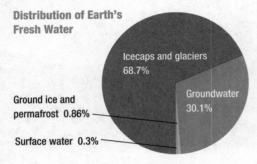

Distribution of Earth's Fresh Water

- Icecaps and glaciers 68.7%
- Groundwater 30.1%
- Ground ice and permafrost 0.86%
- Surface water 0.3%

21 Earth's fresh liquid water is found as surface water and _____

Water pollution can come from many different sources.

22 Runoff from farmland into a river is an example of _____ source pollution.

Federal laws set the standards for potable water quality. Water quality is constantly monitored.

23 Dissolved solids, pH, temperature, and dissolved oxygen are measures of _____.

Ensuring a constant supply of water for people can change the environment.

24 A _____ is a body of water that forms when a dam blocks a river.

25 Claims • Evidence • Reasoning Make a claim about the difference between water quality and water supply. Summarize evidence to support the claim and explain your reasoning.

Lesson Review

Vocabulary

Fill in the blank with the term that best completes the following sentences.

1 _____ water is a term used to describe water that is safe to drink.

2 The addition of nutrients to water by human activity is called artificial _____.

3 _____ pollution comes from many small sources.

Key Concepts

Complete the table below with the type of pollution described in each example.

Example	Type of pollution (chemical, thermal, or biological)
4 Identify A person empties an oil can into a storm drain.	
5 Identify A factory releases warm water into a local river.	
6 Identify Untreated sewage is washed into a lake during a rain storm.	

7 Describe Name two ways in which humans can affect the flow of fresh water.

_____

_____

_____

8 Claims • Evidence • Reasoning Make a claim about why water quality needs to be monitored. Support your claim with evidence and explain your reasoning.

_____

_____

_____

Critical Thinking

Use this graph to answer questions 9 and 10.

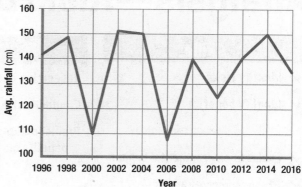

Average Yearly Precipitation in Florida from 1996 to 2016

Source: National Climatic Data Center

9 Analyze Which year had the least precipitation?

_____

10 Infer What effect might many years of low precipitation have on water supply?

_____

_____

11 Claims • Evidence • Reasoning Make a claim about whether a single person or animal could be a cause of point-source pollution. Use evidence to support your claim and explain your reasoning.

_____

_____

_____

_____

12 Claims • Evidence • Reasoning In times of hot, dry, weather, some cities may ban the use of garden sprinklers. Make a claim about why this rule would be made. Summarize evidence to support the claim and explain your reasoning.

_____

_____

_____

S.T.E.M. ENGINEERING & TECHNOLOGY
Analysis—Risk/Benefit

Skills
✔ Identify risks
✔ Identify benefits
Evaluate cost of technology
✔ Evaluate environmental impact
✔ Propose improvements
✔ Propose risk reduction
✔ Compare technologies
✔ Communicate results

Objectives
Research a desalination process.
Conduct a risk/benefit analysis of a desalination process.
Predict actions that may be taken to decrease the risks or improve the benefits of desalination.

Identifying Risks and Benefits of Desalination

Although our planet has a lot of water, vast areas of Earth are dry. Most of the water is too salty to use for drinking or to grow crops. Millions of people struggle to get enough drinking water. Many countries cannot grow enough food because of water shortages. If we could find an inexpensive and safe way to turn salt water into fresh water, people in drier parts of the world could benefit. Fresh water could be used to irrigate crops, and some dry areas could be turned into productive farmland. The removal of salt from salt water is called *desalination*. However, desalination technology is not appropriate for all areas of the world. There are a number of difficulties associated with this technology.

The Sahara Desert

1 Brainstorm What is a benefit of getting fresh water from the sea?

_____

_____

_____

_____

_____

What Methods of Desalination Are Being Tried?

Thousands of desalination facilities exist worldwide. More than a dozen methods of desalination can be used effectively. However, most desalination occurs by the *multistage flash distillation* process. In this method, seawater is boiled so that the water turns to steam, leaving the salt behind. Then the steam is cooled and becomes liquid fresh water. This process must be repeated at different temperatures and pressures to remove as much salt as possible. It takes large amounts of energy to boil the water and run the pressure pumps.

Another desalination method is called *reverse osmosis*. Reverse osmosis uses high pressure to force water through a membrane. This membrane does not allow salt and other substances to pass through. So the liquid on the other side of the membrane is fresh water.

2 Apply What resources does multistage flash distillation require?

_____

_____

_____

_____

3 Claims • Evidence • Reasoning Research two desalination methods. Make a claim about the benefits of each method. Summarize evidence to support the claim and explain your reasoning.

_____

_____

Farmland made possible by irrigation

Reverse osmosis module

Water storage tanks

Desalination facility

🤚 **You Try It!** ⟶

Now it's your turn to research a method of desalination and perform a risk/benefit analysis.

 **You Try It!**

Now it's your turn to more thoroughly research a method of desalination and perform a risk/benefit analysis. You will be comparing your analysis with the work of other class members.

Reverse osmosis desalination plant

① Identify Risks

Choose a desalination method to research. As you learn about your chosen desalination method, write down the risks or challenges this method has. They may be financial, social, or anything else that applies. Also, list the web sites you consulted.

_____

_____

_____

_____

_____

② Identify Benefits

What are the benefits to this method that would make it worth pursuing?

_____

_____

_____

_____

③ Evaluate Environmental Impact

How will this technology affect the land? How will it affect the atmosphere? If salt is returned to the sea, how could it affect marine life?

_____

_____

_____

_____

_____

4 Propose Improvements

What could be done to make this method even better? Can it be combined with another technology or process to enhance its benefits?

_____

_____

_____

5 Propose Risk Reduction

Is there anything that can be done to reduce the risks? Would combining it with another technology or process make it safer?

_____

_____

_____

6 Compare Technology

Discuss your analysis with classmates who chose different technologies. Record the ways in which the method you researched seems better or worse than the methods your classmates researched.

_____

_____

_____

7 Communicate Results

Overall, do you think the desalination method you researched should be used much more than it is? What is its best feature? What recommendations would you make about its use, including where it should be located?

_____

_____

_____

_____

_____

_____

Human Impact on the Atmosphere

ESSENTIAL QUESTION

How do humans impact Earth's atmosphere?

By the end of this lesson, you should be able to identify the impact that humans have had on Earth's atmosphere.

Human activities that involve burning fuels, such as driving vehicles and keeping buildings cool, can cause air pollution.

SC.7.E.6.6 Identify the impact that humans have had on Earth, such as deforestation, urbanization, desertification, erosion, air and water quality, changing the flow of water.

 Lesson Labs

Quick Labs
• Collecting Air-Pollution Particles
• Identifying Noise Pollution
• Concrete versus Vegetation

Engage Your Brain

1 Identify Check T or F to show whether you think each statement is true or false.

T   F

☐   ☐   Human activities can cause air pollution.

☐   ☐   Air pollution cannot affect you if you stay indoors.

☐   ☐   Air pollution does not affect places outside of cities.

☐   ☐   Air pollution can cause lung diseases.

2 Analyze The photo above shows the same city as the photo on the left, but on a different day. How are these photos different?

_____

_____

_____

_____

ACTIVE **READING**

3 Apply Use context clues to write your own definitions for the words *contamination* and *quality*.

Example sentence
You can help prevent food <u>contamination</u> by washing your hands after touching raw meat.

contamination:

_____

_____

_____

Example sentence
The good sound <u>quality</u> coming from the stereo speakers indicated they were expensive.

quality:

_____

_____

_____

Vocabulary Terms

• greenhouse effect
• air pollution
• particulate
• smog
• acid precipitation
• air quality

4 Apply As you learn the definition of each vocabulary term in this lesson, create your own definition or sketch to help you remember the meaning of the term.

AIR
What Is It Good For?

Why is the atmosphere important?

If you were lost in a desert, you could survive a few days without food and water. But you wouldn't last more than a few minutes without air. Air is an important natural resource. The air you breathe forms part of Earth's atmosphere. The *atmosphere* (AT•muh•sfeer) is a mixture of gases that surrounds Earth. Most organisms on Earth have adapted to the natural balance of gases found in the atmosphere.

◯ It Provides Gases That Organisms Need to Survive

Oxygen is one of the gases that make up Earth's atmosphere. It is used by most living cells to get energy from food. Every breath you take brings oxygen into your body. The atmosphere also contains carbon dioxide. Plants need carbon dioxide to make their own food through photosynthesis (foh•toh•SYN•thuh•sys).

◯ It Absorbs Harmful Radiation

High-energy radiation from space would harm life on Earth if it were not blocked by the atmosphere. Fast-moving particles, called *cosmic rays,* enter the atmosphere every second. These particles collide with oxygen, nitrogen, and other gas molecules and are slowed down. A part of the atmosphere called the *stratosphere* contains ozone gas. The ozone layer absorbs most of the high-energy radiation from the sun, called *ultraviolet radiation* (UV), that reaches Earth.

◯ It Keeps Earth Warm

Without the atmosphere, temperatures on Earth would not be stable. It would be too cold for life to exist. The **greenhouse effect** is the way by which certain gases in the atmosphere, such as water vapor and carbon dioxide, absorb and reradiate thermal energy. This slows the loss of energy from Earth into space. The atmosphere acts like a warm blanket that insulates the surface of Earth, preventing the sun's energy from being lost. For this reason, carbon dioxide and water vapor are called *greenhouse gases.*

ACTIVE READING

5 Explain How is Earth's atmosphere similar to a warm blanket?

_____

_____

What is air pollution?

The contamination of the atmosphere by pollutants from human and natural sources is called **air pollution**. Natural sources of air pollution include volcanic eruptions, wildfires, and dust storms. In cities and suburbs, most air pollution comes from the burning of fossil fuels such as oil, gasoline, and coal. Oil refineries, chemical manufacturing plants, dry-cleaning businesses, and auto repair shops are just some potential sources of air pollution. Scientists classify air pollutants as either gases or particulates.

ACTIVE READING

6 Identify As you read, underline sources of air pollution.

👁 Visualize It!

7 Analyze Which one of these images could be both a natural or a human source of air pollution? Explain your reasoning.

_____

_____

_____

_____

_____

Factory emissions

Vehicle exhaust

Forest fires and wildfires

◯ Gases

Gas pollutants include carbon monoxide, sulfur dioxide, nitrogen oxide, and ground-level ozone. Some of these gases occur naturally in the atmosphere. These gases are considered pollutants only when they are likely to cause harm. For example, ozone is important in the stratosphere, but at ground level it is harmful to breathe. Carbon monoxide, sulfur dioxide, and nitrogen dioxide are released from burning fossil fuels in vehicles, factories, and homes. They are a major source of air pollution.

◯ Particulates

Particle pollutants can be easier to see than gas pollutants. A **particulate** (per•TIK•yuh•lit) is a tiny particle of solid that is suspended in air or water. Smoke contains ash, which is a particulate. The wind can pick up particulates such as dust, ash, pollen, and tiny bits of salt from the ocean and blow them far from their source. Ash, dust, and pollen are common forms of air pollution. Vehicle exhaust also contains particulates. The particulates in vehicle exhaust are a major cause of air pollution in cities.

It Stinks!

What pollutants can form from vehicle exhaust?

In urban areas, vehicle exhaust is a common source of air pollution. Gases such as carbon monoxide and particulates such as soot and ash are in exhaust fumes. Vehicle exhaust may also react with other substances in the air. When this happens, new pollutants can form. Ground-level ozone and smog are two types of pollutants that form from vehicle exhaust.

ACTIVE READING

8 Identify As you read, underline how ground-level ozone and smog can form.

◯ Ground-Level Ozone

Ozone in the ozone layer is necessary for life, but ground-level ozone is harmful. It is produced when sunlight reacts with vehicle exhaust and oxygen in the air. You may have heard of "Ozone Action Days" in your community. When such a warning is given, people should limit outdoor activities because ozone can damage their lungs.

◯ Smog

Smog is another type of pollutant formed from vehicle exhaust. **Smog** forms when ground-level ozone and vehicle exhaust react in the presence of sunlight. Smog is a problem in large cities because there are more vehicles on the roads. It can cause lung damage and irritate the eyes and nose. In some cities, there can be enough smog to make a brownish haze over the city.

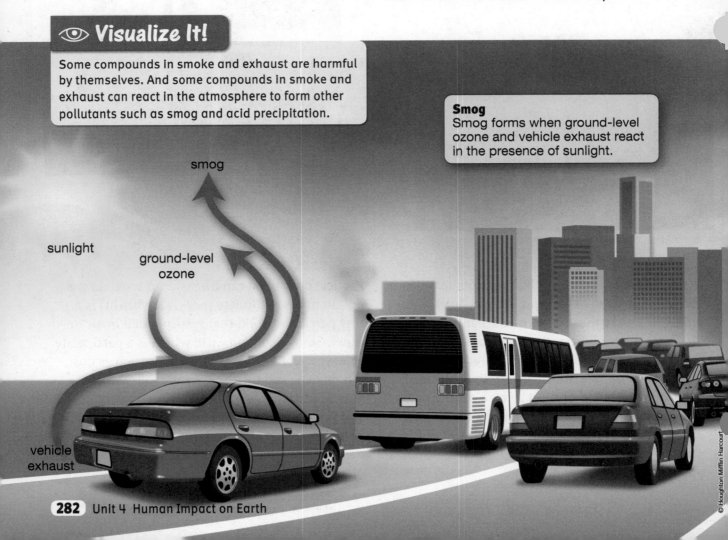

👁 Visualize It!

Some compounds in smoke and exhaust are harmful by themselves. And some compounds in smoke and exhaust can react in the atmosphere to form other pollutants such as smog and acid precipitation.

Smog
Smog forms when ground-level ozone and vehicle exhaust react in the presence of sunlight.

smog

sunlight

ground-level ozone

vehicle exhaust

© Houghton Mifflin Harcourt

How does pollution from human activities produce acid precipitation?

ACTIVE READING

9 Identify As you read, underline how acid precipitation forms.

Precipitation (prih•sip•ih•TAY•shuhn) such as rain, sleet, or snow that contains acids from air pollution is called **acid precipitation**. Burning fossil fuels releases sulfur dioxide and nitrogen oxides into the air. When these gases mix with water in the atmosphere, they form sulfuric acid and nitric acid. Precipitation is naturally slightly acidic. When carbon dioxide in the air and water mix, they form carbonic acid. Carbonic acid is a weak acid. Sulfuric acid and nitric acid are strong acids. They can make precipitation so acidic that it is harmful to the environment.

What are some effects of acid precipitation?

Acid precipitation can cause soil and water to become more acidic than normal. Plants have adapted over long periods of time to the natural acidity of the soils in which they live. When soil acidity rises, some nutrients that plants need are dissolved. These nutrients get washed away by rainwater. Bacteria and fungi that live in the soil are also harmed by acidic conditions.

Acid precipitation may increase the acidity of lakes or streams. It also releases toxic metals from soils. The increased acidity and high levels of metals in water can sicken or kill aquatic organisms. This can disrupt habitats and result in decreased biodiversity in an ecosystem. Acid precipitation can also erode the stonework on buildings and statues.

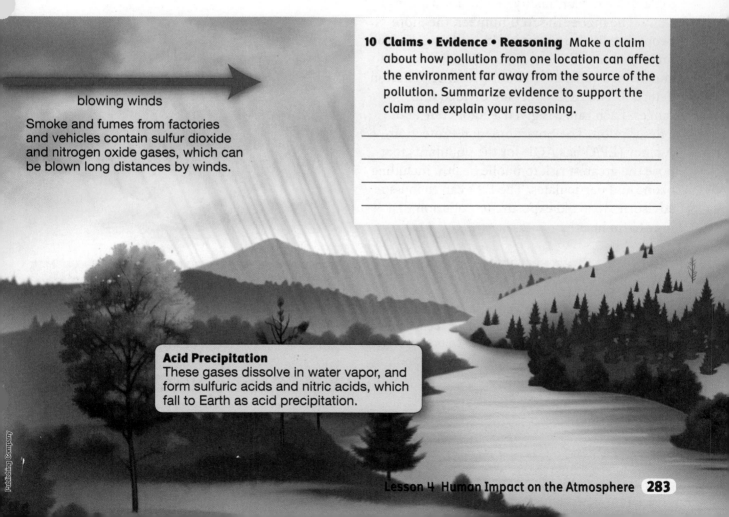

blowing winds

Smoke and fumes from factories and vehicles contain sulfur dioxide and nitrogen oxide gases, which can be blown long distances by winds.

10 Claims • Evidence • Reasoning Make a claim about how pollution from one location can affect the environment far away from the source of the pollution. Summarize evidence to support the claim and explain your reasoning.

_____

_____

_____

_____

Acid Precipitation
These gases dissolve in water vapor, and form sulfuric acids and nitric acids, which fall to Earth as acid precipitation.

Publishing Company

How's the AIR?

What are measures of air quality?

Measuring how clean or polluted the air is tells us about **air quality**. Pollutants reduce air quality. Two major threats to air quality are vehicle exhausts and industrial pollutants. The air quality in cities can be poor. As more people move into cities, the cities get bigger. This leads to increased amounts of human-made pollution. Poor air circulation, such as a lack of wind, allows air pollution to stay in one area where it can build up. As pollution increases, air quality decreases.

◯ Air Quality Index

The Air Quality Index (AQI) is a number used to describe the air quality of a location such as a city. The higher the AQI number, the more people are likely to have health problems that are linked to air pollution. Air quality is measured and given a value based on the level of pollution detected. The AQI values are divided into ranges. Each range is given a color code and a description. The Environmental Protection Agency (EPA) has AQIs for the pollutants that pose the greatest risk to public health, including ozone and particulates. The EPA can then issue advisories to avoid exposure to pollution that may harm health.

Indoor Air Pollution

The air inside a building can become more polluted than the air outside. This is because buildings are insulated to prevent outside air from entering the building. Some sources of indoor air pollution include chlorine and ammonia from household cleaners and formaldehyde from furniture. Harmful chemicals can be released from some paints and glues. Radon is a radioactive gas released when uranium decays. Radon can seep into buildings through gaps in their foundations. It can build up inside well-insulated buildings. *Ventilation*, or the mixing of indoor and outside air, can reduce indoor air pollution. Another way to reduce indoor air pollution is to limit the use of items that create the pollution.

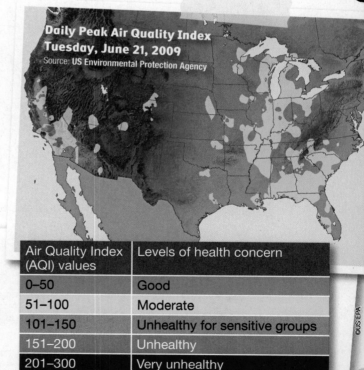

Daily Peak Air Quality Index
Tuesday, June 21, 2009
Source: US Environmental Protection Agency

Air Quality Index (AQI) values	Levels of health concern
0–50	Good
51–100	Moderate
101–150	Unhealthy for sensitive groups
151–200	Unhealthy
201–300	Very unhealthy

Source: US Environmental Protection Agency

Color codes based on the Air Quality Index show the air quality in different areas.

👁 Visualize It!

11 Recommend If you were a weather reporter using this map, what would you recommend for people living in areas that are colored orange? Explain your reasoning.

_____

_____

_____

_____

12 State Your Claim If this were your house, make a claim about three actions you could take to decrease the sources of indoor air pollution.

_____

_____

_____

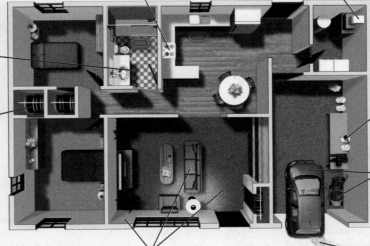

Nitrogen oxides from unvented gas stove, wood stove, or kerosene heater

Chlorine and ammonia from household cleaners

Chemicals from dry cleaning

Formaldehyde from furniture, carpeting, particleboard, and foam insulation

Fungi and bacteria from dirty heating and air conditioning ducts

Chemicals from paint strippers and thinners

Gasoline from car and lawn mower

Carbon monoxide from car left running

How can air quality affect health?

Daily exposure to small amounts of air pollution can cause serious health problems. Children, elderly people, and people with asthma, allergies, lung problems, and heart problems are especially vulnerable to the effects of air pollution. The short-term effects of air pollution include coughing, headaches, and wheezing. Long-term effects, such as lung cancer and emphysema, are dangerous because they can cause death.

13 Claims • Evidence • Reasoning Think about the community in which you live. Make a claim about different things in your community and the surrounding areas that might affect the air quality where you live. Summarize evidence to support the claim and explain your reasoning.

Air Pollution and Your Health

Short-term effects	Long-term effects
coughing	asthma
headaches	emphysema
difficulty breathing	allergies
burning/itchy eyes	lung cancer
	chronic bronchitis

14 Identify Imagine you are walking next to a busy road where there are a lot of exhaust fumes. Circle the effects listed in the table that you are most likely to have while walking.

Things Are CHANGING

How are humans changing Earth's climate?

The burning of fossil fuels releases greenhouse gases, such as carbon dioxide, into the atmosphere. The atmosphere today contains about 43% more carbon dioxide than it did in the mid-1700s, and that level continues to increase. Average global temperatures have also risen in recent decades.

Many people are concerned about how the greenhouse gases from human activities add to the observed trend of increasing global temperatures. Earth's atmosphere and other systems work together in complex ways, so it is hard to know exactly how much the extra greenhouse gases change the temperature. Climate scientists make computer models to understand the effects of climate change. Models predict that average global temperatures are likely to rise another 4.5 °C (8.0 °F) by the year 2100.

A Sunlight (radiant energy) passes through the windows of the car.

B Energy as heat is trapped inside by the windows.

C The temperature inside the car increases.

👁 Visualize It!

15 Synthesize How is a car with closed windows a good analogy of the atmosphere's greenhouse effect?

_____

_____

_____

_____

What are some predicted effects of climate change?

ACTIVE READING

16 Identify As you read, underline some effects of an increasing average global temperature.

Scientists have already noticed many changes linked to warmer temperatures. For example, some glaciers and the Arctic sea ice are melting at the fastest rates ever recorded. A warmer Earth will lead to changes in rainfall patterns, rising sea levels, and possibly more severe storms. These changes will have many negative impacts for life on Earth. Other predicted effects include drought in some regions and increased precipitation in others. Farming practices and the availability of food is also expected to be impacted by increased global temperatures. Such changes will likely have political and economic effects on the world, especially in developing countries.

Melt water pours from an iceberg that broke away from the Jakobshavn Glacier in West Greenland.

How is the ozone layer affected by air pollution?

In the 1980s, scientists reported an alarming discovery about Earth's protective ozone layer. Over the polar regions, the ozone layer was thinning. Chemicals called *chlorofluorocarbons* (klor•oh•flur•oh•kar•buhns) (CFCs) were causing ozone to break down into oxygen, which does not block harmful ultraviolet (UV) rays. The thinning of the ozone layer allows more UV radiation to reach Earth's surface. UV radiation is dangerous to organisms, including humans, as it causes sunburn, damages DNA (which can lead to cancer), and causes eye damage.

CFCs once had many industrial uses, such as coolants in refrigerators and air-conditioning units. CFC use has now been banned, but CFC molecules can stay in the atmosphere for about 100 years. So, CFCs released from a spray can 30 years ago are still harming the ozone layer today.

The dark blue area on this map shows the size of the ozone hole over the South Pole.

17 Infer How might these penguins near the South Pole be affected by the ozone hole?

_____

_____

_____

Source: NASA

Satellite image of Arctic summer sea ice in September 1979.

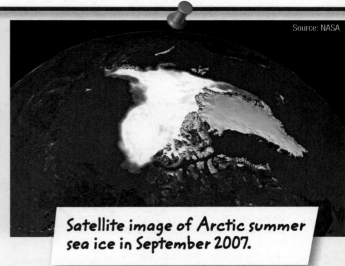

Source: NASA

Satellite image of Arctic summer sea ice in September 2007.

 18 Claims • Evidence • Reasoning Make a claim about how melting sea ice effects people living in coastal areas. Summarize evidence to support the claim and explain your reasoning.

_____

_____

Visual Summary

To complete this summary, fill in the blanks with the correct word or phrase. You can use this page to review the main concepts of the lesson.

Human activities are a major cause of air pollution.

19 Two types of air pollutants are gases and _____.

Human Impact
on the **Atmosphere**

Car exhaust is a major source of air pollution in cities.

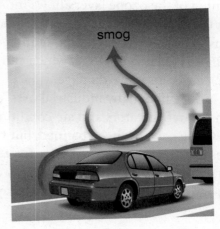

20 _____ is formed when exhausts and ozone react in the presence of sunlight.

Air quality and levels of pollution can be measured.

Air Quality Index (AQI) values	Levels of health concern
0–50	Good
51–100	Moderate
101–150	Unhealthy for sensitive groups
151–200	Unhealthy
201–300	Very unhealthy

21 As pollution increases, _____ decreases.

Climate change may lead to dramatic changes in global weather patterns.

22 The melting of polar ice is one effect of _____.

23 Claims • Evidence • Reasoning Make a claim about the following statement: Each of your breaths, every tree that is planted, and every vehicle on the road affects the composition of the atmosphere. Use evidence to support your claim and explain your reasoning.

_____

_____

(t) ©Steve Cole/PhotoDisc/Getty Images; (b) ©NASA/Goddard Space Flight Center Scientific Visualization Studio. Thanks to Rob Gerston (GSFC) for providing the data.

Lesson Review

Vocabulary

Draw a line to connect the following terms to their definitions.

1 Air pollution

2 Greenhouse effect

3 Air quality

4 Particulate

5 Smog

A tiny particle of solid that is suspended in air or water

B the contamination of the atmosphere by the introduction of pollutants from human and natural sources

C pollutant that forms when ozone and vehicle exhaust react with sunlight

D a measure of how clean or polluted the air is

E the process by which gases in the atmosphere, such as water vapor and carbon dioxide, absorb and release energy as heat

Key Concepts

6 Identify List three effects that an increase in urbanization can have on air quality.

_____

_____

_____

7 Relate How are ground-level ozone and smog related?

_____

_____

_____

8 Claims • Evidence • Reasoning Make a claim about how human health is affected by changes in air quality. Provide evidence to support the claim, and explain your reasoning.

_____

_____

_____

Critical Thinking

Use this graph to answer the following questions.

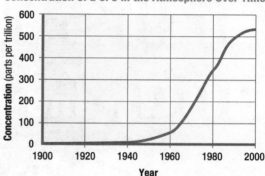

Concentration of a CFC in the Atmosphere Over Time

9 Analyze At what time in the graph did CFCs begin building up in the atmosphere?

_____

_____

10 Synthesize Since the late 1970s, the use of CFCs has been reduced, with a total ban in 2010. But CFCs can stay in the atmosphere for up to 100 years. In the space below, draw a graph showing the concentration of CFCs in the atmosphere over the next 100 years.

11 Claims • Evidence • Reasoning Make a claim about the importance of humans controlling the amount of human-made pollution. Summarize evidence to support the claim, and explain your reasoning.

_____

_____

_____

_____

_____

Protecting Earth's Water, Land, and Air

How can Earth's resources be used wisely?

By the end of this lesson, you should be able to summarize the value of conserving Earth's resources and the effect that wise stewardship has on land, water, and air resources.

Picking up litter to clean streams or rivers is one way we can help preserve Earth's natural resources.

SC.7.E.6.6 Identify the impact that humans have had on Earth, such as deforestation, urbanization, desertification, erosion, air and water quality, changing the flow of water.

Lesson Labs

Quick Labs
- Cleaning Water
- How Can an Oil Spill Be Cleaned Up?
- Soil Erosion

 Engage Your Brain

1 Predict Check T or F to show whether you think each statement is true or false.

T   F

☐   ☐   Conservation is the overuse of natural resources.

☐   ☐   It is everybody's job to be a good steward of Earth's resources.

☐   ☐   Reforestation is the planting of trees to repair degraded lands.

☐   ☐   Alternative energy sources, like solar power, increase the amount of pollution released into the air.

2 Describe Have you ever done something to protect a natural resource? Draw a picture showing what you did. Include a caption.

ACTIVE READING

3 Synthesize You can often guess the meaning of a word from its context, or how it is used in a sentence. Use the sentence below to guess the meaning of the word *stewardship*.

Example sentence
<u>Stewardship</u> of water resources will ensure that there is plenty of clean water for future generations.

stewardship:

_____

_____

Vocabulary Terms

- conservation
- stewardship

4 Apply As you learn the definition of each vocabulary term in this lesson, create your own definition or sketch to help remember the meaning of the term.

Keeping It Clean

What are conservation and stewardship?

In the past, some people have used Earth's resources however they wanted, without thinking about the consequences. They thought it didn't matter if they cut down hundreds of thousands of trees or caught millions of fish. They also thought it didn't matter if they dumped trash into bodies of water. Now we know that it does matter how we use resources. Humans greatly affect the land, water, and air. If we wish to keep using our resources in the future, we need to conserve and care for them.

○ Conservation: Wise Use of Resources

Conservation (kahn•sur•VAY•shuhn) is the wise use of natural resources. By practicing conservation, we can help make sure that resources will still be around for future generations. It is up to everybody to conserve and protect resources. When we use energy or create waste, we can harm the environment. If we conserve whenever we can, we reduce the harm we do to the environment. We can use less energy by turning off lights, computers, and appliances. We can reuse shopping bags, as in the picture below. We can recycle whenever possible, instead of just throwing things away. By doing these things, we take fewer resources from Earth and put less pollution into the water, land, and air.

ACTIVE READING

5 Identify As you read, underline the definitions of *conservation* and *stewardship*.

👁 **Visualize It!**

6 Describe How are the people in the picture below practicing conservation?

_____

_____

_____

This old tire is being used as a planter instead of being thrown away.

○ Stewardship: Managing Resources

Stewardship (stoo•urd•SHIP) is the careful and responsible management of a resource. If we are not good stewards, we will use up a resource or pollute it. Stewardship of Earth's resources will ensure that the environment stays clean enough to help keep people and other living things healthy. Stewardship is everybody's job. Governments pass laws that protect water, land, and air. These laws determine how resources can be used and what materials can be released into the environment. Individuals can also act as stewards. For example, you can plant trees or help clean up a habitat in your community. Any action that helps to maintain or improve the environment is an act of stewardship.

7 Compare Fill in the Venn diagram to compare and contrast conservation and stewardship.

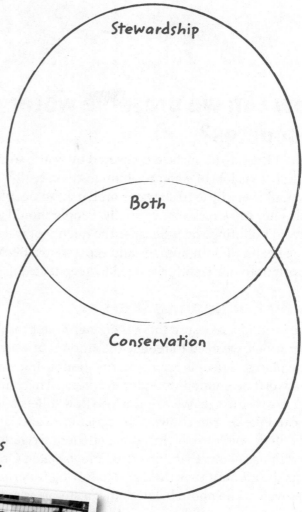

Stewardship

Both

Conservation

Turning empty lots into gardens improves the environment and provides people with healthy food.

Sea turtles are endangered. Scientists help sea turtles that have just hatched find their way to the sea.

◉ Visualize It!

8 Identify How is the person in the picture to the right practicing stewardship?

_____

_____

_____

Water Wise!

How can we preserve water resources?

Most of the Earth's surface is covered by water, so you might think there is lots of water for humans to use. However, there is actually very little fresh water on Earth, so people should use freshwater resources very carefully. People should also be careful to avoid polluting water because the quality of water is important to the health of both humans and ecosystems. Because water is so important to our health, we need to keep it clean!

◯ By Conserving Water

If we want to make sure there is enough water for future generations, we need to reduce the amount of water we use. In some places, if people aren't careful about using water wisely, there soon won't be enough water for everyone. There are many ways to reduce water usage. We can use low-flow toilets and showerheads. We can take shorter showers. In agriculture and landscaping, we can reduce water use by installing efficient irrigation systems. We can also use plants that don't need much water. Only watering lawns the amount they need and following watering schedules saves water. The photo below shows a simple way to use less water—just turn off the tap while brushing your teeth!

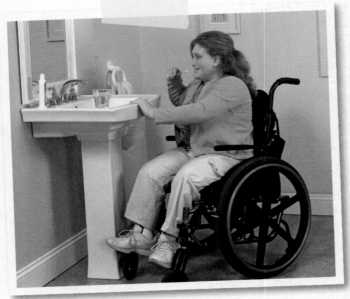

➕➖✖️➗ Do the Math

You Try It

9 Calculate How much fresh water is on Earth?

Solve
Each square on the grid equals 1%. Use the grid to fill in the percentage of each type of water found on Earth.

Earth's Water

▨ Salt water _____

▨ Ice (fresh water) _____

▨ Fresh liquid water _____

10 State Your Claim Make a claim about some ways you can reduce the amount of water you use.

• Turn off the tap when brushing my teeth.

• _____
  _____

• _____
  _____

• _____
  _____

○ With Water Stewardship

Humans and ecosystems need clean water. The diagram below shows how a community keeps its drinking water clean. The main way to protect drinking water is to keep pollution from entering streams, lakes, and other water sources. Laws like the Clean Water Act and Safe Drinking Water Act were passed to protect water sources. These laws indicate how clean drinking water must be and limit the types of chemicals that businesses and private citizens can release into water. These laws also help finance water treatment facilities. We can help protect water by not throwing chemicals in the trash or dumping them down the drain. We can also use nontoxic chemicals whenever possible. Reducing the amount of fertilizer we use on our gardens also reduces water pollution.

For healthy ecosystems and safe drinking water, communities need to protect water sources. The first step to protecting water sources is keeping them from becoming polluted.

Protecting Water Resources

Water testing makes sure water is safe for people to drink. It also helps us find out if there is a pollution problem that needs to be fixed.

Water treatment plants remove pollution from wastewater before it is reused or put back into the environment.

Without clean water to drink, people can get sick. Clean water is also important for agriculture and natural ecosystems.

◉ Visualize It!

11 Claims • Evidence • Reasoning
Make a claim about what steps a community should take to manage its water resources. Use evidence to support your claim and explain your reasoning.

_____

_____

This Land Is Your Land

ACTIVE READING

12 Identify As you read this page and the next, underline ways that we can protect land resources.

How can we preserve land resources?

People rely on land resources for recreation, agriculture, transportation, commerce, industry, and housing. If we manage land resources carefully, we can make sure that these resources will be around for generations and continue to provide resources for humans to use. We also need to make sure that there are habitats for wild animals. To do all these things, we must protect land resources from overuse and pollution. Sometimes we need to repair damage that is already done.

○ Through Preservation

Preservation of land resources is very important. *Preservation* means protecting land from being damaged or changed. Local, state, and national parks protect many natural areas. These parks help ensure that many species survive. Small parks can protect some species. Other species, such as predators, need larger areas. For example, wolves roam over hundreds of miles and would not be protected by small parks. By protecting areas big enough for large predators, we also protect habitats for many other species.

Yosemite National Park is one of the oldest national parks in the country. Like other national, state, and local parks, Yosemite was formed to preserve natural habitats.

Think Outside the Book

13 Claims • Evidence • Reasoning Plant and animal species depend on land resources. Make a claim about how you can help an endangered plant or animal species living in your area. Summarize evidence to support the claim and explain your reasoning

○ Through Reforestation

People use the wood from trees for many things. We use it to make paper and to build houses. We also use wood to heat homes and cook food. In many places, huge areas of forest were cut down to use the wood and nothing was done to replant the forests. Now when we cut trees down, they are often replanted, as in the picture at right. We also plant trees in areas where forests disappeared many years ago in order to help bring the forests back. The process of planting trees to reestablish forestland is called *reforestation*. Reforestation is important, but we can't cut down all forests and replant them. It is important to keep some old forests intact for the animals that need them to survive.

Reforestation

○ Through Reclamation

In order to use some resources, such as coal, metal, and minerals, the resources first have to be dug out of the ground. In the process, the land is damaged. Sometimes, large areas of land are cleared and pits are dug to reach the resource. Land can also be damaged in other ways, including by development and agriculture. *Reclamation* is the process by which a damaged land area is returned to nearly the condition it was in before people used it. Land reclamation, shown in the lower right photo, is required for mines in many states once the mines are no longer in use. Many national and state laws, such as the Surface Mining and Reclamation Act and the Resource Conservation and Recovery Act, guide land reclamation.

A mine being reclaimed

👁 Visualize It!

14 Claims • Evidence • Reasoning Make claims about the similarities between reforestation and reclamation. Summarize evidence to support your claims and explain your reasoning

_____

_____

_____

_____

One way to reduce urban sprawl is to locate homes and businesses close together.

◯ Through Reducing Urban Sprawl

Urban sprawl is the outward spread of suburban areas around cities. As we build more houses and businesses across a wider area, there is less land for native plants and animals. Reducing urban sprawl helps to protect land resources. One way to reduce sprawl is to locate more people and businesses in a smaller area. A good way to do this is with vertical development—that means constructing taller buildings. Homes, businesses, and even recreational facilities can be placed within high-rise buildings. We also can reduce sprawl using mixed-use development. This development creates communities with businesses and houses very close to one another. Mixed-use communities are also better for the environment, because people can walk to work instead of driving.

◯ Through Recycling

Recycling is one of the most important things we can do to preserve land resources. *Recycling* is the process of recovering valuable materials from waste or scrap. We can recycle many of the materials that we use. By recycling materials like metal, plastic, paper, and glass, we use fewer raw materials. Recycling aluminum cans reduces the amount of bauxite that is mined. We use bauxite in aluminum smelting. Everyone can help protect land resources by recycling. Lots of people throw away materials that can be recycled. Find out what items you can recycle!

Bauxite mine

15 Apply Aluminum is mined from the ground. Recycling aluminum cans decreases the need for mining bauxite. Paper can also be recycled. How does recycling paper preserve trees?

_____

_____

◯ Through Using Soil Conservation Methods

Soil conservation protects soil from erosion or degradation by overuse or pollution. For example, farmers change the way they plow in order to conserve soil. Contour plowing creates ridges of soil across slopes. The small ridges keep water from eroding soils. In strip cropping, two types of crops are planted in rows next to each other to reduce erosion. Terracing is used on steep hills to prevent erosion. Areas of the hill are flattened to grow crops. This creates steps down the side of the hill. *Crop rotation* means that crops with different needs are planted in alternating seasons. This reduces the prevalence of plant diseases and makes sure there are nutrients for each crop. It also ensures that plants are growing in the soil almost year-round. In no-till farming, soils are not plowed between crop plantings. Stalks and cover crops keep water in the soils and reduce erosion by stopping soil from being blown away.

ACTIVE READING

16 Identify As you read this page, underline five methods of soil conservation.

👁 Visualize It!

Terracing involves building leveled areas, or steps, to grow crops on.

In contour plowing, crop rows are planted in curved lines along land's natural contours.

Strip cropping prevents erosion by creating natural dams that stop water from rushing over a field.

17 Analyze Which two soil conservation techniques would be best to use on gentle slopes?

☐ contour plowing

☐ crop terracing

☐ strip cropping

18 Analyze Which soil conservation technique would be best to use on very steep slopes?

☐ contour plowing

☐ crop terracing

☐ strip cropping

Into Thin Air

How can we reduce air pollution?

Polluted air can make people sick and harm organisms. Air pollution can cause the atmosphere to change in ways that are harmful to the environment and to people. There are many ways that we can reduce air pollution. We can use less energy. Also, we can develop new ways to get energy that produces less pollution. Everybody can help reduce air pollution in many different ways.

○ Through Energy Conservation

Energy conservation is one of the most important ways to reduce air pollution. Fossil fuels are currently the most commonly used energy resource. When they are burned, they release pollution into the air. If we use less energy, we burn fewer fossil fuels.

There are lots of ways to conserve energy. We can turn off lights when we don't need them. We can use energy-efficient lightbulbs and appliances. We can use air conditioners less in the summer and heaters less in the winter. We can unplug electronics when they are not in use. Instead of driving ourselves to places, we can use public transportation. We can also develop alternative energy sources that create less air pollution. Using wind, solar, and geothermal energy will help us burn less fossil fuel.

ACTIVE READING

19 Identify Underline the sentences that explain the relationship between burning fossil fuels and air pollution.

Using public transportation, riding a bike, sharing rides, and walking reduce the amount of air pollution produced by cars.

Many cities, such as Los Angeles, California, have air pollution problems.

Energy can be produced with very little pollution. These solar panels help us use energy from the sun and replace the use of fossil fuels.

(bkgd) ©Ulf Wallin/Stone/Getty Images; (t) ©Elenarmi/Shutterstock; (b) ©Michael Dwyer/Alamy;

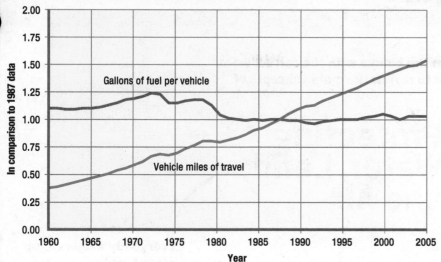

Vehicle Fuel Consumption and Miles Traveled, 1960–2005

In comparison to 1987 data

Gallons of fuel per vehicle

Vehicle miles of travel

Source: U.S. Department of Transportation

Visualize It!

20 Claims • Evidence • Reasoning
Make a claim about how vehicle fuel consumption in comparison to miles traveled has changed since 1960. Use evidence to support your claim and explain your reasoning.

_____

_____

_____

_____

_____

_____

Through Technology

There are lots of ways to generate energy without creating much air pollution. By developing these alternative energy sources, we can reduce the amount of pollution created by burning fossil fuels. Wind turbines generate clean power. So do solar panels that use energy from the sun. We also can use power created by water flowing through rivers or moving with the tides. Geothermal energy from heat in Earth's crust can be used to generate electricity. Hybrid cars get energy from their brakes and store it in batteries. They burn less gas and release less pollution. Driving smaller cars that can go farther on a gallon of gas also reduces air pollution.

New technologies, such as this compact fluorescent lightbulb (CFL), help limit air pollution. CFL bulbs use less energy to make the same amount of light.

Through Laws

Governments in many countries work independently and together to reduce air pollution. They monitor air quality and set limits on what can be released into the air. In the United States, the Clean Air Act limits the amount of toxic chemicals and other pollutants that can be released into the atmosphere by factories and vehicles. It is up to the Environmental Protection Agency to make sure that these limits are enforced. Because air isn't contained by borders, some solutions must be international. The Kyoto Protocol is a worldwide effort to limit the release of greenhouse gases—pollution that can warm the atmosphere.

21 Summarize List three ways air pollution can be reduced.

• _____

_____

_____

• _____

_____

_____

• _____

_____

_____

Visual Summary

To complete this summary, fill in the blanks with the correct word or phrase. You can use this page to review the main concepts of the lesson.

Protecting Water, Land, and Air

Water resources are important to our health.

22 A community's water supply can be protected by:

- conserving water
- preventing pollution
- _____
- treating wastewater

Land resources are used to grow food and make products.

23 Land resources can be protected by:

- preservation
- reclamation and reforestation
- reducing urban sprawl
- _____
- soil conservation

Everybody needs clean air to breathe.

24 The main way to reduce air pollution is to:

_____
_____
_____
_____
_____
_____

25 Claims • Evidence • Reasoning Make claims about how you personally act as a steward of water, land, and air resources. Summarize evidence to support your claims and explain your reasoning

Vocabulary

Fill in the blank with the term that best completes the following sentences.

1 _____ is the wise use of natural resources.

2 _____ is the careful and responsible management of a resource.

Key Concepts

3 **Claims • Evidence • Reasoning** How can water pollution be prevented? Use evidence to support your claims and explain your reasoning.

_____

_____

_____

Fill in the table below.

Example	Type of land resource conservation
4 Identify A county creates a park to protect a forest.	
5 Identify A mining company puts soil back in the hole and plants grass seeds on top of it.	
6 Identify A logging company plants new trees after it has cut some down.	
7 Identify A plastic milk bottle is turned into planks for a boardwalk to the beach.	
8 Identify Instead of building lots of single houses, a city builds an apartment building with a grocery store.	

9 **Gather Evidence** Technology has helped decrease air pollution in recent years. Summarize evidence to support this claim.

_____

_____

10 **State Your Claim** Make a claim about why it is important to protect Earth's water, land, and air resources.

_____

_____

Critical Thinking

11 **Claims • Evidence • Reasoning** Land reclamation can be expensive. Make a claim about how recycling materials can lead to spending less money on reclamation. Summarize evidence to explain your reasoning.

_____

_____

_____

Use the graph to answer the following question.

Average Water Usage of U.S. Household

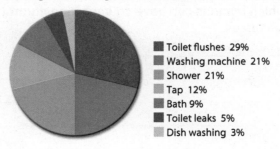

- Toilet flushes 29%
- Washing machine 21%
- Shower 21%
- Tap 12%
- Bath 9%
- Toilet leaks 5%
- Dish washing 3%

12 **Analyze** The graph above shows water use in the average U.S. household. Using the graph, identify three effective ways a household could conserve water.

_____

_____

is important
to preserve

**Protecting Earth's
Water, Land,** and **Air**

Natural
Resources

are affected by

Human Impact
on **Land**

Human Impact
on **Water**

Human Impact
on the
Atmosphere

1 Interpret The Graphic Organizer above shows that humans can have an impact on Earth's natural resources. List two examples of ways in which humans can have an impact on natural resources.

_____

_____

_____

_____

2 Integrate How can erosion on land impact water quality?

_____

_____

_____

_____

3 Claims • Evidence • Reasoning Make a claim about how increasing human population affects land resources, water resources, and the atmosphere. Summarize evidence to support your claim and explain your reasoning.

_____

_____

_____

_____

_____

_____

_____

_____

_____

_____

Vocabulary

Name _____

Check the box to show whether each statement is true or false.

T	F		
☐	☐	**1**	<u>Air quality</u> is a measure of how clean or polluted the air is.
☐	☐	**2**	<u>Potable</u> water is suitable for drinking.
☐	☐	**3**	<u>Conservation</u> is the wise use of natural resources.
☐	☐	**4**	<u>Land degradation</u> is the process by which humans restore damaged land so that it can support the local ecosystem.
☐	☐	**5**	<u>Stewardship</u> of Earth's resources helps make sure that the environment remains healthy.

Key Concepts

Identify the choice that best completes the statement or answers the question.

6 Ms. Chan drew the picture below, which shows a common landscaping practice.

How can this practice cause pollution?

A It pollutes nearby soil when animals track mud from one place to another.

B It pollutes drinking water in the home when chemicals seep into underground pipes.

C It pollutes water when runoff carries chemicals from the soil to local streams and lakes.

D It pollutes the air above the location when chemicals break down and produce gases.

7 Andrea would like to start an environmental conservation club at her school. She is making a poster to describe what the club will do. Which activity could she list that would be part of conservation?

F Learn how to save water.

G Learn how to nurse a sick pet.

H Learn how to build a campfire.

I Learn how to balance a budget.

8 The atmosphere helps regulate Earth's temperature so that life can exist. It also provides the oxygen and carbon dioxide that organisms need to live. Air is an important natural resource that forms part of the atmosphere. Which of these statements provides a **main** reason that air is an important natural resource?

A Air affects surface currents in the oceans.

B Air gives animals and humans a means of transportation.

C Air protects organisms from harmful radiation from the sun.

D Air provides a way for harmful pollutants to move away from Earth.

9 Erosion is the process by which soil and sediment are moved from one place to another. Erosion takes place naturally, but it can be accelerated by human activity. Which of these human activities **least** contributes to land erosion?

F urban sprawl

G planting trees

H surface mining

I improper plowing of furrows

10 The town of Winchester recently built a reservoir that will store drinking water for the town. Which of the following could cause contamination of the water and lead to health-related problems?

A water stewardship

B a water treatment facility

C increase in fertilizer use

D use of nontoxic chemicals

Name _____

11 Air pollution makes it difficult for some people to breathe. It can also cause serious health problems like asthma and allergies. Which of these choices gives the **best** description of air pollution?

F the circulating of pollutants in enclosed spaces

G the long-term health issues related to the quality of the air in cities

H the contamination of the atmosphere by pollutants from human and natural sources

I the pollution that results from changes in the atmosphere, such as the rate of global warming

12 The ozone hole is an area of depleted ozone in Earth's atmosphere. It forms over the Antarctic at the beginning of spring in the Southern Hemisphere, which is August. Which of the following human activities has the **greatest** effect on the ozone in Earth's atmosphere?

A the use of oil in automobile engines

B the use of airplanes in the atmosphere

C the use of satellites in orbit around Earth

D the use of chlorofluorocarbons in refrigeration

13 Ignacio plans to start a recycling program in his neighborhood. He wants to begin by collecting waste materials, such as glass bottles and metal cans. To convince people to help out, he makes a poster explaining how recycling benefits his community. How could recycling waste materials benefit a community?

F It reduces the amount of work that people must do to get rid of wastes.

G It reduces the amount of land area that would be mined for new materials.

H It reduces the amount of land used for storing and recycling waste materials.

I It reduces the amount of energy used because no energy is needed to recycle materials.

Critical Thinking

Answer the following questions in the space provide.

14 The atmosphere is important to life on Earth. Could it be considered a natural resource? Use at least two examples as evidence to support your claim and explain your reasoning.

_____

_____

_____

_____

15 The picture below is of a dam built on a river.

How does a dam affect the surrounding landscape behind and in front of the dam? Explain your reasoning.

_____

_____

How does a dam affect the fish that live breed in that river? Explain your reasoning.

_____

_____

Waves and Light

FLORIDA BIG IDEA 10

Forms of Energy

Radio waves are used to produce a weather map that can track the path and speed of a hurricane.

What Do You Think?

A Doppler Radar uses radio waves to produce a weather map. This allows scientists to track weather systems such as a hurricane. Airport security workers use x-rays to scan luggage for dangerous items. What are some other useful applications of waves in the world around us? As you explore this unit, gather evidence to help you state and support your claim.

Waves and Light

Looking Into Space

The first telescopes were refracting telescopes, which used a pair of lenses to gather light. Today, astronomers also use reflecting telescopes, which gather light with large mirrors, to observe distant objects.

Galileo observing space

1609

Galileo Galilei used a refracting telescope to observe phases of Venus, the moons of Jupiter, the surface of the moon, sunspots, and a supernova.

List other tools that use lenses and think of a use for each one.

_____

_____

_____

_____

_____

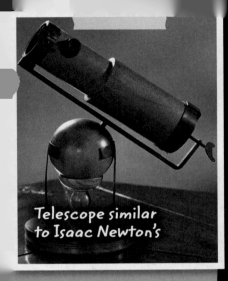

Telescope similar
to Isaac Newton's

Skylab image
of the sun

1973

Telescopes that operate
from space, like the sun-
observing telescope that
was aboard Skylab, can see
all kinds of things we can't
see from Earth.

1668

Isaac Newton built a
reflecting telescope that
used a curved mirror to
gather light. Newton's mirror
did not split light into colors
like the lenses in early
refracting telescopes did.

1990

The orbiting Hubble Space
Telescope can capture detailed
images of objects very far from
Earth. The Hubble Space Telescope
has taken images of the most
distant galaxies astronomers have
ever seen.

Hubble Space
Telescope

⌂ Take It Home!

Eyes to the Sky

Use a pair of binoculars or a telescope to look at
the night sky. Compare what you can see with
magnification to what you can see when looking at
the same part of the sky without magnification. Draw
or write your observations in the chart.

Unmagnified Night Sky	Magnified Night Sky

Waves

ESSENTIAL QUESTION

What are waves?

By the end of this lesson, you should be able to distinguish between types of waves based on medium and direction of motion.

Ocean waves can cause great destruction. This woodblock print illustrates a great wave threatening boats off the coast of Japan.

SC.7.N.1.1 Define a problem from the seventh grade curriculum, use appropriate reference materials to support scientific understanding, plan and carry out scientific investigation of various types, such as systematic observations or experiments, identify variables, collect and organize data, interpret data in charts, tables, and graphics, analyze information, make predictions, and defend conclusions. **SC.7.P.10.3** Recognize that light waves, sound waves, and other waves move at different speeds in different materials.

Lesson Labs

Quick Labs
- Energy in Sound Waves
- Waves on a Spring
- Seeing Vibrations

Exploration Lab
- Sound Idea

S.T.E.M. Lab
- Building a Speaker

Engage Your Brain

1 Predict Check T or F to show whether you think each statement is true or false.

T	F	
☐	☐	The air around you is full of waves.
☐	☐	Ocean waves carry water from hundreds of miles away.
☐	☐	Sound waves can travel across outer space.
☐	☐	Visible light is a wave.

2 Identify Make a list of items in the classroom that are making waves. Next to each item, write what kind of waves you think it is making.

_____

_____

_____

_____

_____

_____

_____

_____

ACTIVE **READING**

3 Distinguish Which of the following definitions of *medium* do you think is most likely to be used in the context of studying waves? Circle your answer.

A of intermediate size

B the matter in which a physical phenomenon takes place

C between two extremes

Vocabulary Terms

- wave
- medium
- longitudinal wave
- transverse wave
- mechanical wave
- electromagnetic wave

4 Apply As you learn the definition of each vocabulary term in this lesson, write your own definition or sketch to help you remember the meaning of the term.

What are waves?

The world is full of waves. Water waves are just one of many kinds of waves. Sound and light are also waves. A **wave** is a disturbance that transfers energy from one place to another.

○ Waves Are Disturbances

Many waves travel by disturbing a material. The material then returns to its original place. A **medium** is the material through which a wave travels.

You can make waves on a rope by shaking the end up and down. The rope is the medium, and the wave is the up-and-down disturbance. As the part of the rope nearest your hand moves, it causes the part next to it to move up and down too. The motion of this part of the rope causes the next part to move. In this way, the wave moves as a disturbance down the whole length of the rope.

Each piece of the rope moves up and down as a wave goes by. Then the piece of rope returns to where it was before. A wave transfers energy from one place to another. It does not transfer matter. The points where the wave is highest are called crests. The points where the wave is lowest are called troughs.

ACTIVE READING

5 Identify Underline the names for the highest and lowest points of a wave.

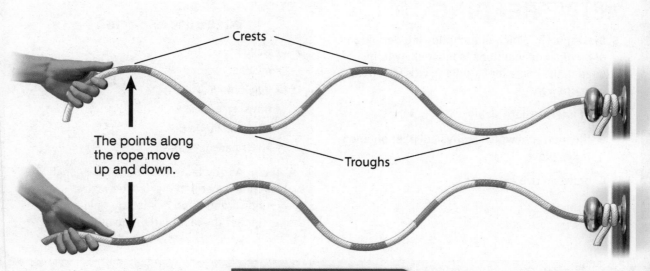

Crests

The points along the rope move up and down.

Troughs

👁 Visualize It!

6 Claims • Evidence • Reasoning Make a claim about what direction the wave travels. Draw an arrow near the rope to show the direction the wave travels as evidence to support your claim and explain your reasoning.

© Houghton Mifflin Harcourt

◯ Waves Are a Transfer of Energy

A wave is a disturbance that transfers energy. Some waves need a medium to transfer energy, such as waves in the ocean that move through water and waves that are carried on guitar or cello strings when they vibrate. Some waves can transfer energy without a medium. One example is visible light. Light waves from the sun transfer energy to Earth across empty space.

👁 Visualize It!

Each snapshot below shows the passage of a wave. The leaf rises and falls as crests and troughs carry it.

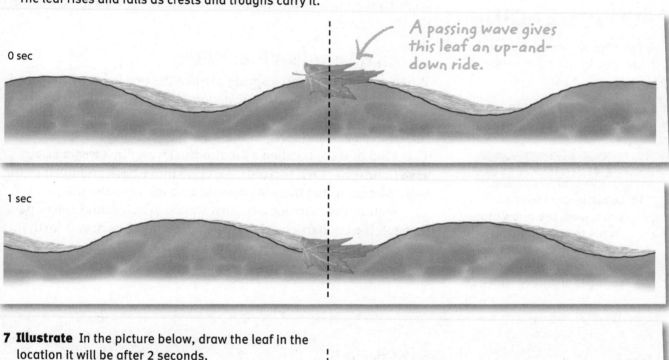

0 sec

A passing wave gives this leaf an up-and-down ride.

1 sec

7 Illustrate In the picture below, draw the leaf in the location it will be after 2 seconds.

2 sec

8 Model In the space below, draw the leaf and wave as they will appear after 3 seconds.

3 sec

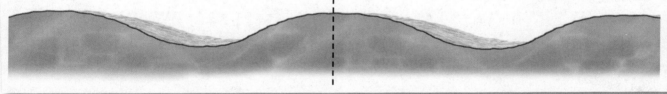

Different Ways

How does a wave transfer energy?

A wave transfers energy in the direction it travels. However, the disturbance may not be in the same direction as the wave. Each wave can be classified by comparing the direction of the disturbance, such as the motion of the medium, with the direction the wave travels.

ACTIVE READING

9 Identify As you read, underline the type of wave that sound is.

◯ As a Longitudinal Wave

When you pull back on a spring toy like the one below, you spread the coils apart and make a *rarefaction*. When you push forward, you squeeze the coils closer together and make a *compression*. The coils move back and forth as the wave passes along the spring toy. This kind of wave is called a longitudinal wave. In a **longitudinal wave** (lahn•jih•TOOD•n•uhl), particles move back and forth in the same direction that the wave travels, or parallel to the wave.

Sound waves are longitudinal waves. When sound waves pass through the air, particles that make up air move back and forth in the same direction that the sound waves travel.

👁 Visualize It!

10 Label In this longitudinal wave, label the arrow that shows the direction the wave travels with a *T*. Label the arrow that shows how the spring is disturbed with a *D*.

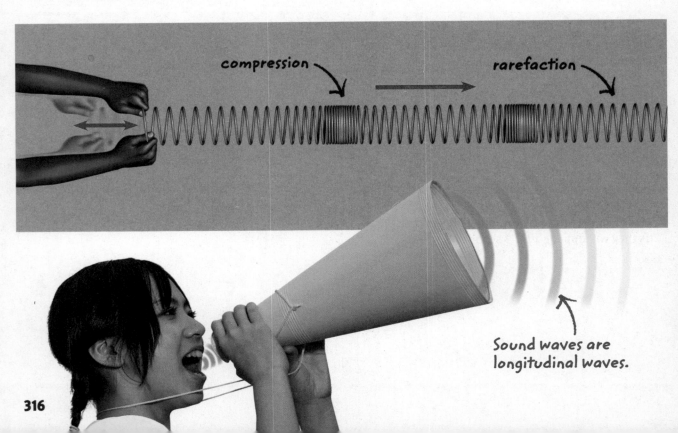

compression

rarefaction

Sound waves are longitudinal waves.

to Transfer Energy

○ As a Transverse Wave

The same spring toy can be used to make other kinds of waves. If you move the end of the spring toy up and down, a wave also travels along the spring. In this wave, the spring's coils move up and down as the wave passes. This kind of wave is called a **transverse wave**. In a transverse wave, particles move perpendicularly to the direction the wave travels.

Transverse waves and longitudinal waves often travel at different speeds in a medium. In a spring toy, longitudinal waves are usually faster. An earthquake sends both longitudinal waves (called P waves) and transverse waves (called S waves) through Earth's crust. In this case, the longitudinal waves are also faster. During an earthquake, the faster P waves arrive first. A little while later, the S waves arrive. The S waves are slower but usually more destructive.

A transverse wave and a longitudinal wave can combine to form another kind of wave called a surface wave. Ripples on a pond are an example of a surface wave.

When these fans do "The Wave," they are modeling the way a disturbance travels through a medium.

12 State Your Claim Make a claim about what type of wave the stadium wave shown above is.

👁 Visualize It!

11 Label In this transverse wave, label the arrow that shows the direction the wave travels with a *T*. Label the arrow that shows how the spring is disturbed with a *D*.

ⓘ Think Outside the Book

13 Identify What do the letters *S* in S waves and *P* in P waves stand for? Relate this to earthquakes.

Water waves are surface waves, a combination of transverse and longitudinal waves.

Making Waves

What are some types of waves?

As you have learned, waves are disturbances that transfer energy. Waves can be classified by the direction of disturbance. But they can also be classified by what is disturbed.

Mechanical Waves

Most of the waves we have talked about so far are waves in a medium. For water waves, water is the medium. For earthquake waves, Earth is the medium. A wave that requires a medium through which to travel is called a **mechanical wave**.

Some mechanical waves can travel through more than one medium. For example, sound waves can move through air, through water, or even through a solid wall. The waves travel at different speeds in the different media. Sound waves travel much faster in a liquid or a solid than in air.

Mechanical waves can't travel without a medium. Suppose all the air is removed from beneath a glass dome, or bell jar, as in the photograph below. In a vacuum, there is no air to transmit sound waves. The vibrations made inside the bell jar can't be heard.

Electromagnetic Waves

Are there waves that can travel without a medium? Yes. Sunlight travels from the sun to Earth through empty space. Although light waves can travel through a medium, they can also travel without a medium. Light and similar waves are called electromagnetic (EM) waves. An **electromagnetic wave** is a disturbance in electric and magnetic fields. They are transverse waves. Examples of EM waves include

- visible light
- radio waves
- microwaves
- ultraviolet (UV) light
- x-rays

In empty space, all these waves travel at the same speed. This speed, referred to as the speed of light, is about 300 million meters per second!

The sound from the toy cannot be heard because there is no air to transmit the sound.

Visible light is a type of wave called an electromagnetic wave.

Visualize It!

14 Claims • Evidence • Reasoning Classify each of the waves in these three photographs as mechanical or electromagnetic. Summarize evidence to support your claims and explain your reasoning.

Sunlight is a(n)
_____

Water waves are
_____

A towel waving displays a(n)
_____

Vocal sounds are
_____

Music is a(n)
_____

Firelight is a(n)
_____

Visual Summary

To complete this summary, fill in the lines below the statement to correct the statement so that it is true. You can use this page to review the main concepts of the lesson.

Waves are disturbances that transfer energy.

15 The water particles in the wave move to the right, along with the wave.

_____

_____

_____

Waves

Waves can be longitudinal or transverse.

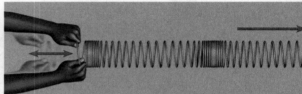

16 The toy above and the toy below both show longitudinal waves.

_____

_____

_____

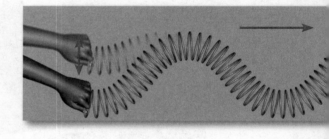

Waves can be mechanical or electromagnetic.

17 This picture shows only examples of mechanical waves.

_____

_____

_____

18 **Claims • Evidence • Reasoning** Consider the following claim: Waves transfer energy but not matter. Do you agree or disagree with this? Summarize evidence to support or refute this claim and explain your reasoning.

Lesson Review

Vocabulary

Circle the term that best completes the following sentences.

1 A wave is a disturbance that transfers *matter/energy*.

2 In a *longitudinal/transverse* wave, the disturbance moves parallel to the direction the wave travels.

3 *Mechanical/Electromagnetic* waves require a medium in which to travel.

Key Concepts

4–6 Identify Name the medium for each of the following types of waves.

Type of wave	Medium
ocean waves	4
earthquake waves	5
sound waves from a speaker	6

7 Describe Explain how transverse waves can be produced on a rope. Then describe how pieces of the rope move as waves pass.

_____

_____

_____

8 Claims • Evidence • Reasoning Make a claim about whether the sun's rays are mechanical or electromagnetic waves. Summarize evidence to support this claim and explain your reasoning.

_____

_____

Critical Thinking

9 Contrast Mechanical waves travel as disturbances in a physical medium. How do electromagnetic waves travel?

_____

_____

_____

Use this image to answer the following questions.

10 Claims • Evidence • Reasoning Even though the phone is ringing, no sound comes out of the jar. Make a claim about the nature of the space inside the jar. Summarize evidence to support this claim and explain your reasoning.

_____

_____

_____

11 Infer What does this same experiment tell you about light waves? Explain your reasoning.

_____

_____

_____

Properties of Waves

ESSENTIAL QUESTION

How can we describe a wave?

By the end of this lesson, you should be able to identify characteristics of a wave and describe wave behavior.

A heartbeat monitor displays a wave, the characteristics of which contain information about a patient's heartbeat.

SC.7.P.10.3 Recognize that light waves, sound waves, and other waves move at different speeds in different materials.

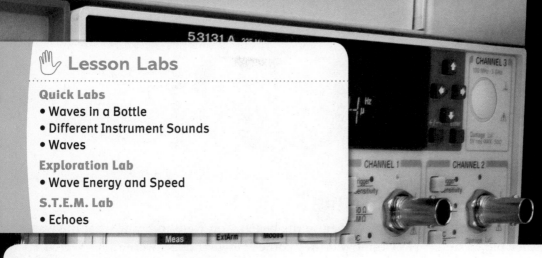

✋ Lesson Labs

Quick Labs
- Waves in a Bottle
- Different Instrument Sounds
- Waves

Exploration Lab
- Wave Energy and Speed

S.T.E.M. Lab
- Echoes

🧠 Engage Your Brain

1 Describe Fill in the blank with the word that you think correctly completes the following sentences.

A guitar amplifier makes a guitar sound

_____

FM radio frequencies are measured in mega- _____

The farther you are from a sound source, the _____ the sound is.

2 Illustrate Draw a diagram of a wave in the space below. How would you describe your wave so that a friend on the phone could duplicate your drawing?

ACTIVE READING

3 Predict Many scientific words also have everyday meanings. For each of the following terms, write in your own words what it means in common use. Then try writing a definition of what it might mean when applied to waves.

Vocabulary Terms

- wave
- amplitude
- wavelength
- wave period
- frequency
- hertz
- wave speed

4 Compare This list contains the vocabulary terms you'll learn in this lesson. As you read, circle the definition of each term.

length:

_____

speed:

_____

period (of time):

_____

Amp It UP!

How can we describe a wave?

Suppose you are talking to a friend who had been to the beach. You want to know what the waves were like. Were they big or small? How often did they come? How far apart were they? Were they moving fast? Each of these is a basic property that can be used to describe waves.

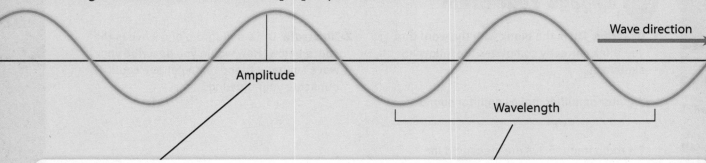

Amplitude

Wave direction

Wavelength

By Its Amplitude

A **wave** is a disturbance that transfers energy from one place to another. As a wave passes, particles in the medium move up and down or back and forth. A wave's **amplitude** is a measure of how far the particles in the medium move away from their normal rest position. The graph above shows a transverse wave. Notice that the amplitude of a wave is also half of the difference between the highest and lowest values.

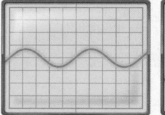 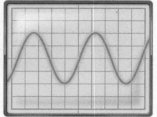

By Its Wavelength

You can use amplitude to describe the height of an ocean wave, for example. But to describe how long the wave is, you need to know its wavelength. The **wavelength** is the distance from any point on a wave to an identical point on the next wave. For example, wavelength is the distance from one crest to the next, from one trough to the next, or between any other two corresponding points. Wavelength measures the length of one cycle, or repetition.

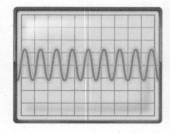 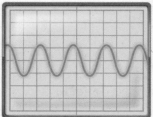

👁 Visualize It!

5 Label Mark the amplitude in the two graphs above. Which wave has the greater amplitude?

_____

6 Label Mark the wavelength in the two graphs above. Which wave has the greater wavelength?

_____

By Its Frequency

Wavelength and amplitude tell you about the size of a wave. Another property tells you how much time a wave takes to repeat. The **wave period** (usually "period") is the time required for one cycle. You can measure the period by finding the time for one full cycle of a wave to pass a given point. For example, you could start timing when one crest passes you and stop when the next crest passes. The time between two crests is the period.

Another way to express the time of a wave's cycle is frequency. The **frequency** of a wave tells how many cycles occur in an amount of time, usually 1 s. Frequency is expressed in **hertz** (Hz). One hertz is equal to one cycle per second. If ten crests pass each second, the frequency is 10 Hz.

> Frequency and period are closely related. Frequency is the inverse of period:
>
> $$\text{frequency} = \frac{1}{\text{period}}$$

Suppose the time from one crest to another—the period—is 5 s. The frequency is then $\frac{1}{5}$ Hz, or 0.2 Hz. In other words, one-fifth (0.2) of a wave passes each second.

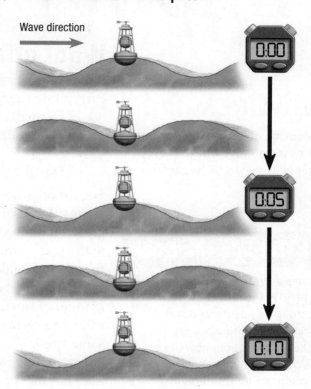

The buoy moves down and back up every five seconds as waves pass.

Wave direction

0:00

0:05

0:10

> Frequency is equal to the number of cycles per unit of time:
>
> $$\text{frequency} = \frac{\text{number of cycles}}{\text{time}}$$

👁 Visualize It!

7 Illustrate On the grid below, draw a wave, and then draw another wave with twice the amplitude.

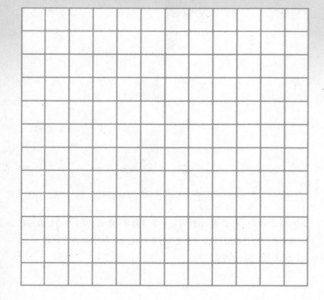

8 Illustrate On the grid below, draw a wave, and then draw another wave with half the wavelength.

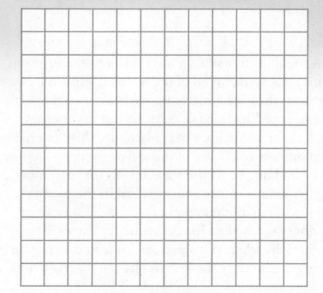

Amp It Down

ACTIVE READING

9 Identify As you read, underline the kind of wave whose energy depends mostly on frequency.

What affects the energy of a wave?

All waves carry energy from one place to another, but some waves carry more energy than others. A leaf falling on water produces waves so small they are hard to see. An earthquake under the ocean can produce huge waves that cause great destruction.

⬤ The Amplitude or The Frequency

For a mechanical wave, amplitude is related to the amount of energy the wave carries. For two similar waves, the wave with greater amplitude carries more energy. For example, sound waves with greater amplitude transfer more energy to your eardrum, so they sound louder.

Greater frequency can also mean greater energy in a given amount of time. If waves hit a barrier three times in a minute, they transfer a certain amount of energy to the barrier. If waves of the same amplitude hit nine times in a minute, they transfer more energy in that minute.

For most electromagnetic (EM) waves, energy is most strongly related to frequency. Very high-frequency EM waves, such as x-rays and gamma rays, carry enough energy to damage human tissue. Lower-frequency EM waves, such as visible light waves, can be absorbed safely by your body.

Energy Loss to a Medium

A medium transmits a wave. However, a medium may not transmit all of the wave's energy. As a wave moves through a medium, particles may move in different directions or come to rest in different places. The medium may warm up, shift, or change in other ways. Some of the wave's energy produces these changes. As the wave travels through more of the medium, more energy is lost to the medium.

Often, higher-frequency waves lose energy more readily than lower-frequency waves. For example, when you stand far from a concert, you might hear only the low-frequency (bass) sounds.

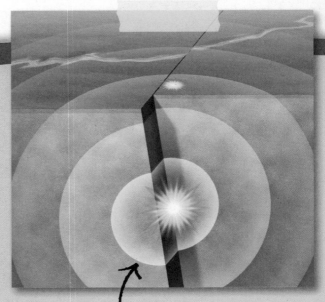

Some of the energy of these earthquake waves is lost to the medium when the ground shifts.

Sound waves expand in three dimensions.

Energy Loss Due to Spreading

So far, we have mostly talked about waves moving in straight lines. But waves usually spread out in more than one dimension. The crests can be drawn as shapes, such as circles or spheres, called *wavefronts*. As each wavefront moves farther from the source, the energy is spread over a greater area. Less energy is available at any one point on the wavefront. If you measure a wave at a point farther from the source, you measure less energy. But the total energy of the wavefront stays the same.

Ripples on a water surface expand in two dimensions.

 11 Predict Which type of wave spreading do you think causes faster energy loss—two-dimensional or three-dimensional? Explain your reasoning.

_____

_____

_____

As the student on the left knocks on the table, the students farther away feel the resulting waves less strongly.

◉ Visualize It!

12 Claims • Evidence • Reasoning Make a claim about what differences the students would observe if they were to repeat their experiment using a longer table. Summarize evidence to support this claim and explain your reasoning.

_____

_____

_____

A Happy Medium

What determines the speed of a wave?

Waves travel at different speeds in different media. For example, sound waves travel at about 340 m/s in air at room temperature, but they travel at nearly 1,500 m/s in water. In a solid, sound waves travel even faster.

○ The Medium in Which It Travels

The speed at which a wave travels—called **wave speed**—depends on the properties of the medium. Specifically, wave speed depends on the interactions of the atomic particles of the medium. In general, waves travel faster in solids than in liquids and faster in liquids than in gases. Interactions, or collisions, between particles happen faster in solids because the medium is more rigid.

How fast the wave travels between particles within the medium depends on many factors. For example, wave speed depends on the density of the medium. Waves usually travel slower in the denser of two solids or the denser of two liquids. The more densely packed the particles are, the more they resist motion, so they transfer waves more slowly.

In a gas, wave speed depends on temperature as well as density. Particles in hot air move faster than particles in cold air, so particles in hot air collide more often. This faster interaction allows waves to pass through hot air more quickly than through the denser cold air. The speed of sound in air at 20 °C is about 340 m/s. The speed of sound in air at 0 °C is slower, about 330 m/s.

Electromagnetic waves don't require a medium, so they can travel in a vacuum. All electromagnetic waves travel at the same speed in empty space. This speed, called the speed of light, is about 300,000,000 m/s. While passing through a medium such as air or glass, EM waves travel more slowly than they do in a vacuum.

ACTIVE **READING**

13 Identify Does sound travel faster or slower when the air gets warmer?

_____

_____

14 Claims • Evidence • Reasoning One diagram shows sound traveling through an air-filled tank. Draw a medium in the second tank in which sound will travel faster than in the air-filled tank. Make a claim about why the medium you have drawn will transmit sound waves faster than air. Summarize evidence to support this claim and explain your reasoning.

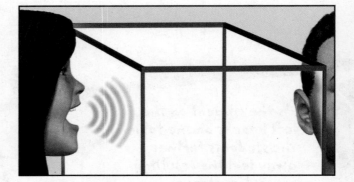

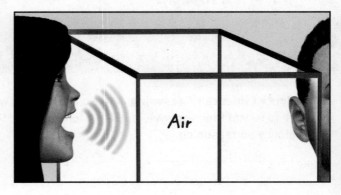

Air

As this person bounces on the trampoline, she models a particle being moved by a wave.

Imagine if the tension on the trampoline were much lower: each bounce would take longer, because the person would sink much lower.

Its Frequency and Wavelength

Wave speed can be calculated from frequency and wavelength. To understand how, it helps to remember that speed is defined as distance divided by time:

As a medium becomes more flexible, it carries waves more slowly.

$$speed = \frac{distance}{time}$$

So if a runner runs 8 m in 2 s, then the runner's speed is 8 m ÷ 2 s = 4 m/s. For a wave, a crest moves a distance of one wavelength in one cycle. The time for the cycle to occur is one period. Using wavelength and period as the distance and time:

$$wave\ speed = \frac{wavelength}{wave\ period}$$

So if a crest moves one wavelength of 8 m in one period of 2 s, the wave speed is calculated just like the runner's speed: 8 m ÷ 2 s = 4 m/s.

Frequency is the inverse of the wave period. So the relationship can be rewritten like this:

$$wave\ speed = frequency \times wavelength$$
$$or$$
$$wavelength = \frac{wave\ speed}{frequency}$$

If you already know the wave speed, you can use this equation to solve for frequency or wavelength.

 **Do the Math**

You Try It

15 Calculate Complete this table relating wave speed, frequency, and wavelength.

Wave speed (m/s)	Frequency (Hz)	Wavelength (m)
20		5
75	15	
	23	16
625		25
	38	20

Visual Summary

To complete this summary, fill in the blanks with the correct word or phrase. You can use this page to review the main concepts of the lesson.

Amplitude tells the amount of displacement of a wave.

Wavelength tells how long a wave is.

Wave period is the time required for one cycle.

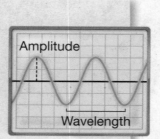

16 _____ = $\dfrac{1}{\text{wave period}}$

17 Hertz is used to express _____

18 One hertz is equal to _____

Wave energy depends on amplitude and frequency.

Most waves lose energy over time as they travel and spread.

20 Some of the wave's energy stays in the _____

Wave Properties

Wave speed depends on the properties of the medium.

In a vacuum, electromagnetic waves all move at the speed of light.

19 wave speed = frequency × _____

21 **Claims • Evidence • Reasoning** Make a claim about how the properties of sound waves change as they spread out in a spherical pattern. Summarize evidence to support this claim and explain your reasoning.

Lesson Review

Vocabulary

Fill in the blank with the correct letter.

1 frequency

_____

2 wavelength

_____

3 wave speed

_____

4 wave period

_____

5 amplitude

_____

A the distance over which a wave's shape repeats

B the maximum distance that particles in a wave's medium vibrate from their rest position

C the time required for one wavelength to pass a point

D the number of wavelengths that pass a point in a given amount of time

E the speed at which a wave travels through a medium

Key Concepts

6 Describe What measures the amount of displacement in a transverse wave?

_____

7 Relate How are frequency and wave period related?

_____

_____

_____

8 Provide What does the energy of an electromagnetic wave depend on?

_____

9 Infer Sound travels slower in colder air than it does in warmer air. Why does the speed of sound depend on air temperature? Explain your reasoning.

_____

_____

Critical Thinking

Use this diagram to answer the following questions. The frequency of the wave is 0.5 Hz.

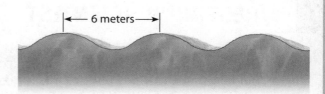

|← 6 meters →|

10 Analyze What is the wavelength of these waves?

_____

11 Calculate What is the speed of these waves?

_____

12 Solve If you were sitting in a boat as these waves passed by, how many seconds would pass between wave crests?

_____

13 Claims • Evidence • Reasoning Make a claim about how the energy of the sound wave changes as it moves farther away from its source. Summarize evidence to support this claim and explain your reasoning.

_____

_____

_____

14 Claims • Evidence • Reasoning A wave has a low speed but a high frequency. Make a claim about the wavelength of this wave. Summarize evidence to support this claim and explain your reasoning.

_____

_____

_____

15 Predict How do you know the speed of an electromagnetic wave in a vacuum?

_____

_____

Publishing Company

PEOPLE **IN SCIENCE**

SC.7.N.1.5 Describe the methods used in the pursuit of a scientific explanation as seen in different fields of science such as biology, geology, and physics.

James West

RESEARCH SCIENTIST

James West's parents wanted him to be a medical doctor, but he wanted to study physics. His father was sure he'd never find a job that way. But Dr. West wanted to study what he loved. He did study physics, and he did find a job. He worked for Bell Laboratories and developed a microphone called the electret microphone. Today, Dr. West's microphone is in almost all telephones, cell phones, and other equipment that records sound.

Dr. West's interest in the microphone started with a question about hearing. A group of scientists wanted to know how close together two sounds could be before the ear would not be able to tell them apart. At the time, there was no earphone sensitive enough for their tests. Dr. West and fellow scientist Dr. Gerhard Sessler found that they could make a more sensitive microphone by using materials called *electrets*. Electrets are the electrical counterparts of permanent magnets. Electrets can store electric charge. This eliminates the need for a battery. The new microphones were cheaper, more reliable, smaller, and lighter than any microphone before them.

Dr. West enjoys the thrill of discovery. He should know. To date, he holds more than 250 U.S. and foreign patents. In 1999 he was inducted into the National Inventors Hall of Fame. Dr. West retired from Bell Laboratories in 2001 and is now on the faculty at Johns Hopkins University. He has won many awards for his work, including both the Silver and Gold Medals from the Acoustical Society of America, The National Medal of Technology and Innovation, and the Benjamin Franklin Medal in Electrical Engineering.

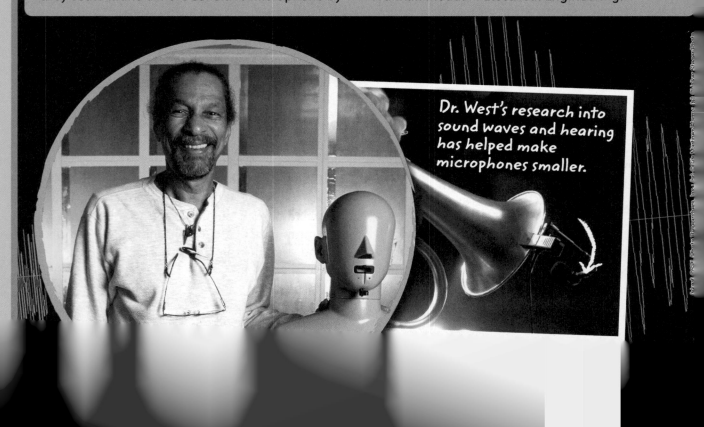

Dr. West's research into sound waves and hearing has helped make microphones smaller.

Dispensing Optician

What You'll Do: Help select and then fit eyeglasses and contact lenses.

Where You Might Work: Medical offices, or optical, department, or club stores

Education: Most training is on the job or through apprenticeships that last two years or longer. Some employers prefer graduates of postsecondary training programs in opticianry.

Other Job Requirements: A good eye for fashion, face shape, and color is a plus, as opticians help people find glasses they like.

Lighting Designer

What You'll Do: Work in theater, television, or film to make what happens on stage or on set visible to audiences. Lighting designers also use lighting and shadow to create the right tone or mood.

Where You Might Work: Theaters, television and film studios and sets, concerts and other special events

Education: A diploma or certificate in lighting design or technical stage management from a college or performing arts institute

Other Job Requirements: Experience lighting stage productions, the ability to work in a team

PEOPLE IN SCIENCE NEWS

ELY Silk

A New Light on Microscopy

Doctors and medical researchers use fluorescent microscopes to see colored or fluorescent dyes in medical research. These microscopes use expensive and dangerous mercury light bulbs to illuminate the dyes. But Ely Silk, a retired computer programmer and inventor in Florida, found a less expensive source of light.

When the mercury bulb on his microscope died, Silk replaced it with many differently colored light-emitting diodes (LEDs). Each inexpensive LED emits light of a different wavelength. The LEDs cost only a couple of dollars each and are much safer than mercury bulbs. Yet they still provide the light needed to view the fluorescent dyes. Now, researchers can use the LED microscopes to really light up their dyes!

Houghton Mifflin Harcourt Publishing Company

The **Electromagnetic Spectrum**

ESSENTIAL **QUESTION**

What is the relationship between various EM waves?

By the end of this lesson, you should be able to distinguish between the parts of the electromagnetic spectrum.

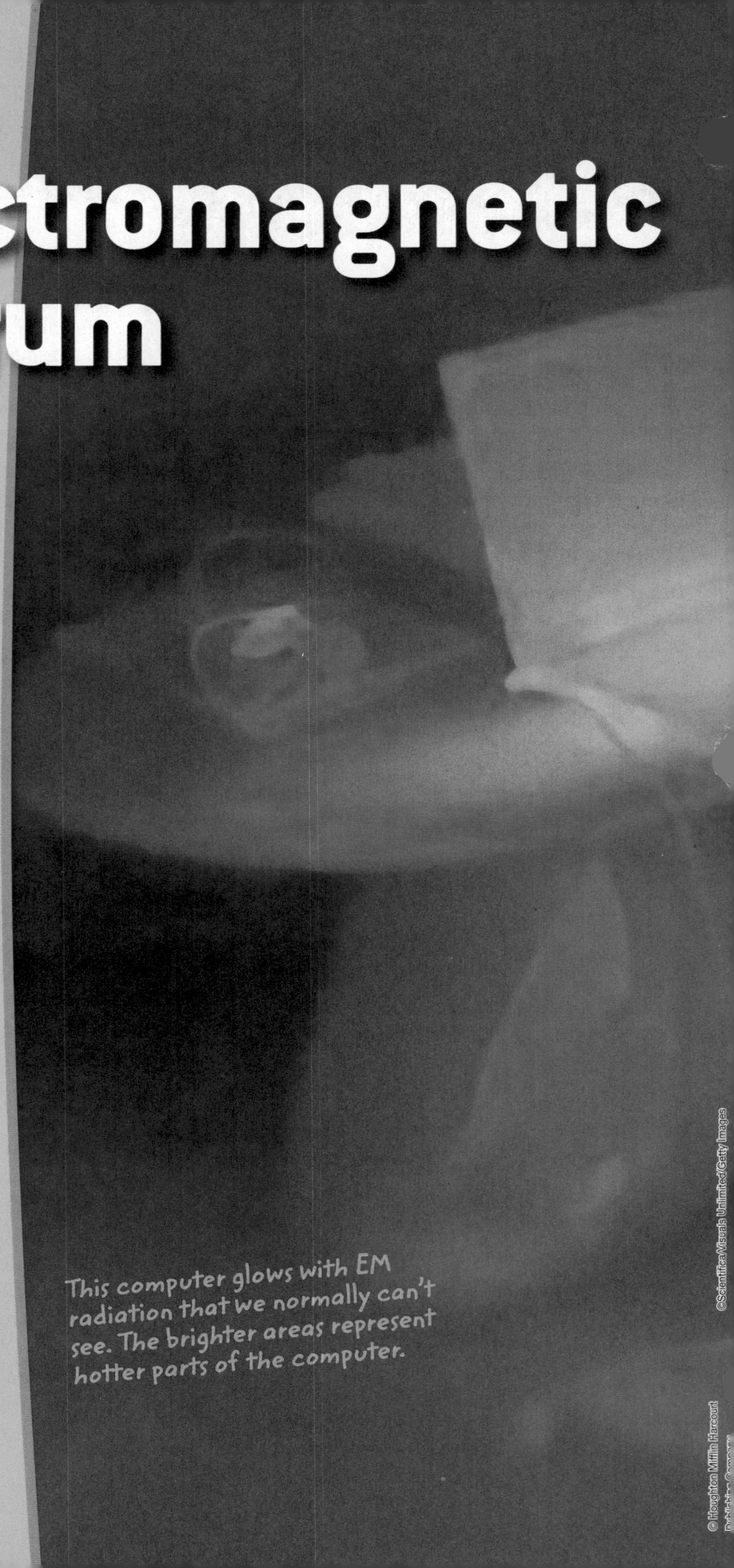

This computer glows with EM radiation that we normally can't see. The brighter areas represent hotter parts of the computer.

SC.7.P.10.1 Illustrate that the sun's energy arrives as radiation with a wide range of wavelengths, including infrared, visible, and ultraviolet, and that white light is made up of a spectrum of many different colors.

© Scientifica/Visuals Unlimited/Getty Images

© Houghton Mifflin Harcourt

Engage Your Brain

1 Select Circle the word or phrase that best completes each of the following sentences:

Radio stations transmit (*radio waves*/*gamma rays*).

The dentist uses (*infrared light*/*x-rays*) to examine your teeth.

Intense (*visible light*/*ultraviolet light*) from the sun can damage your skin.

2 Predict Imagine that humans had not realized there are other parts of the electromagnetic spectrum besides visible light. How would your day today be different without technology based on other parts of the EM spectrum?

_____

_____

_____

_____

_____

_____

ACTIVE READING

3 Synthesize You can often define an unknown word if you know the meaning of its word parts. Use this table of word parts to make an educated guess about the meanings given.

Word part	Meaning
ultra-	beyond
infra-	below
electro-	related to electricty
-magnetic	related to magnetism

What word means "beyond violet"?

_____

What word means "below red"?

_____

What word means "related to electricity and magnetism"?

_____

Vocabulary Terms

• radiation
• electromagnetic spectrum
• infrared
• ultraviolet

4 Apply As you learn the definition of each vocabulary term in this lesson, think of an example of a real-world use. Practice writing the term and its definition, and then writing or drawing a sketch of the example next to the definition.

Electromagnetic Light Show

What is the nature of light?

Light is a type of energy that travels as waves, but light waves are not disturbances in a medium. Light waves are disturbances in electric and magnetic fields. If you have felt the static cling of fabric and the pull of a magnet, then you have experienced electric and magnetic fields. Because these fields can exist in empty space, light does not need a medium in which to travel.

When an electrically charged particle vibrates, it disturbs the electric and magnetic fields around it. These disturbances, called electromagnetic (EM) waves, carry energy away from the charged particle. The disturbances are perpendicular to each other and to the direction the wave travels. **Radiation** (ray•dee•AY•shuhn) is the transfer of energy as EM waves.

In a vacuum, all EM waves move at the same speed: 300,000,000 m/s, called the speed of light. That's fast enough to circle Earth more than seven times in one second!

Although light and other EM waves do not need a medium, they can travel through many materials. EM waves travel more slowly in a medium such as air or glass than in a vacuum.

👁 Visualize It!

7 Label Mark and label the wavelength and amplitude of the disturbances in the fields.

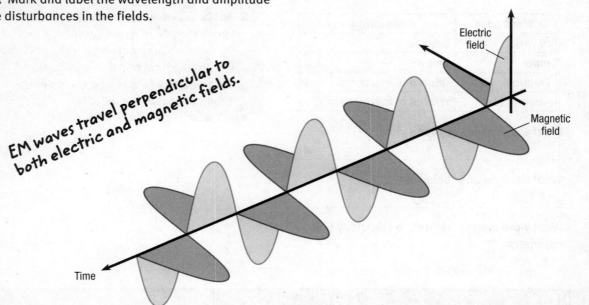

EM waves travel perpendicular to both electric and magnetic fields.

Electric field

Magnetic field

Time

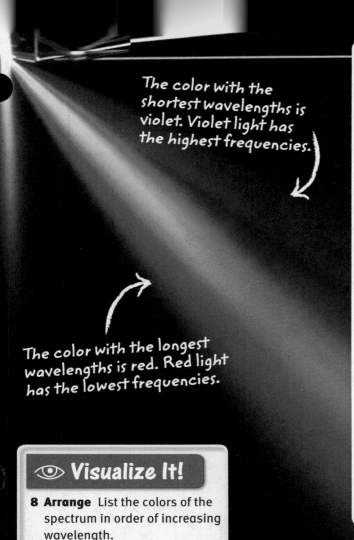

The color with the shortest wavelengths is violet. Violet light has the highest frequencies.

The color with the longest wavelengths is red. Red light has the lowest frequencies.

What determines the color of light?

Light comes in many colors, from red to violet. But what is different about each color of light? Like all waves, light has wavelengths. Different wavelengths of light are interpreted by our eyes as different colors. The shortest wavelengths are seen as violet. The longest wavelengths are seen as red. Even the longest wavelengths we can see are still very small—less than one ten-thousandth of a centimeter.

White light is what we perceive when we see all the wavelengths of light at once, in equal proportions. A prism can split white light into its component colors, separating the colors by wavelength. The various wavelengths of light can also be combined to produce white light.

Our eyes only register three color ranges of light, called the primary colors—red, green, and blue. All other colors we see are a mixture of these three colors. A television or computer screen works by sending signals to make small dots, called pixels, give off red, green, and blue light.

◉ Visualize It!

8 Arrange List the colors of the spectrum in order of increasing wavelength.

_____

_____

_____

_____

_____

_____

_____

9 Select What combination of primary colors do we perceive as yellow?

_____

_____

Red, green, and blue light combine to appear white.

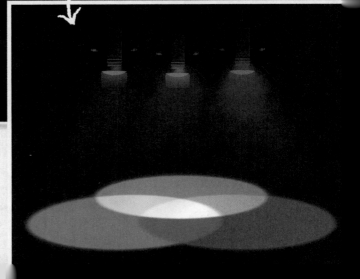

Invisible Colors

What are the parts of the EM spectrum?

EM waves are measured by frequency or by wavelength. The light waves we see are EM waves. However, visible light represents only a very small part of the range of frequencies (or wavelengths) that an EM wave can have. This range is called the **electromagnetic (EM) spectrum**. These other EM waves are the same type of wave as the light we're used to. They're just different frequencies.

Two parts of the spectrum are close to visible light. **Infrared**, or IR, light has slightly longer wavelengths than red light. **Ultraviolet**, or UV, light has slightly shorter wavelengths than violet light.

The Electromagnetic Spectrum

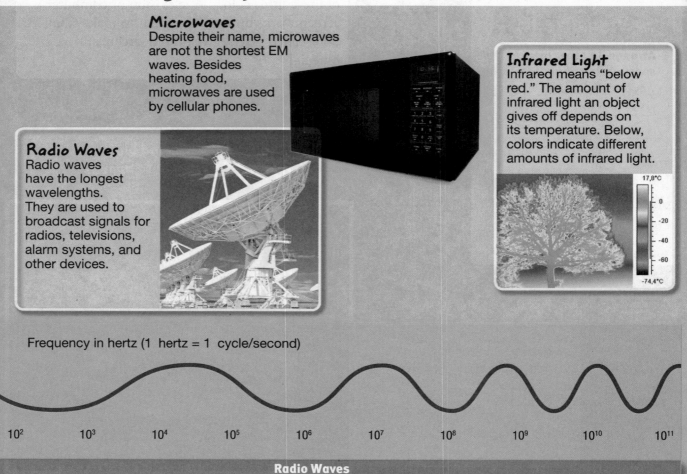

Microwaves
Despite their name, microwaves are not the shortest EM waves. Besides heating food, microwaves are used by cellular phones.

Infrared Light
Infrared means "below red." The amount of infrared light an object gives off depends on its temperature. Below, colors indicate different amounts of infrared light.

17,8°C
0
-20
-40
-60
-74,4°C

Radio Waves
Radio waves have the longest wavelengths. They are used to broadcast signals for radios, televisions, alarm systems, and other devices.

Frequency in hertz (1 hertz = 1 cycle/second)

10^2 10^3 10^4 10^5 10^6 10^7 10^8 10^9 10^{10} 10^{11}

Radio Waves

Microwaves

The inner part of these flowers reflects UV light differently than the outer part. A bee's eyes are sensitive to UV light, and the bee can see the difference. However, human eyes cannot detect UV light. Our eyes can detect yellow light, and the center and edges of the flower reflect yellow light equally, so we see an all-yellow flower.

Human eyes see the flowers as entirely yellow.

A bee's eyes see a pattern in UV light.

Think Outside the Book

10 Incorporate The flower shows designs that are visible to bees, which can see light in the ultraviolet range. Research and explain how this adaptation leads to a symbiotic relationship between the flowers and bees.

Visible Light
Visible light is all the colors of the EM spectrum we can see. It is the narrowest part of the EM spectrum.

Ultraviolet Light
Ultraviolet means "beyond violet." Some animals can see ultraviolet light.

X-Rays
X-rays can pass through most living tissue, but are absorbed by bones.

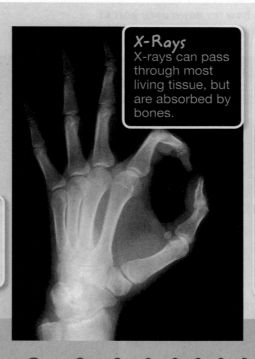

Gamma Rays
Gamma rays can be used to treat illnesses and in making medical images.

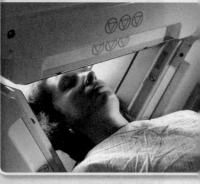

10^{12} 10^{13} 10^{14} 10^{15} 10^{16} 10^{17} 10^{18} 10^{19} 10^{20}

Infrared Light | **Ultraviolet Light** | **Gamma Rays**

Visible Light | **X-Rays**

(t) ©Bjorn Horsfell/Photo Researchers, Inc.; (ml) ©Jim Wehtje/Photodisc/Getty Images; (mr) ©James King-Holmes/Photo Researchers, Inc.

© Houghton Mifflin Harcourt Publishing Company

How much of the sun's energy reaches us?

The sun gives off huge amounts of energy in the form of EM radiation. More of this energy is in the narrow visible light range than any other part of the spectrum, but the sun gives off some radiation in every part of the spectrum.

ACTIVE READING

11 Identify What prevents most of the sun's gamma rays from reaching us?

_____

👁 Visualize It!

The illustration shows how far down each part of the EM spectrum penetrates Earth's atmosphere.

◯ Earth Shields Us from Some EM Radiation

Between the sun and us lies Earth's atmosphere. In order for us to see anything, some of the sun's light must make it through the atmosphere. However, not all wavelengths of light penetrate the atmosphere equally. The atmosphere blocks most of the higher-frequency radiation like x-rays and gamma rays from reaching us at the ground level, while allowing most of the visible light to reach us. There is a "window" of radio frequencies that are barely blocked at all, and this is why the most powerful ground-based telescopes are radio telescopes.

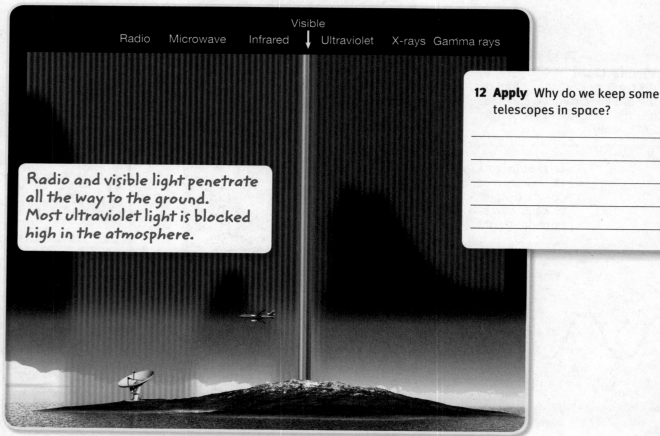

Radio   Microwave   Infrared   Visible   Ultraviolet   X-rays   Gamma rays

Radio and visible light penetrate all the way to the ground. Most ultraviolet light is blocked high in the atmosphere.

12 Apply Why do we keep some telescopes in space?

_____

_____

_____

_____

Star Bright

13 Gather Evidence A student claims that it might be less dangerous to wear no sunglasses than to wear sunglasses that do not block UV light. Summarize evidence to support the claim.

_____

_____

_____

Astronauts need extra protection from EM radiation in space.

We Shield Ourselves from Some Radiation

The atmosphere blocks much of the sun's radiation, but not all. Some EM radiation can be dangerous to humans, so we take extra steps to protect ourselves. Receiving too much ultraviolet (UV) radiation can cause sunburn, skin cancer, or damage to the eyes, so we use sunscreen and wear UV-blocking sunglasses to protect ourselves from the UV light that passes through the atmosphere. Hats, long-sleeved shirts, and long pants can protect us, too.

We need this protection even on overcast days because UV light can travel through clouds. Even scientists in Antarctica, one of the coldest places on Earth, need to wear sunglasses, because fresh snow reflects about 80% of UV light back up to where it might strike their eyes.

Outer space is often thought of as being cold, but despite this, one of the biggest dangers to astronauts is from overheating! Outside of Earth's protective atmosphere, the level of dangerous EM radiation is much higher. And, in the vacuum of space, it's much harder to dispose of any energy, because there's no surrounding matter (like air) to absorb the extra energy. This is one reason why astronauts' helmets have a thin layer of pure gold. This highly reflective gold layer reflects unwanted EM radiation away.

Frequency Asked Questions

How much energy does EM radiation have?

What makes some EM waves safe, and some dangerous? The answer is that different frequencies of EM waves carry different amounts of energy.

◯ Higher Frequency Means More Energy

The energy of an EM wave depends on its frequency. High-frequency, short-wavelength EM waves have more energy than low-frequency, long-wavelength waves.

◯ More Energy Means More Dangerous

A high-frequency EM wave carries a lot of energy, so it has the possibility of damaging living tissue. But a low-frequency wave carries much less energy, and is safer. This is why radio waves (which have the lowest frequencies) are used so often, such as in walkie-talkies and baby monitors. In contrast, UV light causes sunburn unless you have protection, and when working with even higher-energy waves like x-rays, special precautions must be taken, such as wearing a lead apron to block most of the rays.

> ### Think Outside the Book
>
> **15 Apply** On a separate sheet of paper, write a short story where the main character needs protection from two different kinds of EM radiation.

ACTIVE **READING**

14 Claims • Evidence • Reasoning Make a claim about what kinds of EM waves are most dangerous to humans. Summarize evidence that would support this claim and explain your reasoning.

Radio waves pass through humans safely.

UV waves can cause damage to living tissue.

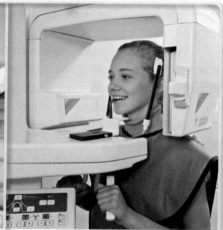

X-rays require extra safety.

Fire in the Sky

The sun constantly streams out charged particles. Earth has a strong magnetic field. When particles from the sun strike Earth, the magnetic field funnels them together, accelerating them. When these particles collide with the atmosphere, they give off electromagnetic radiation in the form of light, and near the poles where they usually come together, a beautiful display called an *aurora* (uh•RAWR•uh) sometimes lights up the sky.

Winds of Change
The stream of electrically charged particles from the sun is called the *solar wind*.

What a Gas!
An aurora produced by nitrogen atoms may have a blue or red color, while one produced by oxygen atoms is green or brownish-red.

Pole Position
At the North Pole, this phenomenon is called the *aurora borealis* (uh•RAWR•uh bawr•ee•AL•is), or northern lights. At the south pole, it is called the *aurora australis* (uh•RAWR•uh aw•STRAY•lis), or southern lights.

ⓘ Extend

16 Relate Which color of aurora gives off higher-energy light, green or red?

17 Explain Why don't we see auroras on the moon? Explain your reasoning

18 Claims • Evidence • Reasoning Make a claim about whether auroras occur on other planets. Summarize evidence that would support this claim and explain your reasoning.

Visual Summary

To complete this summary, fill in the blanks with the correct word or phrase. You can use this page to review the main concepts of the lesson.

The **Electromagnetic Spectrum**

Different wavelengths of light appear as different colors.

19 The color of the longest visible wavelength is _____

20 The color of the shortest visible wavelength is _____

Higher-frequency waves carry more energy. This makes them more dangerous.

21 The energy of an electromagnetic (EM) wave is proportional to its _____

EM waves exist along a spectrum.

22 The waves with the longest wavelengths are _____ waves.

23 The waves with the shortest wavelengths are _____

10^0 10^{19}

Radio Waves   **Gamma Rays**

24 Claims • Evidence • Reasoning Suppose you are designing a device to transmit information without wires. Make a claim about which part of the EM spectrum would be best for this device. Summarize evidence that would support this claim and explain your reasoning.

Lesson Review

Vocabulary

Fill in the blanks with the terms that best complete the following sentences.

1 The transfer of energy as electromagnetic waves is called

_____

2 The full range of wavelengths of EM waves is called the _____

_____

3 _____ radiation lies at frequencies just below the frequencies of visible light.

Key Concepts

4 Describe What is an electromagnetic wave?

_____

_____

5 Organize What are the highest-frequency and lowest-frequency parts of the EM spectrum?

_____

_____

6 Compare How fast do different parts of the EM spectrum travel in a vacuum?

_____

_____

Suppose you like to listen to two different radio stations. The opera station broadcasts at 90.5 MHz and the rock and roll station broadcasts at 107.1 MHz.

7 Support Your Claim Which station's signal has waves with longer wavelengths? Provide evidence to support your claim.

_____

8 Support Your Claim Which station's signal has waves with higher energy? Provide evidence to support your claim.

_____

Use the graph to answer the following questions.

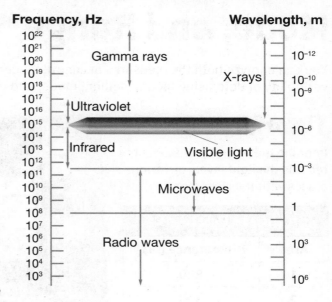

9 State Your Claim How would you classify an EM wave with a frequency of 10^7 Hz?

_____

10 State Your Claim How would you classify an EM wave with a wavelength of 10^{-12} m?

_____

11 Apply What is white light?

_____

_____

Critical Thinking

12 Claims • Evidence • Reasoning Suppose you want to detect x-rays coming from the sun. Make a claim about the best location to place the detector. Summarize evidence that would support this claim and explain your reasoning.

_____

_____

_____

SC.7.N.1.1 Define a problem from the seventh grade curriculum, use appropriate reference materials to support scientific understanding, plan and carry out scientific investigation of various types, such as systematic observations or experiments, identify variables, collect and organize data, interpret data in charts, tables, and graphics, analyze information, make predictions, and defend conclusions.

Mean, Median, Mode, and Range

You can analyze both the measures of central tendency and the variability of data using mean, median, mode, and range.

Tutorial

Imagine that a group of students records the light levels at various places within a classroom.

Classroom Light Levels

Area	Illuminance (lux)
1	800
2	300
3	150
4	300
5	200

Mean The mean is the sum of all of the values in a data set divided by the total number of values in the data set. The mean is also called the *average*.	$$\frac{800 + 300 + 150 + 300 + 200}{5}$$ **mean** = 350 lux
Median The median is the value of the middle item when data are arranged in order by size. In a range that has an odd number of values, the median is the middle value. In a range that has an even number of values, the median is the average of the two middle values.	If necessary, reorder the values from least to greatest: 150, 200, **300**, 300, 800 → ← **median** = 300 lux
Mode The mode is the value or values that occur most frequently in a data set. If all values occur with the same frequency, the data set is said to have no mode. Values should be put in order to find the mode.	If necessary, reorder the values from least to greatest: 150, 200, 300, 300, 800 The value 300 occurs most frequently. **mode** = 300 lux
Range The range is the difference between the greatest value and the least value of a data set.	800 − 150 **range** = 650 lux

You Try It!

The data table below shows the data collected for rooms in three halls in the school.

Illuminance (lux)				
	Room 1	**Room 2**	**Room 3**	**Room 4**
Science Hall	150	250	500	400
Art Hall	300	275	550	350
Math Hall	200	225	600	600

1

Using Formulas Find the mean, median, mode, and range of the data for the school.

2

Claims • Evidence • Reasoning The school board is considering replacing the lights because some people claim that parts of the school are too poorly lit. However, others claim that the lighting in the school is acceptable. Summarize evidence from the school's data that would support each of these claims and explain your reasoning.

_____

_____

_____

_____

_____

_____

_____

_____

_____

_____

_____

📖 Language Arts Connection

On flashcards, write sentences that use the keywords *mean, median, mode,* and *range.* Cover the keywords with small sticky notes. Review each sentence, and determine if it provides enough context clues to determine the covered word. If necessary, work with a partner to improve your sentences.

Interactions of Light

ESSENTIAL QUESTION

How does light interact with matter?

By the end of this lesson, you should be able to explain how light and matter can interact.

These windows allow different colors of light to pass through. The colorful pattern is then reflected off the floor inside.

SC.7.N.1.1 Define a problem from the seventh grade curriculum, use appropriate reference materials to support scientific understanding, plan and carry out scientific investigation of various types, such as systematic observations or experiments, identify variables, collect and organize data, interpret data in charts, tables, and graphics, analyze information, make predictions, and defend conclusions. **SC.7.P.10.2** Observe and explain that light can be reflected, refracted, and/or absorbed. **SC.7.P.10.3** Recognize that light waves, sound waves, and other waves move at different speeds in different materials.

Quick Labs
• Why Is the Sky Blue?
• Filtering Light
• Refraction with Water

Exploration Lab
• Images from Convex Lenses

S.T.E.M. Lab
• Light Maze

Engage Your Brain

1 Predict Check T or F to show whether you think each statement is true or false.

T	F	
☐	☐	Light cannot pass through solid matter.
☐	☐	A white surface absorbs every color of light.
☐	☐	Light always moves at the same speed.

2 Identify Unscramble the letters below to find words about interactions between light and matter. Write your words on the blank lines.

OCRLO _____

RIORMR _____

NABORIW _____

TTRACSE _____

CENFOLRETI _____

ACTIVE READING

3 Synthesize You can often define an unknown word if you know the meaning of its word parts. Use the word parts and sentence below to make an educated guess about the meanings of the words *transmit, transparent,* and *translucent*.

Word part	Meaning
trans-	through
-mit	send
-par	show
-luc	light

transmit:

_____

transparent:

_____

translucent:

_____

Vocabulary Terms
• transparent   • reflection
• translucent   • refraction
• opaque   • scattering
• absorption

4 Apply As you learn the definition of each vocabulary term in this lesson, create your own definition or sketch to help you remember the meaning of the term.

Shedding Light

How can matter interact with light?

Interactions between light and matter produce many common but spectacular effects, such as color, reflections, and rainbows. Three forms of interaction play an especially important role in how people see light.

ACTIVE READING

5 Identify As you read, underline three words that describe how well matter transmits light.

Matter Can Transmit Light

Recall that light and other electromagnetic waves can travel through empty space. When light encounters a material, it can be passed through the material, or transmitted. The medium can transmit all, some, or none of the light.

Matter that transmits light is **transparent** (tranz•PAHR•uhnt). Air, water, and some types of glass are transparent materials. Objects can be seen clearly through transparent materials.

Translucent (tranz•LOO•suhnt) materials transmit light but do not let the light travel straight through. The light is scattered into many different directions. As a result, you can see light through translucent materials, but objects seen through a translucent material look distorted or fuzzy. Frosted glass, some lamp shades, and tissue paper are examples of translucent materials.

Objects can be seen clearly through transparent glass.

Objects look distorted when seen through translucent glass.

Think Outside the Book

6 Discuss Write a short story in which it is important that a piece of glass is translucent or transparent.

© Houghton Mifflin Harcourt Publishing Company

(t) ©Redmond Durrell/Alamy; (b) ©George Diebold/Photographer's Choice/Getty Images

on the Matter

Matter Can Absorb Light

Opaque (oh•PAYK) materials do not let any light pass through them. Instead, they reflect light, absorb light, or both. Many materials, such as wood, brick, or metal, are opaque. When light enters a material but does not leave it, the light is absorbed. **Absorption** is the transfer of light energy to matter.

The shirt at right absorbs the light that falls on it, and so the shirt is opaque. However, absorption is not the only way an object can be opaque.

The shirt is opaque, because light does not pass through it. We can't see the table underneath.

👁 Visualize It!

7 Claims • Evidence • Reasoning Make a claim about whether the table in the photo at the right is transparent, translucent, or opaque. Summarize evidence to support the claim and explain your reasoning.

_____

_____

Matter Can Reflect Light

You see an object only when light from the object enters your eye. However, most objects do not give off, or emit, light. Instead, light bounces off the object's surface. The bouncing of light off a surface is called **reflection**.

Most objects have a surface that is at least slightly rough. When light strikes a rough surface, such as wood or cloth, the light reflects in many different directions. Some of the reflected light reaches your eyes, and you see the object.

Light bounces at an angle equal to the angle at which it hit the surface. When light strikes a smooth or shiny surface such as a mirror, it reflects in a uniform way. As a result, a mirror produces an image. Light from a lamp might be reflected by your skin, then be reflected by a mirror, and then enter your eye. You look at the mirror and see yourself.

Light is reflected by the girl's face and by the mirror.

👁 Visualize It!

8 Identify What is the difference between the way light interacts with the shirt above and the way light interacts with the mirror at right?

_____

_____

Color Me Impressed!

What determines the color of objects we see?

Visible light includes a range of colors. Light that includes all colors is called white light. When white light strikes an object, the object can transmit some or all of the colors of light, reflect some or all of the colors, and absorb some or all of the colors.

○ The Light Reflected or Absorbed

The perceived color of an object is determined by the colors of light reflected by the object. For example, a frog's skin absorbs most colors of light, but reflects most of the green light. When you look in the direction of the frog, the green light enters your eyes, so the frog appears green.

An object that reflects every color appears white. An object that absorbs every color appears black.

The frog's body is green because it reflects green light while absorbing other colors of light.

○ The Light Transmitted

The color of a transparent or translucent object works differently than it does for opaque objects. Some materials may absorb some colors but let other colors pass through. Green plastic, for example, does not appear green because it reflects green light, but rather, because it transmits green light while absorbing other colors of light. When you look toward a bottle made of green plastic, the transmitted green light reaches your eyes. Therefore, the bottle looks green.

Some matter can absorb visible light but let other kinds of electromagnetic waves pass through. For example, radio waves can easily pass through walls that are opaque to visible light. X-rays pass through skin and muscle, but are stopped by denser bone.

The bottle is green because it allows green light to pass through while absorbing other colors of light.

Think Outside the Book

9 Diagram Use colored pencils, crayons, or markers to draw light shining on an object. Draw arrows showing the colors of incoming light and which colors are reflected.

© Houghton Mifflin Harc

The Available Light

Sometimes the perceived color of an object depends on the light available in the area. You may have been in a room with a red light bulb. The glass around the bulb filters out all colors except red, plus some orange and yellow. An object that reflects red light would still appear red under such a light bulb. But an object that absorbed all red, orange, and yellow light would appear gray or black. We can't see colors of light that aren't there to be reflected to our eyes!

Filtered Light

Below, the light from the bulb is being filtered before shining on a frog.

The light bulb emits, or gives off, light in all colors.

A filter blocks some colors, transmitting only red light and some orange and yellow light.

The frog absorbs the red, orange, and yellow light, and reflects no light.

◉ Visualize It!

10 Claims • Evidence • Reasoning
Make a claim about whether the frog will look green under the red light. Summarize evidence to support this claim and explain your reasoning.

_____

_____

_____

_____

_____

_____

Light changes direction when it leaves the water, making the straw look broken.

©Keith Leighton/Alamy

What happens when light waves interact with matter?

You have already learned that light can pass through a transparent medium. But when light waves pass through a medium, the medium can change properties of the light.

○ Light Slows When It Passes Through Matter

You may have learned that light always travels at the same speed in a vacuum. This speed, about 300,000,000 m/s, is called the *speed of light*. However, light travels slower in a medium. Light travels only about three-fourths as fast in water as in a vacuum, and only about two-thirds as fast in glass as in a vacuum.

Although light of all wavelengths travels at the same speed in a vacuum, the same is not true in a medium. When light enters a medium from a vacuum, shorter wavelengths are slowed more than longer wavelengths. In a medium, the speed of violet light is less than the speed of red light.

○ Light Changes Direction

A straight object, such as the straw in the picture above, looks bent or broken when part of it is underwater. Light from the straw changes direction when it passes from water to glass and from glass to air. **Refraction** (ri•FRAK•shuhn) is the change in direction of a wave as it passes from one medium into another at an angle.

Your brain always interprets light as traveling in a straight line. You perceive the straw where it would be if light traveled in a straight line. The light reflected by the straw in air does travel in a straight line to your eye. But the light from the lower part of the straw changes direction when it passes into air. It refracts, causing the illusion that the bottom part of the straw in a water glass is disconnected from the top part.

Refraction is due to the change in speed as a wave enters a new medium. In glass, light's speed depends on wavelength. When light passes through a glass prism, the light waves with shorter wavelengths change direction more than waves with longer wavelengths. So, a prism separates light into a spectrum of colors.

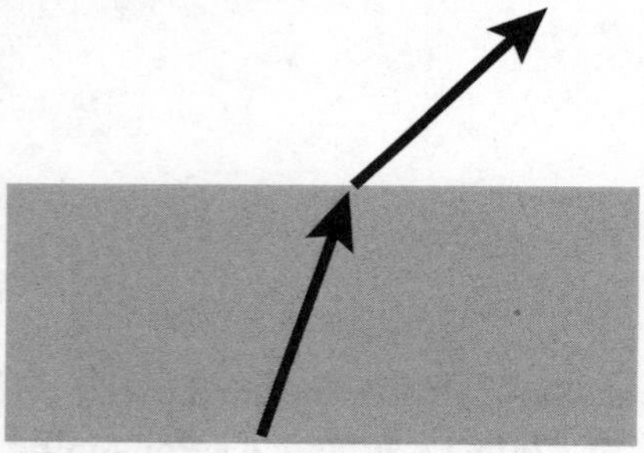

Think Outside the Book

11 **Apply** When a bird tries to catch a fish, it must account for refraction. Draw a picture like the one above to show the path of light from the fish to the bird. Then trace the path backward to show where the fish appears to be to the bird.

12 **Claims • Evidence • Reasoning** Make a claim about which color of light will bend the least when passing through a prism. Summarize evidence to support this claim and explain your reasoning.

© Houghton Mifflin Harcourt Publishing Company

○ Light Scatters

You don't see a beam of light shining through clear air. But if the beam of light shines through fog, some of the light is sent in many different directions. Some enters your eye, and you see the beam. **Scattering** occurs when light is sent in many directions as it passes through a medium. Dust and other small particles can scatter light.

The color of the sky is due to scattered light. Particles of air scatter short wavelengths—blue and violet light—more than long wavelengths. As sunlight passes through air, blue light is scattered first. The blue light appears to come from all directions, and so the sky appears blue. When the sun is near the horizon in the sky, sunlight passes through more of the atmosphere. As the light passes through more and more air, almost all light of short wavelengths is scattered. Only the longest wavelengths are left. The sun and the sky appear yellow, orange, or red.

ACTIVE **READING**

13 Identify What color of light is scattered most easily by the atmosphere?

We can see the light beam coming out of the lighthouse because the fog scatters the light.

In the diagram below, the red lines represent paths of light from the sun. The black brackets show the amount of atmosphere the light must pass through to reach our eyes.

In the evening, sunlight travels through a lot of air. The blue light scatters, leaving only redder light.

The daytime sky appears blue because air scatters blue light more than it does other colors.

Not to scale

Visual Summary

To complete this summary, circle the correct word to complete each statement. You can use this page to review the main concepts of the lesson.

Matter can transmit, reflect, or absorb light.

14 Matter that transmits no light is (transparent/translucent/opaque).

Interactions of Light

The color of an object depends on what colors of light it reflects or transmits.

15 A frog in white light appears green because it (reflects/absorbs/transmits) green light and (reflects/absorbs/transmits) other colors of light.

A transparent medium can bend, scatter, or change the speed of light.

16 The bending of light is called (reflection/refraction/scattering).

17 Claims • Evidence • Reasoning Suppose you are looking at a yellow fish in a fish tank. The tank is next to a window. Make a claim about the path that light takes in order for you to see the fish, starting at the sun and ending at your eyes. Summarize evidence to support the claim and explain your reasoning.

Lesson Review

Vocabulary

Fill in the blank with the term that best completes the following sentences.

1 An object appears fuzzy when seen through a(n) _____ material.

2 A(n) _____ material lets light pass through freely.

3 The bouncing of light off a surface is called _____

4 The bending of light when it changes media is called _____

5 _____ occurs when light changes direction after colliding with particles of matter.

Key Concepts

6 **Identify** For each picture below, identify the material enclosing the sandwich as transparent, translucent, or opaque.

a. _____

b. _____

c. _____

d. _____

7 **State Your Claim** Which material in the pictures above reflects the most light?

_____

8 **State Your Claim** Which material in the pictures above absorbs the most light?

_____

Critical Thinking

9 **Claims • Evidence • Reasoning** Make a claim about whether a mirror's surface is transparent, translucent, or opaque. Summarize evidence to support the claim and explain your reasoning.

_____
_____
_____
_____

10 **Apply** Why does a black asphalt road become hotter than a white cement sidewalk in the same amount of sunlight? Explain your reasoning.

_____
_____
_____
_____
_____
_____
_____

11 **Explain** Why is the sky blue?

_____
_____
_____
_____
_____

12 **Explain** Red, green, and blue light rays each enter a drop of water from the same direction. Make a claim about which light ray's path will bend the most and which will bend the least as it passes through the drop. Summarize evidence to support each claim and explain your reasoning.

_____
_____
_____

SC.7.N.1.1 Define a problem from the seventh grade curriculum, use appropriate reference materials to support scientific understanding, plan and carry out scientific investigation of various types, such as systematic observations or experiments, identify variables, collect and organize data, interpret data in charts, tables, and graphics, analyze information, make predictions, and defend conclusions.

S.T.E.M. ENGINEERING & TECHNOLOGY

Engineering Design Process

Skills
Identify a need
Conduct research
✔ Brainstorm solutions
✔ Select a solution
Design a prototype
✔ Build a prototype
✔ Test and evaluate
✔ Redesign to improve
✔ Communicate results

Objectives
Identify different uses of mirrors and lenses.
Use mirrors and lenses to design and build a periscope.
Test and evaluate the periscope you built.

Building a Periscope

A *periscope* is a device that uses mirrors and lenses to help people see around obstacles. You might be surprised to learn how many other important technologies benefit from mirrors and lenses.

Early Uses of Mirrors and Lenses

For many centuries, people have used mirrors and lenses to bend light. In ancient times, people used shiny metal to see their reflections and pieces of curved glass to start fires. In the 17th century, scientists began using lenses and mirrors to make telescopes, microscopes, and other devices that helped them make new discoveries.

In 1610, Italian astronomer Galileo used a two-lens telescope to discover Jupiter's moons.

1 Identify List devices that use mirrors, lenses, or a combination of both. Then describe the purpose of each device, and identify whether it uses mirrors, lenses, or both.

Device	Purpose	Mirrors, Lenses, or Both
telescope	magnifies far away objects	both

Lasers

Mirrors bend light by reflecting it in a different direction. Lenses bend light by slowing it as it passes through the lens material. Many modern technologies also take advantage of mirrors and lenses. Devices such as DVD players and barcode scanners operate by using laser light. A *laser* is a device that produces a coherent beam of light of a specific wavelength, or color. Laser light is created in a chamber that has mirrors on each end. A single color of light is produced by reflecting light back and forth between the two mirrors. The distance between the mirrors determines the wavelength of light that is amplified. When the light is of the proper wavelength, it can exit the transparent center of one of the mirrors. Lenses are often found in devices that use laser light. Lenses can focus the laser light in devices such as DVD players.

2 Claims • Evidence • Reasoning Conduct research and make a claim about how laser light functions in a device that you use every day. Summarize evidence to support your claim and explain your reasoning.

_____

_____

Periscopes

A periscope is another type of device that uses mirrors and lenses. The mirrors in a periscope bend light in order to allow a person to see around obstacles or above water. Most people think of periscopes in submarines, but periscopes are also used to see over walls or around corners, to see out of parade floats, and to see inside pipes or machinery.

Submarine periscopes use lenses and mirrored prisms to allow people to see above the water without surfacing.

This device uses mirrors and lasers to measure the wind speed during an aircraft test. Wind speed is measured as the laser interacts with dust in the wind.

 You Try It!

Now it's your turn to use mirrors and lenses to design and build a periscope.

 **You Try It!**

Mirrors are used to bend light, and lenses are used to focus light. Now it's your turn to use mirrors and lenses to design and build a periscope that can see at least six inches above eye level.

① Brainstorm Solutions

A You will build a periscope to see things at least six inches above eye level. Brainstorm some ideas about how your periscope will work. Check a box in each row below to get started.

Length of periscope: ☐ 6 inches ☐ 12 inches ☐ other _____

Shape of periscope: ☐ tube ☐ box ☐ other _____

User will look with: ☐ one eye ☐ both eyes _____

Your periscope: ☐ will ☐ will not magnify objects

B Once you have decided what your periscope needs to do, look at the materials available to you, and brainstorm how you can build your periscope. Write down the materials you will use and how you will use them.

_____

_____

_____

② Select a Solution

Choose one of the ideas that you brainstormed. In the space below, draw a sketch of how your prototype periscope will be constructed. Include arrows to show the path of light through your periscope.

S.T.E.M. ENGINEERING & TECHNOLOGY

③ Build a Prototype

Use your materials to assemble the periscope according to your design. Write down the steps you took to assemble the parts.

_____

_____

_____

_____

④ Test, Evaluate, and Redesign to Improve

Test your periscope, and fill in the first row of the table below. Make any improvements, and test your periscope again, filling in an additional row of the table for each revised prototype.

Prototype	What I saw through the periscope	Improvements to be made
1		
2		
3		

⑤ Communicate Results

Write a paragraph summarizing what you wanted the periscope to do, how you designed and built it, whether the finished periscope worked as planned, and how you made improvements.

_____

_____

_____

_____

_____

_____

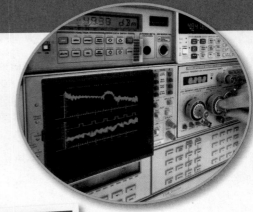

The Electromagnetic Spectrum

is arranged based on the energy of

Waves

are influenced by

Properties of **Waves**

Interactions of **Light**

are influenced by

1 Interpret The Graphic Organizer above shows that the properties of waves are influenced by the energy of waves. Name two properties of waves that affect the energy of waves.

_____

_____

_____

2 Predict When you look in a mirror, you see the reflection of visible light. Would you expect that ultraviolet light would be reflected by a mirror? Explain your reasoning.

_____

_____

_____

3 Claims • Evidence • Reasoning Make a claim about how the energy of a microwave compares to the energy of a gamma ray. Summarize evidence to support your claim and explain your reasoning.

_____

_____

_____

_____

_____

4 Synthesize Is a radio wave a longitudinal wave or a transverse wave?

_____

_____

_____

Vocabulary

Name _____

Fill in each blank with the term that best completes the following sentences.

1 Light travels as a(n) _____ wave.

2 The distance from the crest of one wave to the crest of the next wave is the

_____

3 _____, the number of waves produced in a given amount of time, is expressed in hertz.

4 Sound is a(n) _____ wave because it cannot travel without a medium.

5 The maximum distance that the particles of a medium move away from their rest position is a measure of a wave's _____

Key Concepts

Identify the choice that best completes the statement or answers the question.

6 Heather puts a straw into a glass of water. She notices that when she looks through the glass and the water from the side, the straw appears to be broken. Which term **best** explains why the straw looks like it is broken?

A absorption

C scattering

B refraction

D transmission

7 The energy generated by the sun travels to Earth as electromagnetic waves. Because the radiation from the sun travels to Earth in varying wavelengths, scientists consider them to be a spectrum. Which statement describes an electromagnetic wave with a long wavelength?

F It has a high frequency and low energy.

G It has a high frequency and high energy.

H It has a low frequency and can travel through a vacuum.

I It has a low frequency and needs a medium to travel through.

8 The diagram below shows a wave. The features of the wave are labeled A, B, C, and D.

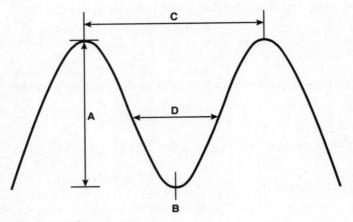

Which label identifies the wavelength?

A A

B B

C C

D D

9 Kana shines a light onto paper as shown in the figure below. The light contains both blue and red wavelengths of light.

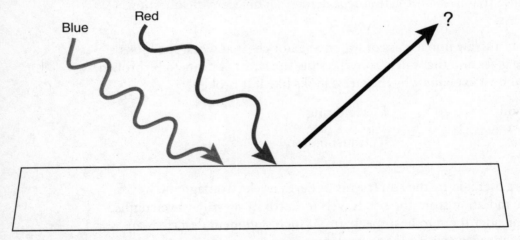

If the paper is blue, what color (or colors) of light bounces off the paper?

F only red

G only blue

H both red and blue

I neither red nor blue

Name _____

10 Habib looks around his classroom at different objects. Which object reflects almost all of the light that strikes it?

A white poster board

B clear window glass

C bright overhead light

D black construction paper

11 Electromagnetic energy travels through space as waves. The electromagnetic spectrum includes all electromagnetic waves, arranged according to frequency and wavelength. Which of these is an example of an electromagnetic wave?

F radio wave

G sound wave

H ocean wave

I gravitational pull

12 Emma measured the maximum displacement of a wave that she made by moving the end of a string up and down. What property of a wave was she measuring?

A period

B frequency

C amplitude

D wavelength

13 Ava covers a flashlight with a piece of thick, black paper. Why doesn't she see the light when she turns on the flashlight?

F The paper absorbs most of the light.

G The paper refracts most of the light.

H The paper reflects most of the light.

I The paper transmits most of the light.

14 Isabella researched how waves travel through the ground during an earthquake. She drew a diagram of one, called an S wave, moving through Earth's crust.

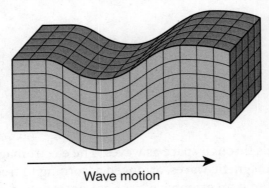

Wave motion

Based on her diagram, what kind of wave is an S wave?

A light

B sound

C longitudinal

D transverse

Critical Thinking

Answer the following questions in the space provided.

15 Some waves carry more energy than others. Which wave has more energy, a loud sound or a quiet sound? Why? Use evidence to support your claim and explain your reasoning.

_____

_____

16 Tafari worked one summer on a ship that set weather buoys in the ocean. He watched how the buoys moved in the water.

Which wave property describes why the buoys bobbed up and down?

Which wave property determines how fast the buoys bobbed in the water?

He observed that when the wind blew harder, the ocean waves were larger, and the buoys moved away from the ship. Did the buoys move as a result of the ocean waves? Summarize evidence to support your claim and explain your reasoning.

_____

_____

_____

_____

Energy and Heat

A Thermogram shows the relative temperature of objects. It can be used to detect heat loss in a house.

FLORIDA **BIG IDEA 11**

Energy Transfer and Transformations

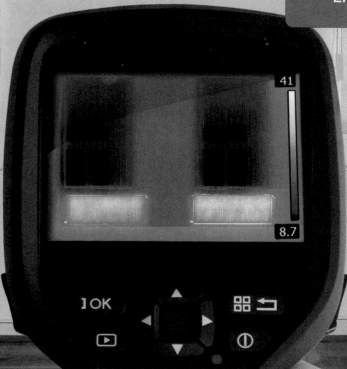

What Do You Think?

See all the red areas in this thermogram? These areas show where energy (in the form of heat) is escaping through gaps around windows and doors. Why is it important to reduce this loss of energy from a home? As you explore this unit, gather evidence to help you state and support a claim.

Energy and Heat

Saving Energy

Humans use many sources of energy in our everyday lives. For example, we need electricity to see at night, fuel to keep our cars running, and food to nourish our bodies. But we need to be careful in our use of energy resources. And you can help!

① Ask a Question

How can individuals avoid wasting energy resources at home?

Make a list of all the sources of energy, such as electricity or natural gas, used in your home. Then, write down what those energy sources are used for, and estimate how much your family uses them each week. For example: "We use natural gas for cooking on our stove approximately three hours each week." Can your family reduce energy consumption in any areas? Work with your family to develop your ideas.

Using a programmable thermostat can help conserve energy.

② Think About It

What is one source of energy used in your home?

_____

_____

Where is energy used most often in your school?

_____

_____

_____

Where is energy used most often in your home?

_____

_____

_____

_____

What are some possible areas in the home and at school where energy usage can be easily reduced?

_____

_____

_____

_____

③ Apply Your Knowledge

A Choose some of the places you identified in your home. Develop strategies for reducing the amount of energy your family uses in those areas.

Area	Strategy

B Apply the strategies you listed above. Track how your energy usage changes as you conserve energy. Examine your utility bill if you have access to it.

_____

_____

_____

_____

_____

Solar panels can convert energy from the sun into a form that can be used in a home.

🏠 Take It Home!

As a class, create an energy conservation plan for your school. Implement it in your class and track how much energy you have saved. Share your results with your school.

Energy Conversion and Conservation

ESSENTIAL QUESTION

How is energy conserved?

By the end of this lesson, you should be able to analyze how energy is conserved through transformations between different forms.

The energy in rocket fuel is changed into energy that allows this rocket to blast off.

SC.7.P.11.2 Investigate and describe the transformation of energy from one form to another. **SC.7.P.11.3** Cite evidence to explain that energy cannot be created nor destroyed, only changed from one form to another.

 Engage Your Brain

1 Explain Draw a diagram that shows what you think happens when a light bulb is turned on. When making your diagram, think about what happens to the energy.

2 Describe What do you know about energy? Using the first letters of the word *energy*, make an acrostic poem that describes energy.

E _____

N _____

E _____

R _____

G _____

Y _____

ACTIVE **READING**

3 Apply Many scientific terms, such as *transformation* and *efficiency*, also have everyday meanings. Use context clues to write your own definition for each underlined word.

Example sentence
After she learned how to play soccer, she went through a complete <u>transformation</u>. Now she practices every day.

transformation:

_____

_____

Example sentence
He finished all of his homework in two hours, and he got everything correct. I wish that I could work with such <u>efficiency</u>.

efficiency:

_____

_____

Vocabulary Terms

- energy transformation
- law of conservation of energy
- efficiency

4 Apply As you learn the definition of each vocabulary term in this lesson, create your own definition or sketch to help you remember the meaning of the term.

Perfect Form

What are some forms of energy?

Remember that energy is the ability to cause change. Energy is measured in joules (J). Energy can come in many different forms. Some common forms of energy are discussed below.

ACTIVE READING

5 Identify As you read, underline examples of energy provided in the text.

○ Mechanical Energy

Mechanical energy is the sum of an object's kinetic energy and potential energy. The energy that a car has while moving is mechanical energy, as is the energy a book has on top of a desk.

○ Sound Energy

Sound energy results from the vibration of particles. People are able to detect these tiny vibrations with structures in their ears that vibrate due to the sound. When you hear a car, you are detecting vibrations in the air that transfer sound energy. Sound cannot travel through empty space. If there were no air or other substance between you and the car, then you would not hear sounds from the car.

○ Electromagnetic Energy

Electromagnetic (ee•LEK•troh•mag•NEH•tik) energy is transmitted through space in the form of electromagnetic waves. Electromagnetic waves can be produced by the vibration of electrically-charged particles. Unlike sound, electromagnetic waves can travel through empty space. Light energy is a form of electromagnetic energy. Some examples of electromagnetic energy are visible light, x-rays, and microwaves. X-rays are high-energy waves used by doctors to look at your bones. Microwaves can be used to cook food. The sun releases a large amount of electromagnetic energy, some of which is absorbed by Earth.

The piccolo player is producing sound energy.

Microwaves use electromagnetic energy to warm food.

This solar flare is an example of many forms of energy. The solar flare releases electromagnetic energy and heat energy produced by nuclear energy in the sun.

Chemical Energy

Chemical energy is the energy stored in chemical bonds that hold chemical compounds together. If a molecule's bonds are broken or rearranged, energy is released or absorbed. Chemical energy can be stored in food and in matches.

Thermal Energy and Heat

Thermal energy is the energy an object has due to the motion of its molecules. The faster the molecules in an object move, the more thermal energy the object has. Heat is the energy transferred from an object at a higher temperature to an object at a lower temperature.

Nuclear Energy

The nucleus of an atom is the source of nuclear (NOO•klee•uhr) energy. When an atom's nucleus breaks apart, or when the nuclei of two small atoms join together, energy is released. The energy given off by the sun comes from nuclear energy. In the sun, hydrogen nuclei join to make a helium nucleus. This reaction gives off a huge amount of energy. The sun's light and heat come from these reactions. Without nuclear energy from the sun, life would not exist on Earth.

Think Outside the Book

6 Claims • Evidence • Reasoning
Keep a journal of ten examples of energy that you see throughout the day. Make a claim about the type of energy it is: mechanical, sound, electromagnetic, chemical, thermal, or nuclear. Provide evidence to support your claim, and explain your reasoning.

7 Categorize Fill in the blank parts of the chart below.

Example	Type of Energy
Bicycle going up a hill	
	Electromagnetic
Orchestra music	

Transformers

What is an energy transformation?

An **energy transformation** takes place when energy changes from one form into another form. Any form of energy can change into any other form of energy. Often, one form of energy changes into more than one form. For example, when you rub your hands together, you hear a sound and your hands get warm. The kinetic energy of your moving hands was transformed into both sound energy and thermal energy.

Another example of an energy transformation is when chemical energy is converted in the body. Why is eating breakfast so important? Eating breakfast gives your body the energy needed to help you start your day. Your chemical potential energy comes from the food you eat. Your body breaks down the components of the food to access the energy contained in them. This energy is then changed to the kinetic energy in your muscles. Some of the chemical energy is converted into thermal energy that allows your body to stay warm.

👁 Visualize It!

Some examples of energy transformation are illustrated in this flashlight. Follow the captions to learn how energy is transformed into the light energy that you rely on when you turn on a flashlight!

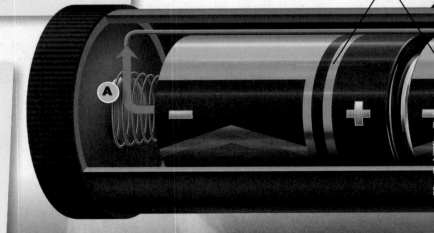

Batteries

A The chemical energy from the batteries is transformed into electrical energy.

8 Claims • Evidence • Reasoning
Identify two other examples of chemical energy being transformed into electrical energy. Provide evidence to support your claim, and explain your reasoning.

_____

_____

Is energy conserved?

A closed system is a group of objects that transfer energy only to one another. For example, a roller coaster can be considered a closed system if it includes everything involved, such as the track, the cars, and the air around them. Energy is conserved in all closed systems. The **law of conservation of energy** states that energy cannot be created or destroyed. It can only change forms. All of the different forms of energy in a closed system always add up to the same total amount of energy. It does not matter how many energy conversions take place.

For example, on a roller coaster some mechanical energy gets transformed into sound and thermal energy as it goes down a hill. The total of the coaster's reduced mechanical energy at the bottom of the hill, the increased thermal energy, and the sound energy, is the same amount of energy as the original amount of mechanical energy. In other words, total energy is conserved.

ACTIVE READING

10 Relate How are energy transformations related to the law of conservation of energy?

_____

_____

_____

_____

i Think Outside the Book

11 Claims • Evidence • Reasoning
Have you ever thought about how a music player works? Make a claim about what type of energy may be used inside of a music player. Provide evidence to support your claim, and explain your reasoning.

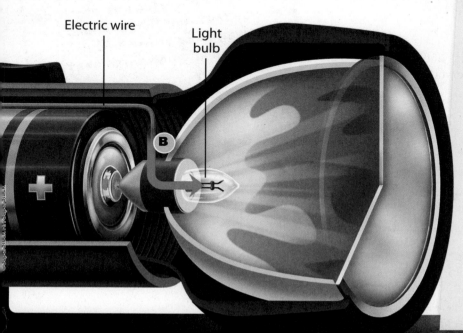

Electric wire

Light bulb

B The electrical energy in the wire is transformed into light energy in the light bulb. Some of the electrical energy is also transferred to the surroundings as heat.

9 Describe Give another example of electrical energy being transformed into light energy.

_____

_____

_____

_____

_____

Efficiency Expert!

How is efficiency measured?

When energy is transformed from one form to another form, some energy is turned into useful energy, but some energy is always transformed into an unintended form. One of the most common unintended forms of energy in an energy transformation is heat. No transformation can ever be 100% efficient. **Efficiency** (ee•FIH•shuhn•see) is the ratio of useful output energy to input energy. Energy efficiency is a comparison of the amount of useful energy after a conversion with the amount of energy before a conversion. Energy efficiency is highly desirable in any system. An efficient process means that as much energy as possible is converted to useful forms of energy. You may have heard that a car is energy efficient if it gets good gas mileage, and that your home may be energy efficient if it is well insulated. Energy conversions that are more efficient waste fewer resources.

unwanted sound energy

unwanted heat energy

The chemical energy in a laptop battery is converted into electrical energy that runs the machine. However, some of the energy is converted into unwanted heat and sound energy.

ACTIVE READING

12 Explain How does the scientific use of the word *efficiency* differ from the everyday use of the word?

_____

_____

⃝ Using a Ratio

Efficiency is the ratio of useful output energy to input energy.

$$\text{Percent efficiency} = \frac{\text{Energy out}}{\text{Energy in}} \times 100\%$$

Energy efficiency is expressed as a percentage. Improving the efficiency of machines is important because greater efficiency results in less waste. If less energy is wasted, less energy is needed to operate a machine. We can use calculations of efficiency to compare different machines to see which is more efficient.

Sample Problem

An old refrigerator required 400 J of energy to give out 50 J of energy. What is its efficiency?

Identify

A. What do you know?

Energy in = 400 J, Energy out = 50 J

B. What do you want to find out? Efficiency

Plan

C. Draw and label a sketch:

400 J ⟶ [ ] ⟶ 50 J

D. Write the formula:

Efficiency = (Energy out / Energy in) × 100%

E. Substitute into the formula:

Efficiency = (50 J / 400 J) × 100%

Solve

F. Calculate and simplify: Efficiency =

(50 J / 400 J) × 100% = 12.5%

G. Check that your units agree:

Answer is a percentage. Efficiency is also a percentage. Units agree.

Answer: 12.5%

You Try It

13 Calculate You would like to replace the refrigerator from the previous problem with a more efficient model. One option requires 300 J of energy and gives out 50 J of energy. What is this refrigerator's efficiency? Is it more efficient than the refrigerator in the previous problem?

Identify

A. What do you know?

B. What do you want to find out?

Plan

C. Draw and label a sketch:

D. Write the formula:

E. Substitute into the formula:

Solve

F. Calculate and simplify:

G. Check that your units agree:

Answer:

This old refrigerator is not as efficient as many new refrigerators that are made today.

Visual Summary

To complete this summary, fill in the blanks with the correct word or phrase. You can use this page to review the main concepts of the lesson.

Energy Conversions

Energy can come in many different forms such as mechanical energy, sound energy, electromagnetic energy, thermal energy, chemical energy, and nuclear energy.

14 A dog running through the yard is an example of_____ energy.

15 Energy is measured in units called _____

One form of energy can transform into another form of energy.

16 Energy cannot be _____ or _____

17 Energy in a flashlight's battery changes from _____ energy to electrical energy.

Efficiency is a ratio of useful output energy to input energy.

$$\text{Percent efficiency} = \left(\frac{\text{Energy out}}{\text{Energy in}} \right) \times 100\%$$

18 No energy transformation can ever be _____ efficient.

19 A common form of unwanted energy in an energy transformation is _____

unwanted sound energy

unwanted heat energy

20 **Claims • Evidence • Reasoning** Describe a process in which energy changes form twice. Make a claim about any unwanted forms of energy produced during the energy transformation. Provide evidence to support your claim, and explain your reasoning.

Lesson Review

Vocabulary

In your own words, define the following terms.

1 Law of conservation of energy:

_____

_____

2 Efficiency:

_____

_____

Key Concepts

3 **Contrast** Describe the difference between nuclear energy and light energy.

_____

_____

_____

4 **Provide** Give an example of an energy conversion. Make sure to discuss which forms of energy are involved.

_____

_____

_____

5 **Describe** Give an example of an energy conversion that produces an unwanted form of energy.

_____

_____

6 **Calculate** Suppose a vacuum cleaner uses 120 J of electrical energy. If 45 J are used to pull air into the vacuum cleaner, how efficient is the vacuum cleaner?

_____

_____

_____

_____

Use this photo to answer the following questions.

7 **Analyze** List one example of each of the following forms of energy found in the photo.

sound energy:

_____

chemical energy:

_____

mechanical energy:

_____

8 **Analyze** List two examples of energy transformations necessary for the sporting event to take place.

_____

_____

_____

Critical Thinking

9 **Claims • Evidence • Reasoning** Make a claim about the statement, "You can move parts of your body because of energy from the sun." Use evidence to support your claim, and explain your reasoning.

_____

_____

_____

_____

Publishing Company

Temperature

ESSENTIAL **QUESTION**

How is temperature related to kinetic energy?

By the end of this lesson, you should be able to relate the temperature of a substance to the kinetic energy of its particles.

SC.7.P.11.1 Recognize that adding heat to or removing heat from a system may result in a temperature change and possibly a change of state. **SC.7.P.11.4** Observe and describe that heat flows in predictable ways, moving from warmer objects to cooler ones until they reach the same temperature.

What does it mean to be hot or cold? You can tell that this environment is cold because there is ice and because the person is in a hat and coat.

Lesson Labs

Quick Lab
• Temperature Change

Engage Your Brain

1 Predict Check T or F to show whether you think each statement is true or false.

T   F

☐   ☐   Solids and liquids are made of particles, but gases are made of air, which is not made of particles.

☐   ☐   Kinetic energy is the energy of motion.

☐   ☐   Kinetic energy depends on mass and speed.

2 Illustrate Think about a time when you were very cold. Then draw a picture of a time when you were very hot. Write a caption about the differences between the two situations.

ACTIVE READING

3 Synthesize Many English words have their roots in other languages. Use the Greek words below to make an educated guess about the meaning of the word *thermometer*. A context sentence is provided for help. Then, write a sentence using the word correctly.

Greek word	Meaning
thermos	warm
metron	to measure

Example sentence
This <u>thermometer</u> indicates that it is 72 °F in this room.

Define thermometer:

_____

Sentence with thermometer:

_____

Vocabulary Terms

• kinetic theory of matter
• temperature
• degree
• thermometer

4 Identify This list contains the key terms you'll learn in this lesson. As you read, circle the definition of each term.

Particle Party

What is the kinetic theory of matter?

All matter is made of atoms. These particles are always moving, even if it doesn't look like they are. The **kinetic theory of matter** states that all of the particles that make up matter are constantly in motion. Because the particles are in motion, they have kinetic energy. The faster the particles are moving, the more kinetic energy they have.

While the particles of matter are constantly moving, the particles move in different directions and at different speeds. This motion is random. Therefore, the individual particles of matter have different amounts of kinetic energy. The average kinetic energy of all these particles takes into account their different random movements. As seen in this picture, solids, liquids, and gases have different average kinetic energies.

This bridge is a solid, so its particles are close together and vibrate.

In this hot pool, the liquid particles are moving around.

The particles in the gas in the air are far apart and moving quickly.

The particles in this cold river water are moving freely.

How do particles move in solids, liquids, and gases?

The kinetic theory of matter explains the motion of particles in solids, liquids, and gases.

- The particles in a solid, such as concrete, are not free to move around very much. They vibrate back and forth in the same position and are held tightly together by forces of attraction.
- The particles in a liquid, such as water in a pool, move much more freely than particles in a solid. They are constantly sliding around and tumbling over each other as they move.
- In a gas, such as the air around you, particles are far apart and move around at high speeds. Particles collide with one another, but otherwise they do not interact much.

ACTIVE READING

5 Describe In your own words, describe the difference between the movement of particles in liquids and the movement of particles in gases.

_____
_____
_____
_____

👁 Visualize It!

6 Claims • Evidence • Reasoning Locate another solid, liquid, or gas in this photo. Sketch a representation of the particles that make up the solid, liquid, or gas. Make a claim as to how fast you think the particles might be moving based on temperature. Use evidence to support your answer. Write a caption to explain your reasoning.

_____
_____
_____

Mercury Rising

How does temperature relate to kinetic energy?

Temperature (TEM•per•uh•chur) is a measure of the average kinetic energy of all the particles in an object. In the picture on the previous page, the particle diagrams for two different liquids are shown. For the colder liquid, the particles are moving slower. For the warmer liquid, the particles are moving faster. If an iron is hot, the particles in the solid are vibrating very fast and have a high average kinetic energy. If the iron has a low temperature, the particles in the solid are vibrating more slowly and have a lower average kinetic energy.

Absolute zero is the temperature at which the motion of particles stops. It is not possible to actually reach absolute zero, though temperatures very close to absolute zero have been reached in laboratories.

How is temperature measured?

Suppose you hear on the radio that the temperature outside is 30 degrees. Do you need to wear a warm coat to spend the day outside? The answer depends on the temperature scale being used. There are three common temperature scales, all of which measure the average kinetic energy of particles. These scales are called Celsius, Fahrenheit, and Kelvin. However, 30 degrees on one scale is quite different from 30 degrees on the other scales.

To establish a temperature scale, two known values and the number of units between the values are needed. The freezing and boiling points of pure water are often used as the standard values. These points are always the same under the same conditions, and they are easy to reproduce. In the Celsius and Fahrenheit scales, temperature is measured in units called degrees. **Degrees** (°) are equally spaced units between two points. The space between degrees can vary from scale to scale. In the Kelvin scale, no degree sign is used. Instead, the unit is just called a kelvin. Temperature is measured using an instrument called a **thermometer**.

ACTIVE READING

7 Claims • Evidence • Reasoning Make a claim about how a substance's temperature changes when the average kinetic energy of its particles increases and when it decreases. Use evidence to support your claim, and explain your reasoning.

i Think Outside the Book

8 Produce Write a story about someone who travels from one extreme temperature to another. Make sure to talk about how your character adjusts to the change in temperature. How are the character's daily activities or decisions affected?

Celsius Scale

The temperature scale most commonly used around the world, and often used by scientists, is the Celsius (SEL•see•uhs) scale (°C). This scale was developed in the 1740s by Anders Celsius. On the Celsius scale, pure water freezes at 0 °C and boils at 100 °C, so there are 100 degrees—100 equal units—between these two temperatures.

Fahrenheit Scale

The scale used most commonly in the United States for measuring temperature is the Fahrenheit scale (°F). It was developed in the early 1700s by Gabriel Fahrenheit. On the Fahrenheit scale, pure water freezes at 32 °F and boils at 212 °F. Thus, there are 180 degrees—180 equal units—between the freezing point and the boiling point of water.

Kelvin Scale

A temperature scale used commonly by physicists is the Kelvin scale. This scale was not developed until the 20th century. The equal units in the Kelvin scale are called kelvins, not degrees. On the kelvin scale, pure water freezes at 273 K and boils at 373 K. There are 100 kelvins—100 equal units—between these two temperatures. The lowest temperature on the Kelvin scale is absolute zero, or 0 K.

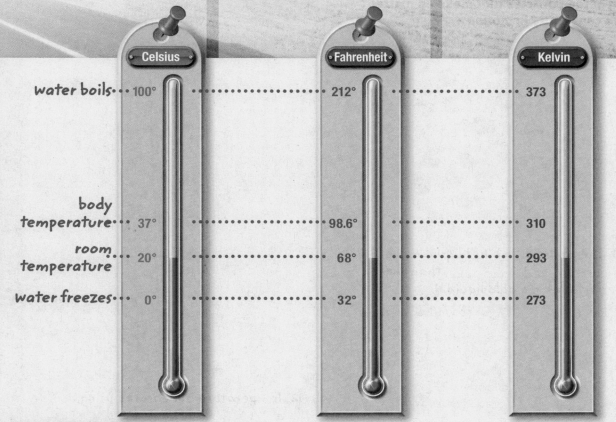

	Celsius	Fahrenheit	Kelvin
water boils	100°	212°	373
body temperature	37°	98.6°	310
room temperature	20°	68°	293
water freezes	0°	32°	273

👁 Visualize It!

9 Identify What is body temperature in the Celsius scale? In the Fahrenheit scale? In the Kelvin scale?

_____

_____

10 Claims • Evidence • Reasoning The water in swimming pools is typically about 80 °F. Mark this temperature on the Fahrenheit thermometer above. Make a claim about what temperature this is in the Celsius and Kelvin scales. Support your claim with evidence, and explain your reasoning.

_____

Visual Summary

To complete this summary, fill in the blanks with the correct word. You can use this page to review the main concepts of the lesson.

Temperature

Temperature is a measure of the average kinetic energy of all the particles in an object. Temperature is measured using one of three scales: Celsius, Fahrenheit, or Kelvin.

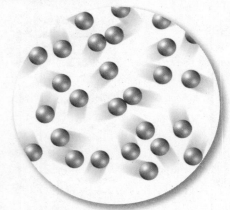

All of the particles that make up matter are constantly in motion.

11 The particles in a hot liquid move _____ than the particles in a cold liquid.

12 Temperature is measured using a _____.

13 Claims • Evidence • Reasoning If a puddle of water is frozen, do particles in the ice have kinetic energy? Use evidence to support your claim and explain your reasoning.

Lesson Review

Vocabulary

For each pair of terms, write a sentence using both words that demonstrates the definition of each word.

1 kinetic theory of matter and temperature

_____

_____

_____

_____

_____

2 thermometer and degree

_____

_____

_____

_____

Key Concepts

3 Relate Describe the relationship between temperature and kinetic energy.

_____

_____

_____

4 Apply Particles in a warmer substance have a _____ average kinetic energy than particles in the substance when it is cooler.

5 Identify What are the three scales used to measure temperature? What are the units of each scale?

_____

_____

_____

_____

Critical Thinking

Use the art below to answer the following questions.

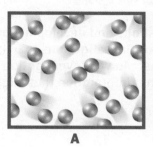 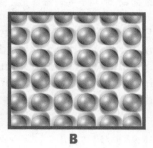

A   B

6 Observe Which illustration represents the substance at a higher temperature? Explain your reasoning.

_____

_____

_____

7 Claims • Evidence • Reasoning Make a claim about what would happen to the particles in illustration A if the substance were chilled and if the particles in illustration B were warmed. Use evidence to support your claim, and explain your reasoning.

_____

_____

_____

_____

8 Claims • Evidence • Reasoning Using your knowledge of the differences between the three different temperature scales, what do you think would happen if a human's body temperature were 98.6 °C? Make a claim about why doctors worry more about a fever of a couple of degrees Celsius than a fever of a couple of degrees Fahrenheit. Provide evidence to support your claim, and explain your reasoning.

_____

_____

_____

_____

THINK SCIENCE

SC.7.N.1.1 Define a problem from the seventh grade curriculum, use appropriate reference materials to support scientific understanding, plan and carry out scientific investigation of various types, such as systematic observations or experiments, identify variables, collect and organize data, interpret data in charts, tables, and graphics analyze information, make predictions, and defend conclusions.

Planning an Investigation

Scientists ask many questions and develop hypotheses about the natural world. They conduct investigations to help answer these questions. A scientist must plan an investigation carefully. The investigation should gather information that might support or disprove the hypothesis.

Tutorial

Use the following steps to help plan an investigation.

① Write a hypothesis.
The hypothesis should offer an explanation for the question that you are asking. The hypothesis must also be testable. If it is not testable, rewrite the hypothesis.

② Identify and list the possible variables in your experiment.
Select the independent variable and the dependent variable. In your investigation, you will change the independent variable to see any effect it may have on the dependent variable.

③ List the materials that you will need to perform the experiment.
This list should also include equipment that you need for safety.

④ Determine the method you will use to test your hypothesis.
Clearly describe the steps you will follow. If you change any part of the procedure while you are conducting the investigation, record the change. Another scientist should be able to follow your procedure to repeat your investigation.

⑤ Analyze the results.
Your data and observations from all of your experiments should be recorded carefully and clearly to maintain credibility. Record how you analyze your results so others can review your work and spot any problems or errors in your analysis.

⑥ Draw conclusions.
Describe what the results of the investigation show. Tell whether the results support your hypothesis.

You Try It!

You are a member of a research team that is trying to design and test a roof system that can maintain a comfortable temperature inside a building during hot days. The system you design and test will be a scale model. To begin, you need to find an answer to the following question: What material will minimize the rate of heat transfer inside a building?

1 Forming a Hypothesis Write down your hypothesis. How does your hypothesis explain or answer your question? Is your hypothesis testable?

_____

_____

_____

_____

2 Identifying Variables List the possible variables in this experiment. Identify dependent variables and independent variables.

_____

_____

_____

_____

3 Selecting Materials What equipment and tools will you need to test this variable? What might happen if you select inappropriate tools?

_____

_____

_____

_____

4 Testing Your Hypothesis What will your system look like? Will it support your testing? You may sketch the system on a separate page.

_____

_____

_____

_____

_____

5 Maintaining Accurate Records What steps will you need to follow in order to test your hypothesis? What kinds of measurements will you collect? What kind of graphic organizer will you use to record your information?

_____

_____

_____

_____

_____

6 Claims • Evidence • Reasoning Make a claim about the material you tested, and use evidence from your data to support your claim. Was your hypothesis helpful? Explain your reasoning.

_____

_____

_____

_____

🏠 Take It Home

Look closely at objects and materials in your home. Write a list of things that help to prevent the transfer of energy as heat. Design an investigation using one or more of these items to learn more about the job they do. Record your observations. Evaluate your results to see if they might point to a further investigation or an improvement to a product. Present your results in a pamphlet.

Thermal Energy and Heat

ESSENTIAL QUESTION

What is the relationship among, heat, temperature, and thermal energy?

By the end of this lesson, you should be able to analyze the relationship between heat, temperature, and thermal energy.

The Afar Depression, in Eastern Africa, is one of the hottest places on Earth. In the summer, temperatures average over 38 °C (100 °F)!

SC.7.N.1.1 Define a problem from the seventh grade curriculum, use appropriate reference materials to support scientific understanding, plan and carry out scientific investigation of various types, such as systematic observations or experiments, identify variables, collect and organize data, interpret data in charts, tables, and graphics, analyze information, make predictions, and defend conclusions. **SC.7.P.11.1** Recognize that adding heat to or removing heat from a system may result in a temperature change and possibly a change of state. **SC.7.P.11.4** Observe and describe that heat flows in predictable ways, moving from warmer objects to cooler ones until they reach the same temperature.

✋ Lesson Labs

Quick Labs
- Simple Heat Engine
- Exploring Thermal Conductivity
- Heat Transfer by Conduction

Exploration Lab
- Changes of State

S.T.E.M. Lab
- Modeling Geothermal Power

🧠 Engage Your Brain

1 Describe Fill in the blanks with the words that you think correctly complete the following sentences.

When you put your hands on a cold object, like a glass of ice water, your hands become

_____ The glass of water

becomes _____ if you

leave your hands on it for a long time. If you leave the glass of ice water out in the sun, the

ice will start to _____

2 Describe Write your own caption for this photo.

_____

_____

_____

ACTIVE **READING**

3 Apply Many scientific words, such as *conductor*, also have everyday meanings. Use context clues to write your own definition for each meaning of the word *conductor*.

Example sentence
That school's band is very good because its <u>conductor</u> is a great teacher.

conductor:

_____

_____

Example sentence
That metal spoon is a good <u>conductor</u>, so it will get hot if you put it into boiling soup.

conductor:

_____

_____

Vocabulary Terms

- **thermal energy**
- **heat**
- **calorie**
- **conduction**
- **conductor**
- **insulator**
- **convection**
- **radiation**

4 Apply As you learn the definition of each vocabulary term in this lesson, create your own definition or sketch to help you remember the meaning of the term.

What is thermal energy?

Thermal energy is the total kinetic energy of all particles in a substance. In the SI system, thermal energy is measured in joules (J). Remember that temperature is not energy, but it does give a measure of the average kinetic energy of all the particles in a substance. If you have two identical glasses of water and one is at a higher temperature than the other, the particles in the hotter water have a higher average kinetic energy. The water at a higher temperature will have a higher amount of thermal energy.

What is the difference between thermal energy and temperature?

Temperature and thermal energy are different from each other. Temperature is related to the average kinetic energy of particles, while thermal energy is the total kinetic energy of all the particles. A glass of water can have the same temperature as Lake Superior, but the lake has much more thermal energy because the lake contains many more water molecules.

After you put ice cubes into a pitcher of lemonade, energy is transferred from the warmer lemonade to the colder ice. The lemonade's thermal energy decreases and the ice's thermal energy increases. Because the particles in the lemonade have transferred some of their energy to the particles in the ice, the average kinetic energy of the particles in the lemonade decreases. Thus, the temperature of the lemonade decreases.

ACTIVE READING

5 Explain What are two factors that determine the thermal energy of a substance?

_____

_____

There are more water molecules in this lake than in the glass of water on the right.

Under Where?

There are fewer water molecules in this glass than in the lake.

6 Apply For each object pair in the table below, circle the object that has more thermal energy. Assume that both objects are at the same temperature.

bowl of soup	small balloon	tiger
pot of soup	large balloon	house cat

Heat It Up!

Energy in the form of heat flows from the warm drinks to the cold ice. The ice melts.

What is heat?

You might think of the word *heat* as having to do with things that feel hot. But heat also has to do with things that feel cold. Heat causes objects to feel hot or cold or to get hot or cold under the right conditions. You probably use the word *heat* every day to mean different things. However, in science, **heat** is the energy transferred from an object at a higher temperature to an object at a lower temperature.

When two objects at different temperatures come into contact, energy is always transferred from the object that has the higher temperature to the object that has the lower temperature. Energy in the form of heat always flows from hot to cold. For example, if you put an ice cube into a glass of water, energy is transferred from the warmer water to the colder ice cube.

7 Apply For each object pair in the table below, draw an arrow in the direction in which energy in the form of heat would flow.

Object 1	Direction of heat flow	Object 2
metal rod		fire
hat		snowman
ice cube		glass of warm water

© Houghton Mifflin Harcourt Publishing Company (t) ©Darren Kemper/Corbis; (b) ©Jose Luis Pelaez Inc/Blend Images/Age Fotostock

Energy in the form of heat flows from the hot fire to the marshmallow. The marshmallow gets so hot that it catches on fire!

Energy in the form of heat flows from the warm mugs to the girls' cold hands. Their hands get warmer.

👁 Visualize It!

8 Claims • Evidence • Reasoning
Make a claim about another heat exchange happening in this picture. Provide evidence to support your claim. Explain your reasoning.

_____

_____

_____

How is heat measured?

Heat is measured in two ways. One way is the calorie (cal). One **calorie** is equal to the amount of energy needed to raise the temperature of 1 g of water by 1 °C. Heat can also be measured in joules (J) because heat is a form of energy. One calorie is equal to 4.18 J.

You probably think of calories in terms of food. However, in nutrition, one Calorie—written with a capital C—is actually one kilocalorie, or 1,000 calories. This means that one Calorie (Cal) contains enough energy to raise the temperature of 1 kg of water by 1 °C. Each Calorie in food contains 1,000 cal of energy.

To find out how many Calories are in an apple, the apple is burned inside an instrument called a calorimeter. A thermometer measures the increase in temperature, which is used to calculate how much energy is released. This amount is the number of Calories.

How is heat related to thermal energy?

Adding or removing heat from a substance will affect its temperature and thermal energy. Heat, however, is not the same as thermal energy and temperature. These are properties of a substance. Heat is the energy involved when these properties change.

Think of what happens when two objects at different temperatures come into contact. Energy as heat flows from the object at the higher temperature to the object at the lower temperature. When both objects come to the same temperature, no more energy as heat flows. Just because the temperature of the two objects is the same does not mean they have the same thermal energy. One object may be larger than the other and thus have more particles in motion.

ACTIVE **READING**

9 Relate What will happen if two objects at different temperatures come into contact?

_____

_____

How can heat affect the state of an object?

The matter that makes up a frozen juice bar is the same whether the juice bar is frozen or has melted. The matter is just in a different form, or state. Remember that the kinetic theory of matter states that the particles that make up matter move around at different speeds. The state of a substance depends on the speed of its particles. Adding energy in the form of heat to a substance may result in a change of state. The added energy may cause the bonds between particles to break. This is what allows the state to change. Adding energy in the form of heat to a chunk of glacier may cause the ice to melt into water. Removing energy in the form of heat from a substance may also result in a change of state.

ACTIVE READING

11 **Predict** What are two ways to change the state of a substance?

_____

_____

i Think Outside the Book

10 **State Your Claim** Have you ever needed to touch a very hot object? What did you use to touch it without burning yourself? Have you ever needed to protect yourself from being cold? What did you use? Compare the objects you used. Make a claim about what they have in common.

Some of this ice is changing state. It is melting into water.

How do polar bears stay warm?

©Arcticphoto//Alamy

© Houghton Mifflin Harcourt Publishing Company

Keep Your Cool

What is conduction?

There are three main ways to transfer energy as heat: conduction, convection, and radiation. **Conduction** is the transfer of energy as heat from one substance to another through direct contact. It occurs any time that objects at different temperatures come into contact with each other. The average kinetic energy of particles in the warmer object is greater than the average kinetic energy of the particles in the cooler object. As the particles collide, some of the kinetic energy of the particles in the warmer object is transferred to the cooler object. As long as the objects are in contact, conduction continues until the temperatures of the objects are equal.

Conduction can also occur within a single object. In this case, energy in the form of heat is transferred from the warmer part of the object to the cooler part of the object. Imagine you put a metal spoon into a cup of hot cocoa. Energy will be conducted from the warm end of the spoon to the cool end until the temperature of the entire spoon is the same.

This is a photo of polar bear hair magnified about 350 times! Notice that it is hollow inside. The air inside is a good insulator.

Conductors

Some materials transfer the kinetic energy of particles better than others. A **conductor** is a material that transfers heat very well. Metals are typically good conductors. You know that when one end of a metal object gets hot, the other end quickly becomes hot as well. Consider pots or pans that have metal handles. A metal handle becomes too hot to touch soon after the pan is placed on a hot stove.

Insulators

An **insulator** (IN•suh•lay•ter) is a material that is a poor conductor of heat. Some examples of insulators are wood, paper, and plastic foam. Plastic foam is a good insulator because it contains many small spaces that are filled with air. A plastic foam cup will not easily transfer energy in the form of heat by conduction. That is why plastic foam is often used to keep hot drinks hot. Think about the metal pan handle mentioned above. It can be dangerous to have handles get hot so quickly. Instead, pot handles are often made of an insulator, such as wood or plastic. Although a plastic handle will also get hot when the pot is on the stove, it takes a much longer time for it to get hot than it would for a metal handle.

12 Classify Decide whether each object below is a conductor or an insulator. Then check the correct box.

Flannel shirt	☐ Conductor
	☐ Insulator
Iron skillet	☐ Conductor
	☐ Insulator
Copper pipe	☐ Conductor
	☐ Insulator
Oven mitt	☐ Conductor
	☐ Insulator

What is convection?

Energy in the form of heat can also be transferred through the movement of gases or liquids. **Convection** (kuhn•VEK•shuhn) is the transfer of energy as heat by the movement of a liquid or gas. In most substances, as temperature increases, the density of the liquid or gas decreases. Convection occurs when a cooler, denser mass of a gas or liquid replaces a warmer, less dense mass of a gas or liquid by pushing it upward.

When you boil water in a pot, the water moves in roughly circular patterns because of convection. The water at the bottom of the pot gets hot because there is a source of heat at the bottom. As the water heats, it becomes less dense. The warmer water rises through the denser, cooler water above it. At the surface, the warm water begins to cool. The particles move closer together, making the water denser. The cooler water then sinks back to the bottom, is heated again, and the cycle repeats. This cycle causes a circular motion of liquids or gases. The motion is due to density differences that result from temperature differences. The motion is called a *convection current*.

What is radiation?

Radiation is another way in which heat can be transferred. **Radiation** is the transfer of energy by electromagnetic waves. Some examples of electromagnetic waves include visible light, microwaves, and infrared light. The sun is the most significant source of radiation that you experience on a daily basis. However, all objects—even you—emit radiation and release energy.

When radiation is emitted from one object and then absorbed by another, the result is often a transfer of heat. Like conduction and convection, radiation can transfer heat from warmer to cooler objects. However, radiation differs from conduction and convection in a very significant way. Radiation can travel through empty space, as it does when it moves from the sun to Earth.

(bkgd) ©NASA; (l) ©Orjan F. Ellingvag/Dagens Naringsliv/Corbis; (tr) ©Howard Davies/Alamy

ACTIVE READING

13 Identify As you read, underline examples of heat transfer.

This pot of boiling water shows how convection currents move.

14 Classify Fill in the blanks in the chart below.

Example	Conduction, Convection, or Radiation
When you put some food in the microwave, it gets hot.	
	Conduction
A heater on the first floor of the school makes the air on the second floor warm.	

© Houghton Mifflin Harcourt Publishing Company

Practical Uses of Radiation

SOCIETY AND TECHNOLOGY

Do you think that you could cook your food using the energy from the sun? Using a device called a solar cooker, you could! A solar cooker works by concentrating the radiation from the sun into a small area using mirrors. Solar cookers aren't just fun to use—they also help some people eat clean food!

In a refugee camp
This woman, who lives in a refugee camp in Sudan, is making tea with water that she boiled in a solar cooker. For many people living far from electricity or a source of clean water, a solar cooker provides a cheap and portable way to sterilize their water. This helps to prevent disease.

As a hobby
This woman demonstrates how her solar cooker works. Many people like to use solar cookers because they do not require any fuel. They also do not release any emissions that are harmful to the planet.

i Extend

15 Claims • Evidence • Reasoning Two examples of radiation are shown in the photos above. Make a claim about the source of the radiation. Use evidence to support your claim, and explain your reasoning.

16 Relate Research other places throughout the world where solar cookers are being used.

17 Produce Explain how solar cookers are useful to society by doing one of the following:
• Make a solar cooker and demonstrate how it works.
• Write a story about a family who uses a solar cooker to stay healthy and safe.

Visual Summary

To complete this summary, circle the correct word or phrase. You can use this page to review the main concepts of the lesson.

Thermal energy is the total kinetic energy of all particles in a substance.

18 If two objects are at the same temperature, the one with more / fewer / the same amount of particles will have a higher thermal energy.

Heat is the energy transferred from an object at a higher temperature to an object at a lower temperature.

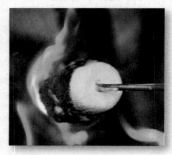

19 Heat always flows from cold to hot / hot to cold / left to right.

Heat

Heat can change the state of a substance.

20 Adding heat to an object causes bonds between particles to form / break / combine. This is what allows the state change.

There are three main ways to transfer energy as heat: conduction, convection, and radiation.

conduction

convection

radiation

21 Conduction is the transfer of energy from a warmer object to a cooler object through a gas / empty space / direct contact.

22 Energy from the sun travels to Earth through conduction / convection / radiation.

23 **Claims • Evidence • Reasoning** Suppose you are outside on a hot day and you move into the shade of a tree. Make a claim to describe which form of energy transfer you are avoiding. Use evidence to explain your reasoning.

Lesson Review

Vocabulary

In your own words, define the following terms.

1 heat

_____

_____

2 thermal energy

_____

_____

3 conduction

_____

_____

4 convection

_____

_____

_____

5 radiation

_____

_____

_____

Use this photo to answer the following questions.

8 Classify Which type of energy transfer is occurring at each lettered area?

A _____

B _____

C _____

Key Concepts

6 Compare What is the difference between heat and temperature?

_____

_____

_____

_____

7 Claims • Evidence • Reasoning Two objects at different temperatures are in contact with each other. Make a claim about what happens to their temperatures. Support your claim with evidence, and explain your reasoning.

_____

_____

_____

_____

Critical Thinking

9 Synthesize Describe the relationships among temperature, heat, and thermal energy.

_____

_____

_____

_____

10 Synthesize Do you think that solids can undergo convection? Explain your reasoning.

_____

_____

_____

_____

_____

SC.7.N.1.1 Define a problem from the seventh grade curriculum, use appropriate reference materials to support scientific understanding, plan and carry out scientific investigation of various types, such as systematic observations or experiments, identify variables, collect and organize data, interpret data in charts, tables, and graphics, analyze information, make predictions, and defend conclusions.

S.T.E.M. ENGINEERING & TECHNOLOGY

Evaluating Technological Systems

Skills	Objectives
✓ Identify inputs	Identify inputs and outputs of a physical system.
✓ Identify outputs	Differentiate between convective and radiative heat transfer.
✓ Identify system processes	Graph temperature data versus time.
✓ Identify system feedback	Analyze and communicate results of an experiment.
Examine system interactions	
Apply system controls	
✓ Communicate results	

Analyzing a Greenhouse

A greenhouse is an enclosed space that maintains a consistent environment and temperature to let people grow plants where the natural climate is not ideal. A greenhouse system needs to heat up and cool off in order to effectively grow plants. How the sun warms a greenhouse involves both radiation and convection. Objects on the ground absorb sunlight and become warm. At the same time, objects cool off primarily in two ways: (1) they get rid of heat by transferring energy as visible light or infrared (in•fruh•RED) light (radiation), or (2) they transfer energy in the form of heat to the air, which then carries it away (convection). A greenhouse retains energy in the form of heat primarily because its roof and walls prevent its warmed air from moving out into the atmosphere.

1 Infer Identify the processes shown at labels A and B as either convection or radiation.

A _____

B _____

Infer Why is convection the main process regulating the temperature in a greenhouse?

_____

_____

_____

_____

Infrared radiation: some escapes; some is reflected.

warm air rises

B

A

cool air sinks

© Houghton Mifflin Harcourt

(bg) ©PhotoStock-Israel/Alamy

Greenhouse Systems

Greenhouses are systems that have inputs and outputs. The inputs are air, water, sunlight, young plants or seeds, and plant nutrients. The outputs are energy in the form of heat and mature plants, fruits, or vegetables. The main uses of greenhouses are agriculture (farming) and horticulture (HOHR•tih•kuhl•cher) (gardening). Typical outputs of agricultural greenhouses are fruits and vegetables. Typical outputs of horticultural greenhouses are ornamental plants and flowers. Greenhouses can vary in size from very large to the size of a shoebox. Gardeners call small greenhouses *cold frames*.

2 Infer Three different types of greenhouses are shown here. Label each type of greenhouse agriculture, horticulture, or cold frame, and list the likely outputs of each.

Ⓐ
_____
_____

Ⓑ
_____
_____

Ⓒ
_____
_____

 You Try It!

Now it's your turn to make a greenhouse and analyze how it works.

✋ You Try It!

Now it's your turn to construct a mini-greenhouse and analyze its inputs, how it heats up, and how its temperature is regulated.

You Will Need

✓ small box, 8 in. (length) x 5 in. (width) x 3 in. (height)

✓ thermometer, digital if possible (1)

✓ marking pens, brown or black

✓ clear plastic wrap

✓ tape or rubber bands

✓ aluminum foil

✓ lamp

① Identify Inputs

What are the inputs of your greenhouse?

_____

② Identify Outputs

What are the outputs of your greenhouse?

_____

_____

③ Identify System Processes

A First, record the room-temperature reading of your thermometer. _____

B Then, begin to construct your greenhouse using the materials listed. With a marking pen, color the inside of your box to simulate the color of dirt.

C Place your thermometer in the box so that it does not touch any part of the box but so that you can still read it. Why should the thermometer not touch the box?

_____

_____

_____

D Using the foil, make a tent-style barrier in the box to shade the thermometer so the lamp does not directly shine on it. Why is it important to shade the thermometer?

_____

_____

_____

E Cover the box with clear plastic wrap, and seal it as best you can with tape or a rubber band to minimize air leaks. Place the lamp above the box to act as the sun.

F What physical processes are involved in your greenhouse system as it accumulates heat energy?

_____
_____
_____
_____

④ Identify System Feedbacks

Record the temperature of the air in the greenhouse every 5 minutes for at least 30 minutes. Add scale values on tick marks to both axes. Then, graph the temperature versus time in the space provided.

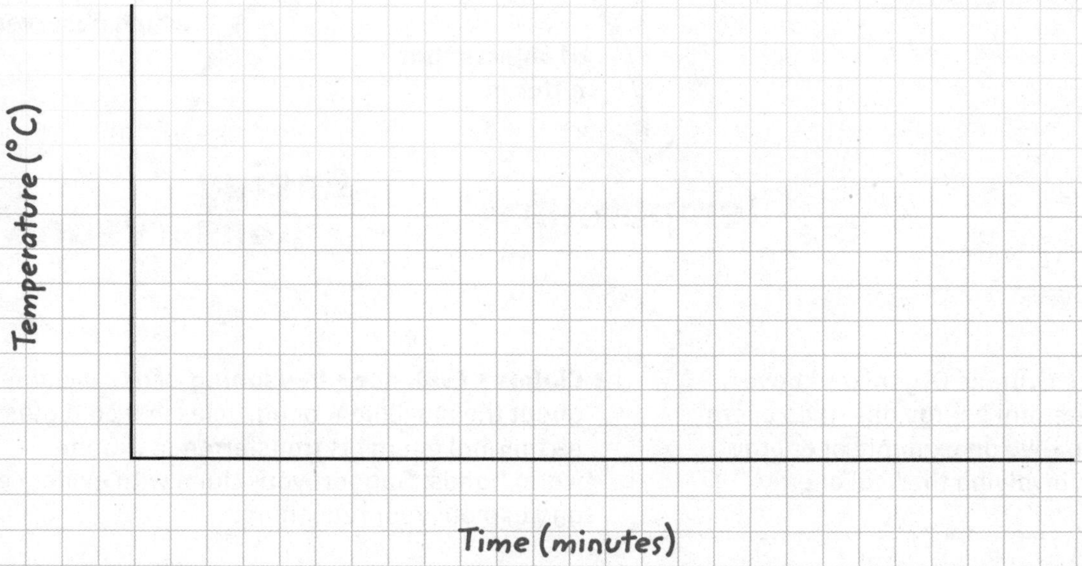

Temperature (°C) vs. Time (minutes)

⑤ Communicate Results

Claims • Evidence • Reasoning Make a claim about what you learned from your greenhouse experiment. Support your claim with evidence, and explain your reasoning.

_____
_____
_____
_____
_____

Heat

is transferred
and changes

↓

Thermal
Energy

of objects that
differ in

which observes

↓

Temperature

Energy
Conservation

1 Interpret The Graphic Organizer above shows that thermal energy observes energy conservation. Give an example of energy conservation involving thermal energy.

_____

_____

_____

_____

2 Compare Describe conductors and insulators in terms of energy.

_____

_____

_____

_____

3 Claims • Evidence • Reasoning Make a claim about the movement of particles in a cold glass as thermal energy is transferred to it from warm hands. Support your claim with evidence and explain your reasoning.

_____

_____

_____

4 Support Your Claim Can you use a thermometer to measure thermal energy? Support your claim with evidence.

_____

_____

_____

_____

Vocabulary

Name _____

Check the box to show whether each statement is true or false.

T	F	
☐	☐	**1** Mechanical energy is the sum of an object's kinetic and potential energy.
☐	☐	**2** The kinetic theory of matter states that all of the particles that make up matter are in a fixed position.
☐	☐	**3** Heat is the energy transferred from an object at a higher temperature to an object at a lower temperature.

Key Concepts

Identify the choice that best completes the statement or answers the question.

4 These two beakers contain the same liquid substance at the same temperature.

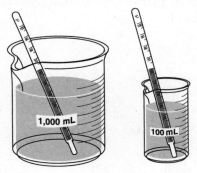

1,000 mL   100 mL

How does the thermal energy of the liquid in the larger beaker compare with the thermal energy of the liquid in the smaller beaker?

A The liquid in the larger beaker has less thermal energy than the liquid in the smaller beaker.

B The liquid in the larger beaker has more thermal energy than the liquid in the smaller beaker.

C The liquid in the larger beaker has the same amount of thermal energy as the liquid in the smaller beaker.

D The exact volume of liquid in each beaker must be known to compare the thermal energy of the liquids.

5 During science class, Sophie measures the temperature of water every minute as it is heating. After a few minutes, the temperature is 82 °C. How far below the boiling point of water is this?

F 8 °C

H 130 °C

G 18 °C

I 191 °C

6 Ella holds an ice cream cone in her hand. She soon notices that her hand begins to feel cold. What is different about the particles that make up her hand?

A They are getting larger.

B They are gaining average energy.

C They are moving slower on average.

D They are joining together.

7 Deval drew the models of particles in a substance shown below. Which model **best** represents the particles in a solid?

F
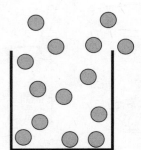

H
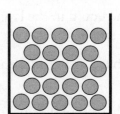

G
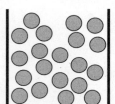

I
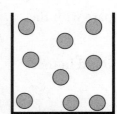

8 Ms. Lewis is a chemist mixing two solutions together. A chemical reaction takes place, and the solution becomes warm. Which statement **best** describes what has happened?

A Energy has been created in the form of thermal energy.

B Energy has been transformed from one form to another.

C More energy has been created than has been destroyed.

D The chemical energy of the solution has been destroyed.

Name _____

9   A group of sheep is grazing in a field. As they eat, the sheep break down the molecules in the grass, which releases energy. Which form of energy is stored in the grass?

   F chemical energy   **H** nuclear energy

   G elastic energy   **I** thermal energy

10 Laith notices that the air in his science classroom is much warmer than the air in his math classroom. Which statement describes how the air particles are different in his colder math classroom?

   A They move faster on average.

   B They are vibrating.

   C They have less average energy.

   D They move more freely.

11 Kito puts his metal spoon into a helping of fresh, hot mashed potatoes as shown in the figure below.

Spoon 20 °C

Mashed potatoes 50 °C

Which process takes place when the two objects come together?

   F The temperature of the spoon increases, but its thermal energy does not change.

   G Energy in the form of heat is transferred from the warmer mashed potatoes to the cooler spoon.

   H The thermal energy of both the mashed potatoes and the spoon increases as heat flows between them.

   I The average temperature of the spoon does not change.

Publishing Company

12 Gordon throws a baseball into the air. It rises, stops momentarily when it reaches its greatest height, and then falls back to the ground. At what point does kinetic energy convert to potential energy?

A when the baseball is rising

B when the baseball is falling

C just after the baseball hits the ground

D while the baseball is at the highest point

13 Damon is a musician playing in a band. At the end of a song, he plucks a single guitar string and the string vibrates rapidly. Which of these statements explains what happens to the kinetic energy of the moving string?

F The kinetic energy is changed into potential energy and stored.

G The kinetic energy is converted to sound energy and thermal energy.

H The kinetic energy is slowly destroyed until no energy remains.

I Some of the energy is converted to sound energy, but the rest is destroyed.

Critical Thinking

Answer the following questions in the space provided.

14 Consider a roller coaster car moving along a track. Is energy conserved in this system? Use evidence of energy transformations in this system and the total energy of the car to support your claim and explain your reasoning.

_____

_____

_____

_____

15 An ice cube sits in an open container of water placed outside on a sunny day.

Make a claim about how adding energy as heat to a system may result in a change of state. Support your claim with evidence and reasoning. Include how the water transfers energy to the ice cube and a comparison of the speeds of particles in the ice, water, and air.

_____

_____

_____

_____

Life over Time

Roseate Spoonbills thrive in shallow waters with muddy bottoms

FLORIDA BIG IDEA 15

Diversity and Evolution of Living Organisms

What Do You Think?

Over time, different life forms change as the environment changes. This happened a number of times in Florida's prehistory. What kinds of organisms do you think lived in prehistoric Florida? As you explore this unit, gather evidence to help you state and support a claim.

Life over Time

Prehistoric Florida

Fossils of land animals in Florida rocks and sediments date back to about 25 million years ago. The fossil record indicates that most of these land animals became extinct in Florida around 10,000 years ago. What do we know about fossils in Florida that are even older than these?

**Age of the Dinosaurs,
(245 million years ago to 65 million years ago)**

The Florida peninsula was covered by ocean. Therefore, only marine fossils can be found in surface rocks of this age. No dinosaur fossils are known.

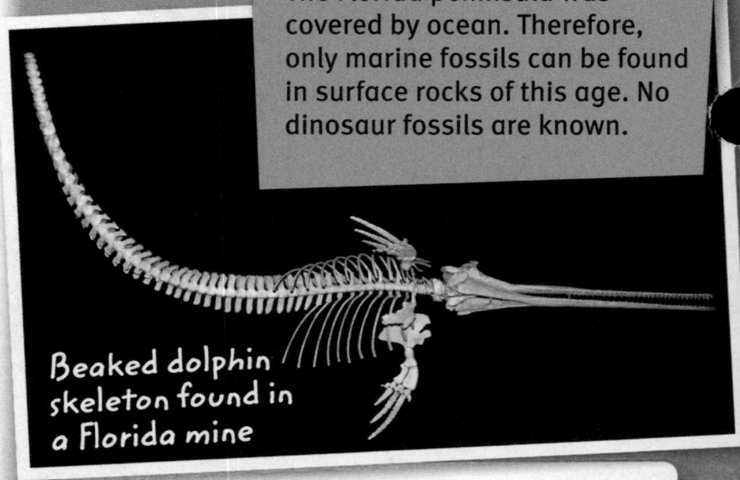

Beaked dolphin skeleton found in a Florida mine

In parts of Florida, the fossils of marine organisms and land animals are found in the same sediment. Why do you think that both types of fossils are found together?

_____
_____
_____
_____
_____
_____
_____
_____

Fossil of a
shark's jaw

Late Cenozoic Era (5 million years ago to Recent)

During the Ice Age, sea level rose and fell. Coral reefs formed in the warm waters off of the southeastern part of the peninsula. Fossils from this time include giant sloths, armadillos, bears, lions, sabertooth cats, and horses. Most of these animals became extinct around 10,000 years ago.

Middle Cenozoic Era (24.5 million years ago to 5 million years ago)

During this time, sea level generally dropped, and more of the Florida peninsula became exposed. Numerous mammals lived in forests and grassy plains. Fossils from this time include horses, rhinoceroses, bears, sabertooth cats, alligators, crocodiles, and birds.

Early Cenozoic Era (65 million years ago to 24.5 million years ago)

Most fossils from this time are marine organisms. These include fossils of shells, corals, sea urchins, sharks, sea turtles, and a very early whale.

Thousands of years ago, the Florida landscape looked like a cool, dry, and open savannah.

🏠 Take It Home!

Your Neighborhood Through Time

Your neighborhood probably hasn't been around since the age of the dinosaurs but it has also changed over time. Do some research to find out when your town was founded. Create a timeline similar to the one above that shows the details of what changes your neighborhood and town might have experienced over time.

Theory of Evolution by Natural Selection

ESSENTIAL QUESTION

What is the theory of evolution by natural selection?

By the end of this lesson, you should be able to describe the role of genetic and environmental factors in the theory of evolution by natural selection.

Because this grass snake's skin color looks like the plant stalk, it is able to hide from predators! This form of camouflage is the result of natural selection.

SC.7.L.15.1 Recognize that fossil evidence is consistent with the scientific theory of evolution that living things evolved from earlier species. **SC.7.L.15.2** Explore the scientific theory of evolution by recognizing and explaining ways in which genetic variation and environmental factors contribute to evolution by natural selection and diversity of organisms. **SC.7.L.15.3** Explore the scientific theory of evolution by relating how the inability of a species to adapt within a changing environment may contribute to the extinction of that species.ards

Lesson Labs

Quick Labs
- Analyzing Survival Adaptations
- Survive or Go Extinct
- Modeling Natural Selection

Exploration Lab
- Environmental Change and Evolution

 Engage Your Brain

1 Predict Check T or F to show whether you think each statement is true or false.

T F
☐ ☐ Fur color can help prevent an animal from being eaten.

☐ ☐ The amount of available food can affect an organism's survival.

☐ ☐ Your parents' characteristics are not passed on to you.

☐ ☐ A species can go extinct if its habitat is destroyed.

2 Infer How do you think this bird and this flower are related? Explain your answer.

_____
_____
_____

ACTIVE **READING**

3 Synthesize You can often define an unknown word by clues provided in the sentence. Use the sentence below to make an educated guess about the meaning of the word *artificial*.

Example sentence:
Many people prefer real sugar to <u>artificial</u> sweeteners made by humans.

artificial:

_____
_____
_____
_____
_____

Vocabulary Terms
- **evolution**
- **artificial selection**
- **natural selection**
- **variation**
- **mutation**
- **adaptation**
- **extinction**

4 Apply As you learn the definition of each vocabulary term in this lesson, create your own definition or sketch to help you remember the meaning of the term.

Darwin's Voyage

What did Darwin observe?

Charles Darwin was born in England in 1809. When he was 22 years old, Darwin graduated from college with a degree in theology. But he was also interested in plants and animals. Darwin became the naturalist—a scientist who studies nature—on the British ship HMS *Beagle*.

During his voyage, Darwin observed and collected many living and fossil specimens. He made some of his most important observations on the Galápagos Islands of South America. He kept a log that was later published as *The Voyage of the Beagle*. With the observations he made on this almost five-year journey, Darwin formed his idea about how biological evolution could happen.

In biology, **evolution** refers to the process by which populations change over time. A population is all of the individuals of a species that live in an area at the same time. A species is a group of closely related organisms that can mate to produce fertile offspring. Darwin developed a hypothesis, which eventually became a theory, of how evolution takes place.

Darwin left England on December 27, 1831. He returned 5 years later.

The plants and animals on the Galápagos Islands differed from island to island. This is where Darwin studied birds called finches.

ENGLAND

EUROPE

NORTH AMERICA

ATLANTIC OCEAN

AFRICA

Galápagos Islands

Equator

SOUTH AMERICA

Cape of Good Hope

i Think Outside the Book

5 Explore Trace Darwin's route on the map, and choose one of the following stops on his journey: Galápagos Islands, Andes Mountains, Australia. Do research to find out what plants and animals live there. Then write an entry in Darwin's log to describe what he might have seen.

Differences among Species

Darwin collected birds from the Galápagos Islands and nearby islands. He observed that these birds differed slightly from those on the nearby mainland of South America. And the birds on each island were different from the birds on the other islands. Careful analysis back in England revealed that they were all finches! Eventually, Darwin suggested that these birds may have evolved from one species of finch.

Darwin observed differences in beak size among finches from different islands. Many years later, scientists confirmed that these differences related to the birds' diets. Birds with shorter, heavier beaks could eat harder foods than those with thinner beaks.

This cactus finch has a narrow beak that it can use in many ways, including to pull grubs and insects from holes in the cactus.

This vegetarian finch has a curved beak, ideal for taking large berries from a branch.

ASIA

👁 Visualize It!

6 Claims • Evidence • Reasoning
Make a claim about how the pointed beak of this woodpecker finch helps it to get food. Summarize evidence to support the claim and explain your reasoning.

_____

_____

Woodpecker finch

INDIAN OCEAN

AUSTRALIA

Darwin saw many plants and animals that were found only on certain continents such as Australia.

km 0   1,000   2,000

mi 0   1,000   2,000

NEW ZEALAND

Darwin's Homework

What other ideas influenced Darwin?

The ideas of many scientists and observations of the natural world influenced Darwin's thinking. Darwin drew on ideas about Earth's history, the growth of populations, and observations of how traits are passed on in selective breeding. All of these pieces helped him develop his ideas about how populations could change over time.

Organisms Pass Traits On to Offspring

Farmers and breeders have been producing many kinds of domestic animals and plants for thousands of years. These plants and animals have traits that the farmers and breeders desire. A *trait* is a form of an inherited characteristic. For example, the length of tail feathers is an inherited characteristic, and short or long tail feathers are the corresponding traits. The practice by which humans select plants or animals for breeding based on desired traits is **artificial selection**. Artificial selection shows that traits can change. Traits can also spread through populations.

7 List Darwin studied artificial selection in the pigeons that he bred. List three other domestic animals that have many different breeds.

_____

_____

_____

_____

_____

This chicken has been bred to have large tail feathers and a big red comb.

This chicken has been bred to have large head feathers.

This chicken has been bred to have feathers on its feet.

ACTIVE READING

8 Identify As you read, underline the names of other important thinkers who influenced Darwin's ideas.

Organisms Acquire Traits

Scientist Jean-Baptiste Lamarck thought that organisms could acquire and pass on traits they needed to survive. For example, a man could develop stronger muscles over time. If the muscles were an advantage in his environment, Lamarck thought the man would pass on this trait to his offspring. Now we know that acquired traits are not passed on to offspring because these traits do not become part of an organism's DNA. But the fact that species change, and the idea that an organism's traits help it survive, shaped Darwin's ideas.

9 Claims • Evidence • Reasoning Make a claim about how the strength of your muscles is partly an acquired trait and partly dependent on DNA. Summarize evidence to support the claim and explain your reasoning.

_____

_____

These rock layers formed over millions of years.

Earth Changes over Time

The presence of different rock layers, such as those in the photo, show that Earth has changed over time. Geologist Charles Lyell hypothesized that small changes in Earth's surface have occurred over hundreds of millions of years. Darwin reasoned that if Earth were very old, then there would be enough time for very small changes in life forms to add up.

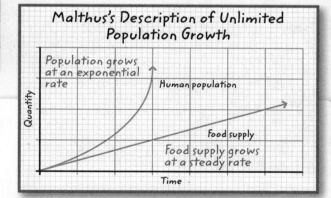

Malthus's Description of Unlimited Population Growth

Population grows at an exponential rate

Human population

Food supply

Food supply grows at a steady rate

Quantity

Time

👁 Visualize It!

10 Claims • Evidence • Reasoning Make a claim about population growth. Use evidence from the graph to support the claim and explain your reasoning.

A Struggle for Survival Exists

After his journey, Darwin read an essay about population growth by economist Thomas Malthus. The essay helped Darwin understand how the environment could influence which organisms survive and which organisms die. All populations are affected by factors that limit population growth, such as disease, predation, and competition for food. Darwin reasoned that the survivors probably have traits that help them survive and that some of these traits could be passed on from parent to offspring.

Natural Selection

What are the four parts of natural selection?

Darwin proposed that most evolution happens through the natural selection of advantageous traits. **Natural selection** is the process by which organisms that inherit advantageous traits tend to reproduce more successfully than other organisms do. There are four parts that contribute to the process of evolution by natural selection—overproduction, genetic variation, selection, and adaptation.

Overproduction

When a plant or animal reproduces, it usually makes more offspring than the environment can support. For example, a female jaguar may have up to four pups at a time. Only some of them will survive to adulthood, and a smaller number of them will successfully reproduce.

11 Claims • Evidence • Reasoning Make a claim about a natural reason for low survival rates of jaguar cubs. Summarize evidence to support the claim and explain your reasoning.

_____

_____

_____

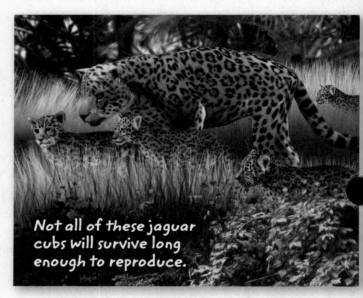

Not all of these jaguar cubs will survive long enough to reproduce.

Variation exists in the jaw sizes of these two jaguars. This variation will be passed on to the next generation.

Genetic Variation

Within a population there are natural differences, or variations, in traits. For example, in the two jaguar skulls to the left, one has a larger jaw than the other. This difference results from a difference in the genetic material of the jaguars. Genetic variations can be passed on from parent to offspring. An important source of variation is a mutation, or change in genetic material.

With each new generation, genetic variation introduces changes to the traits of a population. Greater genetic variation in a population increases the chance that some individuals will have traits that can help them survive environmental changes or diseases. Traits that enhance an individual's ability to reproduce will also increase the chance of survival of a species.

Selection

Individuals try to get the resources they need to survive. These resources include food, water, space and, in most cases, mates for reproduction. About 11,000 years ago, jaguars faced a shortage of food because the climate changed and many prey species died out. A genetic variation in jaw size then became important for survival. Jaguars with larger jaws could eat hard-shelled reptiles when other prey were hard to find.

Individuals with a particular trait, such as a large jaw, are more likely to survive long enough to reproduce. As a result, the trait is "selected" for becoming more common in the next generation of offspring.

A larger jaw makes it easier for this jaguar to eat hard-shelled turtles.

12 Summarize How did large jaws and teeth become typical traits of jaguars?

_____

_____

_____

Adaptation

An inherited trait that helps an organism survive and reproduce in its environment is an **adaptation**. Adaptation is the selection of naturally occurring trait variations in populations. Jaguars with larger jaws were able to survive and reproduce when food was hard to find. As natural selection continues, adaptations grow more common in the population with each new generation, and new adaptations may arise. Over time, the population becomes better adapted to the environment.

Large jaw size is one adaptation of jaguars.

13 Explain In the table below, explain how each part of natural selection works.

Principle of natural selection	How it works
overproduction	
genetic variation	
selection	
adaptation	

Publishing Company

Well-adapted

How do species change over time?

In order for a population to change, some individuals have to be genetically different from other members of the population. Mutations are one of the main sources of genetic variation. Offspring sometimes inherit a gene that has a slight mutation, or change, from the gene the parent has. Mutations can be harmful, helpful, or have no effect. Beneficial mutations help individuals survive and reproduce.

Over Generations, Adaptations Become More Common

ACTIVE **READING**

14 Identify Underline examples of adaptations.

Adaptations are inherited traits that help organisms survive and reproduce. At first, an adaptation is rare. For example, imagine a population of birds in which some birds have shorter beaks. If more birds with shorter beaks survive and reproduce than birds with longer beaks, more birds in the next generation will probably have short beaks. The number of individuals with the adaptation would continue to increase. Some adaptations, such as a duck's webbed feet, are physical. Other adaptations are inherited behaviors that help an organism find food, protect itself, or reproduce.

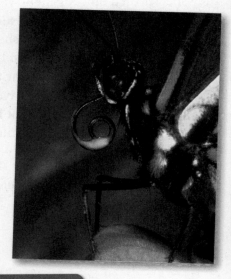

👁 Visualize It!

15 Claims • Evidence • Reasoning Write a claim about how this butterfly's long mouth part helps it to survive. Summarize evidence to support the claim and explain your reasoning.

_____

_____

_____

_____

The male frigate bird uses his red throat pouch to attract a female, which could lead to reproduction.

Genetic Differences Add Up

Parents and offspring often have small genetic differences between them. Over many generations, the small differences can add up. These differences accumulate so that organisms alive now are often very different from their ancestors. As a result, there is great diversity among organisms. For example, the antibiotic penicillin was able to kill many types of bacteria in the 1950s. Today, some of those species of bacteria are now completely resistant to penicillin. The genetic makeup of these bacterial populations has changed. New fossil discoveries and new information about genes add to scientists' understanding of natural selection and evolution.

© Houghton Mifflin Harcourt

What happens to species as the environment changes?

Certain environments favor certain traits. Consider a snake population with either brown- or green-colored snakes. In a forest that has many dead leaves on the ground, brown snakes will blend in better than green snakes will. But in an area with more grass, the green snakes may be better at hiding from predators. Changes in environmental conditions can affect the survival of organisms with a particular trait. Environmental changes can also lead to diversity of organisms by increasing the number of species.

Dinosaurs went extinct 65 million years ago.

Adaptations Can Allow a Species to Survive

All organisms have traits that allow them to survive in specific environments. For example, plants have xylem tissue that carries water up from the roots to the rest of the plant.

If the environment changes, a species is more likely to survive if it has genetic variation. For example, imagine a species of grass in which some plants need less water than others. If the environment became drier, many grass plants would die, but the plants that needed less water might survive. These plants might eventually become a new species if they cannot reproduce with the plants that needed more water.

Some Species May Become Extinct

If no individuals have traits that help them to survive and reproduce in the changed environment, a species will become extinct. **Extinction** occurs when all members of a species have died. Greater competition, new predators, and the loss of habitat are examples of environmental changes that can lead to extinction. Some extinctions are caused by natural disasters. Because a natural disaster can destroy resources quickly, organisms may die no matter what adaptations they have. The fossil record shows that many species have become extinct in the history of life on Earth.

👁 Visualize It!

Environmental change has affected the environmental conditions near the North Pole.

16 Claims • Evidence • Reasoning
How has ice cover near the North Pole changed in the last few decades? Use evidence from the image to support your claim and explain your reasoning.

_____

17 Claims • Evidence • Reasoning
Make a claim about how you think environmental change will affect species that live in the surrounding area. Use evidence to support the claim and explain your reasoning.

_____

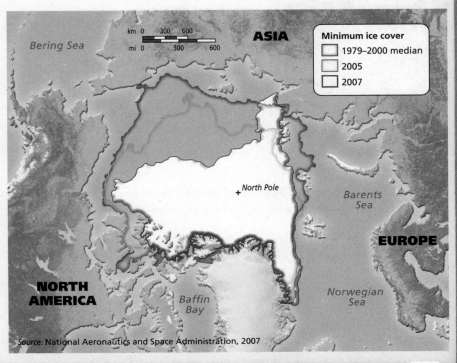

Minimum ice cover
- 1979–2000 median
- 2005
- 2007

Bering Sea · ASIA · North Pole · Barents Sea · EUROPE · NORTH AMERICA · Baffin Bay · Norwegian Sea

Source: National Aeronautics and Space Administration, 2007

Visual Summary

To complete this summary, circle the correct word. You can use this page to review the main concepts of the lesson.

Darwin's theory of natural selection was influenced by his own observations and the work of other scientists.

Evolution is Change over Time

18 Through natural / artificial selection, breeders choose the traits that are passed on to the next generation.

The theory of evolution by natural selection states that organisms with advantageous traits produce more offspring.

Many extinctions have occurred over the course of Earth's history.

20 Because of environmental change, dinosaurs eventually became mutated / extinct.

19 Natural selection can act only on acquired traits / inherited variation.

21 Claims • Evidence • Reasoning Make a claim about how the environment influences natural selection. Summarize evidence to support the claim and explain your reasoning.

Lesson Review

Vocabulary

Use a term from the lesson to complete the sentences below.

1 The four parts of natural selection are overproduction, _____, selection, and adaptation.

2 _____ is the process by which populations change over time.

3 The hollow bones of birds, which keep birds lightweight for flying, is an example of a(n) _____

Key Concepts

4 **Summarize** Describe Darwin's observations on the Galápagos islands during his voyage on the HMS *Beagle*.

_____

_____

_____

5 **Claims • Evidence • Reasoning** How does environmental change affect the survival of a species? Summarize evidence to support your claim and explain your reasoning.

_____

_____

_____

_____

6 **Compare** Why are only inherited traits, not acquired ones, involved in the process of natural selection?

_____

_____

_____

7 **Describe** What is the relationship between mutation, natural selection, and adaptation?

_____

_____

Critical Thinking

Use the diagram to answer the following question.

8 **Apply** How is each of these lizards adapted to its environment?

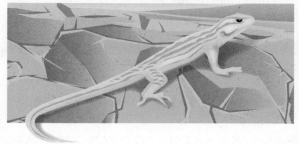

_____

_____

9 **Claims • Evidence • Reasoning** Make a claim about what might happen to a population of rabbits in a forest if a new predator moved to the forest. Cite evidence to support the claim and explain your reasoning.

_____

_____

_____

THINK **SCIENCE**

SC.7.N.1.3 Distinguish between an experiment (which must involve the identification and control of variables) and other forms of scientific investigation and explain that not all scientific knowledge is derived from experimentation.

Scientific Debate

Not all scientific knowledge is gained through experimentation.
It is also the result of a great deal of debate and confirmation.

Tutorial

As you prepare for a debate, look for information from the following sources.

Controlled Experiments Consider the following points when planning or examining the results of a controlled experiment.

- Only one factor should be tested at a time. A factor is anything in the experiment that can influence the outcome.

- Samples are divided into experimental group(s) and a control group. All of the factors of the experimental group(s) and the control group are the same except for one variable.

- A variable is a factor that can be changed. If there are multiple variables, only one variable should be changed at a time.

Independent Studies The results of a different group may provide stronger support for your argument than your own results. And using someone else's results helps to avoid the claim that your results are biased. Bias is the tendency to think about something from only one point of view. The claim of bias can be used to argue against your point.

Comparison with Similar Objects or Events
If you cannot gather data from an experiment to help support your position, finding a similar object or event might help. The better your example is understood, the stronger your argument will be.

Read the passage below and answer the questions.

Many people want to protect endangered species but do not agree on the best methods to use. Incubating, or heating eggs to ensure hatching, is commonly used with bird eggs. It was logical to apply the same technique to turtle eggs. The Barbour's map turtle is found in Florida, Georgia, and Alabama. To help more turtles hatch, people would gather eggs and incubate them. However, debate really began when mostly female turtles hatched. Were efforts to help the turtles really harming them? Scientists learned that incubating eggs at 25°C (77°F) produces males and at 30°C (86°F) produces females. As a result, conservation programs have stopped artificially heating the eggs.

1 What is the variable described in the article about Barbour's map turtles?

_____

_____

2 Write a list of factors that were likely kept the same between the sample groups described in the article.

_____

_____

_____

3 What argument could people have used who first suggested incubating the turtle eggs?

_____

_____

_____

You Try It!

Fossils from the Burgess Shale Formation in Canada include many strange creatures that lived over 500 million years ago. The fossils are special because the soft parts of the creatures were preserved. Examine the fossil of the creature *Marrella* and the reconstruction of what it might have looked like.

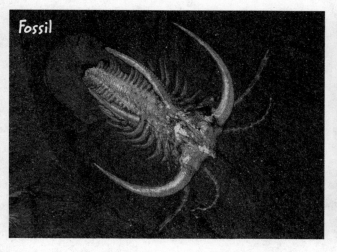

Fossil

Reconstruction

1 Recognizing Relationships Find four features on the reconstruction that you can also identify in the fossil. Write a brief description of each feature.

_____

_____

_____

_____

_____

2 Claims • Evidence • Reasoning *Marrella* is extinct. How do you think *Marrella* behaved when it was alive? What did it eat? How did it move? Summarize evidence you can use to support your claim and explain your reasoning.

_____

_____

_____

_____

_____

3 Communicating Ideas Share your description with a classmate. Discuss and debate your positions. Complete the table to show the points on which you agree and disagree.

Agree	Disagree

 Take It Home!

Research more about the creatures of the Burgess Shale Formation. Find at least one other fossil creature and its reconstruction. What do you think the creature was like?

Evidence of Evolution

ESSENTIAL QUESTION

What evidence supports the theory of evolution?

By the end of this lesson, you should be able to describe the evidence that supports the theory of evolution by natural selection.

SC.7.N.1.5 Describe the methods used in the pursuit of a scientific explanation as seen in different fields of science such as biology, geology, and physics. **SC.7.L.15.1** Recognize that fossil evidence is consistent with the scientific theory of evolution that living things evolved from earlier species.

Fossils show us what a dinosaur looks like. This dinosaur lived millions of years ago!

Lesson Labs

Quick Labs
- How Do We Know What Happened When?
- Comparing Anatomy
- The Opposable Thumb

 Engage Your Brain

1 Predict Check T or F to show whether you think each statement is true or false.

T   F
- ☐ ☐ Fossils provide evidence of organisms that lived in the past.
- ☐ ☐ The wing of a bat has similar bones to those in a human arm.
- ☐ ☐ DNA can tell us how closely related two organisms are.
- ☐ ☐ Whales are descended from land-dwelling mammals.

2 Infer This is a Petoskey stone, which is made up of tiny coral fossils. What can you infer if you find a coral fossil on land?

Petoskey stone

_____
_____
_____

ACTIVE READING

3 Synthesize You can often define an unknown word if you understand the parts of the word. Use the words below to make an educated guess about the meaning of the word *fossil record*.

Word	Meaning
fossil	the remains or trace of once-living organisms
record	an account that preserves information about facts or events

fossil record:

_____
_____

Vocabulary Terms
- fossil
- fossil record

4 Apply As you learn the definition of each vocabulary term in this lesson, create your own definition or sketch to help you remember the meaning of the term.

Fossil Hunt

How do fossils form?

Evidence that organisms have changed over time can be found in amber, ice, or sedimentary rock. Sedimentary rock is formed when particles of sand or soil are deposited in horizontal layers. Often this occurs as mud or silt hardens. After one rock layer forms, newer rock layers form on top of it. So, older layers are found below or underneath younger rock layers. The most basic principle of dating such rocks and the remains of organisms inside is "the deeper it is, the older it is."

Amber fossils form when small creatures are trapped in tree sap and the sap hardens.

5 Examine What features of the organism are preserved in amber?

_____

_____

_____

This flying dinosaur is an example of a cast fossil.

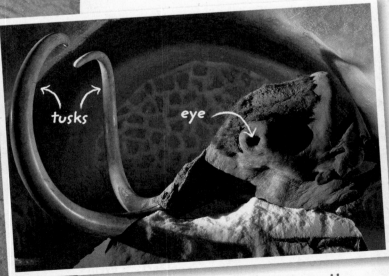

tusks   eye

Because this woolly mammoth was frozen in ice, its skin and hair were preserved.

Many Fossils Form in Sedimentary Rock

Rock layers preserve evidence of organisms that were once alive. The remains or imprints of once-living organisms are called **fossils**. Fossils commonly form when a dead organism is covered by a layer of sediment or mud. Over time, more sediment settles on top of the organism. Minerals in the sediment may seep into the organism and replace the body's material with minerals that harden over time. This process produces a cast fossil. Many familiar fossils are casts of hard parts, such as shells and bones. If the organism rots away completely after being covered, it may leave an imprint of itself in the rock. Despite all of the fossils that have been found, it is rare for an organism to become a fossil. Most often, the dead organism is recycled back into the biological world by scavengers, decomposers, or the process of weathering.

ACTIVE READING

6 Identify As you read, underline the steps that describe how a cast fossil forms.

How do fossils show change over time?

All of the fossils that have been discovered make up the **fossil record**. The fossil record provides evidence about the order in which species have existed through time, and how they have changed over time. By examining the fossil record, scientists can learn about the history of life on Earth.

Despite all the fossils that have been found, there are gaps in the fossil record. These gaps represent chunks of geologic time for which a fossil has not been discovered. Also, the transition between two groups of organisms may not be well understood. Fossils that help fill in these gaps are *transitional fossils*. The illustration on the right is based on a transitional fossil.

Fossils found in newer layers of Earth's crust tend to have physical or molecular similarities to present-day organisms. These similarities indicate that the fossilized organisms were close relatives of the present-day organisms. Fossils from older layers are less similar to present-day organisms than fossils from newer layers are. Most older fossils are of earlier life-forms such as dinosaurs, which don't exist anymore.

◉ Visualize It!

A transitional form between fish and four-legged land vertebrates may be this creature called *Tiktaalik roseae.*

7 Claims • Evidence • Reasoning Make a claim about the environment in which this organism lived. Summarize evidence to support the claim and explain your reasoning.

_____

_____

8 Explain Your Reasoning How is this organism like both a fish and a four-legged vertebrate, such as an amphibian? Explain your reasoning.

_____

_____

Houghton Mifflin Harcourt Publishing Company

More clues . . .

What other evidence supports evolution?

Many fields of study provide evidence that modern species and extinct species share an ancestor. A *common ancestor* is the most recent species from which two different species have evolved. Structural data, DNA, developmental patterns, and fossils all support the theory that populations change over time. Sometimes these populations become new species. Biologists observe that all living organisms have some traits in common and inherit traits in similar ways. Evidence of when and where those ancestors lived and what they looked like is found in the fossil record.

Common Structures

Scientists have found that related organisms share structural traits. Structures reduced in size or function may have been complete and functional in the organism's ancestor. For example, snakes have traces of leglike structures that are not used for movement. These unused structures are evidence that snakes share a common ancestor with animals like lizards and dogs.

Scientists also consider similar structures with different functions. The arm of a human, the front leg of a cat, and the wing of a bat do not look alike and are not used in the same way. But as you can see, they are similar in structure. The bones of a human arm are similar in structure to the bones in the front limbs of a cat and a bat. These similarities suggest that cats, bats, and humans had a common ancestor. Over millions of years, changes occurred. Now, these bones perform different functions in each type of animal.

ACTIVE **READING**

9 List What is a common ancestor?

_____

_____

_____

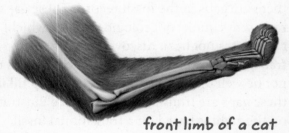

front limb of a bat

front limb of a cat

👁 Visualize It!

10 Relate Do you see any similarities between the bones of the bat and cat limbs and the bones of the human arm? If so, use the colors of the bat and cat bones to color similar bones in the human arm. If you don't have colored pencils, label the bones with the correct color names.

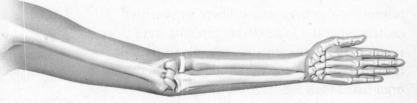

Similar DNA

The genetic information stored in an organism's DNA determines the organism's traits. Because an organism's DNA stays almost exactly the same throughout its entire lifetime, scientists can compare the DNA from many organisms. The greater the number of similarities between the molecules of any two species, the more recently the two species most likely shared a common ancestor.

Recall that DNA determines which amino acids make up a protein. Scientists have compared the amino acids that make up cytochrome c proteins in many species. Cytochrome c is involved in cellular respiration. Organisms that have fewer amino acid differences are more likely to be closely related.

Frogs also have cytochrome c proteins, but they're a little different from yours.

Cytochrome C Comparison	
Organism	Number of amino acid differences from human cytochrome c
Chimpanzee	0
Rhesus monkey	1
Whale	10
Turtle	15
Bullfrog	18
Lamprey	20

Source: M.Dayhoff, *Atlas of Protein Sequence and Structure*

👁 Visualize It!

11 **Claims • Evidence • Reasoning** The number of amino acids in human cytochrome c differs between humans and the species at left. Make a claim about which two species are the least closely related to humans. Cite evidence to support the claim and explain your reasoning.

_____

_____

_____

_____

Developmental Similarities

The study of development is called *embryology*. Embryos undergo many physical and functional changes as they grow and develop. If organisms develop in similar ways, they also likely share a common ancestor.

Scientists have compared the development of different species to look for similar patterns and structures. Scientists think that such similarities come from an ancestor that the species have in common. For example, at some time during development, all animals with backbones have a tail. This observation suggests that they shared a common ancestor.

These embryos are at a similar stage of development.

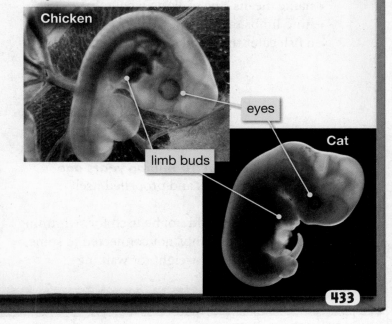

Chicken

eyes

limb buds

Cat

How do we know organisms are related?

Scientists examine organisms carefully for clues about their ancestors. In a well-studied example, scientists looked at the characteristics of whales that made them different from other ocean animals. Unlike fish and sharks, whales breathe air, give birth to live young, and produce milk. Fossil and DNA evidence support the hypothesis that modern whales evolved from hoofed mammals that lived on land.

Fossil Evidence

Scientists have examined fossils of extinct species that have features in between whales and land mammals. These features are called *transitional characters.* None of these species are directly related to modern whales. But their skeletons suggest how a gradual transition from land mammal to aquatic whale could have happened.

Ⓐ *Pakicetus*   **52 million years ago**
- whale-shaped skull and teeth adapted for hunting fish
- ran on four legs
- ear bones in between those of land and aquatic mammals

Ⓑ *Ambulocetus natans*   **50 million years ago**
- name means "the walking whale that swims"
- hind limbs that were adapted for swimming
- a fish eater that lived on water and on land

Ⓒ *Dorudon*   **About 40 million years ago**
- lived in warm seas and propelled itself with a long tail
- tiny hind legs could not be used for swimming
- pelvis and hind limbs not connected to spine, could not support weight for walking

Unused Structures

Most modern whales have pelvic bones and some have leg bones. These bones do not help the animal move.

Molecular Evidence

The DNA of whales is very similar to the DNA of hoofed mammals. Below are some DNA fragments of a gene that makes a type of milk protein.

Hippopotamus   **TCC TGGCA GTCCA GTGGT**

Humpback whale **CCC TGGCA GTGCA GTGCT**

12 Identify Circle the pairs of nitrogen bases (G, T, C, or A) that differ between the hippopotamus and humpback whale DNA.

13 Infer How do you think these bones are involved in a whale's movement?

_____

_____

_____

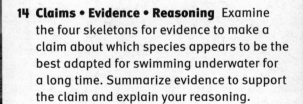

Modern Whale   *Present day*

- no hind limbs, front limbs are flippers
- some whales have tiny hip bones left over from their hoofed-mammal ancestors
- breathe air with lungs like other mammals do

14 Claims • Evidence • Reasoning Examine the four skeletons for evidence to make a claim about which species appears to be the best adapted for swimming underwater for a long time. Summarize evidence to support the claim and explain your reasoning.

_____

_____

_____

_____

_____

_____

_____

Visual Summary

To complete this summary, circle the correct word. You can use this page to review the main concepts of the lesson.

Evidence of Evolution

Fossil evidence shows that life on Earth has changed over time.

> **15** The remains of once-living organisms are called fossils / ancestors.

Evolutionary theory is also supported by structural, genetic, and developmental evidence.

> **16** Similarities / Differences in internal structures support evidence of common ancestry.

Scientists use evidence from many fields of research to study the common ancestors of living organisms.

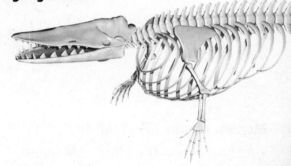

> **17** The tiny leg bones / large dorsal fins of modern whales are an example of unused structures.

18 Claims • Evidence • Reasoning How does the fossil record provide evidence of the diversity of life? Summarize evidence to support the claim and explain your reasoning.

Lesson Review

Vocabulary

1 Which word means "the remains or imprints of once-living organisms found in layers of rock?"

_____

2 Which word means "the history of life in the geologic past as indicated by the imprints or remains of living things?"

_____

Key Concepts

3 Identify What are two types of evidence that suggest that evolution has occurred?

_____

_____

4 Explain How do fossils provide evidence that evolution has taken place?

_____

_____

_____

5 Apply What is the significance of the similar number and arrangement of bones in a human arm and a bat wing?

_____

_____

_____

Critical Thinking

6 Imagine If you were a scientist examining the DNA sequence of two unknown organisms that you hypothesize share a common ancestor, what evidence would you expect to find?

_____

_____

_____

Use this table to answer the following questions.

Cytochrome C Comparison	
Organism	Number of amino acid differences from human cytochrome c
Chimpanzee	0
Turtle	15
Tuna	21

Source: M. Dayhoff, *Atlas of Protein Sequence and Structure*

7 Claims • Evidence • Reasoning Make a claim about how related tuna, turtles, and chimpanzees are to humans. Use evidence to support the claim and explain your reasoning.

_____

_____

_____

_____

8 Explain Your Reasoning If there are no differences between the amino acid sequences in the cytochrome c protein of humans and chimpanzees, why aren't we the same species? Explain your reasoning.

_____

_____

_____

_____

9 Explain Your Reasoning Explain why the pattern of differences that exists from earlier to later fossils in the fossil record supports the claim that evolution has taken place on Earth.

_____

_____

_____

_____

Life over Time

is described by

Evidence of **Evolution**   **supports the**   **Theory** of **Evolution**

1 Support Your Claim The Graphic Organizer above shows that life over time is described by evidence of evolution. Name two types of evidence that support evolution.

_____

_____

_____

_____

2 Claims • Evidence • Reasoning Make a claim about how the finches that Darwin observed of the Galápagos Islands show evidence of evolution. Summarize evidence to support the claim and explain your reasoning.

_____

_____

_____

_____

3 Compare How is natural selection different from evolution?

_____

_____

_____

_____

_____

_____

4 Explain The fossil record reveals changes over time in the environment. Why might a scientist studying evolution be interested in how the environment has changed over time?

_____

_____

_____

_____

_____

Vocabulary

Name _____

Fill in each blank with the term that best completes the following sentences.

1 _____ is the difference in inherited traits an organism has from others of the same species.

2 The _____ is made up of fossils that have been discovered around the world.

Key Concepts

Identify the choice that best completes the statement or answers the question.

3 While exploring a rock formation, Hiroto finds a rock that has footprints pressed into it. A geologist tells Hiroto that the rock is millions of years old. Which of these statements is **correct** about Hiroto's find?

A It is not a fossil because footprints are not fossils.

B It is not a fossil because only whole organisms are fossils.

C It is a fossil only if Hiroto finds actual parts of the organism in rocks nearby.

D It is a fossil because footprints of organisms from million of years ago are considered to be fossils.

4 The diagram below shows a model of the proposed relationships between some groups of ancient and modern mammals. Branch points represent when two species diverged from the proposed common ancestor.

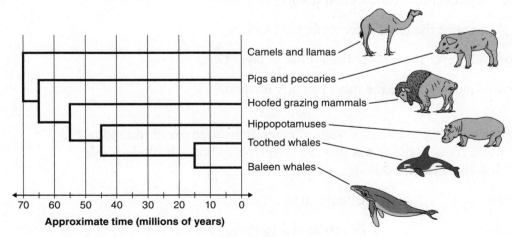

Which of these organisms is **most closely** related to whales?

F bison

H hippo

G camel

I pig

5 Which of these conditions is **least likely** to cause a species to become extinct due to environmental changes?

    A less genetic variation   **C** specific food preferences

    B more genetic variation   **D** more competition for food

6 The diagram below shows a portion of the fossil record in sedimentary rock. Different rock layers and fossils are clearly visible.

Which of these statements is **true** of the fossils and rock layers shown in the diagram?

    F Layer B contains the second-oldest fossils.

    G Layer A contains the most recently formed fossils.

    H The fossils in layer B are older than those in layer D.

    I The fossils in layer D are the most recently formed.

7 When farmers want two desirable traits in cows, they often breed individuals that have those traits in the hopes that the offspring will have both desirable traits. What is this practice called?

    A variation   **C** natural selection

    B adaptation   **D** artificial selection

8 Ronald observes a sparrow's nest in a shrub outside his home. The table below describes his findings.

Week	Observations
1	Six eggs were laid in the nest.
3	Five eggs hatched, and one egg did not hatch.
4	One of the chicks disappeared.
7	Three of the chicks learned to fly, and another one disappeared.

What part of natural selection did Ronald observe?

F adaptation

H selection

G overproduction

I variation

9 Environmental changes may lead to the evolution of a species. Polar bears live in the Arctic. Ice in the Arctic is melting fast, reducing the range where the polar bear can live. If polar bears do not have adaptations that allow them to survive these changes, what may happen to them?

A They may become extinct.

B They may overpopulate.

C They may change the environment.

D They may become another species.

10 Juan is studying fossils. His teacher wrote the following statements on the board and asked the students to put them in the correct order to describe how fossils are formed.

1. Minerals seep into the organism's body and replace it with stone.

2. The organism completely decomposes, leaving behind an imprint.

3. An organism dies, and its body is covered with a layer of sediment.

4. Time passes, and sediment layers continue to build up on the organism.

Which is the correct order of events for fossil formation?

F 3, 4, 1, 2

H 1, 3, 2, 4

G 2, 3, 4, 1

I 3, 2, 1, 4

11 At the zoo, Anya observes that the red kangaroos are of several sizes and colors. What characteristic of populations is Anya observing?

A adaptation   **C** selection

B evolution   **D** variation

Critical Thinking

Answer the following questions in the space provided.

12 Darwin's theory of natural selection consists of four important parts. Describe the four essential parts of natural selection.

_____

_____

_____

_____

13 Charles Darwin studied the finches of the Galápagos Islands and found that their beaks vary in shape and size.

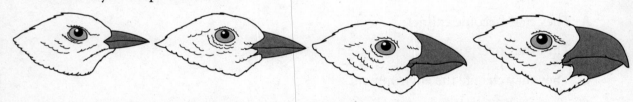

Darwin found that the finches that ate mostly insects had long, narrow beaks. Finches that ate mostly seeds had shorter, broad beaks to crush seeds. Are the four types of finches shown above the result of natural selection? Use specific evidence to support your claim and explain your reasoning.

_____

_____

_____

_____

Reproduction and Heredity

FLORIDA **BIG IDEA 16**

Heredity and Reproduction

The seeds of a papaya allow it to reproduce more papayas with similar traits.

What Do You Think?

Every organism— such as these papayas—that reproduces shares traits with its offspring. How are qualities passed on from generation to generation? As you explore this unit, gather evidence to help you state and support your claim.

Reproduction and Heredity

CITIZEN SCIENCE
Pass It On

Heredity was a mystery that scientists worked to crack over hundreds of years. The modern field of genetics is vital to the understanding of hereditary diseases. The study of genetics can also predict which traits will be passed from parent to offspring.

1856–1863
Many people consider Gregor Mendel to be the Father of Modern Genetics. His famous pea plant experiments, conducted from 1856–1863, helped to illustrate and establish the laws of inheritance.

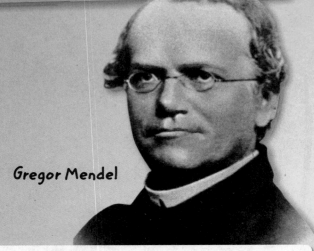

Gregor Mendel

Can you predict the traits Mendel might have examined in pea plants? What traits might a fruit or vegetable plant inherit from a parent plant?

_____

_____

_____

_____

_____

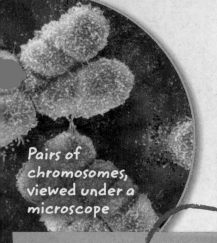
Pairs of chromosomes, viewed under a microscope

Fruit fly

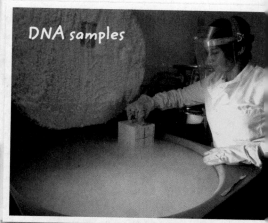
DNA samples

1882
Walther Flemming discovered chromosomes while observing the process of cell division. He didn't know it, but chromosomes pass characteristics from parents to offspring.

1908
Thomas Hunt Morgan was the first to actually realize that chromosomes carry traits. Morgan's fruit fly studies established that genes are located on chromosomes. Studies using fruit flies are still happening.

2003
Our DNA carries information about all of our traits. In fact, the human genome is made up of 20,000–25,000 genes! In 2003, the Human Genome Project successfully mapped the first human genome.

 Take It Home!

Making Trait Predictions

1 Think About It

Different factors influence appearance. Family members may look similar in some ways but different in others. What factors influence a person's appearance?

_____
_____
_____

2 Ask Some Questions

Can you spot any physical characteristics, like bent or straight pinky fingers, that people in your family share?

_____
_____
_____
_____

3 Make A Plan

Consider the characteristics that are most distinctive in your family. How can you trace the way these characteristics have been passed through the family? Design an investigation of hereditary characteristics in your family.

_____
_____
_____
_____

Describe how these characteristics might be the same or different as they are passed on to offspring. What factors might influence this? Make notes here, and illustrate your descriptions on a separate sheet of paper.

_____
_____
_____
_____

Mitosis

ESSENTIAL **QUESTION**

How do cells divide?

By the end of this lesson, you should be able to relate the process of mitosis to its functions in single-celled and multicellular organisms.

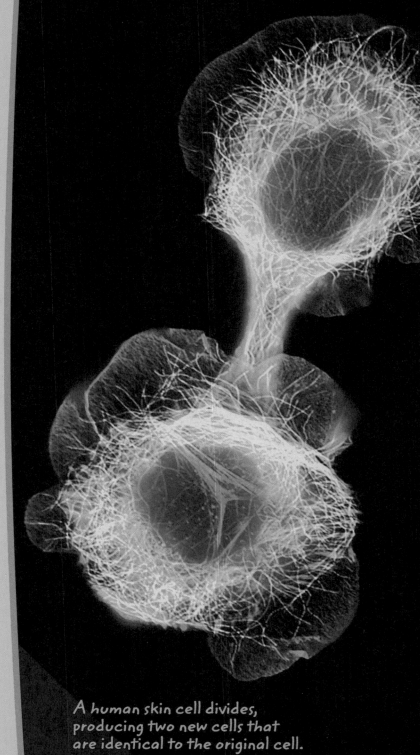

SC.7.L.16.3 Compare and contrast the general processes of sexual reproduction requiring meiosis and asexual reproduction requiring mitosis.

A human skin cell divides, producing two new cells that are identical to the original cell.

 Engage Your Brain

1 Predict Check T or F to show whether you think each statement is true or false.

T	F	
☐	☐	Single-celled organisms can reproduce by cell division.
☐	☐	The only function of cell division is reproduction.
☐	☐	In multicellular organisms, cell division can help repair injured areas.
☐	☐	Cell division produces two cells that are different from each other.

2 Infer An old sequoia tree weighs many tons and has billions of cells. These trees start out as tiny seeds. Predict how these trees get so large.

_____

_____

_____

_____

ACTIVE **READING**

3 Synthesize You can often define an unknown word if you know the meaning of its word parts. Use the word parts and sentence below to make an educated guess about the meaning of the word *cytokinesis*.

Word part	Meaning
cyto-	hollow vessel
-kinesis	division

Example sentence
When a dividing cell undergoes cytokinesis, two cells are produced.

cytokinesis:

_____

_____

_____

Vocabulary Terms
• DNA
• chromosomes
• cell cycle
• interphase
• mitosis
• cytokinesis

4 Apply As you learn the definition of each vocabulary term in this lesson, write your own definition or make a sketch to help you remember the meaning of the term.

Splitsville!

Why do cells divide?

Cell division happens in all organisms. Cell division takes place for different reasons. For example, single-celled organisms reproduce through cell division. In multicellular organisms, cell division is involved in growth, development, and repair, as well as reproduction.

Reproduction

Cell division is important for asexual reproduction, which involves only one parent organism. In single-celled organisms, the parent divides in two, producing two identical offspring. In single-celled and some multicellular organisms, offspring result when a parent organism buds, producing offspring. In multicellular organisms, reproduction by cell division can include plant structures such as runners and plantlets.

Growth and Repair

One characteristic of all living things is that they grow. You are probably bigger this year than you were last year. Your body is made up of cells. Although cells themselves grow, most growth in multicellular organisms happens because cell division produces new cells.

Cell division also produces cells for repair. If you cut your hand or break a bone, the damaged cells are replaced by new cells that form during cell division.

👁 Visualize It!

5 Claims • Evidence • Reasoning Take a look at the photos below. Underneath each photo, make a claim about how cell devision plays a role in what is taking place. Summarize evidence to support your claim, and explain your reasoning.

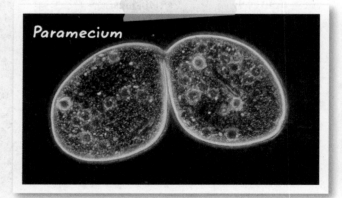

Paramecium

Starfish

Role of cell division:

_____

_____

_____

Role of cell division:

_____

_____

_____

What happens to genetic material during cell division?

The genetic material in cells is called DNA (deoxyribonucleic acid). A **DNA** molecule contains the information that determines the traits that a living thing inherits and needs to live. It contains instructions for an organism's growth, development, and activities. In eukaryotes, DNA is found in the nucleus.

During most of a cell's life cycle, DNA, along with proteins, exists in a complex material called *chromatin* (KROH•muh•tin). Before cell division, DNA is duplicated, or copied. Then, in an early stage of cell division, the chromatin is compacted into visible structures called **chromosomes** (KROH•muh•sohmz). A duplicated chromosome consists of two identical structures called *chromatids* (KROH•muh•tidz). The chromatids are held together by a *centromere* (SEN•truh•mir).

6 Describe What happens to DNA before cell division?

_____

_____

_____

_____

Chromatin
Chromatin is made up of DNA and proteins.

DNA
DNA is found in the nucleus of a eukaryotic cell.

👁 Visualize It!

7 State Your Claim Make a claim about what happens to chromatin in the early stages of cell division.

_____

_____

Around and Around

What are the stages of the cell cycle?

The life cycle of an organism includes birth, growth, reproduction, and death. The life cycle of a eukaryotic cell, called the **cell cycle**, can be divided into three stages: interphase, mitosis, and cytokinesis. During the cell cycle, a parent cell divides into two new cells. The new cells are identical to the parent.

ACTIVE READING

8 Identify As you read, underline the main characteristics of each stage of the cell cycle.

○ Interphase

The part of the cell cycle during which the cell is not dividing is called **interphase** (IN•ter•fayz). A lot of activity takes place in this stage of the cell's life. The cell grows to about twice the size it was when it was first produced. It also produces various organelles. The cell engages in normal life activities, such as transporting materials into the cell and getting rid of wastes.

Changes that occur during interphase prepare a cell for division. Before a cell can divide, DNA must be duplicated. This ensures that, after cell division, each new cell gets an exact copy of the genetic material in the original cell.

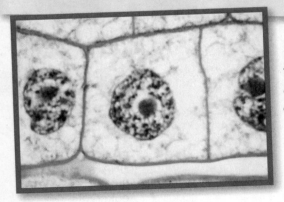

During interphase, the cell carries out normal life activities.

INTERPHASE

ACTIVE READING

9 Describe What happens during interphase?

_____

_____

_____

_____

_____

Mitosis

In eukaryotic cells, **mitosis** (my•TOH•sis) is the part of the cell cycle during which the nucleus divides. Prokaryotes do not undergo mitosis because they do not have a nucleus. Mitosis results in two nuclei that are identical to the original nucleus. So, the two new cells formed after cell division have the same genetic material. During mitosis, chromosomes condense from chromatin. When viewed with a microscope, chromosomes are visible inside the nucleus. At the end of mitosis, the cell has two identical sets of chromosomes in two separate nuclei.

MITOSIS

Prophase

Metaphase

Anaphase

Telophase

During mitosis, the cell's nucleus divides into two identical nuclei.

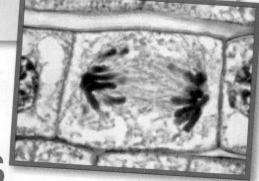

CYTOKINESIS

Cytokinesis

Cytokinesis (sy•toh•kuh•NEE•sis) is the division of the parent cell's cytoplasm. Cytokinesis begins during the last step of mitosis. During cytokinesis, the cell membrane pinches inward between the new nuclei. Eventually, it pinches all the way, forming two complete cells.

In a cell that has a cell wall, such as a plant cell, a cell plate forms. The cell plate becomes cell membranes that separate the new cells. New cell walls form where the plate was.

During cytokinesis, the cytoplasm divides and two new cells are produced.

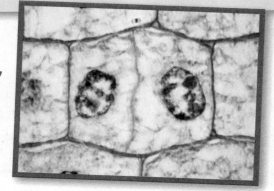

👁 Visualize It!

10 Support Your Claim In what stage does a cell spend most of its time? What evidence in the diagram supports this claim?

_____

Phasing Out

What are the phases of mitosis?

Mitosis has four phases: prophase (PROH•fayz), metaphase (MET•uh•fayz), anaphase (AN•uh•fayz), and telophase (TEE•luh•fayz). By the end of these phases, the cell will have two identical nuclei and cytokinesis will begin.

ACTIVE READING

11 Identify As you read, underline the major events that take place in each phase of mitosis.

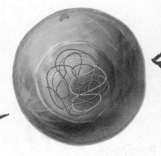

During interphase, DNA is duplicated.

Prophase

During prophase, the chromatin in the nucleus of a cell condenses and becomes visible under a microscope. Each chromosome consists of two chromatids held together by a centromere. The membrane around the nucleus breaks down.

Prophase

Metaphase

During metaphase, chromosomes line up in the middle of the cell. Centromeres of the chromosomes are the same distance from each side of the cell.

Metaphase

Anaphase

During anaphase, the chromatids separate. They are pulled to opposite sides of the cell. Each side of the cell ends up with a complete set of chromosomes.

Anaphase

12 Model With a small group, write a play that acts out the steps of mitosis. Trade your play with another group, and perform the play for your classmates.

Both new cells start the cycle again.

After mitosis, cytokinesis results in two new cells.

Telophase

Telophase

The last phase of mitosis is telophase. A new nuclear membrane forms around each group of chromosomes. So, the cell now has two identical nuclei. The chromosomes become less condensed. Cytokinesis begins during this phase.

13 List Use the table below to draw a picture for each step of the cell cycle.

Step	Drawing
Interphase	
Mitosis: Prophase	
Mitosis: Metaphase	
Mitosis: Anaphase	
Mitosis: Telophase	
Cytokinesis	

Visual Summary

To complete this summary, fill in the blanks with the correct word or phrase. You can use this page to review the main concepts of the lesson.

During the cell cycle, cells divide to produce two identical cells.

14 Three reasons that cells divide are

_____

_____

_____

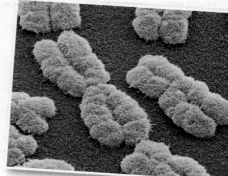

DNA is duplicated before cell division.

15 Loose chromatin is compacted into

_____ ,

each of which has two

_____ that

are held together by a centromere.

Mitosis

The cell cycle is the life cycle of a cell.

16 They lack nuclei, so prokaryotes do not undergo _____

17 The cell produces organelles during

_____

18 _____ results in the formation of two new cells.

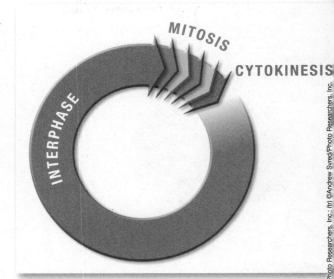

19 **Claims • Evidence • Reasoning** A student claims that the number of chromosomes inside the nucleus of a cell decreases by half during mitosis. Summarize evidence to support or refute this claim and explain your reasoning.

Lesson Review

Vocabulary

Fill in the blanks with the term that best completes the following sentences.

1 _____ provides the information for cell growth and function.

2 The cell spends most of its time in the _____ stage of the cell cycle.

3 After _____ , the nucleus of the parent cell has divided into two new nuclei.

4 A _____ is the condensed, visible form of chromatin.

Key Concepts

5 Relate What happens in a cell during interphase?

_____

_____

_____

6 Compare Describe the functions of cell division in single-celled and multicellular organisms.

_____

_____

_____

7 Claims • Evidence • Reasoning Why is it important for DNA to be duplicated before mitosis? State your claim. Summarize evidence to support your claim and explain your reasoning.

_____

_____

_____

Critical Thinking

Use the figures below to answer the questions that follow.

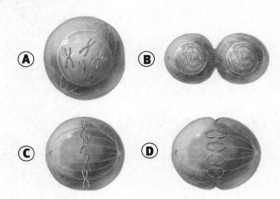

8 Sequence Starting with prophase, what is the correct order of the four diagrams above?

_____

9 Identify What phase is shown in each of the diagrams above?

_____

_____

_____

10 Describe What is happening to the cell in diagram B?

_____

_____

_____

_____

11 Claims • Evidence • Reasoning Make a claim about what would happen if a cell went through mitosis but not cytokinesis. Summarize evidence to support your claim and explain your reasoning.

_____

_____

_____

_____

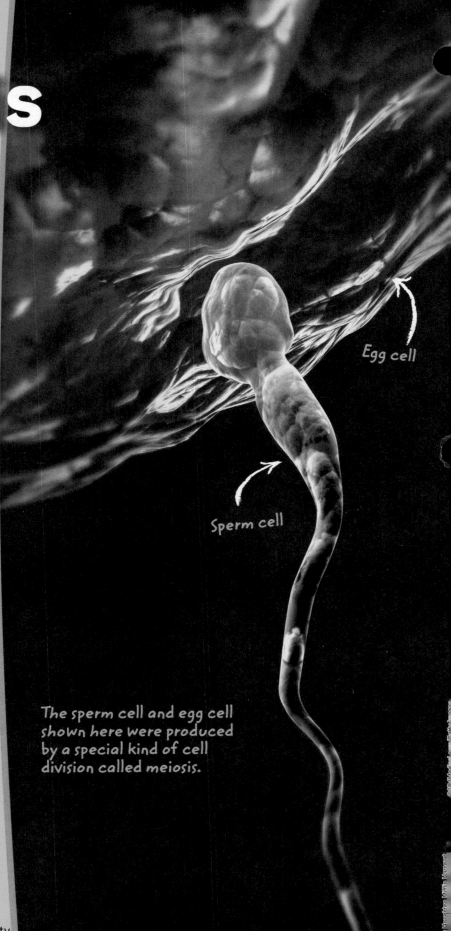

Meiosis

ESSENTIAL QUESTION

How do cells divide for sexual reproduction?

By the end of this lesson, you should be able to describe the process of meiosis and its role in sexual reproduction.

The sperm cell and egg cell shown here were produced by a special kind of cell division called meiosis.

Egg cell

Sperm cell

SC.7.L.16.3 Compare and contrast the general processes of sexual reproduction requiring meiosis and asexual reproduction requiring mitosis.

 **Lesson Labs**

Quick Labs
• Crossover and Meiosis
• Meiosis Flipbook

 Engage Your Brain

1 Predict Check T or F to show whether you think each statement is true or false.

T	F	
☐	☐	The offspring of sexual reproduction have fewer chromosomes than their parents have.
☐	☐	During sexual reproduction, two cells combine to form a new organism.
☐	☐	Sex cells are produced by cell division.
☐	☐	Sex cells have half the normal number of chromosomes.

2 Calculate Organisms have a set number of chromosomes. For example, humans have 46 chromosomes in body cells and half that number (23) in sex cells. In the table below, fill in the number of chromosomes for different organisms.

Organism	Full set of chromosomes	Half set of chromosomes
Human	46	23
Fruit fly		4
Chicken		39
Salamander	24	
Potato	48	

ACTIVE **READING**

3 Synthesize You can often define an unknown word if you know the meaning of its word parts. Use the word parts and the sentence below to make an educated guess about the meaning of the term *homologous*.

Word part	Meaning
homo-	same
-logos	word, structure

Example sentence
Homologous chromosomes are a pair of chromosomes that look similar and have the same genes.

homologous:

_____

_____

_____

Vocabulary Terms
• **homologous chromosomes**
• **meiosis**

4 Apply As you learn the definition of each vocabulary term in this lesson, write your own definition or make a sketch to help you remember the meaning of the term.

Number Off!

How do sex cells differ from body cells?

Before sexual reproduction can take place, each parent produces sex cells. *Sex cells* have half of the genetic information that body cells have. Thus, when the genetic information from two parents combines, the offspring have a full set of genetic information. The offspring will have the same total number of chromosomes as each of its parents.

ACTIVE **READING**

5 Relate Describe sex cells.

_____

_____

Chromosome Number

In body cells, most chromosomes are found in pairs that have the same structure and size. These **homologous chromosomes** (huh•MAHL•uh•guhs KROH•muh•sohmz) carry the same genes. A homologous chromosome pair may have different versions of the genes they carry. One chromosome pair is made up of *sex chromosomes*. Sex chromosomes control the development of sexual characteristics. In humans, these chromosomes are called X and Y chromosomes. Cells with a pair of every chromosome are called *diploid* (DIP•loyd). Many organisms, including humans, have diploid body cells.

This photo shows the 23 chromosome pairs in a human male. Body cells contain all of these chromosomes. Sex cells contain one chromosome from each pair.

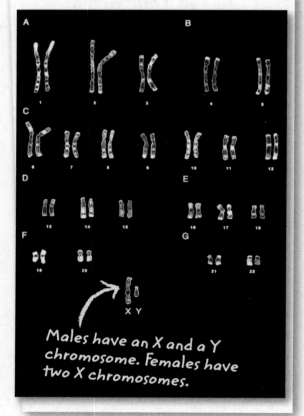

Males have an X and a Y chromosome. Females have two X chromosomes.

👁 Visualize It!

6 State Your Claim The cell shown is a body cell that has two pairs of homologous chromosomes. Make claim about how it is different than a sex cell by drawing a sex cell.

Body cell

Sex cell

Why do organisms need sex cells?

Most human body cells contain 46 chromosomes. Think about what would happen if two body cells were to combine. The resulting cell would have twice the normal number of chromosomes. A sex cell is needed to keep this from happening.

Sex cells are also known as *gametes* (GAM•eetz). Gametes contain half the usual number of chromosomes—one chromosome from each homologous pair and one sex chromosome. Cells that contain half the usual number of chromosomes are known as *haploid* (HAP•loyd).

Gametes are found in the reproductive organs of plants and animals. An egg is a gamete that forms in female reproductive organs. The gamete that forms in male reproductive organs is called a sperm cell.

How are sex cells made?

You know that body cells divide by the process of mitosis. Mitosis produces two new cells, each containing exact copies of the chromosomes in the parent cell. Each new cell has a full set of chromosomes. But to produce sex cells, a different kind of cell division is needed.

Meiosis

A human egg and a human sperm cell each have 23 chromosomes. When an egg is joined with, or *fertilized* by, a sperm cell, a new diploid cell is formed. This new cell has 46 chromosomes, or 23 pairs of chromosomes. One set is from the mother, and the other set is from the father. The newly formed diploid cell may develop into an offspring. **Meiosis** (my•OH•sis) is the type of cell division that produces haploid sex cells such as eggs and sperm cells.

👁 Visualize It!

For the example of fertilization shown, the egg and sperm cells each have one chromosome.

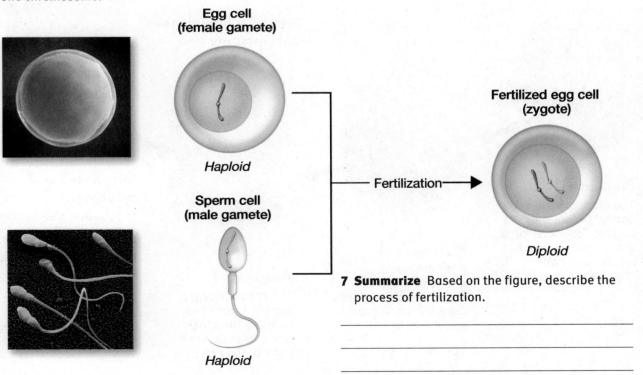

Egg cell
(female gamete)

Haploid

Sperm cell
(male gamete)

Haploid

Fertilized egg cell
(zygote)

← Fertilization →

Diploid

7 Summarize Based on the figure, describe the process of fertilization.

_____

_____

_____

One Step at a Time

What are the stages of meiosis?

Meiosis results in the formation of four haploid cells. Each haploid cell has half the number of chromosomes found in the original cell. Meiosis has two parts: meiosis I and meiosis II.

Meiosis I

Remember that homologous chromosomes have the same genes, but they are not exact copies of each other. Before meiosis I begins, each chromosome is duplicated, or copied. Each half of a duplicated chromosome is called a *chromatid* (KROH•muh•tid). Chromatids are connected to each other by *centromeres* (SEN•truh•mirz). Duplicated chromosomes are drawn in an **X** shape. Each side of the **X** represents a chromatid, and the point where they touch is the centromere.

During meiosis I, pairs of homologous chromosomes and sex chromosomes split apart into two new cells. These cells each have one-half of the chromosome pairs and their duplicate chromatids. The steps of meiosis I are shown below.

ACTIVE READING

8 Sequence As you read, underline what happens to chromosomes during meiosis.

Duplicated homologous chromosomes

Half of a homologous chromosome pair

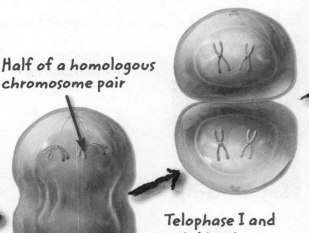

Prophase I
The chromosomes are copied before meiosis begins. The duplicated chromosomes, each made up of two chromatids, pair up.

Metaphase I
After the nuclear membrane breaks down, the chromosome pairs line up in the middle of the cell.

Anaphase I
The chromosomes separate from their partners, and then move to opposite ends of the cell.

Telophase I and cytokinesis
The nuclear membranes re-form, and the cell divides into two cells. The chromatids are still joined.

👁 Visualize It!

9 Claims • Evidence • Reasoning How does meiosis II differ from meiosis I? Summarize evidence to support your claim and explain your reasoning.

_____

_____

_____

_____

Centromere

Chromatid

Prophase II
The chromosomes are not copied again before meiosis II. The nuclear membrane breaks down.

Metaphase II
The chromosomes line up in the middle of each cell.

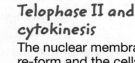

Anaphase II
The chromatids are pulled apart and move to opposite sides of the cell.

Telophase II and cytokinesis
The nuclear membranes re-form and the cells divide. Four new haploid cells are formed. Each has half the usual number of chromosomes.

Think Outside the Book

10 Summarize Work with a partner to make a poster that describes all the steps of meiosis.

Meiosis II

Meiosis II involves both of the new cells formed during meiosis I. The chromosomes of these cells are not copied before meiosis II begins. Both of the cells divide during meiosis II. The steps of meiosis II are shown above.

Meiosis II results in four haploid sex cells. In male organisms, these cells develop into sperm cells. In female organisms, these cells become eggs. In females of some species, three of the cells are broken down and only one haploid cell becomes an egg.

11 Identify At the end of meiosis II, how many cells have formed?

_____

How does meiosis compare to mitosis?

The processes of meiosis and mitosis are similar in many ways. However, they also have several very important differences.

- Only cells that will become sex cells go through meiosis. All other cells divide by mitosis.
- During meiosis, chromosomes are copied once, and then the nucleus divides twice. During mitosis, the chromosomes are copied once, and then the nucleus divides once.
- The cells produced by meiosis contain only half of the genetic material of the parent cell—one chromosome from each homologous pair and one sex chromosome. The cells produced by mitosis contain exactly the same genetic material as the parent—a full set of homologous chromosomes and a pair of sex chromosomes.

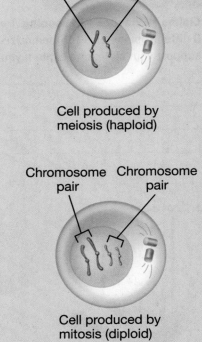

Single chromosome   Single chromosome

Cell produced by meiosis (haploid)

Chromosome pair   Chromosome pair

Cell produced by mitosis (diploid)

12 Gather Evidence Using the table below, provide evidence that shows how meiosis and mitosis are alike and different.

Characteristic	Meiosis	Mitosis
Number of nuclear divisions		
Number of cells produced		
Number of chromosomes in new cells (diploid or haploid)		
Type of cell produced (body cell or sex cell)		
Steps of the process		

© Houghton Mifflin Harcourt

Down Syndrome

Down syndrome is a genetic disease. It is usually caused by an error during meiosis. During meiosis, the chromatids of chromosome 21 do not separate. So, a sex cell gets two copies of chromosome 21 instead of one copy. When this sex cell joins with a normal egg or sperm, the fertilized egg has three copies of chromosome 21 instead of two copies.

1   2   3   4   5

6   7

11   12

Beating the Odds
Down syndrome causes a number of health problems and learning difficulties, but many people with Down syndrome have fulfilling lives.

One Too Many
Someone who has Down syndrome has three copies of chromosome 21 instead of two copies.

18

20   21   22

i Extend

13 Identify What type of error in meiosis causes Down syndrome?

14 Claims • Evidence • Reasoning Research the characteristics of Down syndrome. Make a claim about how a person can overcome some of the difficulties caused by this disorder. Summarize evidence to support your claim

and explain your reasoning.

15 Recommend Research the Special Olympics. Then make an informative brochure, poster, or oral presentation that describes how the Special Olympics gives people with Down syndrome and other disabilities the chance to compete in sports.

Visual Summary

To complete this summary, fill in the blanks with the correct word or phrase. You can use this page to review the main concepts of the lesson.

Meiosis

Meiosis produces haploid cells that can become sex cells.

16 List the steps of meiosis I.

_____

_____

_____

_____

17 List the steps of meiosis II.

_____

_____

_____

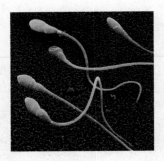

Sex cells have half as many chromosomes as body cells.

18 Sex cells produced by males are called _____, and sex cells produced by females are called _____

Mitosis and meiosis have similarities and differences.

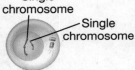

Single chromosome — Single chromosome

Cell produced by meiosis (haploid)

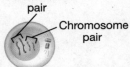

Chromosome pair — Chromosome pair

Cell produced by mitosis (diploid)

19 During _____, chromosomes are copied once and the nucleus divides twice.

20 During _____, chromosomes are copied once and the nucleus divides once.

21 Claims • Evidence • Reasoning What would happen if mitosis occurred in sex cells instead of meiosis? Summarize evidence to support your claim and explain your reasoning.

Lesson Review

Vocabulary

Fill in the blanks with the term that best completes the following sentences.

1 _____ chromosomes are found in body cells but not sex cells.

2 The process of _____ produces haploid cells.

Key Concepts

3 Compare How does the number of chromosomes in sex cells compare with the number of chromosomes in body cells?

_____

_____

_____

4 Identify What is the function of meiosis?

_____

_____

_____

5 List Identify the steps of meiosis.

_____

_____

_____

_____

_____

6 Claims • Evidence • Reasoning How are mitosis and meiosis alike and different? Summarize evidence to support your claim and explain your reasoning.

_____

_____

_____

_____

Critical Thinking

Use the figure to answer the following questions.

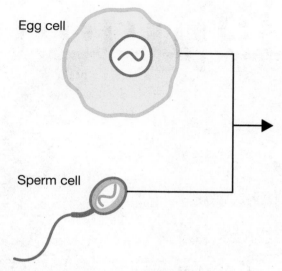

Egg cell

Sperm cell

7 Identify By what process did these cells form?

_____

8 Identify How many chromosomes does a body cell for the organism shown have?

_____

9 Predict Draw a picture of the cell that would form if the sperm cell fused with the egg cell. What is this cell called?

10 Claims • Evidence • Reasoning What would happen if meiosis did not occur? State your claim. Summarize evidence to support this claim and explain your reasoning.

_____

_____

_____

Sexual and Asexual Reproduction

ESSENTIAL QUESTION

How do organisms reproduce?

By the end of this lesson, you should be able to describe asexual and sexual reproduction and list the advantages and disadvantages of each.

Female wolf spiders carry their young on their backs for a short period of time after the young hatch.

SC.7.L.16.3 Compare and contrast the general processes of sexual reproduction requiring meiosis and asexual reproduction requiring mitosis.

Publishing Company

✋ Lesson Labs

Quick Labs
- Reproduction and Diversity
- Create a Classification System

Engage Your Brain

1 Predict Check T or F to show whether you think each statement is true or false.

T	F	
☐	☐	Reproduction requires two parents.
☐	☐	Some organisms reproduce by cell division.
☐	☐	New plants can grow from parts of a parent plant, such as roots and stems.
☐	☐	Offspring of two parents always look like one of their parents.

2 Describe How is the young wolf in the photo below similar to its mother?

_____

_____

_____

_____

ACTIVE **READING**

3 Synthesize You can often define an unknown word if you know the meaning of its word parts. Use the word parts and sentence below to make an educated guess about the meaning of the word *reproduction*.

Word part	Meaning
re-	again
produce	to make
-ion	act or process

Example sentence
Flowers are plant organs that are used for reproduction.

reproduction:

_____

_____

Vocabulary Terms

- **asexual reproduction**
- **sexual reproduction**
- **fertilization**

4 Apply As you learn the definition of each vocabulary term in this lesson, write your own definition or make a sketch to help you remember the meaning of the term.

One Becomes Two

What is asexual reproduction?

An individual organism does not live forever. The survival of any species depends on the ability to reproduce. Reproduction lets genetic information be passed on to new organisms. Reproduction involves various kinds of cell division.

Most single-celled organisms and some multicellular organisms reproduce asexually. In **asexual reproduction** (ay•SEHK•shoo•uhl ree•pruh•DUHK•shuhn), one organism produces one or more new organisms that are identical to itself. These organisms live independently of the original organism. The organism that produces the new organism or organisms is called a *parent*. Each new organism is called an *offspring*. The parent passes on all of its genetic information to the offspring. So, the offspring produced by asexual reproduction are genetically identical to their parents. They may differ only if a genetic mutation happens.

ACTIVE **READING**

5 Relate Describe the genetic makeup of the offspring of asexual reproduction.

_____

_____

_____

Dandelions usually reproduce asexually. The dandelions in this field may all be genetically identical!

i Think Outside the Book

6 Summarize Research five organisms that reproduce asexually. Make informative flash cards that describe how each organism reproduces asexually. When you have finished, trade flashcards with a classmate to learn about five more organisms.

How do organisms reproduce asexually?

Organisms reproduce asexually in many ways. In prokaryotes, which include bacteria and archaea, asexual reproduction happens by cell division. In eukaryotes, which include single-celled and multicellular organisms, asexual reproduction is a more involved process. It often involves a type of cell division called *mitosis* (my•TOH•sis). Mitosis produces genetically identical cells.

Binary Fission

Binary fission (BY•nuh•ree FISH•uhn) is the form of asexual reproduction in prokaryotes. It is a type of cell division. During binary fission, the parent organism splits in two, producing two new cells. Genetically, the new cells are exactly like the parent cell.

Budding

During *budding,* an organism develops tiny buds on its body. A bud grows until it forms a new full-sized organism that is genetically identical to the parent. Budding is the result of mitosis. Eukaryotes such as single-celled yeasts and multicellular hydras reproduce by budding.

Spores

A *spore* is a specialized cell that can survive harsh conditions. Both prokaryotes and eukaryotes can form spores. Spores are produced asexually by one parent. Spores are light and can be carried by the wind. In the right conditions, a spore develops into an organism, such as a fungus.

Vegetative Reproduction

Some plants are able to reproduce asexually by *vegetative reproduction.* Mitosis makes vegetative reproduction possible. New plants may grow from stems, roots, or leaves. Runners are aboveground stems from which a new plant can grow. Tubers are underground stems from which new plants can grow. Plantlets are tiny plants that grow along the edges of a plant's leaves. They drop off the plant and grow on their own.

👁 Visualize It!

7 Claims • Evidence • Reasoning Pick one of the pictures below. Make a claim about how the type of asexual reproduction shown can help the organism reproduce quickly. Summarize evidence to support your claim and explain your reasoning.

Bacteria reproduce by binary fission.

Hydras reproduce by budding.

Spores can survive long periods of time in harsh conditions.

New potato plants can grow from tubers.

Two Make One

What is sexual reproduction?

Most multicellular organisms can reproduce sexually. In **sexual reproduction** (SEHK•shoo•uhl ree•pruh•DUHK•shuhn), two parents each contribute a sex cell to the new organism. Half the genes in the offspring come from each parent. So, the offspring are not identical to either parent. Instead, they have a combination of traits from each parent.

ACTIVE READING

8 Identify As you read, underline the male and female sex cells.

Fertilization

Usually, one parent is male and the other is female. Males produce sex cells called *sperm cells*. Females produce sex cells called *eggs*. Sex cells are produced by a type of cell division called *meiosis* (my•OH•sis). Sex cells have only half of the full set of genetic material found in body cells.

A sperm cell and an egg join together in a process called **fertilization** (fer•tl•i•ZAY•shuhn). When an egg is fertilized by a sperm cell, a new cell is formed. This cell is called a *zygote* (ZY•goht). It has a full set of genetic material. The zygote develops into a new organism. The zygote divides by mitosis, which increases the number of cells. This increase in cells produces growth. You are the size that you are today because of mitosis.

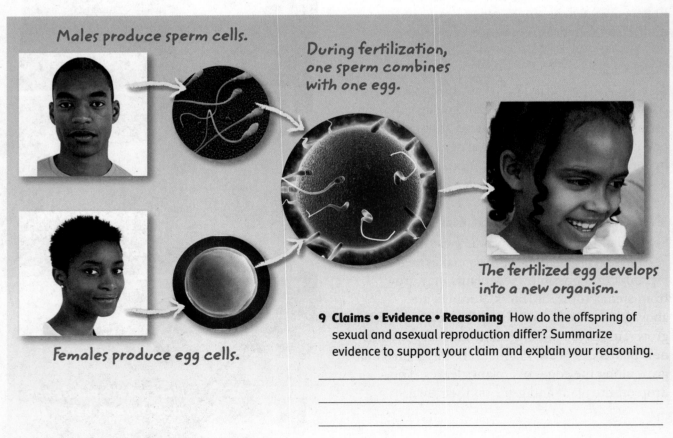

Males produce sperm cells.

During fertilization, one sperm combines with one egg.

The fertilized egg develops into a new organism.

Females produce egg cells.

9 Claims • Evidence • Reasoning How do the offspring of sexual and asexual reproduction differ? Summarize evidence to support your claim and explain your reasoning.

_____

_____

_____

'egg cell with sperm) ©Stocktrek Images, Inc./Alamy

(man, woman, and child) ©Image Source/Getty Images; (sperm cells) ©Juergen Berger/

© Houghton Mifflin Harcou

Odd Reproduction

It may seem like only single-celled organisms undergo asexual reproduction. However, many multicellular organisms reproduce asexually.

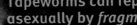

Original arm

Appearing Act

Some organisms, such as aphids, reproduce asexually by *parthenogenesis*. A female produces young without fertilization.

Newly grown body and arms

Falling to Pieces

Tapeworms can reproduce asexually by *fragmentation*. Each segment of the worm can become a new organism if it breaks off of the worm.

Seeing Stars

Organisms such as starfish reproduce asexually by *regeneration*. Even a small part of the starfish can grow into a new organism.

ⓘ Extend

10 Identify Which types of asexual reproduction involve part of an organism breaking off?

11 Investigate Research the advantages and disadvantages of a type of reproduction shown on this page.

12 Claims • Evidence • Reasoning A female shark was left alone in an aquarium tank. She was not pregnant when placed in the tank. Later scientists were surprised to find a baby shark in the tank. Make a claim about what type of reproduction took place in this scenario. Summarize evidence to explain your reasoning.

Added Advantage

What are the advantages of each type of reproduction?

Organisms reproduce asexually, sexually, or both. Each type of reproduction has advantages. For example, sexual reproduction involves complex structures, such as flowers and other organs. These are not needed for asexual reproduction. But the offspring of sexual reproduction may be more likely to survive in certain situations. Read on to find out more about the advantages of each.

13 Compare Use the Venn diagram below to compare asexual and sexual reproduction.

Asexual Reproduction

_____
_____
_____
_____

Both

_____
_____
_____
_____

Sexual Reproduction

_____
_____
_____

Advantages of Asexual Reproduction

Asexual reproduction has many advantages. First, an organism can reproduce very quickly. Offspring are identical to the parent. So, it also ensures that any favorable traits the parent has are passed on to offspring. Also, a parent organism does not need to find a partner to reproduce. Finally, all offspring—not just females—are able to produce more offspring.

14 List Identify four advantages of asexual reproduction.

_____
_____
_____
_____

Cholla cactuses reproduce asexually by vegetative reproduction. They drop off small pieces that grow into new plants.

Cats reproduce sexually. Offspring are similar to, but not exactly like, their parents.

Advantages of Sexual Reproduction

Sexual reproduction is not as quick as asexual reproduction. Nor does it produce as many offspring. However, it has advantages. First, it increases genetic variation. Offspring have different traits that improve the chance that at least some offspring will survive. This is especially true if the environment changes. Offspring are not genetically identical to the parents. So, they may have a trait that the parents do not have, making them more likely to survive.

15 Claims • Evidence • Reasoning Make a claim about how increased genetic variation can help some offspring survive. Cite evidence, and explain your reasoning.

_____

_____

_____

_____

_____

Advantages of Using Both Types of Reproduction

Some organisms can use both types of reproduction. For example, when conditions are favorable, many plants and fungi will reproduce asexually. Doing so lets them spread quickly and take over an area. When the environment changes, these organisms will switch to sexual reproduction. This strategy increases the chance that the species will survive. Because of genetic variation, at least some of the offspring may have traits that help them make it through the environmental change.

16 Compare In the table below, place a check mark in the cells that describe a characteristic of asexual or sexual reproduction.

	Quick	Increases chance of survival in changing environments	Produces genetic variation	Doesn't need a partner	Requires complex structures
Asexual reproduction					
Sexual reproduction					

Visual Summary

To complete this summary, circle the correct word that completes each statement. You can use this page to review the main concepts of the lesson.

Reproduction

Asexual reproduction involves one parent.

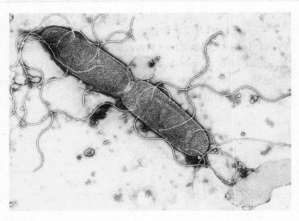

17 The offspring of asexual reproduction are genetically identical / similar to the parent organisms.

18 Prokaryotes reproduce by budding / binary fission.

19 Specialized reproductive structures called runners / spores can survive harsh conditions.

20 A benefit of asexual reproduction is that it is fast / slow.

Sexual reproduction involves two parents.

21 Male organisms produce sex cells called eggs / sperm cells.

22 Male and female sex cells join during fertilization / meiosis.

23 Sexual reproduction increases genetic variation / similarity.

24 Claims • Evidence • Reasoning How can both asexual reproduction and sexual reproduction allow for the survival of a species? Summarize evidence to support your claim and explain your reasoning.

Lesson Review

Vocabulary

Fill in the blanks with the term that best completes the following sentences.

1 After _____ , the zygote develops into a larger organism.

2 An advantage of _____ reproduction is the ability to reproduce quickly.

3 The offspring of _____ reproduction are more likely to survive changes in the environment.

Key Concepts

4 Identify What are some advantages of asexual and sexual reproduction?

_____

_____

_____

_____

_____

5 Compare In sexual reproduction, how do the offspring compare to the parents?

_____

_____

_____

6 Identify List four types of asexual reproduction.

_____

_____

7 Explain Why do some organisms use both types of reproduction?

_____

_____

_____

Critical Thinking

Use the graph to answer the following questions.

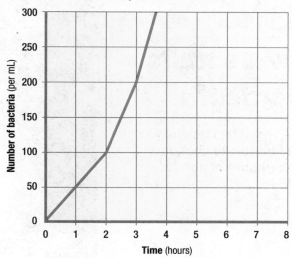

Growth of a Bacterial Population Over Time

8 Infer What type of reproduction is most likely taking place? Explain your reasoning.

_____

_____

9 Claims • Evidence • Reasoning Which advantage of reproduction does the graph show? Summarize evidence to support your claim, and explain your reasoning.

_____

_____

_____

10 Claims • Evidence • Reasoning Make a claim about how the graph might change if the environmental conditions of the bacteria were to suddenly change. Summarize evidence to support your claim, and explain your reasoning.

_____

_____

_____

Publishing Company

Heredity

ESSENTIAL **QUESTION**

How are traits inherited?

By the end of this lesson, you should be able to analyze the inheritance of traits in individuals.

Members of the same family share certain traits. Can you think of some traits that family members share?

SC.7.L.16.1 Understand and explain that every organism requires a set of instructions that specifies its traits, that this hereditary information (DNA) contains genes located in the chromosomes of each cell, and that heredity is the passage of these instructions from one generation to another. **HE.7.C.1.3** Analyze how environmental factors affect personal health. **HE.7.C.1.7** Describe how heredity can affect personal health. **HE.7.C.1.8** Explain the likelihood of injury or illness if engaging in unhealthy/risky behaviors.

Quick Labs
• Gender Determination
• Dominant Alleles

 ## Engage Your Brain

1 Predict Check T or F to show whether you think each statement is true or false.

T F

☐ ☐ Siblings look similar because they each have some traits of their parents.

☐ ☐ Siblings always have the same hair color.

☐ ☐ Siblings have identical DNA.

2 Describe Do you know any identical twins? How are they similar? How are they different?

_____

_____

_____

_____

_____

ACTIVE **READING**

3 Infer Use context clues to write your own definition for the words *exhibit* and *investigate*.

Example sentence
A person with brown hair may also <u>exhibit</u> the trait of brown eye color.

exhibit:

_____

_____

Example sentence
Gregor Mendel began to <u>investigate</u> the characteristics of pea plants.

investigate:

_____

_____

Vocabulary Terms

• heredity
• gene
• allele
• genotype
• phenotype

• dominant
• recessive
• incomplete
  dominance
• codominance

4 Identify This list contains the key terms you'll learn in this lesson. As you read, circle the definition of each term.

Give Peas a Chance

What is heredity?

Imagine a puppy. The puppy has long floppy ears like his mother has, and the puppy has dark brown fur like his father has. How did the puppy get these traits? The traits are a result of information stored in the puppy's genetic material. The passing of genetic material from parents to offspring is called **heredity**.

What did Gregor Mendel discover about heredity?

The first major experiments investigating heredity were performed by a monk named Gregor Mendel. Mendel lived in Austria in the 1800s. Before Mendel became a monk, he attended a university and studied science and mathematics. This training served him well when he began to study the inheritance of traits among the pea plants in the monastery's garden. Mendel studied seven different characteristics of pea plants: plant height, flower and pod position, seed shape, seed color, pod shape, pod color, and flower color. A *characteristic* is a feature that has different forms in a population. Mendel studied each pea plant characteristic separately, always starting with plants that were true-breeding for that characteristic. A true-breeding plant is one that will always produce offspring with a certain trait when allowed to self-pollinate. Each of the characteristics that Mendel studied had two different forms. For example, the color of a pea could be green or yellow. These different forms are called *traits*.

5 Apply Is flower color a characteristic or a trait?

_____

Characteristics of Pea Plants

Characteristic	Traits	
Seed color		
Seed shape		
Pod color		
Flower position		

Traits Depend on Inherited Factors

In his experiments with seed pod color, Mendel took two sets of plants, one true-breeding for plants that produce yellow seed pods and the other true-breeding for plants that produce green seed pods. Instead of letting the plants self-pollinate as they do naturally, he paired one plant from each set. He did this by fertilizing one plant with the pollen of another plant. Mendel called the plants that resulted from this cross the first generation. All of the plants from this first generation produced green seed pods. Mendel called this trait the *dominant* trait. Because the yellow trait seemed to recede, or fade away, he called it the *recessive* trait.

Then Mendel let the first-generation plants self-pollinate. He called the offspring that resulted from this self-pollination the second generation. About three-fourths of the second-generation plants had green seed pods, but about one-fourth had yellow pods. So the trait that seemed to disappear in the first generation reappeared in the second generation. Mendel hypothesized that each plant must have two heritable "factors" for each trait, one from each parent. Some traits, such as yellow seed pod color, could only be observed if a plant received two factors—one from each parent—for yellow pod color. A plant with one yellow factor and one green factor would produce green pods because producing green pods is a dominant trait. However, this plant could still pass on the yellow factor to the next generation of plants.

ACTIVE **READING**

6 Identify As you read, underline Mendel's hypothesis about how traits are passed from parents to offspring.

👁 Visualize It!

7 Claims • Evidence • Reasoning Which pod color is recessive? Summarize evidence to support your claim, and explain your reasoning.

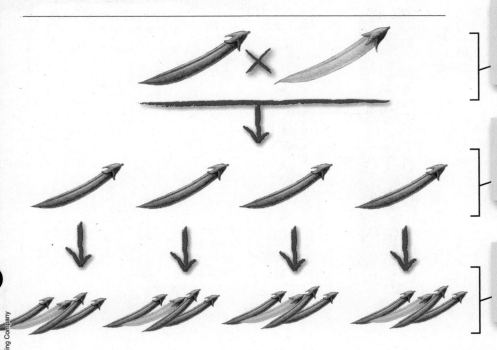

Parent plants Mendel crossed true-breeding green-pod plants with true-breeding yellow-pod plants.

First generation All of the first generation plants had green pods. Mendel let these plants self-pollinate.

Second generation About three-fourths of the second generation had green pods, and one-fourth had yellow pods.

It's in your genes!

Genes are made up of DNA.

How are traits inherited?

Mendel's experiments and conclusions have been the basis for much of the scientific thought about heredity. His ideas can be further explained by our modern understanding of the genetic material DNA. What Mendel called "factors" are actually segments of DNA known as genes!

Genes Are Passed from Parents to Offspring

Genes are segments of DNA found in chromosomes that give instructions for producing a certain characteristic. Humans, like many other organisms, inherit their genes from their parents. Each parent gives one set of genes to the offspring. The offspring then has two versions, or forms, of the same gene for every characteristic—one version from each parent. The different versions of a gene are known as **alleles** (uh•LEELZ). Genes are often represented by letter symbols. Dominant alleles are shown with a capital letter, and recessive alleles are shown with a lowercase version of the same letter. An organism with two dominant or two recessive alleles is said to be *homozygous* for that gene. An organism that has one dominant and one recessive allele is *heterozygous*.

Humans have 23 pairs of chromosomes.

In humans, cells contain pairs of chromosomes. One chromosome of each pair comes from each of two parents. Each chromosome contains sites where specific genes are located.

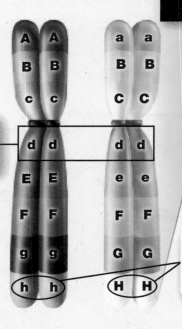

A gene occupies a specific location on both chromosomes in a pair.

👁 Visualize It!

8 Apply Circle a gene pair for which this person is heterozygous.

Alleles are alternate forms of the same gene.

This girl has dimples.

This girl does not have dimples.

9 Apply The girls in this photograph have different types of hair. Is hair type a genotype or a phenotype?

_____

Genes Influence Traits

The alternate forms of genes, called alleles, determine the traits of all living organisms. The combination of alleles that you inherited from your parents is your **genotype** (JEEN•uh•typ). Your observable traits make up your **phenotype** (FEEN•uh•typ). The phenotypes of some traits follow patterns similar to the ones that Mendel discovered in pea plants. That is, some traits are dominant over others. For example, consider the gene responsible for producing dimples, or creases in the cheeks. This gene comes in two alleles: one for dimples and one for no dimples. If you have even one copy of the allele for dimples, you will have dimples. This happens because the allele for producing dimples is dominant. The **dominant** allele contributes to the phenotype if one or two copies are present in the genotype. The no-dimples allele is recessive. The **recessive** allele contributes to the phenotype only when two copies of it are present. If one chromosome in the pair contains a dominant allele and the other contains a recessive allele, the phenotype will be determined by the dominant allele. If you do not have dimples, it is because you inherited two no-dimples alleles—one from each parent. This characteristic shows _complete dominance,_ because one trait is completely dominant over another. However, not all characteristics follow this pattern.

ACTIVE **READING**

11 Identify What is the phenotype of an individual with one allele for dimples and one allele for no dimples?

_____

_____

i Think Outside the Book

10 Summarize Write a short story about a world in which you could change your DNA and your traits. What would be the advantages? What would be the disadvantages?

Many Genes Can Influence a Single Trait

Some characteristics, such as the color of your skin, hair, and eyes, are the result of several genes acting together. Different combinations of alleles can result in different shades of eye color. Because there is not always a one-to-one relationship between a trait and a gene, many traits do not have simple patterns of inheritance.

A Single Gene Can Influence Many Traits

Sometimes, one gene influences more than one trait. For example, a single gene causes the tiger shown below to have white fur. If you look closely, you will see that the tiger also has blue eyes. The gene that affects fur color also influences eye color.

Many genetic disorders in humans are linked to a single gene but affect many traits. For example, the genetic disorder sickle cell anemia occurs in individuals who have two recessive alleles for a certain gene. This gene carries instructions for producing a protein in red blood cells. When a person has sickle cell anemia alleles, the body makes a different protein. This protein causes red blood cells to be sickle or crescent shaped when oxygen levels are low. Sickle-shaped blood cells can stick in blood vessels, sometimes blocking the flow of blood. These blood cells are also more likely to damage the spleen. With fewer healthy red blood cells, the body may not be able to deliver oxygen to the body's organs. All of the traits associated with sickle cell anemia are due to a single gene.

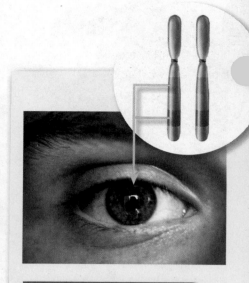

👁 Visualize It!

12 Identify How many genes are responsible for eye color in this example?

_____

This single gene affects the tiger's fur color and eye color.

The Environment Can Influence Traits

Sometimes, the environment influences an organism's phenotype. For example, the arctic fox has a gene that is responsible for coat color. This gene is affected by light. In the winter, there are fewer hours of daylight, and the hairs that make up the arctic fox's coat grow in white. In the summer, when there are more daylight hours, the hairs in the coat grow in brown. In this case, both genes and the environment contribute to the organism's phenotype. The environment can influence human characteristics as well. For example, your genes may make it possible for you to grow to be tall, but you need a healthy diet to reach your full height potential.

Traits that are learned in one's environment are not inherited. For example, your ability to read and write is an acquired trait—a skill you learned. You were not born knowing how to ride a bike, and if you have children, they will not be born knowing how to do it either. They will have to learn the skill just as you did.

ACTIVE **READING**

13 Identify Give an example of an acquired trait.

_____

_____

In the summer, the arctic fox has a brown coat.

In the winter, the arctic fox has a white coat.

14 Claims • Evidence • Reasoning What advantage does white fur give the arctic fox in winter? State your claim. Summarize evidence to support your claim, and explain your reasoning.

_____

_____

_____

Bending the Rules

What are the exceptions to complete dominance?

The characteristics that Mendel chose to study demonstrated complete dominance, meaning that heterozygous individuals show the dominant trait. Some human traits, such as freckles and dimples, follow the pattern of complete dominance, too. However, other traits do not. For traits that show incomplete dominance or codominance, one trait is not completely dominant over another.

Incomplete Dominance

In **incomplete dominance**, each allele in a heterozygous individual influences the phenotype. The result is a phenotype that is a blend of the phenotypes of the parents. One example of incomplete dominance is found in the snapdragon flower, shown below. When a true-breeding red snapdragon is crossed with a true-breeding white snapdragon, all the offspring are pink snapdragons. Both alleles of the gene have some influence. Hair texture is an example of incomplete dominance in humans. A person with one straight-hair allele and one curly-hair allele will have wavy hair.

ACTIVE READING

15 Identify As you read, underline examples of incomplete dominance and codominance.

👁 Visualize It!

16 Claims • Evidence • Reasoning How can you tell that these snapdragons do not follow the pattern of complete dominance? Summarize evidence to support your claim, and explain your reasoning.

_____

_____

_____

_____

Pink snapdragons are produced by a cross between a red snapdragon and a white snapdragon.

Codominance

For a trait that shows **codominance**, both of the alleles in a heterozygous individual contribute to the phenotype. Instead of having a blend of the two phenotypes, heterozygous individuals have both of the traits associated with their two alleles. An example of codominance is shown in the genes that determine human blood types. There are three alleles that play a role in determining a person's blood type: *A, B,* and *O.* The alleles are responsible for producing small particles on the surface of red blood cells called antigens. The *A* allele produces red blood cells coated with A antigens. The *B* allele produces red blood cells coated with B antigens. The *O* allele does not produce antigens. The *A* and *B* alleles are codominant. So, someone with one *A* allele and one *B* allele will have blood cells that are coated with A antigens and B antigens. This person would have type AB blood.

i Think Outside the Book

17 Research Blood type is an important factor when people give or receive blood. Research the meanings of the phrases "universal donor" and "universal recipient." What are the genotypes of each blood type?

ACTIVE READING

18 Identify What antigens coat the red blood cells of a person with type AB blood?

_____

◉ Visualize It!

19 Predict The color of these imaginary fish is controlled by a single gene. Sketch or describe their offspring if the phenotypes follow the pattern of complete dominance, incomplete dominance, or codominance.

Complete dominance (Blue is dominant to yellow.)	Incomplete dominance	Codominance

Visual Summary

To complete this summary, circle the correct word or phrase. You can use this page to review the main concepts of the lesson.

Heredity

Gregor Mendel studied patterns of heredity in pea plants.

20 Traits that seemed to disappear in Mendel's first-generation crosses were dominant / recessive traits.

Inherited genes influence the traits of an individual.

21 An individual with the genotype BB is heterozygous / homozygous.

Phenotypes can follow complete dominance, incomplete dominance, or codominance.

22 When these imaginary fish cross, their offspring are all green. This is an example of codominance / incomplete dominance.

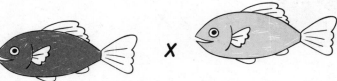

23 Claims • Evidence • Reasoning A child has blonde hair and both of her parents have brown hair. Make a claim about the allele for blonde hair. Summarize evidence to support your claim and explain your reasoning.

Lesson Review

Vocabulary

Draw a line to connect the following terms to their definitions.

1 heredity
_____

2 gene
_____

3 phenotype
_____

A an organism's appearance or other detectable characteristic

B a section of DNA that contains instructions for a particular characteristic

C the passing of genetic material from parent to offspring

Key Concepts

4 Describe What did Mendel discover about genetic factors in pea plants?

_____
_____
_____
_____

5 Describe What is the role of DNA in determining an organism's traits?

_____
_____
_____
_____

6 Apply Imagine that a brown horse and a white horse cross to produce an offspring whose coat is made up of some brown hairs and some white hairs. Which pattern of dominance is this an example of?

_____
_____

7 Identify Give an example of a trait that is controlled by more than one gene.

_____
_____

Use this diagram to answer the following questions.

8 Identify What is the genotype at the Q gene?

_____

9 Apply For which genes is this individual heterozygous?

_____

Critical Thinking

10 Claims • Evidence • Reasoning Consider a person who has Marfan syndrome, which is a genetic disorder. This person has only one allele for this disorder in their genotype. What does this mean about the allele for Marfan syndrome? Summarize evidence to support your claim, and explain your reasoning.

_____
_____

11 Describe Jenny, Jenny's mom, and Jenny's grandfather are all good basketball players. Give an example of an inherited trait and an acquired trait that could contribute to their skill at basketball.

_____
_____

SC.7.N.1.1 Define a problem from the seventh grade curriculum, use appropriate reference materials to support scientific understanding, plan and carry out scientific investigation of various types, such as systematic observations or experiments, identify variables, collect and organize data, interpret data in charts, tables, and graphics, analyze information, make predictions, and defend conclusions.

Interpreting Tables

Visual displays, such as diagrams, tables, or graphs, are useful ways to show data collected in an experiment. A table is the most direct way to communicate this information. Tables are also used to summarize important trends in scientific data. Making a table may seem easy. However, if tables are not clearly organized, people will have trouble reading them. Below are a few strategies to help you improve your skills in interpreting scientific tables.

Tutorial

Use the following instructions to study the parts of a table about heredity in Brittanies and to analyze the data shown in the table.

Offspring from Cross of Black Solid and Liver Tricolor Brittanies		
Color	**Pattern**	**Number of Offspring**
orange and white	solid	1
black and white	solid	1
	tricolor	3
liver and white	solid	1
	tricolor	3

Reading the Title
Every table should have an informative title. By reading the title of the table to the left, we know that the table contains data about the offspring of a cross between a black solid Brittany and a liver tricolor Brittany.

Summarizing the Title
Sometimes it is helpful to write a sentence to summarize a table's title. For example, you could write, "This table shows how puppies that are the offspring of a black solid Brittany and a liver tricolor Brittany might look."

Analyzing the Headings
Row and column headings describe the data in the cells. Headings often appear different from the data in the cells, such as being larger, bold, or being shaded. The row headings in the table to the left organize three kinds of data: the coat color of the puppies, the coat pattern of the puppies, and the number of puppies that have each combination of coat color and pattern.

Describing the Data
In complete sentences, record the information that you read in the table. For example, you could write, "There are five different kinds of offspring. Tricolor puppies are most common, and puppies with a solid coat pattern are least common. There are twice as many tricolor puppies as solid puppies."

Analyzing the Data
Now that you have seen how the table is organized, you can begin to look for trends in the data. Which combinations are most common? Which combinations are least common?

You Try It!

The table below shows the characteristics of Guinea pig offspring. Look at the table, and answer the questions that follow.

Characteristics of Guinea Pig Offspring from Controlled Breeding			
Hair Color	Coat Texture	Hair Length	Number of Guinea Pigs
black	rough	short	27
		long	9
	smooth	short	9
		long	3
white	rough	short	9
		long	3
	smooth	short	3
		long	1

1 Summarizing the Title Circle the title of the table. Write a one-sentence description of the information shown in the table.

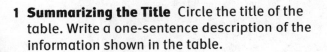

2 Analyzing the Headings Shade the column headings in the table. What information do they show? How many combinations of hair color, coat texture, and hair length are shown?

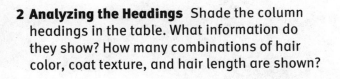

3 Analyzing the Data Circle the most common type of Guinea pig. Box the least common type of Guinea pig. Write sentences to describe the characteristics of each.

4 Applying Mathematics Calculate the total number of Guinea pig offspring. Write this total at the bottom of the table. What percentage of the total number of Guinea pigs has short hair? What percentage of the total number of Guinea pigs has long hair?

5 Claims • Evidence • Reasoning Based on your data from Step 4, which characteristic is dominant in Guinea pigs: long hair or short hair? Summarize evidence to support your claim and explain your reasoning.

6 Applying Concepts What is one advantage of displaying data in tables? What is one advantage of describing data in writing?

Take It Home!

With an adult, practice making tables. You can categorize anything that interests you. Make sure your table has a title and clearly and accurately organizes your data using headings. If possible, share your table with your class.

Punnett Squares and Pedigrees

ESSENTIAL **QUESTION**

How are patterns of inheritance studied?

By the end of this lesson, you should be able to explain how patterns of heredity can be predicted by Punnett squares and pedigrees.

SC.7.L.16.2 Determine the probabilities for genotype and phenotype combinations using Punnett Squares and pedigrees.
HE.7.C.1.3 Analyze how environmental factors affect personal health. **HE.7.C.1.7** Describe how heredity can affect personal health.

These cattle are bred for their long, curly hair, which keeps them warm in cold climates. This trait is maintained by careful breeding of these animals.

Lesson Labs

Quick Labs
- Completing a Punnett Square
- Interpreting Pedigree Charts

Exploration Lab
- Offspring Models

Exploration/S.T.E.M. Lab
- Accuracy of Punnett Square Predictions

 Engage Your Brain

1 Infer Why do you think that children look like their parents?

_____

_____

_____

_____

_____

_____

_____

_____

_____

2 Apply Color or label each circle with the color that results when the two paints mix. As you read the lesson, think about how this grid is similar to and different from a Punnett square.

ACTIVE READING

3 Apply Use context clues to write your own definition for the words *occur* and *outcome*.

Example sentence
Tools can be used to predict the likelihood that a particular genetic combination will <u>occur</u>.

occur:

_____

_____

Example sentence
A Punnett square can be used to predict the <u>outcome</u> of a genetic cross.

outcome:

_____

_____

Vocabulary Terms

- **Punnett square**
- **probability**
- **ratio**
- **pedigree**

4 Apply As you learn the definition of each vocabulary term in this lesson, create your own definition or sketch to help you remember the meaning of the term.

Squared Away

How are Punnett squares used to predict patterns of heredity?

When Gregor Mendel studied pea plants, he noticed that traits are inherited in patterns. One tool for understanding the patterns of heredity is a diagram called a *Punnett square*. A **Punnett square** is a graphic used to predict the possible genotypes of offspring in a given cross. Each parent has two alleles for a particular gene. An offspring receives one allele from each parent. A Punnett square shows all of the possible allele combinations in the offspring.

The Punnett square below shows how alleles are expected to be distributed in a cross between a pea plant with purple flowers and a pea plant with white flowers. The top of the Punnett square shows one parent's alleles for this trait (*F* and *F*). The left side of the Punnett square shows the other parent's alleles (*f* and *f*). Each compartment within the Punnett square shows an allele combination in potential offspring. You can see that in this cross, all offspring would have the same genotype (*Ff*). Because purple flower color is completely dominant to white flower color, all of the offspring would have purple flowers.

ACTIVE READING

5 Identify In a Punnett square, where are the parents' alleles written?

_____

_____

_____

_____

_____

This Punnett square shows the possible offspring combinations in pea plants with different flower colors.

Key:

F Purple flower allele

f White flower allele

Genotype: FF
Phenotype: purple flower

Genotype: ff
Phenotype: white flower

One parent's alleles

The other parent's alleles

	F	F
f	Ff	Ff
f	Ff	Ff

6 Apply Fill in the genotypes and phenotypes of the parents and offspring in this Punnett square. Sketch the resulting offspring possibilities in the white boxes below. (Hint: Assume complete dominance.)

Key:

R Round pea allele

r Wrinkled pea allele

Genotype: _____

Phenotype: _____

Genotype: _____

Phenotype: _____

	R	r
R	Genotype: _____ Phenotype: _____	Genotype: _____ Phenotype: _____
r	Genotype: _____ Phenotype: _____	Genotype: _____ Phenotype: _____

7 Explain Your Reasoning What does each compartment of the Punnett square represent? Explain your reasoning.

_____

_____

_____

_____

_____

_____

_____

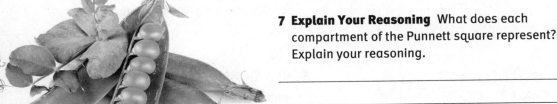

How can a Punnett square be used to make predictions about offspring?

A Punnett square does not tell you what the exact results of a certain cross will be. A Punnett square only helps you find the probability that a certain genotype will occur. **Probability** is the mathematical chance of a specific outcome in relation to the total number of possible outcomes.

Probability can be expressed in the form of a **ratio** (RAY•shee•oh), an expression that compares two quantities. A ratio written as 1:4 is read as "one to four." The ratios obtained from a Punnett square tell you the probability that any one offspring will get certain alleles. Another way of expressing probability is as a *percentage*. A percentage is like a ratio that compares a number to 100. A percentage states the number of times a certain outcome might happen out of a hundred chances.

1:4 is the ratio of red squares to total squares.

Do the Math

Sample Problem

In guinea pigs, the dominant *B* allele is responsible for black fur, while the recessive *b* allele is responsible for brown fur. Use the Punnett square to find the probability of this cross resulting in offspring with brown fur.

	B	b
b	Bb	bb
b	Bb	bb

Identify

A. What do you know?

Parent genotypes are Bb and bb. Possible offspring genotypes are Bb and bb.

B. What do you want to find out?

Probability of the cross resulting in offspring with brown fur

Plan

C. Count the total number of offspring allele combinations: 4

D. Count the number of allele combinations that will result in offspring with brown fur: 2

Solve

E. Write the probability of offspring with brown fur as a ratio: 2:4

F. Rewrite the ratio to express the probability out of 100 off spring by multiplying each side of the ratio by the same number (such as 25): 50:100

G. Convert the ratio to a percentage: 50%

Answer: 50% chance of offspring with brown fur

Do the Math

You Try It

8 Calculate This Punnett square shows a cross between two *Bb* guinea pigs. What is the probability of the cross resulting in offspring with black fur?

	B	b
B	BB	Bb
b	Bb	bb

Identify

A. What do you know?

B. What do you want to find out?

Plan

C. Count the total number of offspring allele combinations:

D. Count the number of allele combinations that will result in offspring with black fur:

Solve

E. Write the probability of offspring with black fur as a ratio:

F. Rewrite the ratio to express the probability out of 100 offspring by multiplying each side of the ratio by the same number:

G. Convert the ratio to a percentage:

Answer:

9 Claims • Evidence • Reasoning
In the cross above, what is the ratio of each of the possible genotypes? Make a claim by filling in the pie chart at the right. Fill in the key to show which pieces of the chart represent the different genotypes.

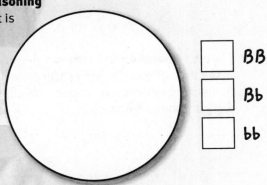

☐ BB

☐ Bb

☐ bb

How can a pedigree trace a trait through generations?

A pedigree is another tool used to study patterns of inheritance. A **pedigree** traces the occurrence of a trait through generations of a family. Pedigrees can be created to trace any inherited trait—even hair color!

Pedigrees can be useful in tracing a special class of inherited disorders known as *sex-linked disorders*. Sex-linked disorders are associated with an allele on a sex chromosome. Many sex-linked disorders, such as hemophilia and colorblindness, are caused by an allele on the X chromosome. Women have two X chromosomes, so a woman can have one allele for colorblindness without being colorblind. A woman who is heterozygous for this trait is called a *carrier,* because she can carry or pass on the trait to her offspring. Men have just one X chromosome. In men, this single chromosome determines if the trait is present.

The pedigree below traces a disease called *cystic fibrosis*. Cystic fibrosis causes serious lung problems. Carriers of the disease have one recessive allele. They do not have cystic fibrosis, but they are able to pass the recessive allele on to their children. If a child receives a recessive allele from each parent, then the child will have cystic fibrosis. Other genetic conditions follow a similar pattern.

ⓘ Think Outside the Book

10 Design Create a pedigree chart that traces the occurrence of dimples in your family or in the family of a friend. Collect information for as many family members as you can.

👁 Visualize It!

Pedigree for Cystic Fibrosis

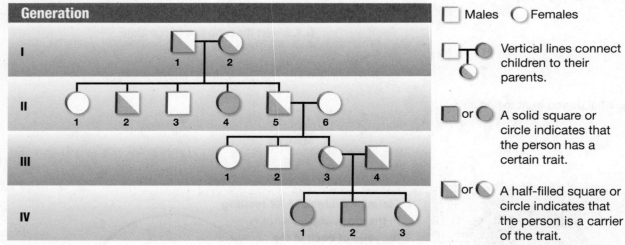

11 Claims • Evidence • Reasoning Does anyone in the third generation have cystic fibrosis? Summarize evidence to support your claim and explain your reasoning.

12 Calculate What is the probability that the child of two carriers will have cystic fibrosis?

Saving the European Mouflon

The European mouflon is an endangered species of sheep. Scientists at the University of Teramo in Italy used genetic tools and techniques to show how the population of mouflon could be preserved.

Maintaining Genetic Diversity

When a very small population of animals interbreeds, there is a greater risk that harmful genetic conditions can appear in the animals. This is one issue that scientists face when trying to preserve endangered species. One way to lower this risk is to be sure that genetically-similar animals do not breed.

Genetics to the Rescue!

Researchers combined the sperm and egg of genetically-dissimilar European mouflons in a laboratory. The resulting embryo was implanted into a mother sheep. By controlling the combination of genetic material, scientists hope to lower the risk of inherited disorders.

ⓘ Extend

13 Claims • Evidence • Reasoning Why are small populations hard to preserve? Summarize evidence to support your claim and explain your reasoning.

14 Research Research another population of animals that has been part of a captive breeding program.

15 Describe Describe these animals and the results of the breeding program by doing one of the following:
- make a poster
- write a song
- write a short story
- draw a graphic novel

Visual Summary

To complete this summary, fill in the blanks with the correct word or phrase. You can use this page to review the main concepts of the lesson.

Predicting Patterns of Inheritance

Punnett squares can be used to make predictions about possible offspring.

	F	F
f	Ff	Ff
f	Ff	Ff

16 A Punnett square shows combinations of different _____ received from each parent.

Pedigrees trace a trait through generations.

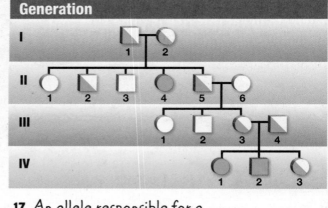

17 An allele responsible for a _____ is found on a sex chromosome.

18 Claims • Evidence • Reasoning How is a heterozygous individual represented in the Punnett square and pedigree shown above? Summarize evidence to support your claim and explain your reasoning.

Vocabulary

Circle the term that best completes the following sentences.

1 A *Punnett square / ratio* is a tool that can be used to predict the genotypes of potential offspring in a given cross.

2 The results from a Punnett square can be used to find the *pedigree / probability* that a certain allele combination will occur in offspring.

3 A mathematical expression that compares one number to another is called a *pedigree / ratio*.

Key Concepts

Use this diagram to answer the following questions.

	G	*G*
g	*Gg*	*Gg*
g	*Gg*	*Gg*

4 Analyze What is gene G responsible for in these fruit flies?

_____

_____

5 Analyze What is the ratio of heterozygous offspring to total offspring in the Punnett square?

6 Define What is a sex-linked disorder?

_____

_____

_____

_____

Critical Thinking

7 Claims • Evidence • Reasoning Imagine a pedigree that traces an inherited disorder found in individuals with two recessive alleles for gene D. The pedigree shows three siblings with the genotypes *DD, Dd,* and *dd.* Did the parents of these three children have the disorder? Summarize evidence to support your claim and explain your reasoning.

_____

_____

_____

8 Explain A *Bb* guinea pig crosses with a *Bb* guinea pig, and four offspring are produced. All of the offspring are black. How could this happen? Explain your reasoning.

_____

_____

_____

9 Synthesize You are creating a pedigree to trace freckles, a recessive trait, in a friend's family. You find out which of her family members have freckles and which do not. When you complete the pedigree, what can you learn about members of your friend's family that you could not tell just by looking at them?

_____

_____

_____

UNIT 8
Summary

Punnett Squares and **Pedigrees** — **predict patterns of** → **Heredity**

Heredity — **which is the passing of traits by** → **Sexual** and **Asexual Reproduction**

Sexual and Asexual Reproduction — **through** → **Meiosis**

Sexual and Asexual Reproduction — **can involve** → **Mitosis**

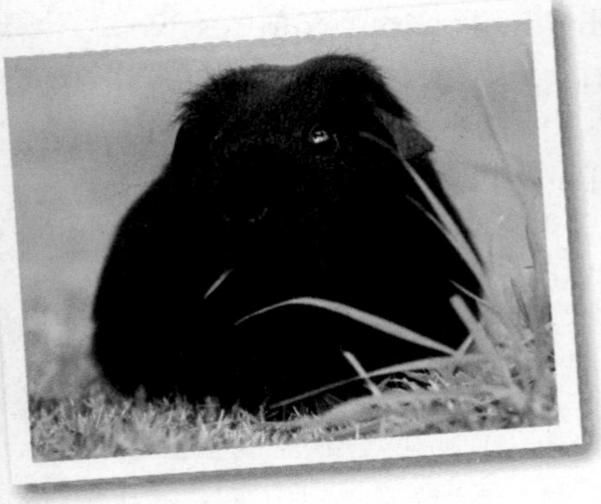

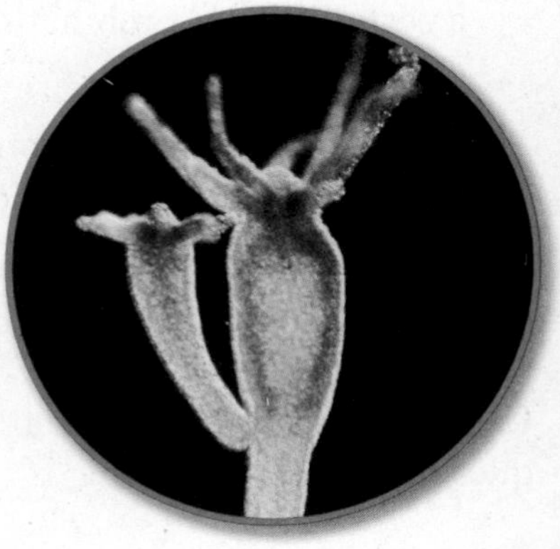

1 Claims • Evidence • Reasoning The Graphic Organizer above shows that Punnett squares are used to make predictions about heredity. Are Punnett squares more useful for predicting the results of sexual or asexual reproduction? State your claim. Summarize evidence to support your claim and explain your reasoning.

2 Compare How are meiosis and mitosis similar? How are they different?

3 Relate Compare the phenotype and genotype of a parent to the phenotype and genotype of its offspring produced by asexual reproduction.

Vocabulary

Name _____

Fill in each blank with the term that best completes the following sentences.

1 The genetic material of all cells is _____

2 A(n) _____ compares or shows the relationship between two quantities.

3 _____ is the process of cell division that results in the formation of cells with half the usual number of chromosomes.

4 The type of reproduction that results in offspring that are genetically identical to the single parent is known as _____ reproduction.

Key Concepts

Identify the choice that best completes the statement or answers the question.

5 Cassie draws flashcards for each phase of mitosis and cytokinesis. Before she can label the backs of the flashcards, Cassie drops them onto the floor. The flashcards get mixed up as shown below.

1   2   3   4   5

In what order should Cassie place the cards to show mitosis from start to finish?

A 1 → 2 → 3 → 4 → 5   **C** 3 → 1 → 5 → 2 → 4

B 2 → 4 → 5 → 1 → 3   **D** 4 → 2 → 1 → 5 → 3

6 Brandy knows that chromosomes behave differently in meiosis and mitosis. What do chromosomes do in meiosis but **not** in mitosis?

F Each chromosome makes an exact copy of itself.

G The homologous chromosomes form pairs.

H Chromosomes line up in the middle of the cell.

I Chromosomes condense, becoming visible under a microscope.

7 Noriko is studying a plant species she found in a forest. She collects leaf samples from a large parent plant and from the smaller offspring that are growing next to it. After running some tests, she finds that the offspring are genetically identical to the parent plant. Which of these statements is **true** about Noriko's find?

A The offspring were produced sexually, and two parents were required.

B The offspring were produced asexually, and two parents were required.

C The offspring were produced sexually, and only one parent was required.

D The offspring were produced asexually, and only one parent was required.

8 Examine the Punnett square below.

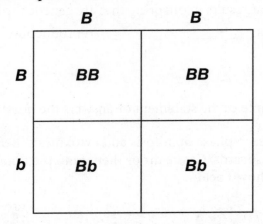

Which of the following choices gives the alleles of the parents shown here?

F *BB* and *BB*

G *BB* and *Bb*

H *Bb* and *Bb*

I *Bb* and *bb*

9 Delia is teaching her sister about important molecules in the body. She tells her sister that one molecule provides a set of instructions that determines characteristics, such as eye color or hair color. Which molecule is Delia describing?

A DNA

B glucose

C gamete

D spore

Name _____

10 The diagram below shows the results of crossing a pea plant with smooth seeds and a pea plant with wrinkled seeds.

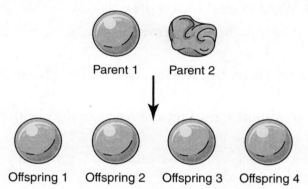

Parent 1   Parent 2

Offspring 1   Offspring 2   Offspring 3   Offspring 4

What can be determined from the results of the experiment?

F Smooth shape and wrinkled shape are both recessive traits.

G Smooth shape and wrinkled shape are both dominant traits.

H Smooth shape is a dominant trait, and wrinkled shape is a recessive trait.

I Smooth shape is a recessive trait, and wrinkled shape is a dominant trait.

11 Lucinda decides to investigate what would happen if there is an error at different stages of the cell cycle. She examines interphase, mitosis, and cytokinesis. Which of these statements describes what is **most likely** to happen if DNA is not duplicated during interphase?

A The new cells would be more numerous.

B The new cells would have too many chromosomes.

C The new cells would have too many nuclei.

D The new cells would have too few chromosomes.

12 A species of rabbit can have brown fur or white fur. One rabbit with two alleles for brown fur (*BB*) has brown fur. A second rabbit with two alleles for white fur (*bb*) has white fur. Which statement is true about the alleles *B* and *b*?

F They are on two different genes.

G They result in the same phenotype.

H They are two different versions of the same gene.

I They provide identical instructions for a characteristic.

13 Leah cuts a small stem from an azalea plant and gives it to John. John takes the cutting home and plants it in his garden. In a few months, the small stem has grown into a full-sized, new plant. Which of these choices correctly describes this situation?

A Leah's plant reproduced by budding and is genetically different than the plant in John's garden.

B Leah's plant reproduced by binary fission and is genetically different than the plant in John's garden.

C Leah's plant reproduced by spore formation and is genetically identical to the plant in John's garden.

D Leah's plant reproduced by vegetative reproduction and is genetically identical to the plant in John's garden.

Critical Thinking

Answer the following question in the space provided.

14 Describe two advantages and disadvantages of asexual reproduction.

_____

_____

_____

_____

15 Jake made a pedigree to trace the traits of straight and curly hair in his family.

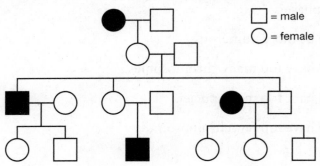

□ = male
○ = female

A shaded circle or square in Jake's pedigree represents a person with straight hair. Make a claim about whether straight hair is controlled by a dominant allele or a recessive allele. Use evidence to support your claim and explain your reasoning. How do you know that straight hair is not sex-linked?

_____

_____

_____

_____

_____

DNA and Modern Genetics

This crop of soybeans has been genetically modified to make them herbicide resistant.

FLORIDA **BIG IDEA 16**

Heredity and Reproduction

What Do You Think?

We can change the genetic make up of organisms to have traits that we desire, such as better flavor or nutrition. Should foods from genetically modified organisms be labeled accordingly? As you explore this unit, find evidence to make and support a claim.

UNIT 9

DNA and Modern Genetics

Solved with Forensics

Modern crime labs use genetics, the study of how traits are inherited, to interpret evidence found at the scene of a crime. In the following scenario, a bike has been stolen and you will use genetic evidence to figure out what happened.

Stolen! Have you seen my bike?

1 Ask A Question

What should a detective at a crime scene look for?

Determine what types of evidence a detective could find at a crime scene. Consider that some evidence might be microscopic! In this case, you have found an empty juice box and a lock of hair.

WARNING
SEALED EVIDENCE
DO NOT TAMPER

② Think About It

List some of the traits (like fingerprints) that are unique to every individual.

_____

_____

_____

_____

What biological evidence might be found on the juice box and lock of hair left behind at the crime scene? What could they tell you about the crime?

_____

_____

_____

_____

_____

🏠 Take It Home!

Find out how DNA forensics is applied in our justice system. How accurate is it? Has it been used to reverse any court decisions or overturn any convictions?

③ Apply Your Knowledge

A The hair sample you gathered is in a sealed bag. Why is it important to protect samples?

_____

_____

_____

B When lab technicians analyze DNA, it doesn't have a name on it. How can you match your sample to an individual and solve the crime?

_____

_____

_____

C Can forensics determine for sure that the person identified by the evidence committed the crime? Explain your reasoning.

_____

_____

_____

DNA Structure and Function

ESSENTIAL QUESTION

What is DNA?

By the end of this lesson, you should be able to describe the structure and main functions of DNA.

SC.7.N.1.1 Define a problem from the curriculum, use appropriate reference materials to support scientific understanding, plan and carry out scientific investigation of various types, such as systematic observations or experiments, identify variables, collect and organize data, interpret data in charts, tables, and graphics, analyze information, make predictions, and defend conclusions.
SC.7.N.1.5 Describe the methods used in the pursuit of a scientific explanation as seen in different fields of science such as biology, geology, and physics.
SC.7.L.16.1 Understand and explain that every organism requires a set of instructions that specifies its traits, that this hereditary information (DNA) contains genes located in the chromosomes of each cell, and that heredity is the passage of these instructions from one generation to another.
HE.7.C.1.3 Analyze how environmental factors affect personal health.

This bacterium was treated with a special chemical, causing a twisted maze of DNA to burst from the cell.

 Lesson Labs

Quick Labs
• Modeling DNA
• Mutations Cause Diversity

Exploration Lab
• Extracting DNA

Engage Your Brain

1 Predict Check T or F to show whether you think each statement is true or false.

T	F	
☐	☐	DNA is found in the cells of all living things.
☐	☐	All DNA mutations are harmful.
☐	☐	The cell can make copies of its DNA.

2 Describe DNA is sometimes called the *blueprint of life*. Why do you think that is?

_____

_____

_____

_____

_____

_____

ACTIVE READING

3 Synthesize Many English words have their roots in other languages. Use the Latin words below to make an educated guess about the meanings of the words *replication* and *mutation*.

Latin word	Meaning
mutare	to change
replicare	to repeat

Example sentence
DNA can undergo <u>mutation</u>.

mutation:

_____

_____

Example sentence
Before cell division, DNA <u>replication</u> occurs.

replication:

_____

_____

Vocabulary Terms

• DNA
• nucleotide
• replication
• mutation
• RNA
• ribosome

4 Identify This list contains the key terms you'll learn in this lesson. As you read, circle the definition of each term.

Cracking the CODE

ATTAGCGATCACTAAATTA

What is DNA?

The genetic material of a cell contains information needed for the cell's growth and other activities. It also determines the inherited characteristics of an organism. The genetic material in cells is contained in a molecule called deoxyribonucleic (dee•OK•see•ry•boh•noo•KLAY•ik) acid, or **DNA** for short. You could compare the information in DNA to the books in your local library. You might find a book describing how to bake a cake or complete your favorite video game. The books, however, don't actually do any of those things—you do. Similarly, the "books" that make up the DNA "library" carry the information that a cell needs to function, grow, and divide. However, DNA doesn't do any of those things. Proteins do most of the work of a cell and also make up much of the structure of a cell.

Scientists describe DNA as containing a code. A *code* is a set of rules and symbols used to carry information. For example, your computer uses a code of ones and zeroes that is translated into numbers, letters, and graphics on a computer screen. To understand how DNA functions as a code, you first need to learn about the structure of the DNA molecule.

ACTIVE READING

5 Identify As you read, underline the meaning of the word *code*.

DNA Timeline

Review this timeline to learn about some of the important scientific contributions to our understanding of DNA.

1875   **1900**   **1925**

1869 Friedrich Miescher identifies a substance that will later be known as DNA.

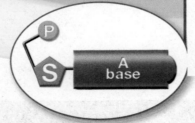

1919 Phoebus Levene publishes a paper on nucleic acids. His research helps scientists determine that DNA is made up of sugars, phosphate groups, and four nitrogen-containing bases: adenine, thymine, guanine, and cytosine. Bases are often referred to by their first letter: A, T, C, or G. Each base has a different shape.

6 Support Your Claim In this model, what do *P, S,* and *A bases* represent?

_____

_____

© Houghton Mifflin Harcourt

How was DNA discovered?

The discovery of the structure and function of DNA did not happen overnight. Many scientists from all over the world contributed to our current understanding of this important molecule. Some scientists discovered the chemicals that make up DNA. Others learned how these chemicals fit together. Still others determined the three-dimensional structure of the DNA molecule. The timeline below shows some of the key steps in this process of discovery.

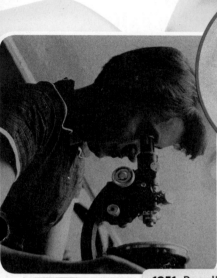

An image of DNA produced by using x-rays.

1951 Rosalind Franklin and Maurice Wilkins make images of DNA using x-rays. When an x-ray passes through the molecule, the ray bends and creates a pattern that is captured on film.

1953 James Watson and Francis Crick use Chargaff's rules and the x-ray images of DNA to conclude that DNA looks like a long, twisted ladder. They build a large-scale model of DNA using simple materials from their laboratory.

1950

1975

1950 Erwin Chargaff observes that the amount of guanine always equals the amount of cytosine, and the amount of adenine equals the amount of thymine. His findings are now known as *Chargaff's rules*.

1952 Alfred Hershey and Martha Chase perform experiments with viruses to confirm that DNA, not proteins, carries genetic information.

(r) ©A. Barrington Brown/Photo Researchers, Inc.

Publishing Company

Unraveling**DNA**

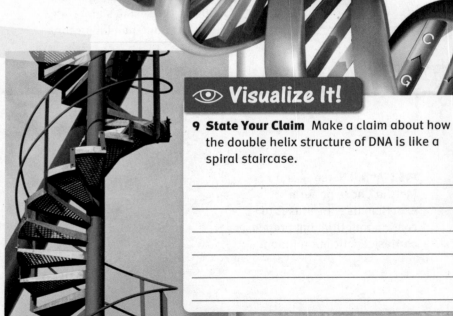

DNA is found in the nucleus of eukaryotic cells.

What does DNA look like?

The chemical components that make up DNA are too small to be observed directly. But experiments and imaging techniques have helped scientists to infer the shape of DNA and the arrangement of its parts.

The Shape of DNA Is a Double Helix

The structure of DNA is a twisted ladder shape called a *double helix*. The two sides of the ladder, often referred to as the DNA backbone, are made of alternating sugars and phosphate groups. The rungs of the ladder are made of a pair of bases, each attached to one of the sugars in the backbone.

ACTIVE **READING**

8 Describe Where are phosphate groups found in a DNA molecule?

_____

_____

The DNA molecule has a double-helix shape.

👁 Visualize It!

9 State Your Claim Make a claim about how the double helix structure of DNA is like a spiral staircase.

_____

_____

_____

_____

_____

© Houghton Mifflin Harcourt

DNA Is Made Up of Nucleotides

A base, a sugar, and a phosphate group make a building block of DNA known as a **nucleotide**. These repeating chemical units join together to form the DNA molecule. There are four different nucleotides in DNA, identified by their bases: adenine (A), thymine (T), cytosine (C), and guanine (G). Because of differences in size and shape, adenine always pairs with thymine (A-T) and cytosine always pairs with guanine (C-G). These paired, or *complementary*, bases fit together like two pieces of a puzzle.

The order of the nucleotides in DNA is a code that carries information. The DNA code is read like a book. *Genes* are segments of DNA that relate to a certain trait. Each gene has a starting point and an ending point, with the DNA code being read in one direction. The bases A, T, C, and G form the alphabet of the code. The code stores information about which proteins the cells should build. The types of proteins your body makes help to determine your traits.

10 Apply Place boxes around the bases that pair with each other.

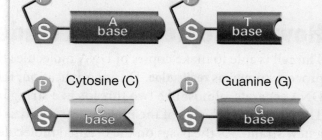

Adenine (A)   Thymine (T)

Cytosine (C)   Guanine (G)

11 Devise The bases are often referred to simply by their initials—A, T, C, and G. The phrase "all tigers can growl" may help you remember them. Think of another phrase that uses words starting with A, T, C, and G that could help you remember the bases. Write your phrase below.

_____

_____

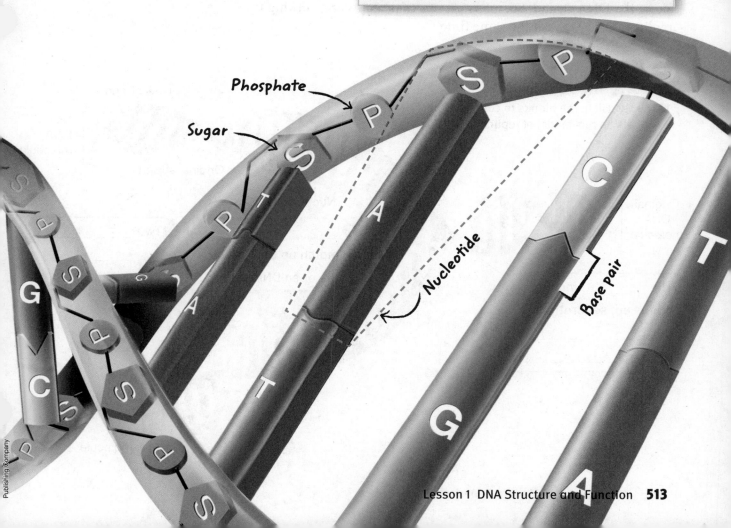

Phosphate

Sugar

Nucleotide

Base pair

Replication and

How are copies of DNA made?

The cell is able to make copies of DNA molecules through a process known as **replication**. During replication, the two strands of DNA separate, almost like two threads in a string being unwound. The bases on each side of the molecule are used as a pattern for a new strand. As the bases on the original molecule are exposed, complementary nucleotides are added. For example, an exposed base containing adenine attaches to a nucleotide containing thymine. When replication is complete, there are two identical DNA molecules. Each new DNA molecule is made of one strand of old DNA and one strand of new DNA.

When are copies of DNA made?

Before a cell divides, it copies the DNA so that each new daughter cell will have a complete set of instructions. Our cells can replicate DNA in just a few hours. How? Replication begins in many places along the DNA strand. So, many groups of proteins are working to replicate your DNA at the same time.

👁 Visualize It!

12 Apply Fill in the blanks to complete the labels on this model of replicating DNA.

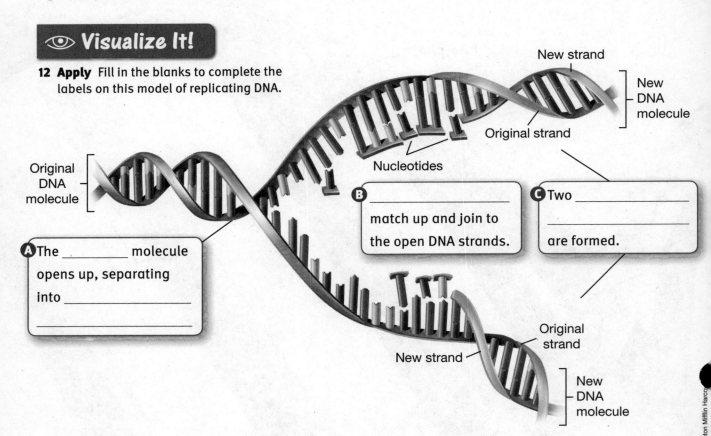

New strand

New DNA molecule

Original strand

Nucleotides

B _____ match up and join to the open DNA strands.

C Two _____ _____ are formed.

Original DNA molecule

A The _____ molecule opens up, separating into _____ _____

Original strand

New strand

New DNA molecule

Mutation

What are mutations?

Changes in the number, type, or order of bases on a piece of DNA are known as **mutations**. Sometimes, a base is left out. This kind of change is known as a *deletion*. Or, an extra base might be added. This kind of change is an *insertion*. The most common mutation happens when one base replaces another. This kind of change is known as a *substitution*.

How do mutations happen? Given the large number of bases in an organism's DNA, it is not surprising that random errors can occur during replication. However, DNA can also be damaged by physical or chemical agents called *mutagens*. Ultraviolet light and the chemicals in cigarette smoke are examples of mutagens.

Cells make proteins that can fix errors in DNA. But sometimes a mistake isn't corrected, and it becomes part of the genetic code. Mutations to DNA may be beneficial, neutral, or harmful. A *genetic disorder* results from mutations that harm the normal function of a cell. Some of these disorders, such as Tay-Sachs disease and sickle-cell anemia, are *inherited*, or passed on from parent to offspring. Other genetic disorders result from mutations that occur during a person's lifetime. Most cancers fall into this category.

👁 Visualize It!

13 Apply Place a check mark in the box to indicate which type of mutation is being shown.

Original sequence

(A) ☐ deletion ☐ insertion ☐ substitution

(B) ☐ deletion ☐ insertion ☐ substitution

(C) ☐ deletion ☐ insertion ☐ substitution

This snake has albinism, a condition in which the body cannot make the pigments that give color to the skin and eyes.

14 Claims • Evidence • Reasoning Albinism is an inherited genetic disorder. Make a claim about what traits you would see in the offspring of this snake. Summarize evidence to support the claim and explain your reasoning.

_____

_____

_____

_____

Protein Factory

What is the role of DNA and RNA in building proteins?

Imagine that you are baking cookies. You have a big cookbook that contains the recipe. If you take the book with you into the kitchen, you risk damaging the book and losing important instructions. You only need one page from the book, so you copy the recipe on a piece of paper and leave the cookbook on the shelf. This process is similar to the way that the cell uses DNA to build proteins. First, some of the information in the DNA is copied to a separate molecule called ribonucleic acid, or **RNA**. Then, the copy is used to build proteins. Not all the instructions are needed all the time. In eukaryotes, the DNA is protected inside the cell's nucleus.

Like DNA, RNA has a sugar-phosphate backbone and the bases adenine (A), guanine (G), and cytosine (C). But instead of thymine (T), RNA contains the base uracil (U). Also, the sugar found in RNA is different from the one in DNA. There are three types of RNA: messenger RNA, ribosomal RNA, and transfer RNA. Each type of RNA has a special role in making proteins.

ACTIVE READING

15 Identify As you read, number the sentences that describe the steps of transcription.

Transcription: The Information in DNA Is Copied to Messenger RNA

When a cell needs a set of instructions for making a protein, it first makes an RNA copy of the necessary section of DNA. This process is called *transcription*. Transcription involves DNA and messenger RNA (mRNA). Only individual genes are transcribed, not the whole DNA molecule. During transcription, DNA is used as a template to make a complementary strand of mRNA. The DNA opens up where the gene is located. Then RNA bases match up to complementary bases on the DNA template. When transcription is complete, the mRNA is released and the DNA molecule closes.

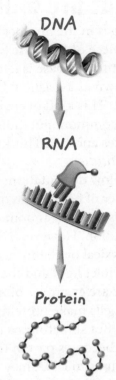

DNA

RNA

Protein

RNA uses the genetic information stored in DNA to build proteins.

mRNA

Cell nucleus

A During transcription, DNA is used as a template to make a complementary strand of mRNA. In eukaryotes, the mRNA then exits the nucleus.

Translation: The Information in Messenger RNA Is Used to Build Proteins

Once the mRNA has been made, it is fed through a protein assembly line within a ribosome. A **ribosome** is a cell organelle made of ribosomal RNA (rRNA) and protein. As mRNA passes through the ribosome, transfer RNA (tRNA) molecules deliver amino acids to the ribosome. Each group of three bases on the mRNA strand codes for one amino acid. So the genetic code determines the order in which amino acids are brought to the ribosome. The amino acids join together to form a protein. The process of making proteins from RNA is called *translation*.

B A ribosome attaches to an mRNA strand at the beginning of a gene.

tRNA

Amino acid

Ribosome

C A tRNA molecule enters the ribosome. Three bases on the tRNA match up to 3 complementary bases on the mRNA strand. The bases on the mRNA strand determine which tRNA and amino acid move into the ribosome.

Chain of amino acids

Chain of amino acids is released

D The tRNA transfers its amino acid to a growing chain. Then, the tRNA is released. The ribosome moves down the mRNA and the process repeats.

E Once the ribosome reaches the end of the gene, the chain of amino acids is released.

16 Apply Fill in the table below by placing check marks in the appropriate boxes and writing the product of transcription and translation.

Process	What molecules are involved?				What is the product?
Transcription	☐ DNA	☐ mRNA	☐ tRNA	☐ ribosome	
Translation	☐ DNA	☐ mRNA	☐ tRNA	☐ ribosome	

Visual Summary

To complete this summary, fill in the blanks with the correct word or phrase. You can use this page to review the main concepts of the lesson.

DNA has a double-helix shape and is made up of nucleotides.

DNA Structure and Function

17 The four bases in DNA nucleotides are

_____

_____

_____

_____

The cell can make copies of DNA.

18 DNA replication happens before cells _____

DNA and RNA are involved in making proteins.

20 The two processes involved in making proteins from the DNA code are

DNA can mutate.

19 Three types of DNA mutations are _____

_____

_____

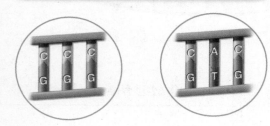

21 **Claims • Evidence • Reasoning** Make a claim about how a mutation in the DNA could affect the proteins made by the cell. Summarize evidence to support the claim and explain your reasoning.

Lesson Review

Vocabulary

In your own words, define the following terms.

1 A(n) _____ of DNA consists of a sugar, a phosphate, and a nitrogen-containing base.

2 A(n) _____ is a change in the base sequence of a DNA molecule.

Key Concepts

Draw a line to connect the following scientists to their contributions to our understanding of DNA.

3 Erwin Chargaff

4 Rosalind Franklin and Maurice Wilkins

5 James Watson and Francis Crick

A took x-ray images of DNA molecule

B proposed a double-helix model of DNA

C found that the amount of adenine equals the amount of thymine and that the amount of guanine equals the amount of cytosine

6 Identify How does the structure of RNA differ from the structure of DNA?

_____

_____

7 Identify When does DNA replication occur?

_____

_____

8 Describe Name the three types of RNA and list their roles in making proteins.

_____

_____

9 Identify What can cause DNA mutations?

_____

_____

Critical Thinking

Use this diagram to answer the following questions.

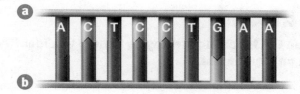

ⓐ A C T C C T G A A
ⓑ

10 Describe What is the sequence of bases on DNA strand *b*, from left to right?

_____

11 Apply This segment of DNA is transcribed to form a complementary strand of mRNA. The mRNA then undergoes translation. How many amino acids would the RNA code for?

_____

_____

12 Claims • Evidence • Reasoning After many cell divisions, a segment of DNA has more base pairs than it originally did. Make a claim about how this could happen. Summarize evidence to support the claim and explain your reasoning.

_____

_____

13 Explain Your Reasoning Why must DNA replicate?

_____

_____

Publishing Company

SC.7.N.1.1 Define a problem from the curriculum, use appropriate reference materials to support scientific understanding, plan and carry out scientific investigation of various types, such as systematic observations or experiments, identify variables, collect and organize data, interpret data in charts, tables, and graphics, analyze information, make predictions, and defend conclusions. SC.7.N.1.4 Identify test variables (independent variables) and outcome variables (dependent variables) in an experiment.

Identifying Variables

When you are analyzing or designing a scientific experiment, it is important to identify the variables in the experiment. Usually, an experiment is designed to discover how changing one variable affects another variable. In a scientific investigation, the independent variable is the factor that is purposely changed. The dependent variable is the factor that changes in response to the independent variable.

Tutorial

Use the following strategies to help you identify the variables in an experiment.

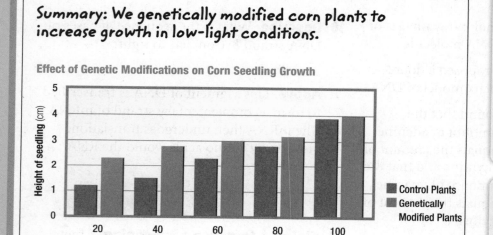

Summary: We genetically modified corn plants to increase growth in low-light conditions.

Effect of Genetic Modifications on Corn Seedling Growth

■ Control Plants
■ Genetically Modified Plants

Reading a Summary The published results of an experiment usually include a brief summary. You should be able to identify the variables from it. In the summary to the left, the independent variable is the DNA of the corn plants, and the dependent variable is the height of the plants.

Analyzing a Graph Making a graph can be a very effective way to show the relationship between variables. For a bar graph, the independent variable is usually shown on the *x*-axis, or the horizontal axis. The dependent variable is usually shown on the *y*-axis, or the vertical axis.

Describing the Data When you read a graph, describing the information in complete sentences can help you to identify the variables. For example, you could write, "In the first 80 hours, the genetically modified corn plants grew much more quickly than the control plants grew. But by 100 hours, both kinds of plants were about the same height. This shows that the effect of the independent variable was greatest during the first 80 hours of plant growth."

Identifying the Effects of Variables Look closely at the graph. Notice that the genetically modified seedlings grew more quickly than the control seedlings, but the effects were greatest in the early part of the experiment. A variable's effect is not always constant throughout an experiment.

You Try It!

The passage below describes the process of gel electrophoresis. Use the description to answer the question that follows.

> During gel electrophoresis, DNA is broken into separate fragments. These fragments are added to a gel. When an electric current is applied to the gel, the fragments travel different distances through the gel. The size of the DNA fragments determines how far they travel. Smaller fragments travel farther than larger fragments do. Scientists can use these data to identify unknown samples of DNA.

1 Reading a Summary Identify the variables described in the passage.

_____

_____

The graph below shows the results of DNA analysis using gel electrophoresis. Look at the graph, and answer the questions that follow.

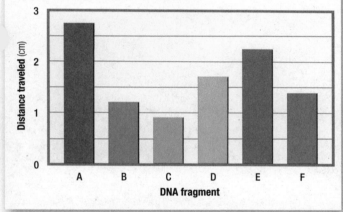

Distance Traveled by DNA Fragments

2 Analyzing a Graph Which variables are shown in the graph? Circle the axis that shows the dependent variable.

_____

_____

3 Analyzing the Data What is the relationship between the size of the DNA fragments and the distance they traveled? Circle the DNA fragment that is the smallest.

_____

_____

4 Applying Mathematics Calculate the average distance that the DNA fragments traveled. How much farther than the average distance did the smallest DNA fragment travel?

5 Claims • Evidence • Reasoning Why is it important to limit the number of variables in an experiment? Summarize evidence to support a claim and explain your reasoning.

_____

_____

_____

_____

_____

 Take It Home!

With an adult, plan and conduct a simple experiment that includes an independent variable and a dependent variable. Record your results and graph your data if possible. Then share your results with the class.

Biotechnology

ESSENTIAL QUESTION

How does biotechnology impact our world?

By the end of this lesson, you should be able to explain how biotechnology impacts human life and the world around us.

SC.7.L.16.4 Recognize and explore the impact of biotechnology (cloning, genetic engineering, artificial selection) on the individual, society and the environment.

These glowing bands contain fragments of DNA that have been treated with a special chemical. This chemical glows under ultraviolet light, allowing scientists to see the DNA.

(bkgd) ©Sinclair Stammers/Photo Researchers, Inc; (t) ©David Hoffman Photo Library/Alamy

© Houghton Mifflin Harcourt
Publishing Company

 Lesson Labs

Quick Labs
- Matching Codes
- How Can a Simple Code Be Used to Make a Product?

PRIVATE LAND
GMO TRIAL
KEER OFF

Engage Your Brain

1 Predict Fill in the blanks with the word or phrase you think correctly completes the following sentences.

A medical researcher might study DNA in order to learn _____

_____

_____

A crime scene investigator might study DNA in order to learn _____

_____

_____

2 Apply *GMO* stands for "genetically modified organism." Write a caption to accompany the following photo.

_____

_____

_____

ACTIVE **READING**

3 Apply Use context clues to write your own definition for the words *inserted* and *technique*.

Example sentence
Using special technologies, a gene from one organism can be <u>inserted</u> into the DNA of another.

inserted:

_____

_____

Example sentence
Cloning is a <u>technique</u> in which the genetic information of an organism is copied.

technique:

_____

_____

Vocabulary Terms
- biotechnology
- artificial selection
- genetic engineering
- clone

4 Apply As you learn the definition of each vocabulary term in this lesson, create your own definition or sketch to help you remember the meaning of the term.

Bio**TECHNOLOGY**

Protective clothing keeps this geneticist safe as he works with infectious particles.

This scientist works inside of a greenhouse. He breeds potato plants.

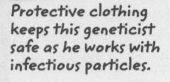

Think Outside the Book

5 Research Research careers in biotechnology. Choose a career that you might like to have and share it with your class. You may choose to present your findings in one of the following ways:
- a poster
- a computer presentation
- a play
- a short essay

What is biotechnology?

A forensic scientist makes copies of DNA from a crime scene. A botanist breeds flowers for their bright red blooms. A geneticist works to place a human gene into the DNA of bacteria. What do these processes have in common? They are all examples of biotechnology. **Biotechnology** is the use and application of living things and biological processes. In the past 40 years, new technologies have allowed scientists to directly change DNA. But biotechnology is not a new scientific field. For thousands of years, humans have been breeding plants and animals and using bacteria and yeast to ferment foods. These, too, are examples of biotechnology.

ACTIVE **READING**

6 Identify Name three examples of biotechnology.

_____

_____

_____

Different dog breeds are produced by artificial selection.

What are some applications of biotechnology?

Biotechnology processes fall into some broad categories. Artificial selection, genetic engineering, and cloning are some of the most common techniques.

Artificial Selection

For thousands of years, humans have been carefully selecting and breeding certain plants and animals that have desirable traits. Over many generations, horses have gotten faster, pigs have gotten leaner, and corn has become sweeter. **Artificial selection** is the process of selecting and breeding organisms that have certain desired traits. Artificial selection is also known as *selective breeding*.

Artificial selection can be successful as long as the desirable traits are controlled by genes. Animal and plant breeders select for alleles, which are different versions of a gene. The alleles being selected must already be present in the population. People do not change DNA during artificial selection. Instead, they cause certain alleles to become more common in a population. The different dog breeds are a good example of artificial selection. All dogs share a common ancestor, the wolf. However, thousands of years of selection by humans have produced dogs with a variety of characteristics.

👁 Visualize It!

These vegetables have been developed through artificial selection. Their common ancestor is the mustard plant.

kale

broccoli

cabbage

cauliflower

Brussels sprouts

7 Claims • Evidence • Reasoning Why might farmers use artificial selection to develop different types of vegetables? Make a claim, summarize evidence to support the claim, and explain your reasoning.

_____

_____

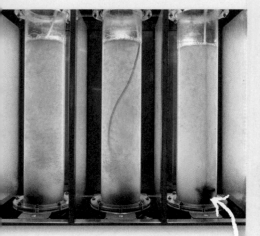

Scientists have engineered algal cells to contain more energy-storing fats. As a result, they may serve as a biofuel alternative to fossil fuels in the future.

Genetic Engineering

Within the past 40 years, it has become possible to directly change the DNA of an organism. **Genetic engineering** is the process in which a piece of DNA is modified for use in research, medicine, agriculture, or industry. The DNA that is engineered often codes for a certain trait of interest. Scientists can isolate a segment of DNA, change it in some way, and return it to the organism. Or, scientists can take a segment of DNA from one species and transfer it to the DNA of an organism from another species.

ACTIVE **READING**

8 Describe For what purposes can genetic engineering be used?

_____

_____

These genetically modified plant cells produce tiny, biodegradable plastic pellets. The pellets are then collected to make plastic products.

9 Claims • Evidence • Reasoning Traditional plastics are made from petroleum, a nonrenewable resource. Make a claim about the benefits of plastic made by plants over traditional plastic. Summarize evidence to support the claim, and explain your reasoning.

_____

_____

_____

_____

_____

_____

plant cell

plastic pellets

Cloning

A **clone** is an organism, cell, or piece of genetic material that is genetically identical to the one from which it was derived. Cloning has been used to make copies of small traces of DNA found at crime scenes or on ancient artifacts. Also, cloning can be used to copy segments of DNA for genetic engineering.

In 1996, scientists cloned the DNA from one sheep's body cell to produce another sheep named Dolly. The ability to clone a sheep, which is a mammal, raised many concerns about the future uses of cloning, because humans are also mammals. It is important that people understand the science of genetics. Only then can we make informed decisions about how and when the technology should be used.

Dolly was cloned from a body cell of an adult sheep.

10 Apply Review each of the examples of biotechnology below. Then classify each as artificial selection, genetic engineering, or cloning.

Scientists have introduced a gene to the DNA of these fish that causes the fish to glow.	☐ artificial selection ☐ genetic engineering ☐ cloning
A scientist is gathering DNA from clothing found at a crime scene. Then many copies of the DNA sample will be made. This will allow the scientist to better study the DNA. Then the scientist might be able to confirm the identity of the person at the crime scene.	☐ artificial selection ☐ genetic engineering ☐ cloning
Wild carrots have thin, white roots. Over time, carrot farmers have selected carrots that have thick, bright orange roots.	☐ artificial selection ☐ genetic engineering ☐ cloning
Diabetes can be treated in some people with injections that contain the hormone insulin. The gene responsible for producing insulin in humans has been inserted into the DNA of bacteria. These bacteria then produce the human insulin that is used in the injection.	☐ artificial selection ☐ genetic engineering ☐ cloning

Feel the IMPACT!

How does biotechnology impact our world?

Scientists are aware that there are many ethical, legal, and social issues that arise from the ability to use and change living things. Biotechnology can impact both our society and our environment. We must decide how and when it is acceptable to use biotechnology. The examples that follow show some concerns that might be raised during a classroom debate about biotechnology.

> **11 Evaluate** Read the first two examples of biotechnology and what students had to say about their effects on individuals, society, and the environment. Then complete Example 3 by filling in questions or possible effects of the technology.

Example 1

Editing Genes

Many diseases are caused by harmful bacteria. Antibiotics are substances that fight bacteria. Over time, however, many bacteria undergo changes that make them resistant to antibiotics. Scientists are using a technology known as CRISPR to change, or edit, the genes of organisms. By altering the DNA of bacteria such as those shown, scientists may be able to cause harmful bacteria to destroy their own genes.

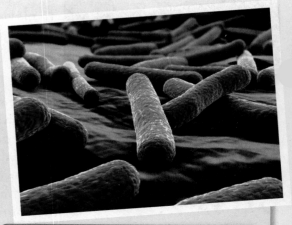

Effects on Individuals and Society

"If harmful bacteria can be engineered to destroy their own DNA, many lives could be saved."

Effects on Environment

"While targeting one organism, other changes might arise that have unpredictable effects on other organisms."

ⓘ Think Outside the Book

> **12 Claims • Evidence • Reasoning** As a class, choose a current event that involves biotechnology. Then hold a debate, making claims and providing evidence about the benefits and risks of technology. Explain your reasoning.

Example 2

Cloning of Pyrenean ibex

The Pyrenean ibex, or bucardo, is an extinct species of mountain goat. In 2009, scientists produced a cloned burcardo. The newborn died within minutes of being born.

Effects on Individuals and Society

"How will we decide when it is appropriate to clone other types of organisms?"

Effects on Environment

"Cloning could restore extinct species and increase populations of endangered species."

Example 3

Tough Plants!

Much of the corn and soybeans grown in the United States is genetically engineered. The plants have bacterial genes that make them more resistant to plant-eating insects.

Effects on Individuals and Society

Effects on Environment

Visual Summary

To complete this summary, circle the correct word or phrase. You can use this page to review the main concepts of the lesson.

Biotechnology

Biotechnology is the use of living things and biological processes.

13 Modern biotechnology techniques can change an organism's DNA / environment.

Aritifical selection, genetic engineering, and cloning are three types of biotechnology.

14 The DNA of the algae on the right has been modified through a technique called cloning / genetic engineering.

Biotechnology impacts individuals, society, and the environment.

15 Creating a clone / gene of an extinct species could impact the environment.

16 **Claims • Evidence • Reasoning** Both artificial selection and genetic engineering produce organisms that have traits that are different from the original organism. Make a claim about how these two techniques differ. Summarize evidence to support the claim and explain your reasoning.

Lesson Review

Vocabulary

In your own words, define the following terms.

1 biotechnology

_____

_____

_____

2 artificial selection

_____

_____

_____

3 clone

_____

_____

_____

Key Concepts

4 Identify Wheat has been bred by farmers for thousands of years to improve its ability to be ground into flour. This is an example of what kind of biotechnology?

A artificial selection

B genetic engineering

C cloning

D PCR

5 Identify Which of the following statements correctly describes why society must carefully consider the use of biotechnology?

A Biotechnology is a relatively new scientific field.

B Biotechnology can impact individuals and the environment.

C The methods of genetic engineering are not well understood.

D Artificial selection is an example of biotechnology.

Critical Thinking

Use this graph to answer the following questions.

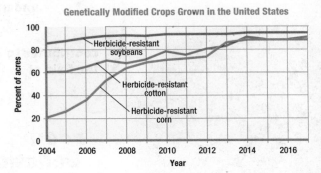

Genetically Modified Crops Grown in the United States

Source: *USDA, 2017*

6 Analyze In 2004, what percentage of soybean crops in the United States were genetically engineered to be herbicide resistant?

_____

7 Analyze From 2004 to 2010, which genetically engineered crop had the greatest increase in acreage?

_____

_____

8 Claims • Evidence • Reasoning Some salmon have been genetically engineered to grow more quickly. The salmon are raised in pens set in rivers or in the sea. Make a claim about how these salmon might impact society and the environment. Summarize evidence to support the claim and explain your reasoning.

_____

_____

_____

Biotechnology

relies on an understanding of

DNA Structure and **Function**

contributes to the field of

Modern Genetics

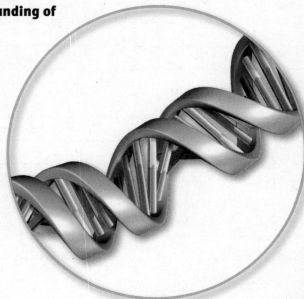

1 Interpret The Graphic Organizer above shows that biotechnology relies on an understanding of the structure and function of DNA. Explain your reasoning.

_____

_____

_____

_____

_____

_____

_____

_____

_____

2 Compare How are DNA replication and DNA cloning similar? How are they different?

_____

_____

_____

_____

3 Claims • Evidence • Reasoning The variety of traits seen in house cats is due in part to artificial selection. What contribution do mutations make to artificial selection? Make a claim about the role of mutations. Summarize evidence to support the claim and explain your reasoning.

_____

_____

_____

_____

Vocabulary

Name _____

Fill in each blank with the term that best completes the following sentences.

1 The genetic material of all cells is _____

2 _____ is the use and application of living things and biological processes.

3 A(n) _____ is an organism, cell, or piece of genetic material that is genetically identical to the one from which it was derived.

Key Concepts

Identify the choice that best completes the statement or answers the question.

4 Terrie is creating a model of DNA. Which of these shapes illustrates how her model should look?

A

C

B

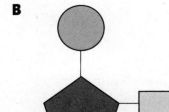

D

5 The diagram below shows an original sequence of DNA and then a mutated sequence of DNA.

Original sequence

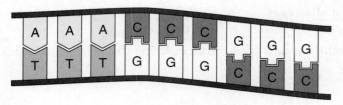

New sequence

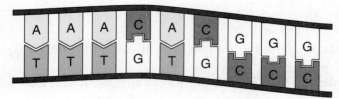

Which type of mutation took place?

F deletion   **H** substitution

G insertion   **I** translation

6 Sickle cell anemia is an inherited disorder. Which of the following is **a true** statement about sickle cell anemia?

A It is never inherited from a parent.

B The mutation occurs during a person's lifetime.

C It is an infectious disease.

D It is caused by a change in the bases in DNA.

7 Alice is studying biological molecules. She isolated a molecule and identified the nucleotide bases adenine, cytosine, guanine, and thymine. Which molecule did Alice isolate?

F DNA   **H** rRNA

G mRNA   **I** tRNA

Name _____

8 Cloning is one type of biotechnology. Which of these choices is an example of cloning?

A Certain chickens are bred for their distinctive feather color.

B Several copies of a fruit fly gene are produced in a laboratory.

C Plants with red flowers are bred with plants with blue flowers.

D Yeast cells are placed under an ultraviolet lamp, causing their DNA to mutate.

9 Luis wants to interview someone who has a career in biotechnology. Which of the following **best** describes a career in biotechnology?

F Athena uses a sophisticated telescope to observe stars.

G Zach tracks the number of fish that inhabit a certain coastal area.

H Vincent modifies the DNA of bacteria to study the function of their genes.

I Lindsey writes computer programs that model the three-dimensional structure of chemical compounds.

10 Dylan is listing the substances that make up DNA. Which of these substances should he list as a nucleotide base found in DNA?

A adenine   **C** sugar

B phosphate   **D** uracil

11 A scientist transfers a fragment of genetic material from one organism to another organism of a different species. What is this process called?

F artificial selection   **H** genetic engineering

G selective breeding   **I** asexual reproduction

12 Rachel is analyzing a DNA sample to identify its base pairs. Her results show that 40% of the sample is adenine. Which other base makes up 40% of the sample?

A cytosine   **C** thymine

B guanine   **D** uracil

13 The following sequence of letters represents the order of bases in a single strand of DNA.

C-T-T-A-G-G-C-T-T-A-C-C-A

Which of these sequences would be the complementary strand that forms during replication?

F G-A-A-T-C-C-G-A-A-T-G-G-T

G C-T-T-A-G-G-C-T-T-A-C-C-A

H T-C-C-G-A-A-T-C-C-G-T-T-G

I A-G-G-C-T-T-A-G-G-C-A-A-C

Critical Thinking

Answer the following questions in the space provided.

14 Describe the major steps of gene transcription and translation. What molecules and organelles are involved in the processes?

_____

_____

_____

_____

_____

15 Rachel's class is debating the impact of biotechnology on people, society, and the environment. Do you think that biotechnology has a positive or negative impact? Provide specific evidence to support your claim and explain your reasoning.

_____

_____

_____

_____

_____

Ecology

FLORIDA BIG IDEA 17

Interdependence

Mangrove roots
are home for fish.

What Do You Think?

Ecosystems consist of living things that depend on each other to survive. How might these fish depend on mangrove roots? How do other interactions between organisms make this ecosystem function? Use information in this unit to help you make a claim with evidence to support your reasoning.

Ecology

Sharing Spaces

Florida provides living space for many kinds of birds. Ospreys are large birds of prey that eat mostly fish. They often nest on telephone poles and other man-made structures. Yellow-rumped warblers are small birds that live in trees and eat insects and berries.

1 Ask A Question

How can organisms affect each other and a whole ecosystem?

An ecosystem is made up of all the living and nonliving things in an environment. Ospreys and yellow-rumped warblers are part of the same ecosystem. With your teacher and your classmates, brainstorm ways in which ospreys and yellow-rumped warblers might affect each other.

Yellow-rumped warbler

② Think About It

Look at the photos of the ospreys in their environment. List at least two resources they need to survive and explain how the ospreys get them.

_____

_____

_____

What are two ways nonliving things could affect yellow-rumped warblers?

_____

_____

_____

Osprey nest

③ Apply Your Knowledge

A List the ways in which yellow-rumped warblers and ospreys share resources.

_____

_____

_____

B Yellow-rumped warblers live in Florida during the winter only. How might the warblers affect other organisms in the ecosystem if they stayed in Florida all year?

_____

_____

_____

_____

C Describe a situation that could negatively affect both the osprey population and the yellow-rumped warbler population.

_____

_____

_____

🏠 Take It Home!

Are ecologists looking for people to report observations in your community? Contact a university near your community to see if you can help gather information about plants, flowers, birds, or invasive species. Then, share your results with your class.

Introduction to Ecology

ESSENTIAL QUESTION

How are different parts of the environment connected?

By the end of this lesson, you should be able to analyze the parts of an environment.

This rain forest is an ecosystem. Hornbills are organisms in the ecosystem that use the trees for shelter.

© Timothy Laman/National Geographic/Getty Images

Lesson Labs

Quick Labs
- Condensation and Evaporation
- Greenhouse Effect
- Climate Determines Plant Life

 Engage Your Brain

1 Describe In your own words, write a list of living or nonliving things that are in your neighborhood.

_____

_____

_____

_____

_____

_____

_____

2 Relate Write a photo caption that compares the ecosystem shown above and the ecosystem shown on the previous page.

_____

_____

_____

_____

ACTIVE READING

3 Synthesize You can often define an unknown word or term if you know the meaning of its word parts. Use the word parts and sentence below to make an educated guess about the meaning of the term *abiotic factor*.

Word part	Meaning
a-	without
bio-	life

Example sentence
In an ecosystem, rocks are an example of an <u>abiotic factor</u> because they are not a living part of the environment.

abiotic factor:

_____

_____

Vocabulary Terms

- ecology
- biotic factor
- abiotic factor
- population
- species
- community
- ecosystem
- biome
- niche
- habitat

4 Apply As you learn the definition of each vocabulary term in this lesson, create your own definition or sketch to help you remember the meaning of the term.

fflin Harcourt
pany

The Web of Life

How are all living things connected?

Organisms need energy and matter to live. Interactions between organisms cause an exchange of energy and matter. This exchange creates a web of life in which all organisms are connected to each other and to their environment. **Ecology** is the study of how organisms interact with one another and with the environment.

Through the Living Environment

Each individual organism has a role to play in the flow of energy and matter. In this way, organisms are connected to all other organisms. Relationships among organisms affect each one's growth and survival. A **biotic factor** is an interaction between organisms in an area. Competition is one way that organisms interact. For example, different kinds of plants might compete for water in the desert.

This desert includes all of the organisms that live there, and all of the living and nonliving things that they need to survive.

This horse is a part of the living environment.

The rocks and air are parts of the nonliving environment.

Through the Nonliving Environment

All organisms rely on the nonliving environment for survival. An **abiotic factor** is a nonliving part of an environment, such as water, nutrients, soil, sunlight, rainfall, or temperature. Some of these are resources that organisms need to grow and survive. For example, plants use sunlight, water, and soil nutrients to make food. Similarly, some organisms rely on soil or rocks for shelter.

Abiotic factors influence where organisms can survive. In a terrestrial environment, temperature and rainfall are important abiotic factors. In aquatic environments, the water's temperature, salt, and oxygen content are important abiotic factors. Changes in these basic abiotic factors affect where organisms can live and how many individuals are able to survive in the environment.

ACTIVE **READING**

5 Explain Your Reasoning How does the environment determine where an organism can survive? Explain your reasoning.

_____

_____

_____

_____

_____

_____

👁 Visualize It!

6 Categorize List the abiotic factors that are present in the photo.

_____ — _____

_____ — _____

7 Relate Choose one abiotic factor that you listed above and explain how the horse interacts with it.

_____

_____

_____

_____

Stay Organized!

What are the levels of organization in the environment?

The environment can be organized into different levels. These levels range from a single organism to all of the organisms and their surroundings in an area. The levels of organization get more complex as more of the environment is considered.

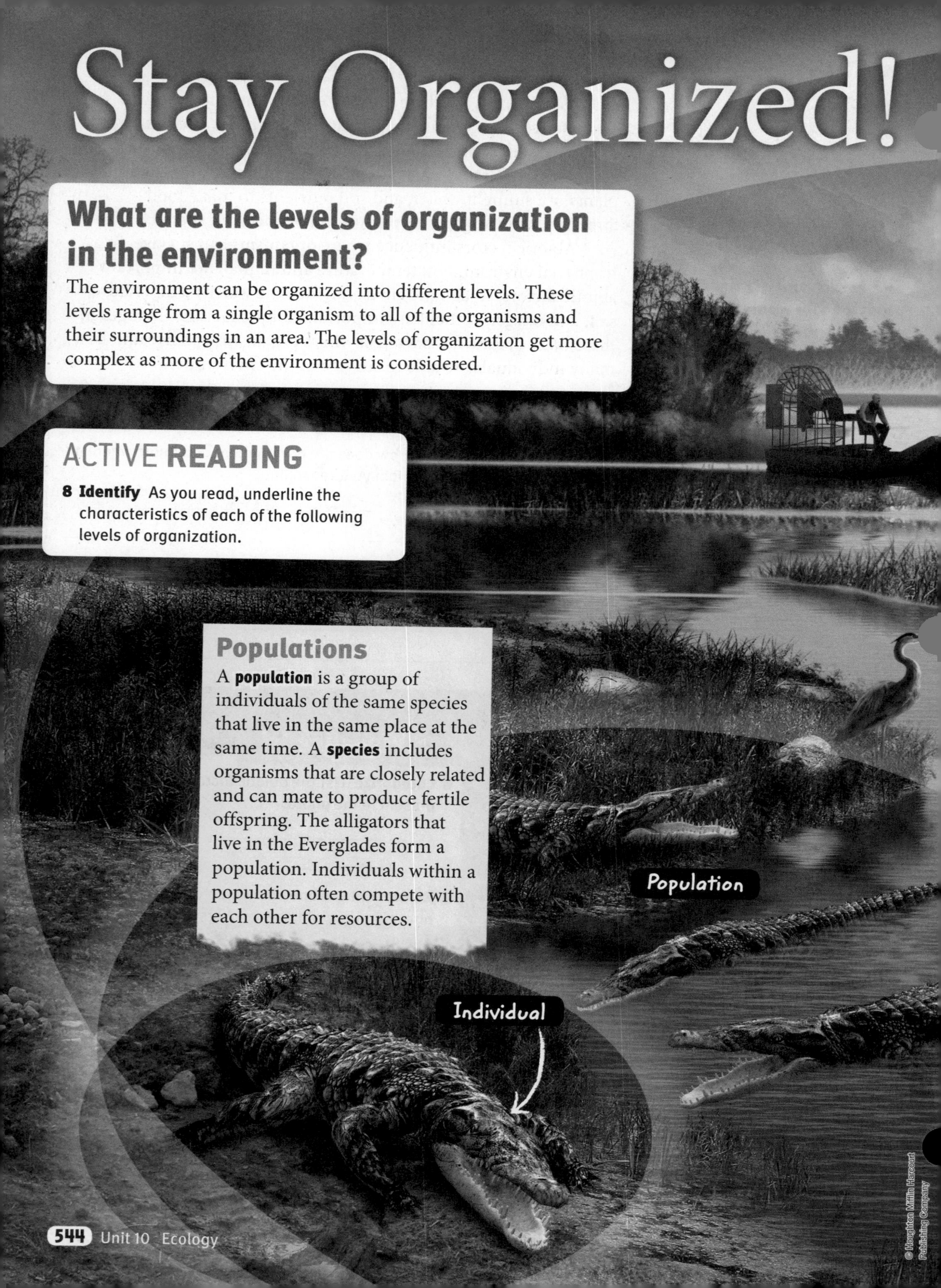

Populations

A **population** is a group of individuals of the same species that live in the same place at the same time. A **species** includes organisms that are closely related and can mate to produce fertile offspring. The alligators that live in the Everglades form a population. Individuals within a population often compete with each other for resources.

Population

Individual

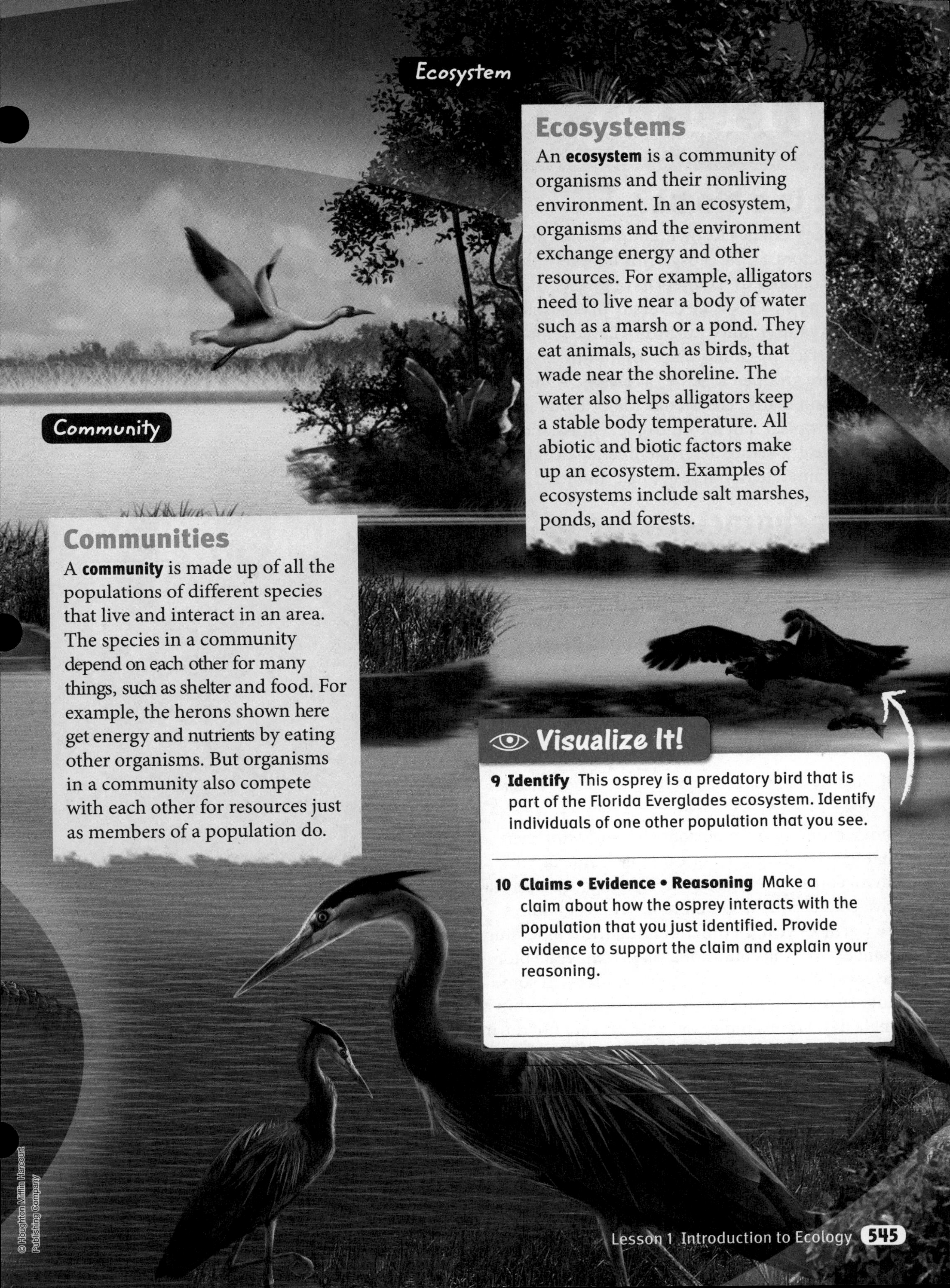

Ecosystem

Ecosystems

An **ecosystem** is a community of organisms and their nonliving environment. In an ecosystem, organisms and the environment exchange energy and other resources. For example, alligators need to live near a body of water such as a marsh or a pond. They eat animals, such as birds, that wade near the shoreline. The water also helps alligators keep a stable body temperature. All abiotic and biotic factors make up an ecosystem. Examples of ecosystems include salt marshes, ponds, and forests.

Community

Communities

A **community** is made up of all the populations of different species that live and interact in an area. The species in a community depend on each other for many things, such as shelter and food. For example, the herons shown here get energy and nutrients by eating other organisms. But organisms in a community also compete with each other for resources just as members of a population do.

👁 Visualize It!

9 Identify This osprey is a predatory bird that is part of the Florida Everglades ecosystem. Identify individuals of one other population that you see.

_____

10 Claims • Evidence • Reasoning Make a claim about how the osprey interacts with the population that you just identified. Provide evidence to support the claim and explain your reasoning.

_____

_____

Think Globally!

What is a biome?

Each ecosystem has its own unique biotic and abiotic factors. Some ecosystems have few plants and are cold and dry. Others have forests and are hot and moist. This wide diversity of ecosystems can be organized into categories. Large regions characterized by climate and communities of species are grouped together as **biomes**. A biome can contain many ecosystems. Major land biomes include tropical rain forest, tropical grassland, temperate grassland, desert, temperate deciduous forest, temperate rain forest, taiga, and tundra.

What characteristics define a biome?

All of the ecosystems in a biome share some traits. They share climate conditions, such as temperature and rainfall, and have similar communities.

Climate Conditions

ACTIVE **READING**

11 Identify As you read, underline the climate factors that characterize biomes.

Temperature is an important climate factor that characterizes biomes. For example, some biomes have a constant temperature. The taiga and tundra have cold temperatures all year. Tropical biomes are warm all year. In other biomes, the temperature changes over the course of a year. Temperate biomes have warm summers and colder winters. In some biomes, major temperature changes occur within a single day. For example, some deserts are hot during the day but cold at night.

Biomes also differ in the amount of precipitation they receive. For example, tropical biomes receive a lot of rainfall, while deserts receive little precipitation. The taiga and tundra have moist summers and dry winters.

This temperate rain forest gets a lot of rainfall. The organisms here have adapted to the wet climate.

ⓘ Think Outside the Book

12 Claims • Evidence • Reasoning Describe your climate and make a list of the living things that are found in natural undeveloped areas nearby. Research which biome has these features. Use evidence to make a claim about the biome you live in and support your reasoning. Look at a biome map to see if your claim matches the biome that is mapped for your location.

Communities of Living Things

Biomes contain communities of living things that have adapted to the climate of the region. Thus, ecosystems within the same biome tend to have similar species across the globe. Monkeys, vines, and colorful birds live in hot and humid tropical rain forests. Grasses, large mammals, and predatory birds inhabit tropical grasslands on several continents.

Only certain types of plants and animals can live in extreme climate conditions. For example, caribou, polar bears, and small plants live in the tundra, but trees cannot grow there. Similarly, the plant and animal species that live in the desert are also unique. Cacti and certain animal species have adaptations that let them tolerate the dry desert climate.

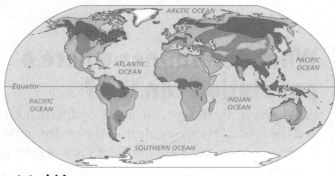

World biomes

- Desert
- Tropical grassland
- Temperate grassland
- Tropical rain forest
- Temperate deciduous forest
- Temperate rain forest
- Taiga
- Tundra

👁 Visualize It!

13 Claims • Evidence • Reasoning The photos below show two different biomes. Use what you learned about the characteristics of biomes to compare these environments. Use evidence to support a claim for categorizing them as different biomes and explain your reasoning.

Compare: _____

_____

_____

_____

_____

_____

_____

Explain your reasoning: _____

_____

_____

_____

_____

_____

_____

Home Sweet Home

What determines where a population can live?

Ecologists study the specific needs of different kinds of organisms and the role each species plays in the environment. Organisms that live in the same area have different ways of getting the resources they need.

Niche

Each population in an ecosystem plays a specific role. A population's **niche** (NICH) is the abiotic conditions under which individuals can survive and the role they play in the ecosystem. For example, one part of a shark population's niche is eating fish.

A **habitat** is the place where an organism usually lives and is part of an organism's niche. The habitat must provide all of the resources that an organism needs to grow and survive. Abiotic factors, such as temperature, often influence whether a species can live in a certain place. Biotic factors, such as the interactions with other organisms that live in the area, also play a role. For example, the habitat of a shark must include populations of fish it can eat.

Two populations cannot occupy exactly the same niche. Even small differences in habitats, roles, and adaptations can allow similar species to live together in the same ecosystem. For example, green and brown anoles sometimes live on the same trees, but they avoid competition by living in different parts of the trees.

14 Relate How is a habitat like a person's address? How is a niche like a person's job?

_____
_____
_____
_____
_____
_____
_____

👁 Visualize It!

15 Claims • Evidence • Reasoning
Describe the prairie dog's niche. How does it find shelter and impact the environment? Summarize evidence to support the claim and explain your reasoning.

_____
_____
_____
_____

Prairie dogs dig burrows in grassy plains. They eat plants and are hunted by predators such as owls and foxes.

© Houghton Mifflin Harcourt Publishing Company

©Raymond K. Gehman/National Geographic/Getty Images

Lizard Invasion

Green anole lizards (*Anolis carolinensis*) have been part of the South Florida ecosystem for a long time. Recently, a closely related lizard, the nonnative brown anole (*Anolis sagrei*), invaded the green anoles' habitat. How do they avoid competing with each other for resources?

Home Base

Green anoles live on perches throughout a tree. Brown anoles live mainly on branches that are close to the ground. If they have to share a tree, green anoles will move away from perches close to the ground. In this way, both kinds of anoles can live in the same tree while avoiding competition with each other.

Intrusive Neighbors

Although brown and green anoles can coexist by sharing their habitats, they do not live together peacefully. For example, brown anoles affect green anoles by eating their young.

ℹ Extend

16 Describe How do green and brown anoles avoid competition? Draw a picture of a tree showing both green and brown anoles living in it.

17 Research What are other examples of two species dividing up the parts of a habitat?

18 Claims • Evidence • Reasoning Make a claim about what would happen if the habitats of the two species overlapped. Present your evidence to support your reasoning in a format such as a short story, a music video, or a play.

Visual Summary

To complete this summary, circle the correct word. You can use this page to review the main concepts of the lesson.

Ecology is the study of the biotic and abiotic factors in an ecosystem, and the relationships between them.

Ecology and Ecosystems

19 In a desert ecosystem, the sand is a(n) biotic / abiotic factor, and a lizard eating an insect is a(n) biotic / abiotic factor.

Every organism has a habitat and a niche.

20 Horses that live in the desert feed on other organisms that live there, such as low, dry shrubs. In this example, the desert is a habitat / niche and the horses' feeding behavior is part of a habitat / niche.

The environment can be organized into different levels, including populations, communities, and ecosystems.

21 Populations of cacti, together with sand and rocks, are included in a desert community / ecosystem.

Biomes are characterized by climate conditions and the communities of living things found within them.

22 Biomes are large / small regions that make up / contain ecosystems.

23 **Claims • Evidence • Reasoning** Name a biotic factor in the desert ecosystem above and make a claim about the effect on the horses if it were removed from the ecosystem. Cite evidence to support your claim and explain your reasoning.

Lesson Review

Vocabulary

1 Explain how the meanings of the terms *biotic factor* and *abiotic factor* differ.

_____

_____

_____

2 In your own words, write a definition for *ecology*.

_____

_____

_____

3 Explain how the meanings of the terms *habitat* and *niche* differ.

_____

_____

_____

Key Concepts

4 Compare What is the relationship between ecosystems and biomes?

_____

_____

_____

5 Explain Within each biome, how can the environment be organized into levels from complex to simple?

_____

_____

6 Explain Your Reasoning How do the populations in a community depend on each other? Explain your reasoning.

_____

_____

_____

7 Identify What factors determine where a population can live?

_____

_____

_____

Critical Thinking

8 Claims • Evidence • Reasoning What might happen in a tropical rain forest biome if the area received very little rain for an extended period of time? Summarize evidence that supports the claim and explains your reasoning.

_____

_____

_____

9 Claims • Evidence • Reasoning Owls and hawks both eat rodents. They are also found in the same habitats. Since no two populations can occupy exactly the same niche, make a claim about how owls and hawks coexist. Summarize evidence that supports the claim and explains your reasoning

_____

Use this graph to answer the following question.

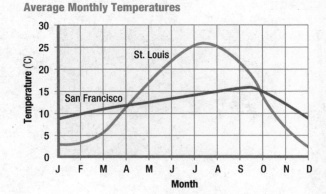

10 Interpret What is the difference in average temperature between the two cities in July?

_____

PEOPLE IN SCIENCE

SC.7.N.1.5 Describe the methods used in the pursuit of a scientific explanation as seen in different fields of science such as biology, geology, and physics.

Kenneth Krysko

ECOLOGIST

Snakes have fascinated Dr. Kenneth Krysko since he was four years old. Now he is an ecologist specializing in herpetology—the study of snakes. You can often find him in the Florida Everglades looking for Burmese pythons. He tracks these pythons to help limit the effect they have on Florida ecosystems.

Burmese pythons can grow to be 6 meters long. They are native to southeast Asia and were illegally brought to Florida as pets. Many owners released them into the wild when the snakes grew too large. The snakes breed well in Florida's subtropical climate. And they eat just about any animal they can swallow, including many native species. Dr. Krysko tracks down these invasive pythons. Through wildlife management, molecular genetics, and other areas of study, he works with other scientists to search for ways to reduce the python population.

Dr. Krysko studies many other invasive species, that is, nonnative species that can do harm in Florida ecosystems. He shares what he learns, including ways to identify and deal with invasive species with other ecologists. Along with invasion ecology, he has done research in reproduction and conservation biology. Dr. Krysko also works as a collections manager in the herpetology division at the Florida Museum of Natural History.

Dr. Krysko works to get a handle on what to do about the invasive pythons.

JOB BOARD

Park Naturalist

What You'll Do: Teach visitors at state and national parks about the park's ecology, geology, and landscape. Lead field trips, prepare and deliver lectures with slides, and create educational programs for park visitors. You may participate in research projects and track organisms in the park.

Where You Might Work: State and national parks

Education: An advanced degree in science and teacher certification

Other Job Requirements: You need to be good at communicating and teaching. Having photography and writing skills helps you prepare interesting educational materials.

Conservation Warden

What You'll Do: Patrol an area to enforce rules, and work with communities and groups to help educate the public about conservation and ecology.

Where You Might Work: Indoors and outdoors in state and national parks and ecologically sensitive areas

Education: A two-year associate's degree or at least 60 fully accredited college-level credits

Other Job Requirements: To work in the wild, good wilderness skills, map-reading, hiking, and excellent hearing are useful.

PEOPLE IN SCIENCE NEWS

Phil McCRORY

Saved by a Hair!

Phil McCrory, a hairdresser in Huntsville, Alabama, asked a brilliant question when he saw an otter whose fur was drenched with oil from the Exxon Valdez oil spill. If the otter's fur soaked up oil, why wouldn't human hair do the same? McCrory gathered hair from the floor of his salon and performed his own experiments. He stuffed hair into a pair of pantyhose and tied the ankles together. McCrory floated this bundle in his son's wading pool and poured used motor oil into the center of the ring. When he pulled the ring closed, not a drop of oil remained in the water! McCrory's discovery was tested as an alternative method for cleaning up oil spills. Many people donated their hair to be used for cleanup efforts. Although the method worked well, the engineers conducting the research concluded that hair is not as useful as other oil-absorbing materials for cleaning up large-scale spills.

Roles in Energy Transfer

ESSENTIAL QUESTION

How does energy flow through an ecosystem?

By the end of this lesson, you should be able to relate the roles of organisms to the transfer of energy in food chains and food webs.

Energy is transferred from the sun to producers, such as kelp. It flows through the rest of the ecosystem.

This fish also needs energy to live. How do you think it gets this energy? From the sun like kelp do?

SC.7.L.17.1 Explain and illustrate the roles of and relationships among producers, consumers, and decomposers in the process of energy transfer in a food web.

Lesson Labs

Quick Labs
• Yeast Action
• Pyramid of Energy

Exploration Lab
• Food Webs

 Engage Your Brain

1 Describe Most organisms on Earth get energy from the sun. How is energy flowing through the ecosystem pictured on the opposite page?

_____

_____

_____

_____

_____

2 Predict List two of your favorite foods. Then, explain how the sun's energy helped make those foods available to you.

_____

_____

_____

_____

_____

ACTIVE **READING**

3 Synthesize You can often define an unknown word if you know the meaning of its word parts. Use the word parts and sentences below to make an educated guess about the meaning of the words *herbivore* and *carnivore*.

Word part	Meaning
-vore	to eat
herbi-	plant
carni-	meat

Example sentence
A koala bear is an <u>herbivore</u> that eats eucalyptus leaves.

herbivore:

_____

_____

_____

Example sentence
A great white shark is a <u>carnivore</u> that eats fish and other marine animals.

carnivore:

_____

_____

_____

Vocabulary Terms

• producer
• decomposer
• consumer
• herbivore

• carnivore
• omnivore
• food chain
• food web

4 Apply As you learn the definition of each vocabulary term in this lesson, create your own definition or sketch to help you remember the meaning of the term.

Get Energized!

How do organisms get energy?

Energy is all around you. Chemical energy is stored in the bonds of molecules and holds molecules together. The energy from food is chemical energy in the bonds of food molecules. All living things need a source of chemical energy to survive.

Think Outside the Book

5 Apply Record what you eat at your next meal. Where do you think these items come from, before they reach the market?

ACTIVE READING

6 Identify As you read, underline examples of producers, decomposers, and consumers.

Producers Convert Energy Into Food

A **producer**, also called an autotroph, uses energy to make food. Most producers use sunlight to make food in a process called photosynthesis. The sun powers most life on Earth. In photosynthesis, producers use light energy to make food from water, carbon dioxide, and nutrients found in water and soil. The food contains chemical energy and can be used immediately or stored for later use. All green plants, such as grasses and trees, are producers. Algae and some bacteria are also producers. The food that these producers make supplies the energy for other living things in an ecosystem.

Decomposers Break Down Matter

An organism that gets energy and nutrients by breaking down the remains of other organisms is a **decomposer**. Fungi, such as the mushrooms on this log, and some bacteria are decomposers. Decomposers are nature's recyclers. By converting dead organisms and animal and plant waste into materials such as water and nutrients, decomposers help move matter through ecosystems. Decomposers make these simple materials available to other organisms.

These mushrooms are decomposers. They break down the remains of plants and animals.

This plant is a producer. Producers make food using light energy from the sun.

Consumers Eat Other Organisms

A **consumer** is an organism that eats other organisms. Consumers use the energy and nutrients stored in other living organisms because they cannot make their own food. A consumer that eats only plants, such as a grasshopper or bison, is called an **herbivore**. A **carnivore**, such as a badger or this wolf, eats other animals. An **omnivore** eats both plants and animals. A *scavenger* is a specialized consumer that feeds on dead organisms. Scavengers, such as the turkey vulture, eat the leftovers of the meals of other animals or eat dead animals.

This wolf is a consumer. It eats other organisms to get energy.

Consumers

👁 Visualize It!

7 List Beside each image, place a check mark next to the word that matches the type of consumer the animal is.

Name: Hedgehog
What I eat: leaves, earthworms, insects

What am I?
☐ herbivore
☐ omnivore
☐ carnivore

Name: Moose
What I eat: grasses, fruits

What am I?
☐ herbivore
☐ omnivore
☐ carnivore

Name: Komodo dragon
What I eat: insects, birds, mammals

What am I?
☐ herbivore
☐ omnivore
☐ carnivore

8 Claims • Evidence • Reasoning Make a claim about how carnivores might be affected if the main plant species in a community were to disappear. Summarize evidence to support the claim and explain your reasoning.

_____

_____

Energy Transfer

How is energy transferred among organisms?

Organisms change energy from the environment or from their food into other types of energy. Some of this energy is used for the organism's activities, such as breathing or moving. Some of the energy is saved within the organism to use later. If an organism is eaten or decomposes, the consumer or decomposer takes in the energy stored in the original organism. Only chemical energy that an organism has stored in its tissues is available to consumers. In this way, energy is transferred from organism to organism.

ACTIVE READING

9 Claims • Evidence • Reasoning When a grasshopper eats grass, only some of the energy from the grass is stored in the grasshopper's body. Make a claim about how the grasshopper uses the rest of the energy. Summarize evidence to support the claim and explain your reasoning. How does the grasshopper use the rest of the energy?

_____

_____

This tree gets its energy from the sun.

This ant eats plants like the mesquite tree, and other insects.

10 Identify By what process does this tree get its energy?

_____

_____

11 Apply What type of energy is this ant consuming?

_____

_____

Energy Flows Through a Food Chain

A **food chain** is the path of energy transfer from producers to consumers. Energy moves from one organism to the next in one direction. The arrows in a food chain represent the transfer of energy, as one organism is eaten by another. Arrows represent the flow of energy from the body of the consumed organism to the body of the consumer of that organism.

Producers form the base of food chains. Producers transfer energy to the first, or primary, consumer in the food chain. The next, or secondary, consumer in the food chain consumes the primary consumer. A tertiary consumer eats the secondary consumer. Finally, decomposers recycle matter back to the soil.

👁 Visualize It!

The photographs below show a typical desert food chain. Answer the following four questions from left to right based on your understanding of how energy flows in a food chain.

This hawk eats the lizard. It is at the top of the food chain.

13 Predict If nothing ever eats this hawk, what might eventually happen to the energy that is stored in its body?

_____

_____

This lizard eats mostly insects.

12 Apply What does the arrow between the ant and the lizard represent?

_____

_____

World Wide Webs

How do food webs show energy connections?

Few organisms eat just one kind of food. So, the energy and nutrient connections in nature are more complicated than a simple food chain. A **food web** is the feeding relationships among organisms in an ecosystem. Food webs are made up of many food chains.

The next page shows a coastal food web. Most of the organisms in this food web live in the water. The web also includes some birds that live on land and eat fish. Tiny algae called phytoplankton form the base of this food web. Like plants on land, phytoplankton are producers. Tiny consumers called zooplankton eat phytoplankton. Larger animals, such as fish and squid, eat zooplankton. At the top of each chain are top predators, animals that eat other animals but are rarely eaten. In this food web, the killer whale is a top predator. Notice how many different energy paths lead from phytoplankton to the killer whale.

ACTIVE READING

14 Identify Underline the type of organism that typically forms the base of the food web.

👁 Visualize It!

15 Apply Complete the statements to the right with the correct organism names from the food web.

ENERGY

ENERGY

Energy flows up the food web when
_____ eat puffins.

Puffins are connected to many organisms in the food web.

Puffins get energy by eating

_____,

_____,

and _____.

Food Web

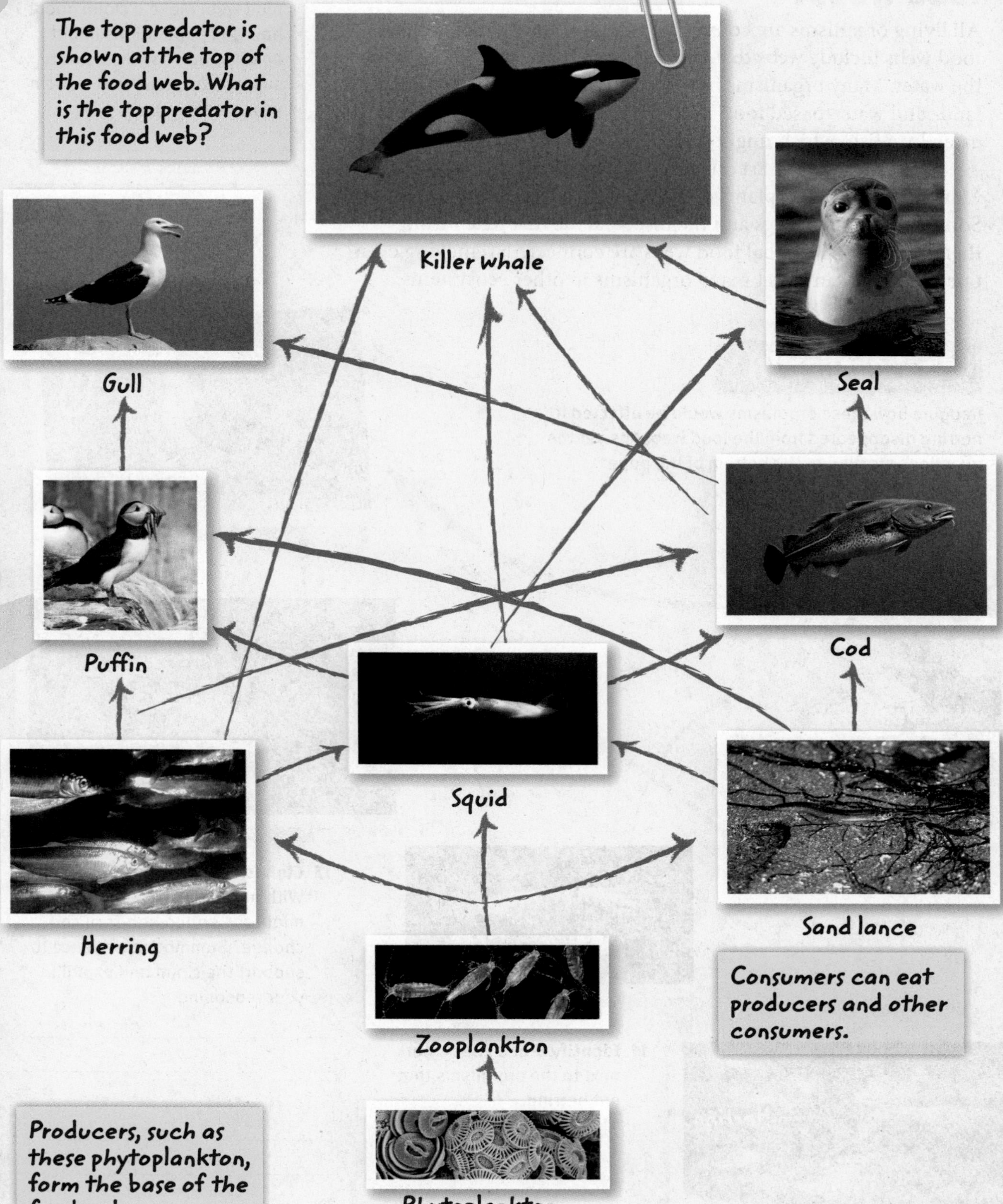

The top predator is shown at the top of the food web. What is the top predator in this food web?

Killer whale

Seal

Gull

Puffin

Cod

Squid

Herring

Sand lance

Zooplankton

Phytoplankton

Consumers can eat producers and other consumers.

Producers, such as these phytoplankton, form the base of the food web.

How are organisms connected by food webs?

All living organisms are connected by global food webs. Global food webs include webs that begin on land and webs that begin in the water. Many organisms have feeding relationships that connect land- and water-based food webs. For example, algae might be eaten by a fish, which might then be eaten by a bird.

Food webs that start on land may also move into the water. Many insects that eat plants on land lay their eggs in the water. Some fish eat these eggs and the insect larvae that hatch from them. Because the global food webs are connected, removing even one organism can affect many organisms in other ecosystems.

18 Claims • Evidence • Reasoning
Gulls don't eat herring but they are still connected by the food web. Make a claim about how gull populations might be affected. Use evidence to support the claim and explain your reasoning.

_____

_____

_____

👁 Visualize It!

Imagine how these organisms would be affected if herring disappeared from the food web. Answer the questions starting at the bottom of the page.

■ Gull

■ Puffin

■ Cod

■ Squid

Herring

16 Identify Put a check mark next to the organisms that eat herring.

17 Claims • Evidence • Reasoning
With no herring to eat, how might the eating habits of cod change? Summarize evidence to support the claim and explain your reasoning.

_____

_____

_____

_____

_____

_____

Dangerous Competition

Sometimes species are introduced into a new area. These invasive species often compete with native species for energy resources, such as sunlight and food.

Full Coverage
The kudzu plant was introduced to stop soil erosion, but in the process it outgrew all the native plants, preventing them from getting sunlight. Sometimes it completely covers houses or cars!

Destructive Zebras
The zebra mussel is one of the most destructive invasive species in the United States. They eat by filtering tiny organisms out of the water, often leaving nothing for the native mussel species.

Across the Grass
The walking catfish can actually move across land to get from one pond to another! As a result, sometimes the catfish competes with native species for food.

ℹ Extend

19 Claims • Evidence • Reasoning Make a claim about how competition between invasive and native species might affect a food web. Summarize evidence to support the claim and explain your reasoning.

20 Describe Give an example of competition for a food resource that may occur in an ecosystem near you.

21 Illustrate Provide an illustration of your example of competition in a sketch or a short story. Be sure to include the important aspects of food webs that you learned in the lesson.

Visual Summary

To complete this summary, circle the correct word. You can use this page to review the main concepts of the lesson.

Energy Transfer in **Ecosystems**

Food Web

Organisms get energy in different ways.

- Producers make their own food.
- Consumers eat other living organisms.
- Decomposers break down dead organisms.

22 Herbivores, carnivores, and omnivores are three types of producers / consumers / decomposers.

Food chains and food webs describe the flow of energy in an ecosystem.

23 All food chains start with producers / consumers / decomposers.

24 **Claims • Evidence • Reasoning** Predict the effects on global food webs if the sun's energy could no longer reach Earth. Use evidence to support the claim and explain your reasoning.

Lesson Review

Vocabulary

Fill in the blanks with the term that best completes the following sentences.

1 _____ is the primary source of energy for most ecosystems.

2 A _____ eats mostly dead matter.

3 A _____ contains many food chains.

4 _____ is the process by which light energy from the sun is converted to food.

Key Concepts

5 Describe What are the roles of producers, consumers, and decomposers in an ecosystem?

_____

_____

_____

_____

6 Explain Your Reasoning What types of organisms typically make up the base, middle, and top of a food web? Explain your reasoning.

_____

_____

_____

7 Describe Identify the two types of global food webs and describe how they are connected.

_____

_____

_____

Use the figure to answer the following questions.

8 Apply Describe the flow of energy in this food chain. Be sure to use the names of the organisms and what role they serve in the food chain (producer, consumer, or decomposer). If an organism is a consumer, identify whether it is an herbivore, carnivore, or omnivore.

_____

_____

9 Apply What do the arrows represent in the figure above?

_____

_____

Critical Thinking

10 Claims • Evidence • Reasoning Give an example of a decomposer, and make a claim about what would happen if decomposers were absent from a forest ecosystem. Summarize evidence to support the claim and explain your reasoning.

_____

_____

11 Claims • Evidence • Reasoning How would a food web be affected if a species disappeared from an ecosystem? Summarize evidence to support your claim and explain your reasoning.

_____

_____

_____

Interactions in Communities

ESSENTIAL QUESTION

How do organisms interact?

By the end of this lesson, you should be able to predict the effects of different interactions in communities.

These birds, called tickbirds, eat ticks and flies on a rhinoceros. This behavior helps the rhino. The ticks are also parasites that sometimes drink the rhino's blood!

SC.7.N.1.1 Define a problem from the seventh grade curriculum, use appropriate reference materials to support scientific understanding, plan and carry out scientific investigation of various types, such as systematic observations or experiments, identify variables, collect and organize data, interpret data in charts, tables, and graphics, analyze information, make predictions, and defend conclusions. SC.7.L.17.2 Compare and contrast the relationships among organisms such as mutualism, predation, parasitism, competition, and commensalism.

✋ Lesson Labs

Quick Labs
• What Organisms Does an Environment Support?
• Measuring Species Diversity
• Biodiversity All Around Us

Exploration Lab
• How Do Populations Interact?
• Change in Populations

⚙ Engage Your Brain

1 Predict Check T or F to show whether you think each statement is true or false.

   T   **F**

☐ ☐ Different animals can compete for the same food.

☐ ☐ Parasites help the organisms that they feed on.

☐ ☐ Some organisms rely on each other for necessities such as food or shelter.

☐ ☐ Organisms can defend themselves against predators that try to eat them.

2 Explain Draw an interaction between two living things that you might observe while on a picnic. Write a caption to go with your sketch.

ACTIVE **READING**

3 Synthesize You can often define an unknown word if you know the meaning of its word parts. Use the word parts and sentence below to make an educated guess about the meaning of the word *symbiosis*.

Word part	Meaning
bio-	life
sym-	together

Example sentence
The relationship between a sunflower and the insect that pollinates it is an example of symbiosis.

symbiosis:

_____

_____

_____

Vocabulary Terms

• predator
• prey
• symbiosis
• mutualism

• commensalism
• parasitism
• competition

4 Apply As you learn the meaning of each vocabulary term in this lesson, create your own definition or sketch to help you remember the meaning of the term.

Feeding Frenzy!

How do predator and prey interact?

Every organism lives with and affects other organisms. Many organisms must feed on other organisms in order to get the energy and nutrients they need to survive. These feeding relationships establish structure in a community.

ACTIVE READING

5 Identify As you read, underline examples of predator–prey adaptations.

Predators Eat Prey

In a predator–prey relationship, an animal eats another animal for energy and nutrients. The **predator** eats another animal. The **prey** is an animal that is eaten by a predator. An animal can be both predator and prey. For example, if a warthog eats a lizard, and is, in turn, eaten by a lion, the warthog is both predator and prey.

Predators and prey have adaptations that help them survive. Some predators have talons, claws, or sharp teeth, which provide them with deadly weapons. Spiders, which are small predators, use their webs to trap unsuspecting prey. Camouflage (CAM•ah•flaj) can also help a predator or prey to blend in with its environment. A tiger's stripes help it to blend in with tall grasses so that it can ambush its prey, and the wings of some moths look just like tree bark, which makes them difficult for predators to see. Some animals defend themselves with chemicals. For example, skunks and bombardier beetles spray predators with irritating chemicals.

This lion is a predator. The warthog is its prey.

Adaptations of Predators and Prey

Most organisms wouldn't last a day without their adaptations. This bald eagle's vision and sharp talons allow it to find and catch prey.

sharp talons

Predators and Prey Populations Are Connected

Predators rely on prey for food, so the sizes of predator and prey populations are linked together very closely. If one population grows or shrinks, the other population is affected. For example, when there are a lot of warthogs to eat, the lion population may grow because the food supply is plentiful. As the lion population grows, it requires more and more food, so more and more warthogs are hunted by the lions. The increased predation may cause the warthog population to shrink. If the warthog population shrinks enough, the lion population may shrink due to a shortage in food supply. If the lion population shrinks, the warthog population may grow due to a lack of predators.

This lion is hunting down the antelope. If most of the antelope are killed, the lions will have less food to eat.

6 Compare Fill in the Venn diagram to compare and contrast predators and prey.

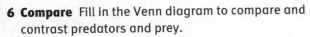

Predators   Both   Prey

_____   _____   _____
_____   _____   _____
_____   _____   _____
_____   _____   _____

Think Outside the Book

7 Claims • Evidence • Reasoning Choose a predator and think about what it eats and how it hunts. Then do one of the following:

- Write a nomination for the predator to be "Predator of the Year." Summarize evidence to support the nomination and explain your reasoning.
- Draw the predator and make a claim about adaptations that help it hunt. Use evidence to support the claim and explain your reasoning.

Don't be surprised if this "leaf" walks away—it's actually an insect.

👁 Visualize It!

8 Claims • Evidence • Reasoning Make a claim about how this insect's appearance might help keep it from getting eaten. Summarize evidence to support the claim and explain your reasoning.

_____
_____
_____
_____

Living Together

What are the types of symbiotic relationships?

A close long-term relationship between different species in a community is called **symbiosis** (sim•bee•OH•sis). In symbiosis, the organisms in the relationship can benefit from, be unaffected by, or be harmed by the relationship. Often, one organism lives in or on the other organism. Symbiotic relationships are classified as mutualism, commensalism, or parasitism.

ACTIVE **READING**

9 Identify As you read, underline examples of symbiotic relationships.

Mutualism

A symbiotic relationship in which both organisms benefit is called **mutualism**. For example, when the bee in the photo drinks nectar from a flower, it gets pollen on its hind legs. When the bee visits another flower, it transfers pollen from the first flower to the second flower. In this interaction, the bee is fed and the second flower is pollinated for reproduction. So, both organisms benefit from the relationship. In this example, the mutualism benefits the bee and the two parent plants that are reproducing.

Bees pollinate flowers. This is an example of mutualism.

Commensalism

A symbiotic relationship in which one organism benefits while the other is unaffected is called **commensalism.** For example, orchids and other plants that often live in the branches of trees gain better access to sunlight without affecting the trees. In addition, the tree trunk shown here provides a living space for lichens, which do not affect the tree in any way. Some examples of commensalism involve protection. For example, certain shrimp live among the spines of the fire urchin. The fire urchin's spines are poisonous but not to the shrimp. By living among the urchin's spines, the shrimp are protected from predators. In this relationship, the shrimp benefits and the fire urchin is unaffected.

Lichens can live on tree bark.

10 Compare How does commensalism differ from mutualism?

_____

_____

_____

_____

12 Claims • Evidence • Reasoning
Observe and take notes about how the organisms in your area interact with one another. Imagine what would happen if one of these organisms disappeared. Write down three effects that you can think of. Cite evidence to support your claims and explain your reasoning.

parasite

host

Parasitism

A symbiotic relationship in which one organism benefits and another is harmed is called **parasitism** (PAR•uh•sih•tiz•uhm). The organism that benefits is the *parasite*. The organism that is harmed is the *host*. The parasite gets food from its host, which weakens the host. Some parasites, such as ticks, live on the host's surface and feed on its blood. These parasites can cause diseases such as Lyme disease. Other parasites, such as tapeworms, live within the host's body. They can weaken their host so much that the host dies.

11 Summarize Using the key, complete the table to show how organisms are affected by symbiotic relationships.

Symbiosis	Species 1	Species 2
Mutualism	+	
	+	0
Parasitism		

Key + organism benefits
0 organism not affected
− organism harmed

Let the Games Begin!

Why does competition occur in communities?

In a team game, two groups compete against each other with the same goal in mind—to win the game. In a biological community, organisms compete for resources. **Competition** occurs when organisms fight for the same limited resource. Organisms compete for resources such as food, water, sunlight, shelter, and mates. If an organism doesn't get all the resources it needs, it could die.

Sometimes competition happens among individuals of the same species. For example, different groups of lions compete with each other for living space. Males within these groups also compete with each other for mates.

Competition can also happen among individuals of different species. Lions mainly eat large animals, such as zebras. They compete for zebras with leopards and cheetahs. When zebras are scarce, competition increases among animals that eat zebras. As a result, lions may steal food or compete with other predators for smaller animals.

ACTIVE READING

13 Identify Underline each example of competition.

14 Predict In the table below, fill in the missing cause and effect of two examples of competition in a community.

Cause	Effect
A population of lions grows too large to share their current territory.	
	Several male hyenas compete to mate with the females present in their area.

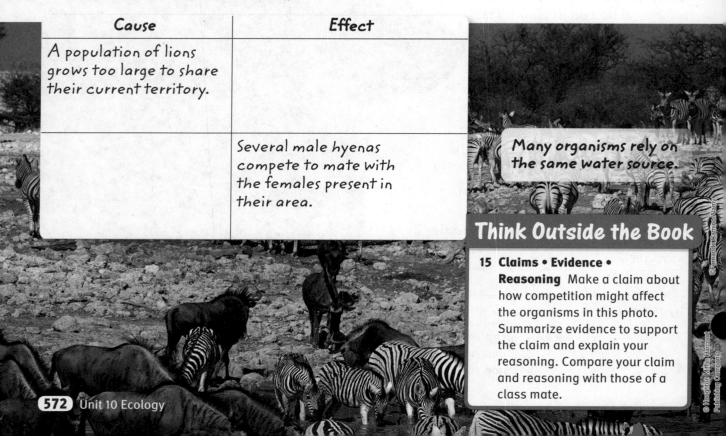

Many organisms rely on the same water source.

Think Outside the Book

15 Claims • Evidence • Reasoning Make a claim about how competition might affect the organisms in this photo. Summarize evidence to support the claim and explain your reasoning. Compare your claim and reasoning with those of a class mate.

Strange Relationships

Glow worms? Blind salamanders? Even creepy crawlers in this extreme cave community interact in ways that help them meet their needs. How do these interactions differ from ones in your own community?

Guano Buffet

Cave swiftlets venture out of the cave daily to feed. The food they eat is recycled as bird dung, or guano, which piles up beneath the nests. The guano feeds many cave dwellers, such as insects. As a result, these insects never have to leave the cave!

A Blind Hunter

Caves are very dark and, over generations, these salamanders have lost the use of their eyes for seeing. Instead of looking for food, they track prey by following water movements.

Sticky Traps

Bioluminescent glow worms make lines of sticky beads to attract prey. Once a prey is stuck, the worm pulls in the line to feast.

ℹ️ Extend

16 Claims • Evidence • Reasoning Make a claim about the type of relationship illustrated in two of the examples shown above. Summarize evidence to support the claim and explain your reasoning.

17 Research Name some organisms in your community and the interactions they have.

18 Create Illustrate two of the interactions you just described by doing one of the following:
- make a poster
- write a song
- write a play
- draw a graphic novel

Visual Summary

To complete this summary, fill in the blanks with the correct word or phrase. You can use this page to review the main concepts of the lesson.

Organisms interact in feeding relationships.

19 Predators eat
_____

Organisms interact in symbiosis—very close relationships between two species.

Mutualism:

Commensalism:

Parasitism:

20 A parasite gets nourishment from its
_____

Interactions in Communities

Organisms interact in competition.

21 Organisms compete for resources such as
_____
_____
_____

Competition can occur between:
Members of the same species   Members of different species

22 Claims • Evidence • Reasoning Make a claim about how interactions can be both beneficial and harmful to the organisms in a community. Summarize evidence to support the claim and explain your reasoning.

Lesson Review

Vocabulary

Fill in the blank with the term that best completes the following sentences.

1 A _____ is an animal that kills and eats another animal, known as prey.

2 A long-term relationship between two different species within a community is called

_____

3 _____ occurs when organisms fight for limited resources.

Key Concepts

Fill in the table below.

Example	Type of symbiosis
4 Identify Tiny organisms called mites live in human eyelashes and feed on dead skin, without harming humans.	
5 Identify Certain bacteria live in human intestines, where they get food and also help humans break down their food.	

6 Claims • Evidence • Reasoning Think of an animal, and list two resources that it might compete for in its community. Make a claim about what adaptations the animal has to compete for these resources. Cite evidence to support the claim and explain your reasoning.

_____

_____

7 Claims • Evidence • Reasoning Make a claim about the relationship between the size of a predator population and the size of a prey population. Cite evidence to support the claim and explain your reasoning.

_____

_____

Critical Thinking

Use this graph to answer the following question.

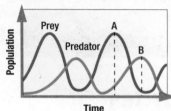

Predator and Prey Populations Over Time

8 Explain Your Reasoning At which point (A or B) on this graph would you expect competition within the predator population to be the highest? Explain your reasoning.

_____

9 Claims • Evidence • Reasoning Think of a resource, and predict what happens to the resource when competition for it increases. Summarize evidence that explains your reasoning and supports the claim.

_____

10 Claims • Evidence • Reasoning Identify a community near where you live, such as a forest, a pond, or your own backyard. Think about the interactions of the organisms in this community. Describe an interaction and identify it as predation, mutualism, commensalism, parasitism, or competition. Summarize evidence that supports the claim and explains your reasoning.

_____

FOCUS ON **FLORIDA**

SC.7.L.17.3 Describe and investigate various limiting factors in the local ecosystem and their impact on native populations, including food, shelter, water, space, disease, parasitism, predation, and nesting sites.

Florida Populations

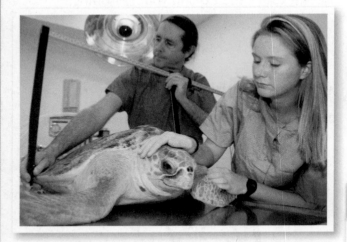

This injured sea turtle is being treated at the Turtle Hospital in Marathon, Florida.

Sea Turtles

Every summer, Florida becomes home to about 50,000 new residents who are famous for their hard shells and amazing swimming skills. Five species of sea turtles, including the loggerhead and leatherback turtles, make nests on the beaches of Florida in May. Two months later, their eggs hatch. The newborn turtles, or hatchlings, emerge from their nests and make their way to the water. The turtles stay in the Gulf Stream for a few years. Hatchlings are vulnerable to fish and seabirds, but even adult sea turtles must watch out for sharks. While their hard shells protect them from most predators, many turtles are injured every year through contact with human beings. Outboard motors can damage a turtle's shell. Fishing nets can trap turtles and drown them. Humans also hunt female turtles for their meat. Human development and construction threaten the habitats of sea turtles. Laws are in place to help protect the declining sea turtle population.

Social Studies Connection

Loggerhead turtles, the most common sea turtle in Florida, usually nest along the east coast of Florida. The hatchling loggerheads migrate to the Gulf Stream. The table shows data collected from a tracking device placed on a loggerhead turtle. Plot the points on the map to see the route the turtle followed.

Tracking Data for Loggerhead Turtle Migration		
Date	**Latitude (°N)**	**Longitude (°W)**
February 6	33	79
February 13	36	74
February 17	38	67
February 23	42	59
March 10	40	49

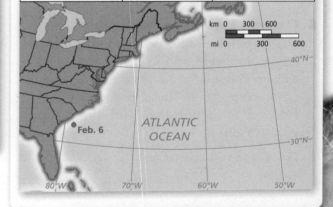

Iguanas on the Loose!

You don't have to go to a zoo or a pet store to see an iguana. Sometimes you can find them in the middle of town! Iguanas are not native to Florida. People originally brought iguanas to Florida as pets. Over time, many were released or escaped, and iguanas now live and reproduce in the wild.

Iguana trappers have been used to capture iguanas, but this reptile population has become harder to control. Florida's subtropical climate is a favorable ecosystem for iguanas. Wild adult iguanas are large and powerful. They do not have many natural predators—alligators, dogs, raccoons, and some birds of prey are the only species that seem to threaten them.

Iguanas pose hazards to humans in several ways. Iguanas can cause structural damage to buildings by burrowing into their foundations. In addition, their wastes contain the salmonella bacteria, which pose a health risk to humans.

Iguanas do not respond well to sudden drops in temperature. At low temperatures, an iguana's metabolism slows down and the iguana appears frozen. However, once the weather warms up, it returns to its regular state. During a cold snap, it seems like it's raining iguanas in Florida as these "frozen" reptiles fall out of trees. Because hundreds of thousands of iguanas live in Florida, you could get caught in an iguana storm!

Wild iguana

Managing Deer

They are about the size of a medium-sized dog, but otherwise look like a deer. Tiny Key deer are unique to one of Florida's ecosystems. And they very nearly disappeared! In the 1930s, the Key deer population was very low. Poaching and hunting meant that only about 50 Key deer were alive. With careful wildlife and habitat management, the current Key deer population is now at 300, but is still considered endangered. A larger population of Key deer means a healthier Florida ecosystem. The endangered Florida panther is a predator of Key deer. So when the Key deer population shrinks, the panther population is also threatened.

Key deer

Take It Home

You are part of a campaign to protect endangered animals of Florida like the leatherback sea turtle, Key deer, or Florida panther. Research one of these animals and create a profile page or blog post about it. Include links to websites for more information on your endangered animal.

(bkgd) ©Klaus Nigge/National Geographic/Getty Images; (t) ©Rick & Nora Bowers/Alamy

Publishing Company

Florida's Ecosystems

ESSENTIAL QUESTION

How do limiting factors affect Florida's ecosystems?

By the end of this lesson, you should be able to explain how limiting factors affect the native populations in Florida's ecosystems.

Human activity near beaches may keep animals such as this leatherback sea turtle from reproducing.

SC.7.N.1.1 Define a problem from the seventh grade curriculum, use appropriate reference materials to support scientific understanding, plan and carry out scientific investigation of various types, such as systematic observations or experiments, identify variables, collect and organize data, interpret data in charts, tables, and graphics, analyze information, make predictions, and defend conclusions. **SC.7.L.17.3** Describe and investigate various limiting factors in the local ecosystem and their impact on native populations, including food, shelter, water, space, disease, parasitism, predation, and nesting sites.

Lesson Labs

Quick Labs
- Life in Moving Water
- Changes in the Intertidal Zone

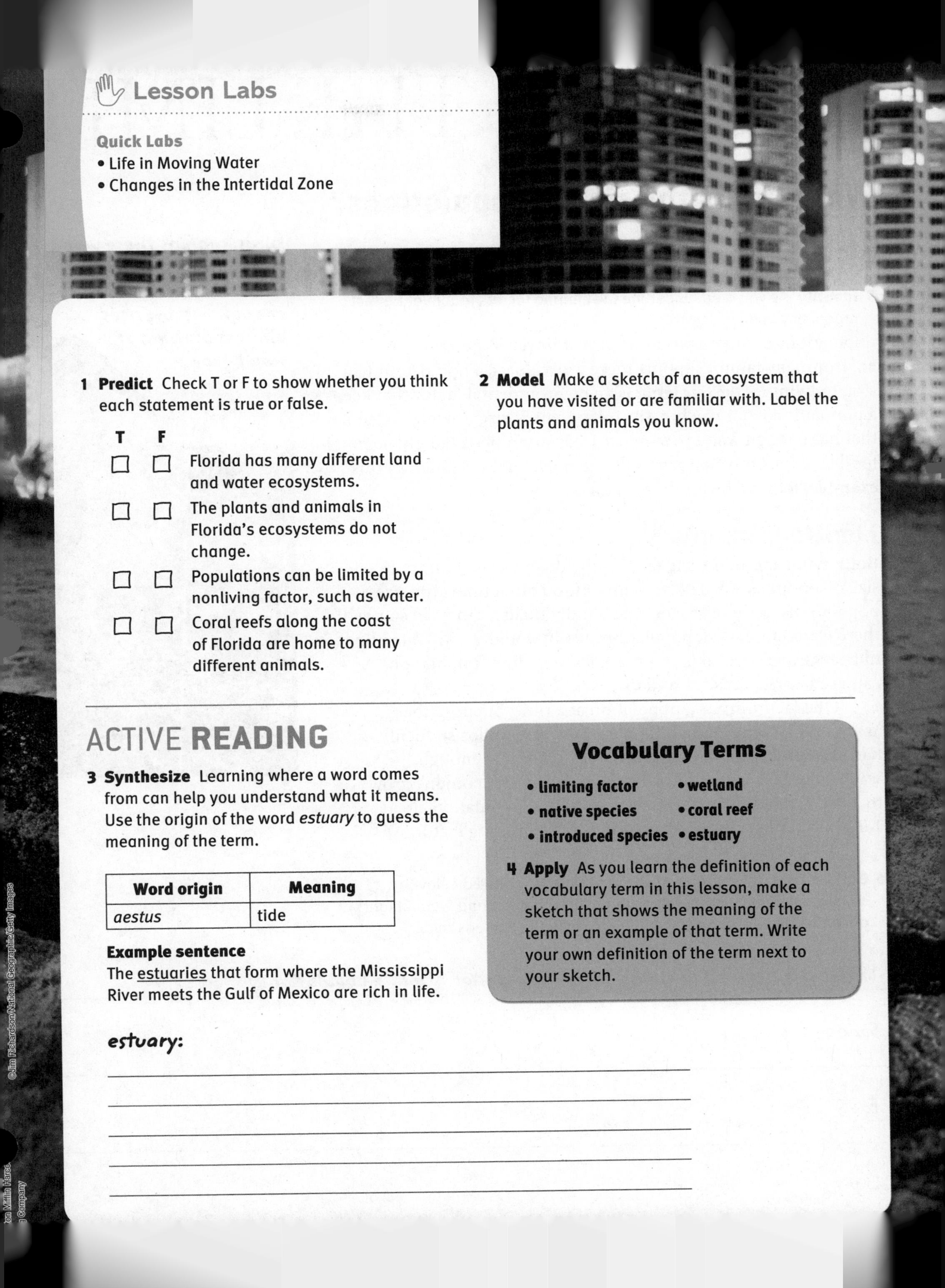

1 Predict Check T or F to show whether you think each statement is true or false.

T	F	
☐	☐	Florida has many different land and water ecosystems.
☐	☐	The plants and animals in Florida's ecosystems do not change.
☐	☐	Populations can be limited by a nonliving factor, such as water.
☐	☐	Coral reefs along the coast of Florida are home to many different animals.

2 Model Make a sketch of an ecosystem that you have visited or are familiar with. Label the plants and animals you know.

ACTIVE **READING**

3 Synthesize Learning where a word comes from can help you understand what it means. Use the origin of the word *estuary* to guess the meaning of the term.

Word origin	Meaning
aestus	tide

Example sentence
The estuaries that form where the Mississippi River meets the Gulf of Mexico are rich in life.

estuary:

____

____

____

____

____

Vocabulary Terms

- **limiting factor**
- **native species**
- **introduced species**
- **wetland**
- **coral reef**
- **estuary**

4 Apply As you learn the definition of each vocabulary term in this lesson, make a sketch that shows the meaning of the term or an example of that term. Write your own definition of the term next to your sketch.

Pushing THE LIMIT

What limits the size of populations?

ACTIVE READING

5 Identify As you read, underline the limiting factors that might affect organisms in an ecosystem.

Populations of organisms don't grow forever. When the environment cannot support more individuals, a population will stop growing. A **limiting factor** is an environmental factor that keeps a population from reaching its full potential size. Imagine a habitat that has enough water to support 1,000 armadillos but only enough food for 500. Only 500 armadillos can live in the habitat. In this example, food is the limiting factor.

Limiting Factors

Both living and nonliving environmental factors can limit the size of a population. The amount of food often limits the size of populations. If there are too many individuals, some will starve. If there were more food, populations likely would grow. Water, light, nutrients, shelter, and living space also can limit populations. So can predators, parasites, and diseases.

One factor limits a population at a time. Suppose the area that had only enough food for 500 armadillos suddenly had enough food for 2,000 armadillos, but only enough water for 1,000 armadillos. The population still couldn't grow to 2,000 armadillos. Water would keep the population at 1,000 armadillos. In this case, water is the limiting factor.

Birds, such as these wood storks, need space for nests. If there aren't enough nesting sites, bird populations won't grow.

6 Explain Your Reasoning For each limiting factor listed below, choose an animal or plant and predict how that limiting factor might affect the population of the organism. Explain your reasoning.

Limiting factor	How does the limiting factor affect a population?
Space	
Food	
Light	

The Burmese python is an introduced species from Asia that is now found in the Everglades.

What are introduced species?

Species that naturally live in an ecosystem are called **native species**. On the other hand, **introduced species** are species that have been brought to an ecosystem by human actions. Some introduced species were brought to new places on purpose. Others traveled in vehicles or on other animals. Escaped or released pets can also start new populations in the wild.

Many introduced species are successful because they do not have predators, parasites, or diseases in the new habitat. Some introduced species may be better competitors for resources than native species. Introduced species may eat native species. As a result, introduced species often are limiting factors.

Many species have been introduced to Florida. For example, Burmese pythons from Asia are now found in the Everglades. Many of these pythons were pets. In the wild, they eat many native animals, such as wading birds, deer, and even alligators! By eating these animals, pythons compete with native predators for food.

Little blue herons are just one of the many native species that Burmese pythons eat.

7 Cause and Effect Use the diagram below to describe how the Burmese python affects Florida's ecosystems.

Effect:
_____
_____

Cause
_____
_____

Effect:
_____
_____

Land, HO!

What are Florida's land ecosystems?

Many species live in Florida's land ecosystems—forests, prairies, beaches, and dunes. Some native species are found nowhere else on Earth. Introduced plants and animals can threaten native species. Different factors limit populations in these ecosystems.

ACTIVE READING

8 Summarize After you read each heading, list organisms and limiting factors in the land ecosystems described.

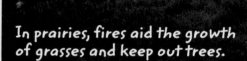

In prairies, fires aid the growth of grasses and keep out trees.

Prairies

Plants such as grasses, sedges, and rushes dominate Florida's prairies. Fire is an important limiting factor on prairies. Fires keep trees from growing. Fires also cause new growth in grasses. Herbivores, which are animals that eat plants, can limit plant populations on prairies.

Who lives here?

_____

_____

What are limiting factors here?

_____

_____

Forests

Longleaf pines, mangroves, cypress, and cabbage palms can be found in Florida's forests. Light, space, and nutrients limit tree and plant populations. Many animals live in forests. Predators such as Florida panthers limit the populations of animals such as deer. Fire is also a limiting factor in forests. Although some species are harmed by fire, other species rely on it. Fire returns nutrients to the soil. A few species, such as sand pines, release seeds only after a fire.

Who lives here?

_____

_____

What are limiting factors here?

_____

_____

In forests, such as this cypress forest, light can be a limiting factor.

Dunes are threatened by human activity.

Dunes

Blowing sand forms dunes along beaches. Low-growing plants that can survive being sprayed with salt water grow here. They hold sand in place, allowing other plants to grow. Steep slopes limit plant growth. Big trees can't grow on dunes. Sand doesn't provide enough support for roots. Dunes are important for nesting birds. Development can limit the space and resources available to organisms. It also damages the plants that hold sand in place.

Who lives here?

_____

_____

What are limiting factors here?

_____

_____

On beaches, many animals live in tunnels in the sand.

Beaches

Beaches are found where land meets water. Most beaches in Florida are sandy. Animals, such as clams and crabs, live under the sand. Birds eat these animals and organisms that wash up on the beach. So, birds can limit populations of some animals. Beaches are nesting sites for sea turtles and birds. Development can decrease the space available for nests.

Who lives here?

_____

_____

What are limiting factors here?

_____

_____

9 Claims • Evidence • Reasoning Make a claim about why fires are important to prairies but not important to dunes. Summarize evidence to support the claim and explain your reasoning.

_____

_____

_____

_____

_____

Gator COUNTRY

What are Florida's freshwater ecosystems?

ACTIVE **READING**

10 Identify As you read, underline factors that limit populations in
Florida's freshwater ecosystems.

Freshwater ecosystems are very important in Florida. They
include lakes, ponds, rivers, streams, and wetlands. Water is a
limiting factor in many of
these ecosystems. Freshwater
ecosystems have different water
depths, speeds of water flow, and
types of organisms. They provide
food and drinking water for people.
People also use them for activities
such as boating and swimming.

Florida has many rivers, canals, and lakes.

A lake near Wekiwa Springs, Florida

Lakes and Ponds

Lakes and ponds are standing bodies of water.
So, water flows very little if at all. Some plants
float on top of the water. Other plants grow in
shallow areas, where they can get light and air. If
the amount of oxygen in lakes and ponds is low,
it can limit populations. When there is enough
oxygen, ponds and lakes support many kinds of
fish. Introduced fish, such as walking catfish, and
introduced plants, such as water hyacinth, can be
found in many lakes and ponds in Florida.

Rivers and Streams

Rivers and streams have flowing water. They
carry nutrients that are important to the
ecosystems that they flow into. Rivers and
streams are home to many organisms, including
the endangered manatee. Shelter is often a
limiting factor in rivers and streams. Rocks
provide hiding places from predators. Rocks
also shelter organisms from currents that would
sweep them away.

Wetlands

The Florida Everglades are wetlands. A **wetland** is an area where land is covered by water for at least part of the year. Water flows slowly in wetlands. Many birds, fish, reptiles, and mammals live in wetlands. Wetland plants help remove wastes and pollution from water. Nutrients limit plant populations. Low oxygen levels and drying up of wetlands can limit fish. Animals and trees rely on *hammocks,* which are areas that are dry most of the year.

11 Apply With a partner, work together to make lists of the animals and plants in a local freshwater ecosystem. Then, identify how water moves through the ecosystem.

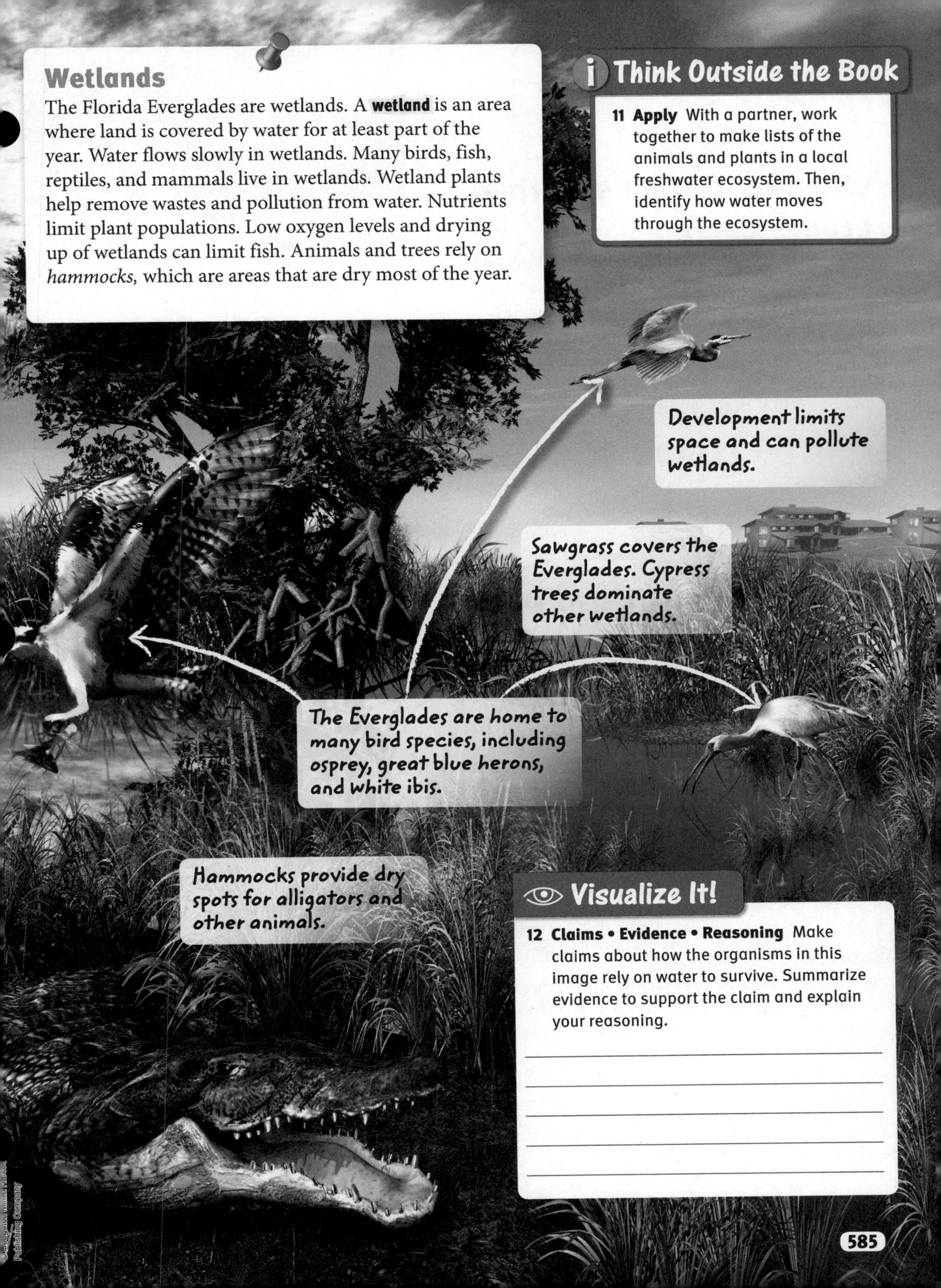

Development limits space and can pollute wetlands.

Sawgrass covers the Everglades. Cypress trees dominate other wetlands.

The Everglades are home to many bird species, including osprey, great blue herons, and white ibis.

Hammocks provide dry spots for alligators and other animals.

Visualize It!

12 Claims • Evidence • Reasoning Make claims about how the organisms in this image rely on water to survive. Summarize evidence to support the claim and explain your reasoning.

_____

_____

_____

_____

_____

Just Add SALT!

What are Florida's marine ecosystems?

The marine, or saltwater, ecosystems of Florida include coral reefs, estuaries (ES•choo•ehr•eez), salt marshes, and mangrove swamps. Florida's marine ecosystems support many species. They provide food and recreation for people. Florida's marine ecosystems are at risk from development and pollution. Both can limit populations.

ACTIVE READING

13 Identify As you read, underline the limiting factors in the ecosystem described.

Coral Reefs

One of the most diverse marine ecosystems is the coral reef. A **coral reef** grows in waters that are warm, shallow, and clear. Coral reefs are made up of the skeletons of tiny animals called *corals*. Tiny protists live inside coral bodies and give coral reefs their color. These protists use light to produce food, which corals can use. Because they need light to grow, water depth and sunlight limit the growth of the protists and coral in reefs.

Reefs are home to many kinds of fish, sea turtles, and other animals such as crabs, shrimps, anemones, urchins, and starfish. A reef may be home to thousands of species. So, space is often a limiting factor. High temperatures and polluted water from land can also limit populations of corals and other reef animals.

◉ Visualize It!

14 Claims • Evidence • Reasoning Make a claim about what limiting factors are present in this coral reef ecosystem. Use evidence to support the claim and explain your reasoning.

_____

_____

_____

_____

Many species of plants and animals live in estuaries.

Grasses dominate salt marshes.

Mangrove populations are limited by nutrients, water, and temperature.

Estuaries

Many streams and rivers flow into the ocean, forming estuaries. An **estuary** is an area where fresh water mixes with salt water. Both grasses and seagrasses grow in estuaries. Many fish lay eggs here, and plants provide shelter for young fish. Birds, turtles, alligators, and many other animals live in estuaries.

Many organisms rely on the nutrients provided by estuaries. So, nutrients are a limiting factor. Populations also are limited by water movement and salt levels in the water. Some species need high salt levels whereas other species, such as alligators, need lower levels.

Salt Marshes

Salt marshes are found along the coast. Grasses and other plants, such as sedges and rushes, live in these areas. Salt marshes are occasionally flooded by tides. This flooding can limit plant populations. Plants do not grow where water is too deep or the ground is wet for too long. Salt levels and nutrients can also limit plants and animals in salt marshes. If oxygen levels in water get too low, they limit the populations of fish and other species.

Mangrove Swamps

Mangrove swamps are found in areas that are flooded by tides and also receive freshwater runoff. They are dominated by mangrove trees. Mangroves need nutrients to survive. Mangroves cannot survive low temperatures. So, temperature also limits mangrove populations.

Mangrove roots often reach below the water. They shelter small fish from predators. For organisms that live in mangrove swamps, the amount of time the area is wet or dry is a limiting factor. Salt levels also limit populations in mangrove swamps.

15 Compare What limiting factors do estuaries, salt marshes, and mangrove swamps have in common?

_____

_____

_____

Visual Summary

To complete this summary, fill in the blanks with the correct word or phrase. You can use this page to review the main concepts of the lesson.

Populations are limited by living and nonliving factors.

16 The Burmese python is a(n) _____ species in the Florida Everglades.

Marine habitats include coral reefs, estuaries, salt marshes, and mangrove swamps.

19 A(n) _____ is an area where fresh water meets salt water.

Florida's Ecosystems

Florida's land ecosystems include forests, prairies, dunes, and beaches.

17 In forests, sunlight is a(n) _____ for plants on the forest floor.

Freshwater ecosystems include lakes, ponds, rivers, streams, and wetlands.

18 The Florida Everglades are an example of a(n) _____.

20 Claims • Evidence • Reasoning Predict what might happen to a native fish species if an introduced fish species that ate the same food was released in a pond. Summarize evidence to support the claim and explain your reasoning.

Lesson Review

Vocabulary

Fill in the blanks with the terms that best complete the following sentence.

1 A(n) _____ is a species that naturally lives in an ecosystem.

2 A(n) _____ is an ecosystem that is covered with water for at least part of the year.

3 A(n) _____ is an ecosystem found in warm, clear salt water.

4 _____ keep populations from reaching their full potential size.

Key Concepts

5 Explain Your Reasoning A population of birds has nesting sites for 500 birds and food for 400 birds. What is the limiting factor for this population? Explain your reasoning.

_____

_____

_____

6 Claims • Evidence • Reasoning Imagine a new species of bird was introduced to the same area as a population of native birds. Make a claim about the effect the introduced species might have on the native species. Summarize evidence to support the claim and explain your reasoning.

_____

_____

_____

7 Explain What characteristics of estuaries make them good places for fish to lay their eggs?

_____

_____

_____

Critical Thinking

8 Explain Your Reasoning Choose an ecosystem near you. List three organisms in the ecosystem and describe limiting factors for each of them. Explain your reasoning.

_____

_____

_____

The graphs below show how the size of a gull population is affected by nesting sites and crabs, which gulls eat. Use the graphs to answer the questions that follow.

Limiting Factors That May Affect Gull Populations

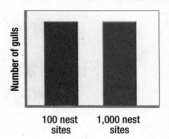
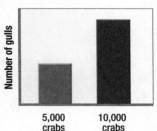

9 Support Your Claim What factor limits the gull population, nesting sites or crabs? Use evidence to support your claim.

_____

_____

_____

10 Claims • Evidence • Reasoning Make a claim about what would happen to the gull population if there were only 10 nest sites. Summarize evidence to support the claim and explain your reasoning.

_____

_____

_____

Introduction to **Ecology**

**include feeding
relationships
that lead to**

Roles in **Energy
Transfer**

Interactions in
Communities

depend on

**Florida's
Ecosystems**

1 Interpret The Graphic Organizer above shows that Florida's ecosystems depend on the transfer of energy. Give an example of an energy transfer in a Florida ecosystem.

_____

_____

_____

_____

_____

2 Claims • Evidence • Reasoning Make a claim about whether organisms compete for abiotic resources. Summarize evidence to support the claim and explain your reasoning.

_____

_____

_____

3 Describe Name a feeding relationship within one of Florida's land ecosystems.

_____

_____

_____

4 Explain Your Reasoning How could introduced species disrupt existing feeding relationships? Explain your reasoning.

_____

_____

_____

_____

Vocabulary

Name _____

Check the box to show whether each statement is true or false.

T	F		
☐	☐	**1**	<u>Competition</u> occurs when organisms try to use the same limited resource.
☐	☐	**2**	A <u>habitat</u> is the role of a population in its community, including its environment and its relationship with other species.
☐	☐	**3**	A <u>food chain</u> is the feeding relationships among all of the organisms in an ecosystem.
☐	☐	**4**	A <u>limiting factor</u> is an environmental factor that increases the growth of a population.

Key Concepts

Identify the choice that best completes the statement or answers the question.

5 Remoras are small fish that attach to sharks but do not harm them. When sharks tear prey apart, remoras eat the leftovers. What relationship do remoras have with sharks?

A mutualism

B parasitism

C commensalism

D predator-prey

6 Ecosystems have producers, decomposers, and consumers. Carnivores and scavengers are both types of consumers in an ecosystem. Which of the following is a characteristic of scavengers that makes them different from carnivores?

F Scavengers eat only plant materials.

G Scavengers are omnivores that always eat live animals.

H Scavengers are omnivores that eat dead plants and animals.

I Scavengers are able to produce their own food when no other food is available.

Publishing Company

7 Mangrove swamps are found along the southern coasts of Florida. A mangrove swamp contains an ecosystem of many organisms living among the large roots of the mangrove trees. This food web shows some of the relationships in that ecosystem.

Mangrove Food Web

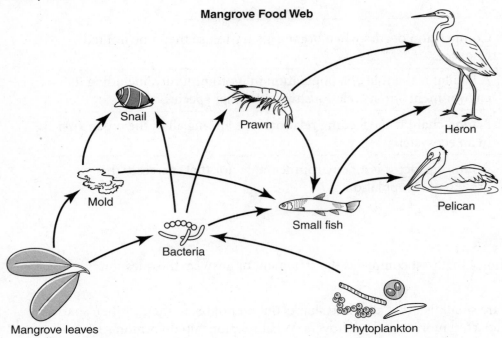

According to the food web, which organism is a producer in the mangrove swamp?

A crab

B mold

C pelican

D phytoplankton

8 Ecological environments can be divided into different levels of organization. From the following choices, identify the correct order from largest to smallest.

F ecosystem, population, community, individual

G community, ecosystem, population, individual

H ecosystem, community, population, individual

I individual, population, community, ecosystem

Name _____

9 Cogongrass, a non-native species of grass, grows in many areas of Florida. Its roots can spread quickly underground. Cogongrass thrives where fires allow it to spread. Which of the following is a negative effect that cogongrass could have on other organisms in its habitat?

A It provides places for animals in the habitat to hide.

B It provides a new source of food for animals in the habitat.

C It replaces native plants that animals depend on for food or shelter.

D It contributes nutrients to the soil in the habitat so that soil organisms can grow.

10 Honeybees are important pollinators of flowers. Mites that live in the bodies of bees can attack honeybee colonies. Some birds, amphibians, and insects eat honeybees. Which of the following relationships is **not** included in the description above?

F parasitism   **H** commensalism

G mutualism   **I** predator-prey

11 Earth's environments include both biotic and abiotic factors that living things need to survive. Large mangrove ecosystems are found along the coastlines in Florida. Which of the following are both abiotic factors in the mangrove ecosystem?

A water and pelican   **C** pelican and crab

B sun and rocks   **D** snail and water

12 The Florida panther used to live in forests, prairies, and swamps over most of the southeastern United States. Now, it lives only in the southern tip of Florida, south of the Caloosahatchee River. Based on this information, what is the **most likely** cause of the decline of the Florida panther population?

F the unintentional introduction of a larger predator

G the break-up of the panther's natural habitat by human settlement

H the weakening of species due to inbreeding

I competition for territory between panthers

Critical Thinking

Answer the following questions in the space provided.

13 Use the diagram to help you answer the following question.

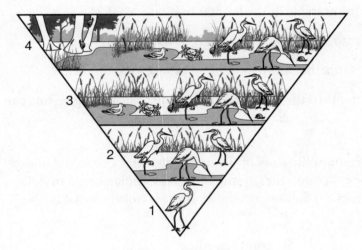

There is a sudden decrease in the food availability for wading birds. Make a claim about how the different levels of organization shown in the diagram will be affected. Summarize evidence to support your claim and explain your reasoning.

_____

_____

_____

_____

14 The diagram below shows how a manatee gets its energy.

| Energy source | Sea grass | Manatee |

What provides the energy for the sea grass, the manatee, and most life on Earth?

_____

What role does the sea grass play in this food chain? _____

According to this diagram, what type of consumer is the manatee? _____

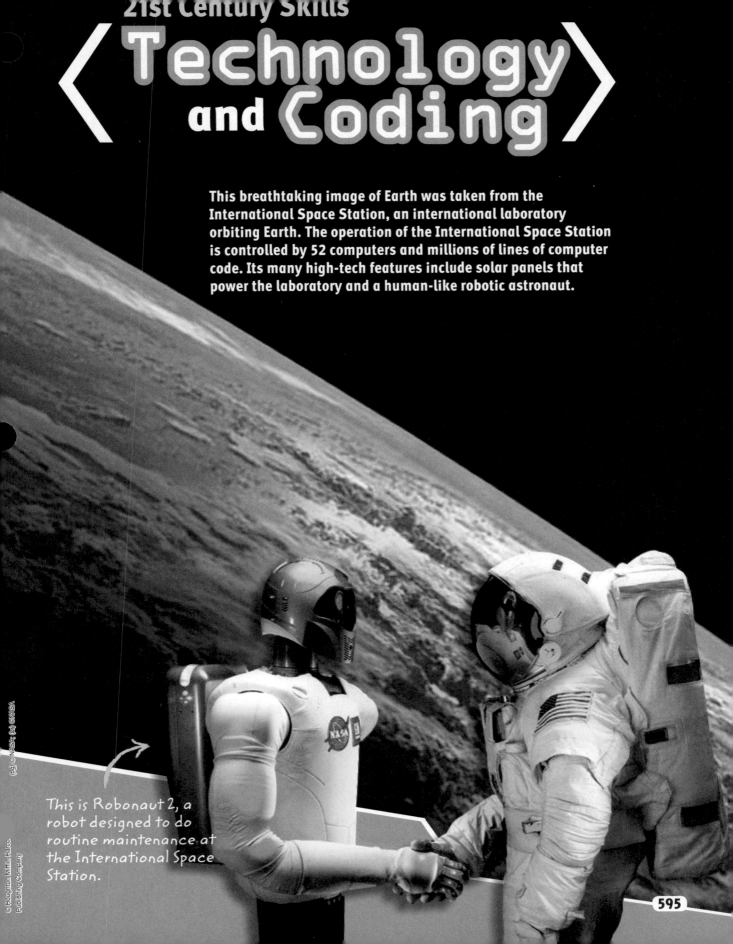

21st Century Skills

⟨Technology⟩
and Coding⟩

This breathtaking image of Earth was taken from the International Space Station, an international laboratory orbiting Earth. The operation of the International Space Station is controlled by 52 computers and millions of lines of computer code. Its many high-tech features include solar panels that power the laboratory and a human-like robotic astronaut.

This is Robonaut 2, a robot designed to do routine maintenance at the International Space Station.

Data Driven

What is computer science?

If you like computer technology and learning about how computers work, computer science might be for you. *Computer science* is the study of computer technology and how data is processed, stored, and accessed by computers. Computer science is an important part of many other areas, including science, math, engineering, robotics, medicine, game design, and 3D animation.

Computer technology is often described in terms of *hardware*, which are the physical components, and *software*, which are the programs or instructions that a computer runs. Computer scientists must understand how hardware and software work together. Computer scientists may develop new kinds of useful computer software. Or they may work with engineers to improve existing computer hardware.

The first electronic computer, the computer ENIAC (Electronic Numerical Integrator And Computer), was developed at the University of Pennsylvania in 1946.

The integrated circuit (IC), first developed in the 1950s, was instrumental in the development of small computer components.

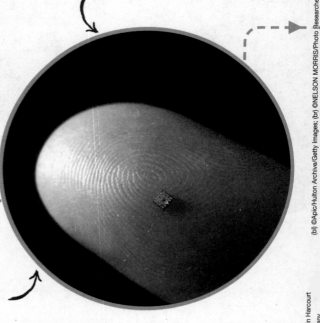

The development of the IC made it possible to reduce the overall size of computers and their components and to increase their processing speed.

How has computer technology changed over time?

Modern digital computer technology is less than 100 years old. Yet in that short amount of time, it has advanced rapidly. The earliest digital computers could perform only a limited number of tasks and were the size of an entire room. Over the decades, engineers continued to develop smaller, faster, and more powerful computers. Today's computers can process hundreds of millions of instructions per second!

Computer scientists and engineers think about what people want or need from computer technology. The most advanced hardware is not useful if people do not know how to use it. So computer scientists and engineers work to create software that is reliable, useful, and easy to use. Today's tablet computers, cell phones, and video game consoles can be used without any special training.

Advances in digital computer technology have helped make computers cheaper and easier to operate, which has allowed many more people to work and play with them.

1 **Claims • Evidence • Reasoning** Make a claim about whether modern computers are simpler or more complex than early computers. Summarize evidence to support the claim and explain your reasoning.

_____

_____

Computer Logic

What do computer scientists do?

Many people enjoy developing computer technology for fun. Learning how to create mobile phone games or Internet-enabled gadgets can be rewarding hobbies. For some people, that hobby may one day become a career in computer science. Working in computer science is a bit like solving a puzzle. Applying knowledge of how computers work to solve real-world problems requires collaboration, creativity, and logical, step-by-step thinking.

This is a kayak folded up.

They collaborate across many disciplines

Computers are valuable tools in math and science because they can perform complex calculations very quickly. Computers are useful to many other fields, too. For example, animators use computer technology to create realistic lighting effects in 3D animated films. Mechanics use computers to diagnose problems in car systems. For every field that relies on special software or computer technology, there is an opportunity for computer scientists and engineers to collaborate and develop solutions for those computing needs. Computer scientists must be able to define and understand the problems presented to them and to communicate and work with experts in other fields to develop the solutions.

Computational origami is a computer program used to model the ways in which different materials, including paper, can be folded. It combines computer science and the art of paper folding to create new technologies, such as this kayak.

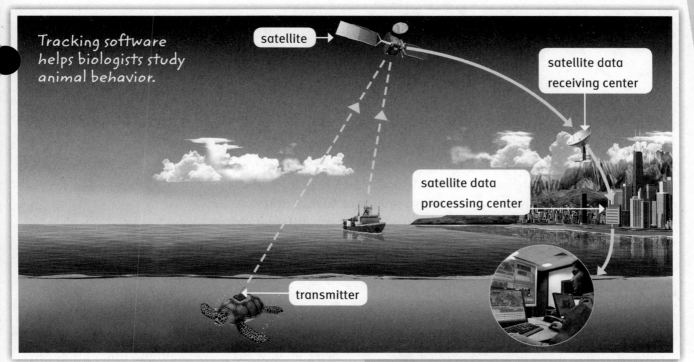

Tracking software helps biologists study animal behavior.

satellite

satellite data receiving center

satellite data processing center

transmitter

They help solve real-world problems

Some computer scientists carry out theoretical research. Others apply computer science concepts to develop software. Theoretical computer science and practical software development help solve real-world problems. For example, biologists need ways to safely and accurately track endangered animals. Computer science theories on artificial intelligence and pattern recognition have been applied to advanced animal-tracking technologies, such as satellite transmitters and aerial cameras. New kinds of image processing software now allow biologists to analyze the collected data in different ways.

They use logical, step-by-step thinking

Computers perform tasks given to them, and they do this very well. But in order to get the results they expect, computer scientists and programmers must write very accurate instructions. Computer science and programming requires logical thinking, deductive reasoning, and a good understanding of cause-and-effect relationships. When designing software, computer scientists must consider every possible user action and how the computer should respond to each action.

2 Support Your Claim Make a claim about how computer science is helping this scientist do her research. Support your claim with evidence from the image.

_____

_____

_____

Transmitters can be attached to animals to help track their movements.

Up to <Code>

How is computer software created?

Imagine that you are using a computer at the library to learn more about the history of electronic music. You use the library's database application to start searching for Internet resources. You also do a search to look for audio recordings. Finally, you open a word processor to take notes on the computer. Perhaps without realizing it, you've used many different pieces of software. Have you ever wondered how computer software is created?

Computer software is designed to address a need

Computer software can help us to learn more about our world. It can be useful to business. Or it can simply entertain us. Whatever its purpose, computer software should fulfill some human want or need. The first steps in creating software are precisely defining the need or want being addressed and planning how the software will work.

Computer software source code is written in a programming language

The instructions that tell a computer how to run video games, word processors, and other kinds of software are not written in a human language. They are written in a special programming language, or *code*. JavaScript, C++, and Python are examples of programming languages. Programming languages—like human languages—must follow certain rules in order to be understood by the computer. A series of instructions written in a programming language is called *source code*.

Identifying what need a computer program addresses is one of the first development steps.

Source code is revised

Sometimes, programmers make mistakes in their code. Many programming environments have a feature that alerts the programmer to certain errors, such as spelling mistakes in commands, missing portions of code, or logical errors in the sequence of instructions. However, many mistakes go undetected, too. Some errors may cause the program to function incorrectly or not at all. When this happens, the programmer must identify the error, correct it, and test the software again.

3 Identify This source code contains an error. Infer where the error is located. What does this code "tell" the computer to do? Write your answers below.

_____

_____

_____

_____

Computer software is user tested and revised

Once the software is created, it must be tested thoroughly to make sure it does not fail or behave in unexpected ways. It must also be tested to ensure that it meets users' needs. The creators of a piece of software might observe how people use it. Or they might ask users to provide feedback on certain features and test the software again.

```
13
14   # Scores are not tied, so check
15   # which player wins the round
16 ▾ if player1_score > player2_score:
17       print ("Player 1 wins!")
18 ▾ else:
19       prnt ("Player 2 wins!")
20

! Syntax error, line 19
```

Test running a program is important for finding and fixing errors in the code.

Play it Safe

How should I work with computers?

It is easy to lose track of time when you're sitting in front of a computer or game console. It's also easy to forget that things you say or do online can be seen and shared by many different people. Here are some tips for using computers safely and responsibly.

✓ Maintain good posture

Time can pass by quickly when you are working on a computer or another device. Balance computer time with other activities, including plenty of physical activity. When you are sitting at a computer, sit upright with your shoulders relaxed. Your eyes should be level with the top of the monitor and your feet should be flat on the ground.

✓ Observe electrical safety

Building your own electronics projects can be fun, but it's important to have an understanding of circuits and electrical safety first. Otherwise, you could damage your components or hurt yourself. The potential for an electrical shock is real when you open up a computer, work with frayed cords, or use ungrounded plugs or attempt to replace parts without understanding how to do so safely. Ask an adult for help before starting any projects. Also, avoid using a connected computer during thunderstorms.

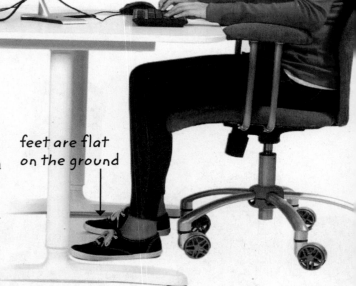

head and neck in a straight, neutral position

shoulders are relaxed

wrists are straight

feet are flat on the ground

Good posture will help you avoid the aches and injuries related to sitting in front of a computer for a long time.

✓ Handle and maintain computers properly

Be cautious when handling and transporting electronic devices. Dropping them or spilling liquids on them could cause serious damage. Keep computers away from dirt, dust, liquids, and moisture. Never use wet cleaning products unless they are specifically designed for use on electronics. Microfiber cloths can be used to clear smudges from device screens. Spilled liquids can cause circuits to short out and hardware to corrode. If a liquid spills on a device, unplug it and switch it off immediately, remove the battery and wipe up as much of the liquid inside the device as possible. Don't switch the device back on until it is completely dry.

✓ Do not post private information online

Talk to your family about rules for Internet use. Do not use the Internet to share private information such as photographs, your phone number, or your address. Do not respond to requests for personal details from people you do not know.

✓ Treat yourself and others with respect

It is important to treat others with respect when on the Internet. Don't send or post messages online that you wouldn't say to someone in person. Unfortunately, not everyone acts respectfully while online. Some people may say hurtful things to you or send you unwanted messages. Do not reply to unwanted messages. Alert a trusted adult to any forms of contact, such as messages or photos, that make you feel uncomfortable.

4 Apply Fill in the chart below with a suitable response to each scenario.

SCENARIO	YOUR RESPONSE
You receive a text message from an online store asking for your home address.	
You've been lying down in front of a laptop, and you notice that your neck is feeling a little sore.	
You need to take a laptop computer with you on your walk to school.	
You want to try assembling a robotics kit with a friend.	
Someone posts unfriendly comments directed at you.	

Career in Computing:
Game Programmer

What do video game programmers do?

Creating your own universe with its own set of rules is fun. Just ask a programmer who works on video games!

What skills are needed in game programming?

A programmer should know how to write code, but there are other important skills a programmer needs as well. An understanding of physics and math is important for calculating how objects move and interact in a game. Game programmers usually work on a team with other people, such as artists, designers, writers, and musicians. They must be able to communicate effectively, and ideally, the programmer should understand the other team members' roles.

How can I get started with game development?

You don't need a big budget or years of experience to try it out. There are books, videos, and websites that can help you get started. When you're first experimenting with game development, start small. Try making a very simple game like Tic-Tac-Toe. Once you've mastered that, you can try something more complex.

5 Claims • Evidence • Reasoning Make a claim about why working on a team would be important to the game development process. Summarize evidence to support the claim and explain your reasoning.

_____

_____

_____

Glossary

Pronunciation Key

Sound	Symbol	Example	Respelling	Sound	Symbol	Example	Respelling
ă	a	pat	PAT	ngk	ngk	bank	BANGK
ā	ay	pay	PAY	ŏ	ah	bottle	BAHT'l
âr	air	care	KAIR	ō	oh	toe	TOH
ä	ah	father	FAH•ther	ô	aw	caught	KAWT
är	ar	argue	AR•gyoo	ôr	ohr	roar	ROHR
ch	ch	chase	CHAYS	oi	oy	noisy	NOYZ•ee
ĕ	e	pet	PET	ŏŏ	u	book	BUK
ĕ (at end of a syllable)	eh	settee lessee	seh•TEE leh•SEE	ōō	oo	boot	BOOT
				ou	ow	pound	POWND
ĕr	ehr	merry	MEHR•ee	s	s	center	SEN•ter
ē	ee	beach	BEECH	sh	sh	cache	CASH
g	g	gas	GAS	ŭ	uh	flood	FLUHD
ĭ	i	pit	PIT	ûr	er	bird	BERD
ĭ (at end of a syllable)	ih	guitar	gih•TAR	z	z	xylophone	ZY•luh•fohn
				z	z	bags	BAGZ
				zh	zh	decision	dih•SIZH•uhn
ī	y eye (only for a complete syllable)	pie island	PY EYE•luhnd	ə	uh	around broken focus	uh•ROWND BROH•kuhn FOH•kuhs
îr	ir	hear	HIR	ər	er	winner	WIN•er
j	j	germ	JERM	th	th	thin they	THIN THAY
k	k	kick	KIK	w	w	one	WUHN
ng	ng	thing	THING	wh	hw	whether	HWETH•er

A

abiotic factor an environmental factor that is not associated with the activities of living organisms (543)
factor abiótico un factor ambiental que no está asociado con las actividades de los seres vivos

absolute dating any method of measuring the age of an event or object in years (222)
datación absoluta cualquier método que sirve para determinar la edad de un suceso u objeto en años

absorption in optics, the transfer of light energy to particles of matter (351)
absorción en la óptica, la transferencia de energía luminosa a las partículas de materia

acid precipitation (AS•id prih•sip•ih•TAY•shun) precipitation, such as rain, sleet, or snow, that contains a high concentration of acids, often because of the pollution of the atmosphere (283)
precipitación ácida precipitación tal como lluvia, aguanieve o nieve, que contiene una alta concentración de ácidos debido a la contaminación de la atmósfera

adaptation a characteristic that improves an individual's ability to survive and reproduce in a particular environment (421)
adaptación una característica que mejora la capacidad de un individuo para sobrevivir y reproducirse en un determinado ambiente

air pollution the contamination of the atmosphere by the introduction of pollutants from human and natural sources (281)
contaminación del aire la contaminación de la atmósfera debido a la introducción de contaminantes provenientes de fuentes humanas y naturales

air quality (AIR KWAHL•ih•tee) a measure of the pollutants in the air that is used to express how clean or polluted the air is (284)
calidad de aire una medida de los contaminantes presentes en el aire que se usa para expresar el nivel de pureza o contaminación del aire

allele (uh•LEEL) one of the alternative forms of a gene that governs a characteristic, such as hair color (480)
alelo una de las formas alternativas de un gene que rige un carácter, como por ejemplo, el color del cabello

amplitude the maximum distance that the particles of a wave's medium vibrate from their rest position (324)
amplitud la distancia máxima a la que vibran las partículas del medio de una onda a partir de su posición de reposo

artificial selection the human practice of breeding animals or plants that have certain desired traits (418, 525)
selección artificial la práctica humana de criar animales o cultivar plantas que tienen ciertos caracteres deseados

asexual reproduction (ay•SEHK•shoo•uhl ree•pruh•DUHK•shuhn) reproduction that does not involve the union of sex cells and in which one parent produces offspring that are genetically identical to the parent (468)
reproducción asexual reproducción que no involucra la unión de células sexuales, en la que un solo progenitor produce descendencia que es genéticamente igual al progenitor

asthenosphere the solid, plastic layer of the mantle beneath the lithosphere; made of mantle rock that flows very slowly, which allows tectonic plates to move on top of it (126)
astenosfera la capa sólida y plástica del manto, que se encuentra debajo de la litosfera; está formada por roca del manto que fluye muy lentamente, lo cual permite que las placas tectónicas se muevan en su superficie

atom the smallest unit of an element that maintains the properties of that element (92)
átomo la unidad más pequeña de un elemento que conserva las propiedades de ese elemento

B

biome (BY•ohm) a large region characterized by a specific type of climate and certain types of plant and animal communities (546)
bioma una región extensa caracterizada por un tipo de clima específico y ciertos tipos de comunidades de plantas y animales

biotechnology (by•oh•tek•NAHL•uh•jee) the use and application of living things and biological processes (524)
biotecnología el uso y la aplicación de seres vivos y procesos biológicos

biotic factor an environmental factor that is associated with or results from the activities of living organisms (542)
factor biótico un factor ambiental que está asociado con las actividades de los seres vivos o que resulta de ellas

C

calorie the amount of energy needed to raise the temperature of 1 g of water 1 °C; the Calorie used to indicate the energy content of food is a kilocalorie (395)
caloría la cantidad de energía que se requiere para aumentar la temperatura de 1 g de agua en 1 °C; la Caloría que se usa para indicar el contenido energético de los alimentos es la kilocaloría

carnivore an organism that eats animals (557)
carnívoro un organismo que se alimenta de animales

cell cycle the life cycle of a cell (450)
ciclo celular el ciclo de vida de una célula

chromosomes (KROH•muh•sohmz) in a eukaryotic cell, one of the structures in the nucleus that are made up of DNA and protein; in a prokaryotic cell, the main ring of DNA (449)
cromosoma en una célula eucariótica, una de las estructuras del núcleo que está hecha de ADN y proteína; en una célula procariótica, el anillo principal de ADN

cleavage in geology, the tendency of a mineral to split along specific planes of weakness to form smooth, flat surfaces (99)
exfoliación en geología, la tendencia de un mineral a agrietarse a lo largo de planos débiles específicos y formar superficies lisas y planas

climate the weather conditions in an area over a long period of time (202)
clima las condiciones del tiempo en un área durante un largo período de tiempo

clone (KLOHN) an organism, cell, or piece of genetic material that is genetically identical to one from which it was derived (527)
clon un organismo, célula o fragmento de material genético que es genéticamente idéntico al organismo, célula o material genético del cual proviene

codominance (koh•DAHM•uh•nuhns) a condition in which two alleles are expressed such that the phenotype of a heterozygous individual is a combination of the phenotypes of the two homozygous parents (485)
codominancia una condición en la que dos alelos están expresados de modo que el fenotipo de un individuo heterocigoto es una combinación de los fenotipos de los dos padres homocigotos

commensalism a relationship between two organisms in which one organism benefits and the other is unaffected (570)
comensalismo una relación entre dos organismos en la que uno se beneficia y el otro no es afectado

community all of the populations of species that live in the same habitat and interact with each other (545)
comunidad todas las poblaciones de especies que viven en el mismo hábitat e interactúan entre sí

competition (kahm•pih•TISH•uhn) ecological relationship in which two or more organisms depend on the same limited resource (572)
competencia la relación ecológica en la que dos o más organismos dependen del mismo recurso limitado

compound a substance made up of atoms or ions of two or more different elements joined by chemical bonds (92)
compuesto una sustancia formada por átomos de dos o más elementos diferentes unidos por enlaces químicos

compression (kuhm•PRESH•uhn) stress that occurs when forces act to squeeze an object (151, 161)
compresión estrés que se produce cuando distintas fuerzas actúan para estrechar un objeto

conduction (kuhn•DUHK•shuhn) the transfer of energy as heat through a material (397)
conducción calor la transferencia de energía en forma de calor a través del contacto directo

conductor (kuhn•DUHK•ter) a material that transfers energy easily (397)
conductor un material a través del cual se transfiere energía

conservation (kahn•sur•VAY•shuhn) the wise use of and preservation of natural resources (292)
conservación el uso inteligente y la preservación de los recursos naturales

consumer an organism that eats other organisms or organic matter (557)
consumidor un organismo que se alimenta de otros organismos o de materia orgánica

convection (kuhn•VECK•shuhn) the movement of matter due to differences in density that are caused by temperature variations; can result in the transfer of energy as heat (125, 140, 398)
convección el movimiento de la materia debido a diferencias en la densidad que se producen por variaciones en la temperatura; puede resultar en la transferencia de energía en forma de calor

convergent boundary the boundary between tectonic plates that are colliding (138)
límite convergente el límite entre placas tectónicas que chocan

coral reef a limestone ridge found in tropical climates and composed of coral fragments that are deposited around organic remains (586)
arrecife de coral una cumbre de piedra caliza ubicada en climas tropicales, formada por fragmentos de coral depositados alrededor de restos orgánicos

core the central part of Earth below the mantle (125)
núcleo la parte central de la Tierra, debajo del manto

crust the thin and solid outermost layer of Earth above the mantle (125)
corteza la capa externa, delgada y sólida de la Tierra, que se encuentra sobre el manto

crystal natural solid substance that has a definite geometric shape (93)
cristal sustancia sólida natural que tiene una forma geométrica definida

cytokinesis (sy•toh•kuh•NEE•sis) the division of the cytoplasm of a cell; cytokinesis follows the division of the cell's nucleus by mitosis or meiosis (451)
citocinesis la división del citoplasma de una célula; la citocinesis ocurre después de que el núcleo de la célula se divide por mitosis o meiosis

data (DAY•tuh) information gathered by observation or experimentation that can be used in calculating or reasoning (23)
datos la información recopilada por medio de la observación o experimentación que puede usarse para hacer cálculos o razonar

decomposer an organism that gets energy by breaking down the remains of dead organisms or animal wastes and consuming or absorbing the nutrients (556)
descomponedor un organismo que, para obtener energía, desintegra los restos de organismos muertos o los desechos de animales y consume o absorbe los nutrientes

deforestation (dee•fohr•ih•STAY•shuhn) the removal of trees and other vegetation from an area (255)
deforestación la remoción de árboles y demás vegetación de un área

deformation (dee•fohr•MAY•shuhn) the bending, tilting, and breaking of Earth's crust; the change in the shape of rock in response to stress (148, 159)
deformación el proceso de doblar, inclinar y romper la corteza de la Tierra; el cambio en la forma de una roca en respuesta a la tensión

degree (dih•GREE) the units of a temperature scale (384)
grado la unidad de una escala de temperatura

dependent variable (dih•PEN•duhnt VAIR•ee•uh•buhl) in a scientific investigation, the factor that changes as a result of manipulation of one or more independent variables (23)
variable dependiente en una investigación científica, el factor que cambia como resultado de la manipulación de una o más variables independientes

deposition the process in which material is laid down (109)
deposición el proceso por medio del cual un material se deposita

desertification (dih•zer•tuh•fih•KAY•shuhn) the process by which human activities or climatic changes make areas more desertlike (255)
desertificación el proceso por el cual las actividades humanas o los cambios climáticos hacen que un área se vuelva más parecida a un desierto

divergent boundary the boundary between two tectonic plates that are moving away from each other (139, 161)
límite divergente el límite entre dos placas tectónicas que se están separando una de la otra

DNA deoxyribonucleic acid, the material that contains the information that determines inherited characteristics (449, 510)
ADN ácido desoxirribonucleico, el material que contiene la información que determina las características que se heredan

dominant (DAHM•uh•nuhnt) describes the allele that is fully expressed when carried by only one of a pair of homologous chromosomes (479)
dominante describe al alelo que contribuye al fenotipo de un individuo cuando una o dos copias del alelo están presentes en el genotipo de ese individuo

earthquake a movement or trembling of the ground that is caused by a sudden release of energy when rocks along a fault move (158)
terremoto un movimiento o temblor del suelo causado por una liberación súbita de energía que se produce cuando las rocas ubicadas a lo largo de una falla se mueven

ecology the study of the interactions of living organisms with one another and with their environment (542)
ecología el estudio de las interacciones de los seres vivos entre sí mismos y entre sí mismos y su ambiente

ecosystem a community of organisms and their abiotic, or nonliving, environment (545)
ecosistema una comunidad de organismos y su ambiente abiótico o no vivo

efficiency (ee•FIH•shuhn•see) a quantity, usually expressed as a percentage, that measures the ratio of work output to work input (376)
eficiencia una cantidad, generalmente expresada como un porcentaje, que mide la relación entre el trabajo de entrada y el trabajo de salida

elastic rebound the sudden return of elastically deformed rock to its undeformed shape (159)
rebote elástico ocurre cuando una roca deformada elásticamente vuelve súbitamente a su forma no deformada

electromagnetic spectrum all of the frequencies or wavelengths of electromagnetic radiation (338)
espectro electromagnético todas las frecuencias o longitudes de onda la radiación electromagnética

electromagnetic wave a wave that consists of electric and magnetic fields that vibrate at right angles to each other (318)
onda electromagnética una onda que está formada por campos eléctricos y magnéticos que vibran formando un ángulo recto unos con otros

element a substance that cannot be separated or broken down into simpler substances by chemical means; all atoms of an element have the same atomic number (92)
elemento una sustancia que no se puede separar o descomponer en sustancias más simples por medio de métodos químicos; todos los átomos de un elemento tienen el mismo número atómico

empirical evidence (em•PIR•ih•kuhl EV•ih•duhns) the observations, measurements, and other types of data that people gather and test to support and evaluate scientific explanations (10)
evidencia empírica las observaciones, mediciones y demás tipos de datos que se recopilan y examinan para apoyar y evaluar explicaciones científicas

energy resource a natural resource that humans use to generate energy (245)
recurso energético un recurso natural que utilizan los humanos para generar energía

energy transformation the process of energy changing from one form into another (374)
transformación de energía el proceso de cambio de un tipo de energía a otro

engineering (en•juh•NIR•ing) the application of science and mathematics to solve real-life problems (44)
ingeniería la aplicación de las ciencias y las matemáticas para resolver problemas de la vida diaria

epicenter (EP•i•sen•ter) the point on Earth's surface directly above an earthquake's starting point, or focus (158)
epicentro el punto de la superficie de la Tierra que queda justo arriba del punto de inicio, o foco, de un terremoto

erosion the process by which wind, water, ice, or gravity transports soil and sediment from one location to another (109)
erosión el proceso por medio del cual el viento, el agua, el hielo o la gravedad transporta tierra y sedimentos de un lugar a otro

estuary an area where fresh water mixes with salt water from the ocean (587)
estuario un área donde el agua dulce de los ríos se mezcla con el agua salada del océano

eutrophication (yoo•TRAWF•ih•kay•shuhn) an increase in the amount of nutrients, such as nitrates, in a marine or aquatic ecosystem (264)
eutrofización un aumento en la cantidad de nutrientes, tales como nitratos, en un ecosistema marino o acuático

evolution the process in which inherited characteristics within a population change over generations such that new species sometimes arise (416)
evolución el proceso por medio del cual las características heredadas dentro de una población cambian con el transcurso de las generaciones de manera tal que a veces surgen nuevas especies

experiment (ik•SPEHR•uh•muhnt) an organized procedure to study something under controlled conditions (20)
experimento un procedimiento organizado que se lleva a cabo bajo condiciones controladas para estudiar algo

extinction the death of every member of a species (423)
extinción la muerte de todos los miembros de una especie

fault (FAWLT) a break in a body of rock along which one block moves relative to another (150, 159)
falla una grieta en un cuerpo rocoso a lo largo de la cual un bloque se mueve respecto de otro

fertilization (fer•tl•i•ZAY•shuhn) the union of a male and female gamete to form a zygote (470)
fecundación la unión de un gameto masculino y femenino para formar un cigoto

focus the location within Earth along a fault at which the first motion of an earthquake occurs (158)
foco el lugar dentro de la Tierra a lo largo de una falla donde ocurre el primer movimiento de un terremoto

folding the bending of rock layers due to stress (149)
plegamiento fenómeno que ocurre cuando las capas de roca se doblan debido a la compresión

food chain the pathway of energy transfer through various stages as a result of the feeding patterns of a series of organisms (559)
cadena alimenticia la vía de transferencia de energía través de varias etapas, que ocurre como resultado de los patrones de alimentación de una serie de organismos

food web a diagram that shows the feeding relationships between organisms in an ecosystem (560)
red alimenticia un diagrama que muestra las relaciones de alimentación entre los organismos de un ecosistema

fossil the trace or remains of an organism that lived long ago, most commonly preserved in sedimentary rock (195, 214, 431)
fósil los indicios o los restos de un organismo que vivió hace mucho tiempo, comúnmente preservados en las rocas sedimentarias

fossil fuel a nonrenewable energy resource formed from the remains of organisms that lived long ago; examples include oil, coal, and natural gas (243, 300)
combustible fósil un recurso energético no renovable formado a partir de los restos de organismos que vivieron hace mucho tiempo; algunos ejemplos incluyen el petróleo, el carbón y el gas natural

fossil record the history of life in the geologic past as indicated by the traces or remains of living things (198, 431)
registro fósil la historia de la vida en el pasado geológico según la indican los rastros o restos de seres vivos

frequency (FRE•kwuhn•see) the number of waves produced in a given amount of time, such as a second (325)
frecuencia el número de ondas producidas en una cantidad de tiempo determinada, como por ejemplo, un segundo

G

gene one set of instructions for an inherited trait (480)
  gene un conjunto de instrucciones para un carácter heredado

genetic engineering a technology in which the genome of a living cell is modified for medical or industrial use (526)
  ingeniería genética una tecnología en la que el genoma de una célula viva se modifica con fines médicos o industriales

genotype (JEEN•uh•typ) the entire genetic makeup of an organism; also the combination of genes for one or more specific traits (481)
  genotipo la constitución genética completa de un organismo; también, la combinación de genes para uno o más caracteres específicos

geologic column an ordered arrangement of rock layers that is based on the relative ages of the rocks and in which the oldest rocks are at the bottom (215)
  columna geológica un arreglo ordenado de capas de rocas que se basa en la edad relativa de las rocas y en el cual las rocas más antiguas están al fondo

greenhouse effect the warming of the surface and lower atmosphere of Earth that occurs when water vapor, carbon dioxide, and other gases absorb and reradiate thermal energy (280)
  efecto invernadero el calentamiento de la superficie y de la parte más baja de la atmósfera, el cual se produce cuando el vapor de agua, el dióxido de carbono y otros gases absorben y vuelven a irradiar la energía térmica

H

habitat the place where an organism usually lives (548)
  hábitat el lugar donde vive normalmente un organismo

half-life the time required for half of a sample of a radioactive isotope to break down by radioactive decay to form a daughter isotope (222)
  vida media el tiempo que se requiere para que la mitad de una muestra de un isótopo radiactivo se descomponga por desintegración radiactiva y forme un isótopo hijo

heat the energy transferred between objects that are at different temperatures (394)
  calor la transferencia de energía entre objetos que están a temperaturas diferentes

herbivore an organism that eats only plants (557)
  herbívoro un organismo que sólo come plantas

heredity (huh•RED•ih•tee) the passing of genetic material from parent to offspring (478)
  herencia la transmisión de material genético de padres a hijos

hertz (HERTS) a unit of frequency equal to one cycle per second (325)
  hertz una unidad de frecuencia que representa un ciclo por segundo

homologous chromosome (huh•MAHL•uh•guhs KROH•muh•sohmz) chromosomes that have the same sequence of genes and the same structure (458)
  cromosoma homólogo cromosomas con la misma secuencia de genes y la misma estructura

hot spot a volcanically active area of Earth's surface, commonly far from a tectonic plate boundary (178)
  mancha caliente un área volcánicamente activa de la superficie de la Tierra que comúnmente se encuentra lejos de un límite entre placas tectónicas

hypothesis (hy•PAHTH•i•sis) a testable idea or explanation that leads to scientific investigation (22)
  hipótesis una idea o explicación que conlleva a la investigación científica y que se puede probar

I

ice core (YS KOHR) a long cylinder of ice obtained from drilling through ice caps or ice sheets; used to study past climates (203)
  testigo de hielo un cilindro largo de hielo que se obtiene al perforar campos de hielo o capas de hielo continentales; se usa para estudiar los climas del pasado

igneous rock rock that forms when magma cools and solidifies (110)
  roca ígnea una roca que se forma cuando el magma se enfría y se solidifica

incomplete dominance (in•kuhm•PLEET DAHM•uh•nuhns) a condition in which two alleles are expressed such that the phenotype of a heterozygous individual is an intermediate of the phenotypes of the two homozygous parents (484)
  dominancia incompleta una condición en la que dos alelos se expresan de modo que el fenotipo de un individuo heterocigoto es intermedio entre los fenotipos de sus dos padres homocigotos

independent variable (in•dih•PEN•duhnt VAIR•ee•uh•buhl) in a scientific investigation, the factor that is deliberately manipulated (23)
  variable independiente en una investigación científica, el factor que se manipula deliberadamente

infrared (in•fruh•RED) electromagnetic wavelengths immediatley outside the red end of the visible spectrum (338)
  infrarrojo longitudes de onda electromagnéticas inmediatamente adyacentes al color rojo en el espectro visible

insulator (IN•suh•lay•ter) a material that reduces or prevents the transfer of energy (397)
aislante un material que reduce o evita la transferencia de energía

interphase (IN•ter•fayz) the period of the cell cycle during which activities such as cell growth and protein synthesis occur without visible signs of cell division (450)
interfase el período del ciclo celular durante el cual las actividades como el crecimiento celular y la síntesis de proteínas existen sin signos visibles de división celular

introduced species a species introduced either by accident or on purpose by human actions into places beyond the species's natural range (581)
especie exótica una especie que se ha introducido en lugares ajenos a su área de distribución natural, ya sea por la acción humana o por accidente

kinetic theory of matter (kuh•NET•ik THEE•uh•ree UHV MAT•er) a theory that states that all of the particles that make up matter are constantly in motion (382)
teoría cinética de la materia una teoría que establece que todas las partículas que forman la materia están en movimiento constante

land degradation (LAND deg•ruh•DAY•shuhn) the process by which human activity and natural processes damage land to the point that it can no longer support the local ecosystem (254)
degradación del suelo el proceso por el cual la actividad humana y los procesos naturales dañan el suelo de modo que el ecosistema local no puede subsistir

lava magma that flows onto Earth's surface; the rock that forms when lava cools and solidifies (172)
lava magma que fluye a la superficie terrestre; la roca que se forma cuando la lava se enfría y se solidifica

law a descriptive statement or equation that reliably predicts events under certain conditions (8)
ley una ecuación o afirmación descriptiva que predice sucesos de manera confiable en determinadas condiciones

law of conservation of energy the law that states that energy cannot be created or destroyed but can be changed from one form to another (375)
ley de la conservación de la energía la ley que establece que la energía ni se crea ni se destruye, sólo se transforma de una forma a otra

life-cycle analysis (LYF SY•kuhl uh•NAL•sis) the evaluation of the materials and energy used for the manufacture, transportation, sale, use, and disposal of a technology (59)
análisis del ciclo de vida la evaluación de los materiales y la energía usados para la fabricación, transporte, veta, uso y eliminación de una tecnología

limiting factor an environmental factor that prevents an organism or population from reaching its full potential of size or activity (580)
factor limitante un factor ambiental que impide que un organismo o población alcance su máximo potencial de distribución o de actividad

lithosphere the solid, outer layer of Earth that consists of the crust and the rigid upper part of the mantle (126)
litosfera la capa externa y sólida de la Tierra que está formada por la corteza y la parte superior y rígida del manto

longitudinal wave (lahn•jih•TOOD•n•uhl) a wave in which the particles of the medium vibrate parallel to the direction of wave motion (317)
onda longitudinal una onda en la que las partículas del medio vibran paralelamente a la dirección del movimiento de la onda

luster the way in which a mineral reflects light (99)
brillo la forma en que un mineral refleja la luz

magma (MAG•muh) the molten or partially molten rock material containing trapped gases produced under the Earth's surface (172)
magma el material rocoso total o parcialmente fundido que contiene gases atrapados que se producen debajo de la superficie terrestre

mantle the layer of rock between the Earth's crust and core (125)
manto la capa de roca que se encuentra entre la corteza terrestre y el núcleo

material resource a natural resource that humans use to make objects or to consume as food and drink (244)
recurso material un recurso natural que utilizan los seres humanos para fabricar objetos o para consumir como alimento o bebida

matter anything that has mass and takes up space (92)
materia cualquier cosa que tiene masa y ocupa un lugar en el espacio

mechanical wave a wave that requires a medium through which to travel (318)
onda mecánica una onda que requiere un medio para desplazarse

medium a physical environment in which phenomena occur (314)
medio un ambiente físico en el que ocurren fenómenos

Publishing Company

meiosis (my•OH•sis) a process in cell division during which the number of chromosomes decreases to half the original number by two divisions of the nucleus, which results in the production of sex cells gametes or spores (459)
meiosis un proceso de división celular durante el cual el número de cromosomas disminuye a la mitad del número original por medio de dos divisiones del núcleo, lo cual resulta en la producción de células sexuales gametos o esporas

mesosphere (MEZ•uh•sfir) 1. the strong, lower part of the mantle between the asthenosphere and the outer core, 2. the layer of the atmosphere between the stratosphere and the thermosphere and in which temperature decreases as altitude increases (126)
mesosfera 1. la parte fuerte e inferior del manto que se encuentra entre la astenosfera y el núcleo externo, 2. la capa de la atmósfera que se encuentra entre la estratosfera y la termosfera, en la cual la temperatura disminuye al aumentar la altitud

metamorphic rock a rock that forms from other rocks as a result of intense heat, pressure, or chemical processes (110)
roca metamórfica una roca que se forma a partir de otras rocas como resultado de calor intenso, presión o procesos químicos

mineral a naturally formed, inorganic solid with a crystalline structure (92)
mineral un sólido inorgánico formado naturalmente que tiene una estructura cristalina

mitosis (my•TOH•sis) in eukaryotic cells, a process of cell division that forms two new nuclei, each of which has the same number of chromosomes (451)
mitosis en las células eucarióticas, un proceso de división celular que forma dos núcleos nuevos, cada uno de los cuales posee el mismo número de cromosomas

model a pattern, plan, representation, or description designed to show the structure or workings of an object, system, or concept (38)
modelo un diseño, plan, representación o descripción cuyo objetivo es mostrar la estructura o funcionamiento de un objeto, sistema o concepto

mutation a change in the structure or amount of the genetic material of an organism (420, 515)
mutación un cambio en la estructura o cantidad del material genético de un organismo

mutualism a relationship between two species in which both species benefit (570)
mutualismo una relación entre dos especies en la que ambas se benefician

native species a species that was not introduced and that naturally occurs in a given ecosystem both in the past and now (581)

especie nativa una especie que no se ha introducido y que se encuentra de forma natural en un ecosistema dado, del pasado o actual

natural resource any natural material that is used by humans, such as water, petroleum, minerals, forests, and animals (242)
recurso natural cualquier material natural que es utilizado por los seres humanos, como agua, petróleo, minerales, bosques y animales

natural selection the process by which individuals that are better adapted to their environment survive and reproduce more successfully than less well adapted individuals do (420)
selección natural el proceso por medio del cual los individuos que están mejor adaptados a su ambiente sobreviven y se reproducen con más éxito que los individuos menos adaptados

niche (NICH) the role of a species in its community, including use of its habitat and its relationships with other species (548)
nicho el papel que juega una especie en su comunidad, incluidos el uso de su hábitat y su relación con otras especies

nonpoint-source pollution pollution that comes from many sources rather than from a single specific site; an example is pollution that reaches a body of water from streets and storm sewers (264)
contaminación no puntual contaminación que proviene de muchas fuentes, en lugar de provenir de un solo sitio específico; un ejemplo es la contaminación que llega a una masa de agua a partir de las calles y los drenajes

nonrenewable resource a resource that forms at a rate that is much slower than the rate at which the resource is consumed (243)
recurso no renovable un recurso que se forma a una tasa que es mucho más lenta que la tasa a la que se consume

nucleotide in a nucleic-acid chain, a subunit that consists of a sugar, a phosphate, and a nitrogenous base (513)
nucleótido en una cadena de ácidos nucleicos, una subunidad formada por un azúcar, un fosfato y una base nitrogenada

observation the process of obtaining information by using the senses; the information obtained by using the senses (21)
observación el proceso de obtener información por medio de los sentidos; la información que se obtiene al usar los sentidos

omnivore an organism that eats both plants and animals (557)
omnívoro un organismo que come tanto plantas como animales

opaque (oh•PAYK) describes an object that is not transparent or translucent; a material through which light cannot pass (351)
opaco término que describe un objeto que no es transparente ni translúcido

P

Pangaea (pan•JEE•uh) the supercontinent that formed 300 million years ago and that began to break up 200 million years ago (133)
Pangea el supercontinente que se formó hace 300 millones de años y que comenzó a separarse hace 200 millones de años

parasitism (PAR•uh•sih•tiz•uhm) a relationship between two species in which one species, the parasite, benefits from the other species, the host, which is harmed (571)
parasitismo una relación entre dos especies en la que una, el parásito, se beneficia de la otra, el huésped, que resulta perjudicada

particulate (per•TIK•yuh•lit) a tiny particle of solid that is suspended in air or water (281)
material particulado una pequeña partícula de material sólido que se encuentra suspendida en el aire o el agua

pedigree a diagram that shows the occurrence of a genetic trait in several generations of a family (496)
pedigrí un diagrama que muestra la incidencia de un carácter genético en varias generaciones de una familia

phenotype (FEEN•uh•typ) an organism's appearance or other detectable characteristic (481)
fenotipo la apariencia de un organismo u otra característica perceptible

plate tectonics the theory that explains how large pieces of the lithosphere, called plates, move and change shape (136)
tectónica de placas la teoría que explica cómo las grandes partes de litosfera, denominadas placas, se mueven y cambian de forma

point-source pollution pollution that comes from a specific site (264)
contaminación puntual contaminación que proviene de un lugar específico

population a group of organisms of the same species that live in a specific geographical area (544)
población un grupo de organismos de la misma especie que viven en un área geográfica específica

potable suitable for drinking (267)
potable que puede beberse

predator an organism that kills and eats all or part of another organism (568)
depredador un organismo que mata y se alimenta de otro organismo o de parte de él

prey an organism that is killed and eaten by another organism (568)
presa un organismo al que otro organismo mata para alimentarse de él

probability the likelihood that a possible future event will occur in any given instance of the event (494)
probabilidad la probabilidad de que ocurra un posible suceso futuro en cualquier caso dado del suceso

producer an organism that can make its own food by using energy from its surroundings (556)
productor un organismo que puede elaborar sus propios alimentos utilizando la energía de su entorno

prototype (PROH•tuh•typ) a test model of a product (47)
prototipo prueba modelo de un producto

Pugh chart (PYOO CHART) a table used to compare the features of multiple items, such as technological products or solutions (60)
tabla de Pugh una tabla que se usa para comparar las características de muchos elementos, como productos o soluciones tecnológicas

Punnett square a graphic used to predict the results of a genetic cross (492)
cuadro de Punnett una gráfica que se usa para predecir los resultados de una cruza genética

R

radiation (ray•dee•AY•shuhn) the transfer of energy as electromagnetic waves (336, 398)
radiación la transferencia de energía en forma de ondas electromagnéticas

radioactive decay the process in which a radioactive isotope tends to break down into a stable isotope of the same element or another element (222)
desintegración radiactiva el proceso por medio del cual un isótopo radiactivo tiende a desintegrarse y formar un isótopo estable del mismo elemento o de otro elemento

radiometric dating (ray•dee•oh•MET•rik DAYT•ing) a method of determining the absolute age of an object by comparing the relative percentages of a radioactive parent isotope and a stable daughter isotope (223)
datación radiométrica un método para determinar la edad absoluta de un objeto comparando los porcentajes relativos de un isótopo radiactivo precursor y un isótopo estable hijo

ratio (RAY•shee•oh) a comparison of two numbers using division (494)
razón comparacion de dos números mediante la división

recessive (rih•SES•iv) in genetics, describes an allele that is expressed only when no dominant allele is present in an individual (479)

recesivo en genética, término que describe un alelo que se expresa sólo cuando no hay un alelo dominante presente en el individuo

reflection the bouncing back of a ray of light, sound, or heat when the ray hits a surface that it does not go through (351)
reflexión el rebote de un rayo de luz, sonido o calor cuando el rayo golpea una superficie pero no la atraviesa

refraction (ri•FRAK•shuhn) the bending of a wave as it passes between two substances in which the speed of the wave differs (354)
refracción el curvamiento de una onda a medida que pasa entre dos sustancias en el que la velocidad de la onda difiere

relative dating any method of determining whether an event or object is older or younger than other events or objects (208)
datación relativa cualquier método que se utiliza para determinar si un acontecimiento u objeto es más viejo o más joven que otros acontecimientos u objetos

renewable resource a natural resource that can be replaced at the same rate at which the resource is consumed (243)
recurso renovable un recurso natural que puede reemplazarse a la misma tasa a la que se consume

replication the duplication of a DNA molecule (514)
replicación la duplicación de una molécula de ADN

reservoir (REZ•uhr•vwohr) an artificial body of water that usually forms behind a dam (269)
represa una masa artificial de agua que normalmente se forma detrás de una presa

ribosome a cell organelle composed of RNA and protein; the site of protein synthesis (517)
ribosoma un organelo celular compuesto de ARN y proteína; el sitio donde ocurre la síntesis de proteínas

rift zone an area of deep cracks that forms between two tectonic plates that are pulling away from each other (114)
zona de rift un área de grietas profundas que se forma entre dos placas tectónicas que se están alejando una de la otra

risk-benefit analysis (risk•BEN•uh•fit uh•NAL•ih•sis) the comparison of the risks and benefits of a decision or product (58)
análisis de riesgo-beneficio la comparación de los riesgos y los beneficios de una decisión o de un producto

RNA ribonucleic acid, a molecule that is present in all living cells and that plays a role in protein production (516)
ARN ácido ribonucleico, una molécula que está presente en todas las células vivas y que juega un papel en la producción de proteínas

rock cycle the series of processes in which rock forms, changes from one type to another, is destroyed, and forms again by geologic processes (111)

ciclo de las rocas la serie de procesos por medio de los cuales una roca se forma, cambia de un tipo a otro, se destruye y se forma nuevamente por procesos geológicos

S

scattering (SKAT•er•ing) the spreading out of light rays in all directions (355)
dispersión la dispersio'n de los rayos de luz en todas las direcciones

sea-floor spreading the process by which new oceanic lithosphere sea floor forms when magma rises to Earth's surface at mid-ocean ridges and solidifies, as older, existing sea floor moves away from the ridge (134)
expansión del suelo marino el proceso por medio del cual se forma nueva litósfera oceánica suelo marino cuando el magma sube a la superficie de la Tierra en las dorsales oceánicas y se solidifica, a medida que el antiguo suelo marino existente se aleja de la dorsal oceánica

sedimentary rock a rock that forms from compressed or cemented layers of sediment (110)
roca sedimentaria una roca que se forma a partir de capas comprimidas o cementadas de sedimento

sexual reproduction (SEHK•shoo•uhl ree•pruh•DUHK•shuhn) reproduction in which the sex cells from two parents unite to produce offspring that share traits from both parents (470)
reproducción sexual reproducción en la que se unen las células sexuales de los dos progenitores para producir descendencia que comparte caracteres de ambos progenitores

shear stress (SHIR STRES) stress that occurs when forces act in parallel but opposite directions, pushing parts of a solid in opposite directions (150)
tensión de corte el estrés que se produce cuando dos fuerzas actúan en direcciones paralelas pero opuestas, lo que empuja las partes de un sólido en direcciones opuestas

smog (SMAHG) air pollution that forms when ozone and vehicle exhaust react with sunlight (282)
esmog contaminación del aire que se produce cuando el ozono y sustancias químicas como los gases de los escapes de los vehículos reaccionan con la luz solar

species (SPEE•seez) a group of organisms that are closely related and can mate to produce fertile offspring (544)
especie un grupo de organismos que tienen un parentesco cercano y que pueden aparearse para producir descendencia fértil

stewardship (stoo•urd•SHIP) behavior that leads to the protection, conservation, and reclamation of natural resources (293)

gestión ambiental responsable comportamiento que hace posible la protección, la conservación y el rescate de los recursos naturales

streak the color of a mineral in powdered form (98)
veta el color de un mineral en forma de polvo

subsidence the sinking of regions of the Earth's crust to lower elevations (114)
hundimiento del terreno el hundimiento de regiones de la corteza terrestre a elevaciones más bajas

superposition (soo•per•puh•ZISH•uhn) a principle that states that younger rocks lie above older rocks if the layers have not been disturbed (209)
superposición un principio que establece que las rocas más jóvenes se encontrarán sobre las rocas más viejas si las capas no han sido alteradas

symbiosis (sim•bee•OH•sis) a relationship in which two different organisms live in close association with each other (570)
simbiosis una relación en la que dos organismos diferentes viven estrechamente asociados uno con el otro

 T

technology (tek•NAHL•uh•jee) the application of science for practical purposes; the use of tools, machines, materials, and processes to meet human needs (45)
tecnología la aplicación de la ciencia con fines prácticos; el uso de herramientas, máquinas, materiales y procesos para satisfacer las necesidades de los seres humanos

tectonic plate a block of lithosphere that consists of the crust and the rigid, outermost part of the mantle (136, 175)
placa tectónica un bloque de litosfera formado por la corteza y la parte rígida y más externa del manto

tectonic plate boundary (tek•THAN•ik PLAYT BOWN•duh•ree) the edge between two or more plates classified as divergent, convergent, or transform by the movement taking place between the plates (159)
límite de placa tectónica el borde entre dos o más placas clasificado como divergente, convergente o transformante por el movimiento que se produce entre las placas

temperature (TEM•per•uh•chur) a measure of how hot or cold something is; specifically, a measure of the average kinetic energy of the particles in an object (384)
temperatura una medida de qué tan caliente o frío está algo; específicamente, una medida de la energía cinética promedio de las partículas de un objeto

tension (TEN•shun) stress that occurs when forces act to stretch an object (151)
tensión estrés que se produce cuando distintas fuerzas actúan para estirar un objeto

theory the explanation for some phenomenon that is based on observation, experimentation, and reasoning; that is supported by a large quantity of evidence; and that does not conflict with any existing experimental results or observations (9)
teoría una explicación sobre algún fenómeno que está basada en la observación, experimentación y razonamiento; que está respaldada por una gran cantidad de pruebas; y que no contradice ningún resultado experimental ni observación existente

thermal energy the total kinetic energy of a substance's atoms (392)
energía térmica la energía cinética de los átomos de una sustancia

thermal pollution a temperature increase in a body of water that is caused by human activity and that has a harmful effect on water quality and on the ability of that body of water to support life (264)
contaminación térmica un aumento en la temperatura de una masa de agua, producido por las actividades humanas y que tiene un efecto dañino en la calidad del agua y en la capacidad de esa masa de agua para permitir que se desarrolle la vida

thermometer an instrument that measures and indicates temperature (384)
termómetro un instrumento que mide e indica la temperatura

trace fossil a fossilized structure, such as a footprint or a coprolite, that formed in sedimentary rock by animal activity on or within soft sediment (197)
fósil traza una estructura fosilizada, como una huella o un coprolito, que se formó en una roca sedimentaria por la actividad de un animal sobre sedimento blando o dentro de éste

trade-off (TRAYD•awf) the giving up of one thing in return for another, often applied to the engineering design process (56)
compensación pérdida de una cosa a cambio de otra, con frecuencia aplicado al proceso de diseño en ingeniería

transform boundary the boundary between tectonic plates that are sliding past each other horizontally (139)
límite de transformación el límite entre placas tectónicas que se están deslizando horizontalmente una sobre otra

translucent (tranz•LOO•suhnt) describes matter that transmits light but that does not transmit an image (350)
traslúcido término que describe la materia que transmite luz, pero que no transmite una imagen

transparent (tranz•PAHR•uhnt) describes matter that allows light to pass through with little interference (350)
transparente término que describe materia que permite el paso de la luz con poca interferencia

transverse wave a wave in which the particles of the medium move perpendicularly to the direction the wave is traveling (317)

onda transversal una onda en la que las partículas del medio se mueven perpendicularmente respecto a la dirección en la que se desplaza la onda

ultraviolet (uhl•truh•VY•uh•lit) electromagnetic wavelengths immediately outside the violet end of the visible range (338)

ultravioleta longitudes de onda electromagnéticas inmediatamente adyacentes al color violeta en el espectro visible

unconformity (uhn•kuhn•FAWR•mih•tee) a break in the geologic record created when rock layers are eroded or when sediment is not deposited for a long period of time (211)

disconformidad una ruptura en el registro geológico, creada cuando las capas de roca se erosionan o cuando el sedimento no se deposita durante un largo período de tiempo

uniformitarianism (yoo•nuh•fohr•mi•TAIR•ee•uh•niz•uhm) a principle that geologic processes that occurred in the past can be explained by current geologic processes (194)

uniformitarianismo un principio que establece que es posible explicar los procesos geológicos que ocurrieron en el pasado en función de los procesos geológicos actuales

uplift the rising of regions of the Earth's crust to higher elevations (114)

levantamiento la elevación de regiones de la corteza terrestre a elevaciones más altas

urbanization (er•buh•nih•ZAY•shuhn) the growth of urban areas caused by people moving into cities (251)

urbanización el crecimiento de las áreas urbanas producido por el desplazamiento de personas hacia las ciudades

variation (vair•ee•AY•shuhn) the occurrence of hereditary or nonhereditary differences between different invidivuals of a population (420, 473)

variabilidad la incidencia de diferencias hereditarias o no hereditarias entre distintos individuos de una población

vent an opening at the surface of the Earth through which volcanic material passes (172)

chimenea una abertura en la superficie de la Tierra a través de la cual pasa material volcánico

volcano a vent or fissure in Earth's surface through which magma and gases are expelled (172)

volcán una chimenea o fisura en la superficie de la Tierra a través de la cual se expulsan magma y gases

water pollution (WAW•ter puh•LOO•shuhn) waste matter or other material that is introduced into water and that is harmful to organisms that live in, drink, or are exposed to the water (264)

contaminación del agua material de desecho u otro material que se introduce en el agua y que daña a los organismos que viven en el agua, la beben o están expuestos a ella

wave a disturbance that transfers energy from one place to another without requiring matter to move the entire distance (314, 324)

onda una perturbacio'n que transfiere energi'a de un lugar a otro sin que sea necesario que la materia se mueva toda la distancia

wavefront the collection of points that are reached at the same instant by a wave propagating through a medium (327)

wave period the time required for one wavelength to pass a given point (325)

período de onda el tiempo que se requiere para que una longitud de onda pase por un punto dado

wave speed the speed at which a wave travels through a medium (328)

rapidez de onda la rapidez a la cual viaja una onda a través de un medio

wavelength the distance between two adjacent crests or troughs of a wave (324)

longitud de onda la distancia entre dos crestas o senos adyacentes de una onda

weathering the natural process by which atmospheric and environmental agents, such as wind, rain, and temperature changes, disintegrate and decompose rocks (109)

meteorización el proceso natural por medio del cual los agentes atmosféricos o ambientales, como el viento, la lluvia y los cambios de temperatura, desintegran y descomponen las rocas

wetland an area of land that is periodically underwater or whose soil contains a great deal of moisture (585)

terreno pantanoso un área de tierra que está periódicamente bajo el agua o cuyo suelo contiene una gran cantidad de humedad

Index